SAMURAI DEEPER KYO

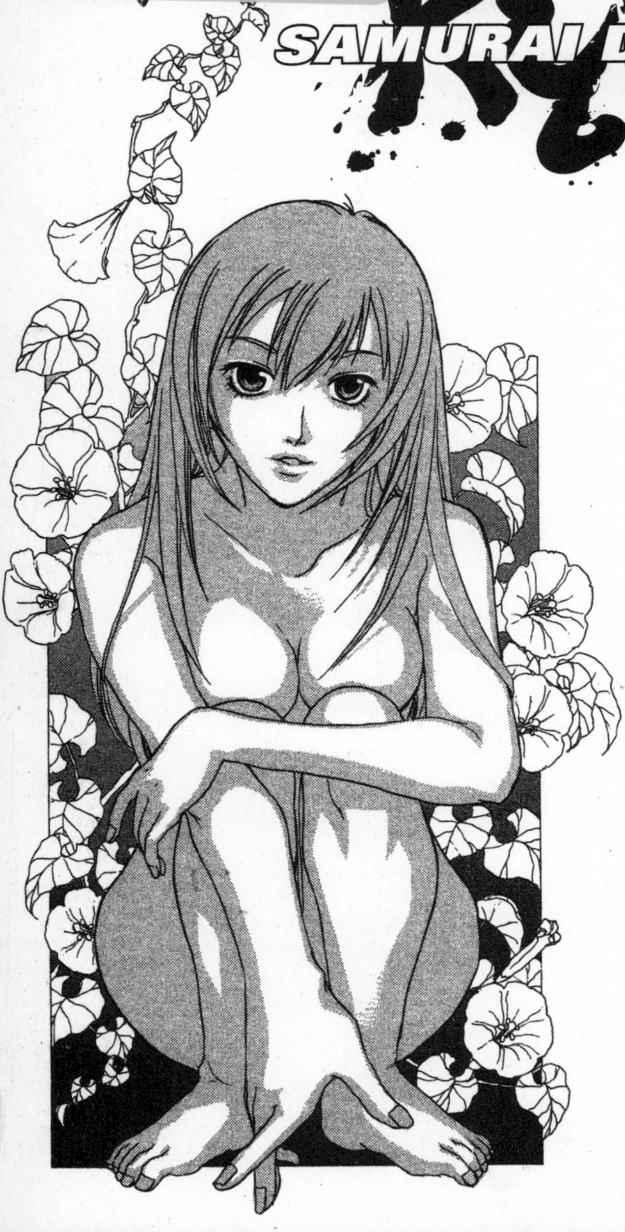

Translator - Alexander O. Smith
Script Editor   Rich Amtower
Copy Editor - Carol Fox
Retouch and Lettering - Jose Macasocol, Jr.
Cover Design - Raymond Makowski
Graphic Designer - James Dashiell

Editor - Jake Forbes
Digital Imaging Manager - Chris Buford
Pre-Press Manager - Antonio DePietro
Production Managers - Jennifer Miller, Mutsumi Miyazaki
Art Director - Matt Alford
Managing Editor - Jill Freshney
VP of Production - Ron Klamert
President & C.O.O. - John Parker
Publisher & C.E.O. - Stuart Levy

E-mail: info@TOKYOPOP.com
Come visit us online at www.TOKYOPOP.com

A  Manga

TOKYOPOP Inc.
5900 Wilshire Blvd. Suite 2000
Los Angeles, CA 90036

Samurai Deeper Kyo Vol. 6

ISBN: 1-59182-542-3

First TOKYOPOP printing: April 2004

10 9 8 7 6 5 4 3 2 1
Printed in the USA

SAMURAI DEEPER Kyo

Vol. 6
by Akimine Kamijyo

TOKYOPOP®

Los Angeles • Tokyo • London

DRAMATIS PERSONAE

...According to Tora.

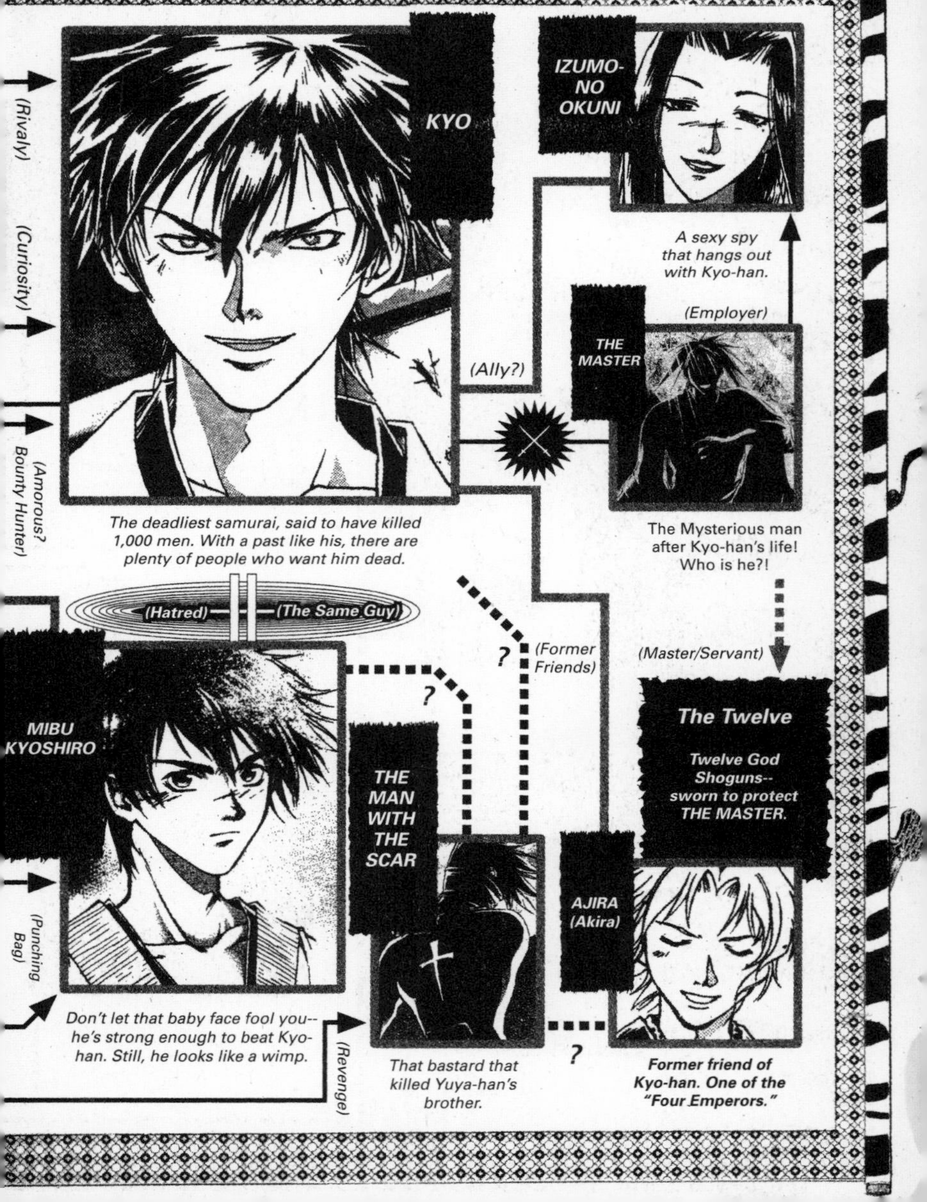
KYO
The deadliest samurai, said to have killed 1,000 men. With a past like his, there are plenty of people who want him dead.
IZUMO-NO OKUNI
A sexy spy that hangs out with Kyo-han.
(Ally?)
(Employer)
THE MASTER
The Mysterious man after Kyo-han's life! Who is he?!
(Master/Servant)
The Twelve
Twelve God Shoguns-- sworn to protect THE MASTER.
(Hatred)
(The Same Guy)
MIBU KYOSHIRO
Don't let that baby face fool you-- he's strong enough to beat Kyo-han. Still, he looks like a wimp.
?
?
(Former Friends)
THE MAN WITH THE SCAR
That bastard that killed Yuya-han's brother.
?
AJIRA (Akira)
Former friend of Kyo-han. One of the "Four Emperors."
(Rivalry)
(Curiosity)
(Amorous? Bounty Hunter)
(Punching Bag)
(Revenge)

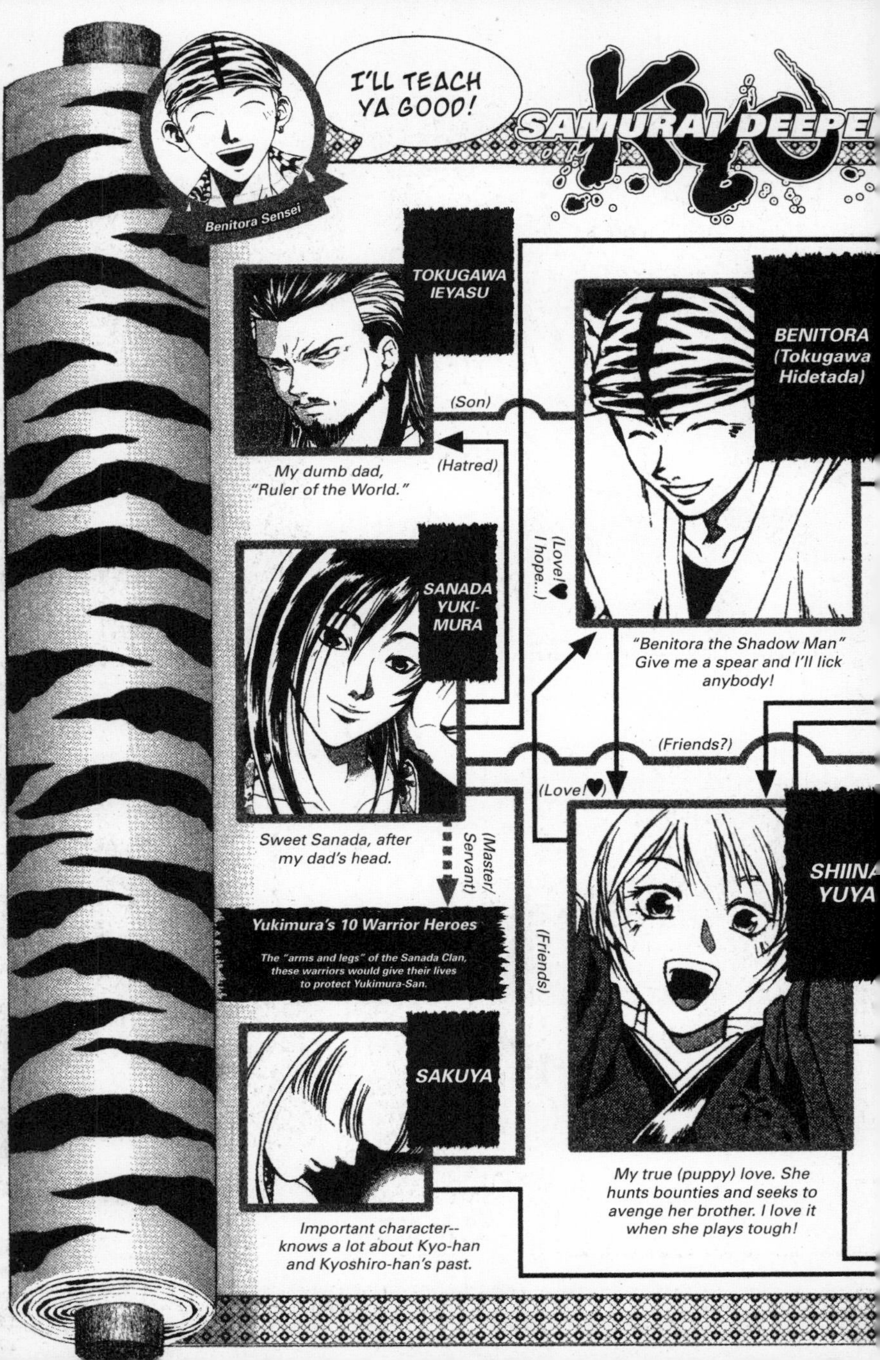
I'LL TEACH YA GOOD!
Benitora Sensei
SAMURAI DEEPER KYO
TOKUGAWA IEYASU
(Son)
(Hatred)
My dumb dad, "Ruler of the World."
BENITORA (Tokugawa Hidetada)
"Benitora the Shadow Man" Give me a spear and I'll lick anybody!
(Love!♥ I hope...)
SANADA YUKI-MURA
Sweet Sanada, after my dad's head.
(Friends?)
(Love!♥)
(Master/ Servant)
Yukimura's 10 Warrior Heroes
The "arms and legs" of the Sanada Clan, these warriors would give their lives to protect Yukimura-San.
(Friends)
SHIINA YUYA
My true (puppy) love. She hunts bounties and seeks to avenge her brother. I love it when she plays tough!
SAKUYA
Important character--knows a lot about Kyo-han and Kyoshiro-han's past.

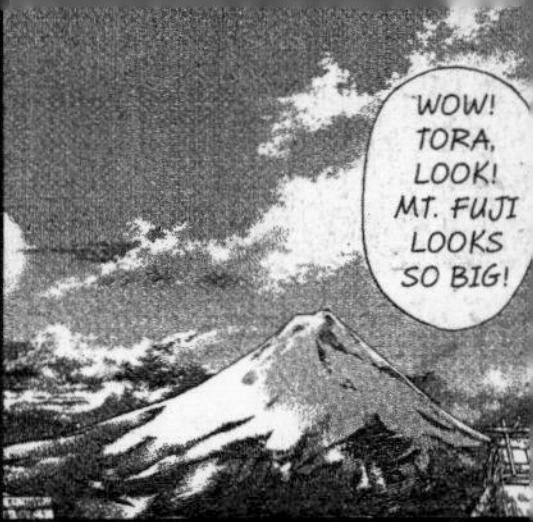
WOW! TORA, LOOK! MT. FUJI LOOKS SO BIG!

Kyo and company have co
to Hakone at the base o
Mt. Fuji, on their way to t
forest of **Aokigahara**
where Kyo's body is said to

There, they meet
a blind samurai
named **Akira,**
who claims to know Kyo.

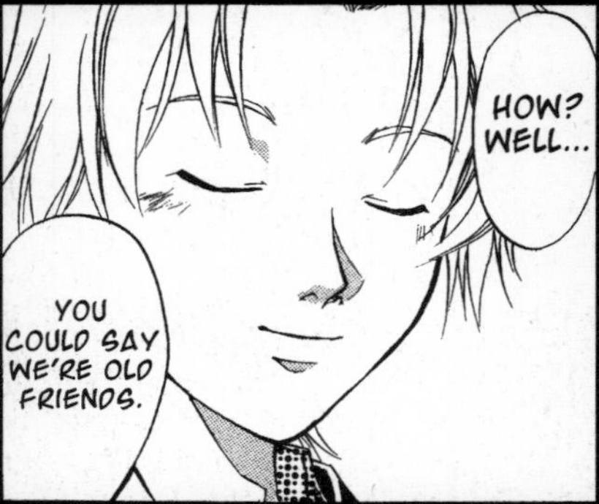
HOW? WELL...
YOU COULD SAY WE'RE OLD FRIENDS.

Now, Akira has
taken the role of
"Ajira,"
one of the
12 God Shoguns,
an elite team
of samurai
called into action
by their leader,
The Master.

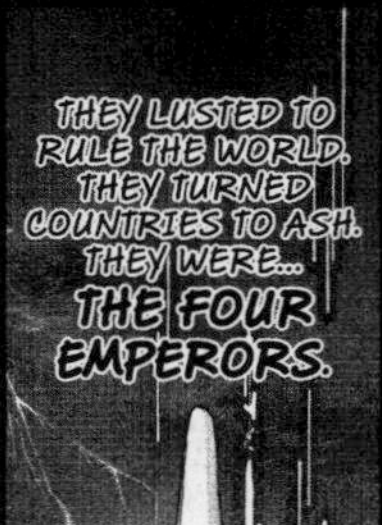
THEY LUSTED TO RULE THE WORLD. THEY TURNED COUNTRIES TO ASH. THEY WERE... THE FOUR EMPERORS.

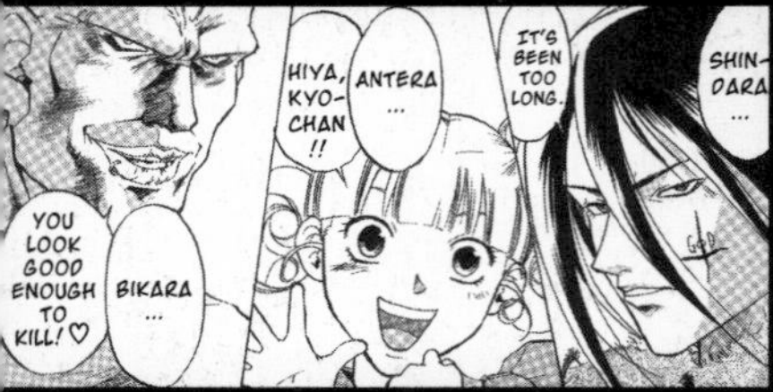
SHIN-DARA ...
IT'S BEEN TOO LONG.
ANTERA ...
HIYA, KYO-CHAN !!
BIKARA ...
YOU LOOK GOOD ENOUGH TO KILL! ♡

Other members of the
God Shoguns have
appeared as well,
but they do not come
to fight Kyo...yet.
They seek his body.

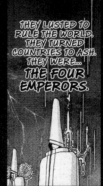

Once Kyo reaches
Aokigahara, he orders
Yuya to leave...

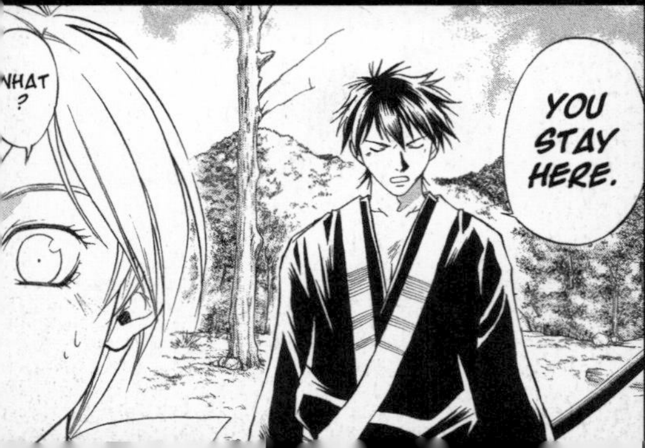
YOU STAY HERE.
HAT ?

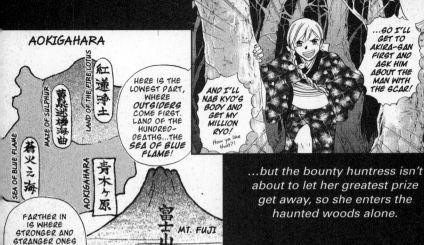

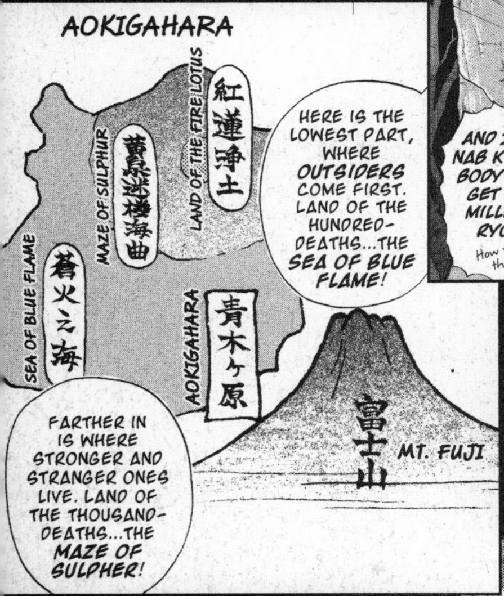
AOKIGAHARA
紅蓮浄土
LAND OF THE FIRE LOTUS
MAZE OF SULPHUR
蒼火之海
SEA OF BLUE FLAME
青木ヶ原
AOKIGAHARA
富士山
MT. FUJI
HERE IS THE LOWEST PART, WHERE OUTSIDERS COME FIRST. LAND OF THE HUNDRED-DEATHS...THE SEA OF BLUE FLAME!
FARTHER IN IS WHERE STRONGER AND STRANGER ONES LIVE. LAND OF THE THOUSAND-DEATHS...THE MAZE OF SULPHER!

Aokigahara is no place for outsiders ...

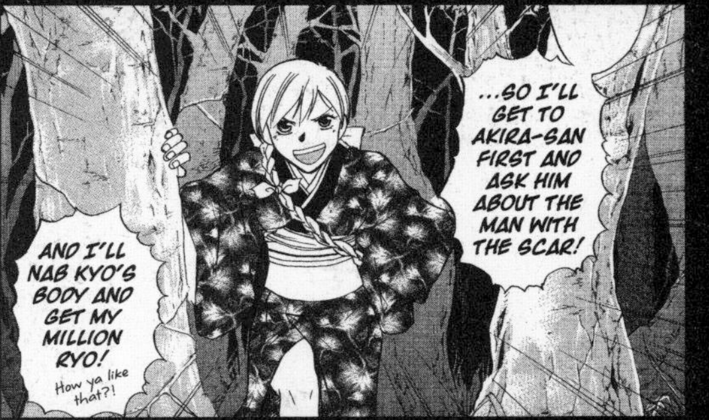
...SO I'LL GET TO AKIRA-SAN FIRST AND ASK HIM ABOUT THE MAN WITH THE SCAR!
AND I'LL NAB KYO'S BODY AND GET MY MILLION RYO!
How ya like that?!

...but the bounty huntress isn't about to let her greatest prize get away, so she enters the haunted woods alone.

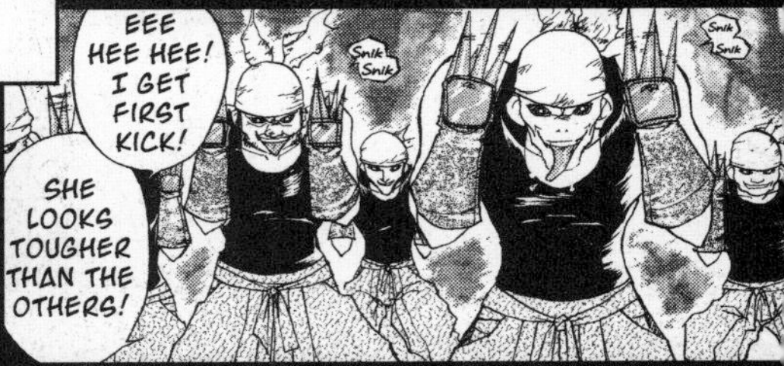
Snik Snik
Snik Snik
EEE HEE HEE! I GET FIRST KICK!
SHE LOOKS TOUGHER THAN THE OTHERS!

...and soon Yuya finds herself at the mercy of the forest's denizens.

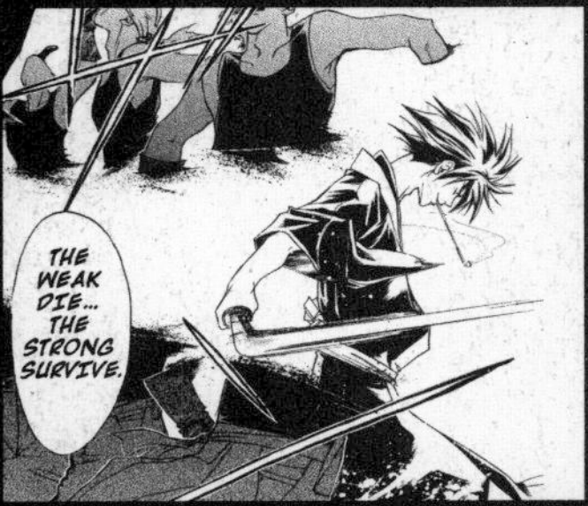
THE WEAK DIE... THE STRONG SURVIVE.

Kyo leaves Benitora and Okuni to save Yuya from the demons...

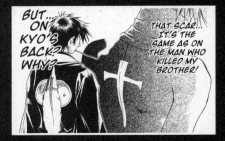

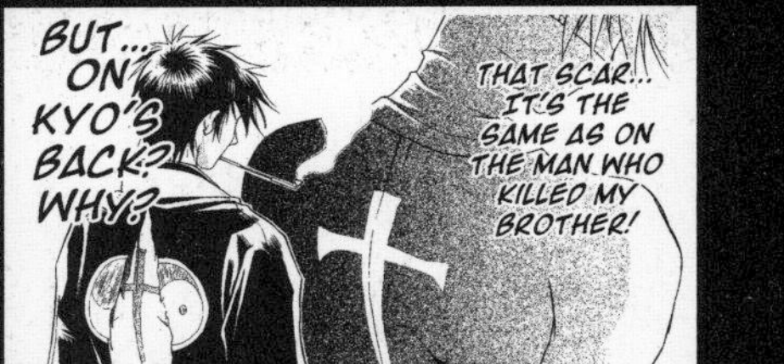
THAT SCAR... IT'S THE SAME AS ON THE MAN WHO KILLED MY BROTHER!
BUT... ON KYO'S BACK? WHY?

...but in the battle, his shirt is ripped, revealing a **shocking mark** to Yuya.

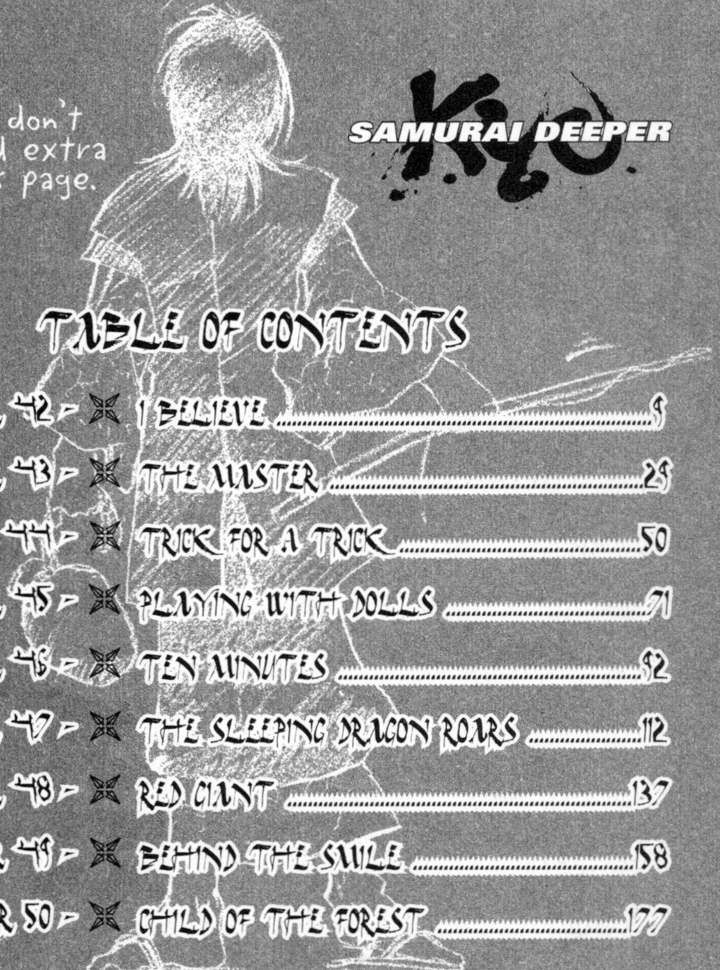
Line-drawing time.
Hey, I don't get paid extra for this page. ♡

SAMURAI DEEPER KYO

TABLE OF CONTENTS

Editors Note:
Dear readers,
Up until now, all names have been listed "Western-style," given name first, family name last. In Japan, names are listed in the reverse order. From this volume on (and in reprints of earlier volumes) the names will be listed Japanese-style. So, for example, the shogun's name would be said as "Tokugawa Ieyasu," NOT "Ieyasu Tokugawa." With many more volumes of Samurai Deeper Kyo to go, we feel that it is better to get it "right" from here on out, rather than continue with the reversed order. We apologize for the inconvenience, but hope you'll appreciate the change.
-The Editor

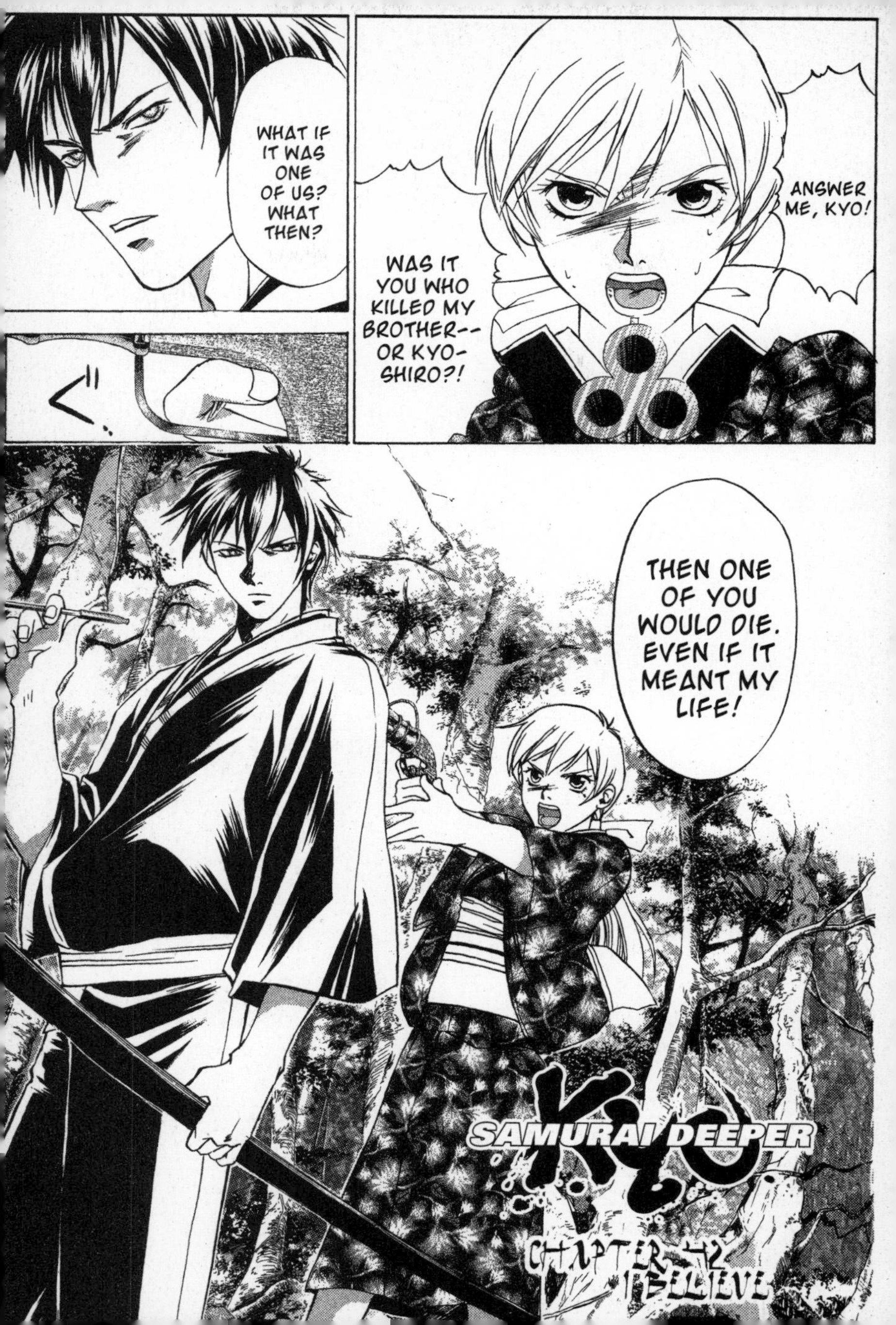
ANSWER ME, KYO!
WAS IT YOU WHO KILLED MY BROTHER-- OR KYO-SHIRO?!
WHAT IF IT WAS ONE OF US? WHAT THEN?
THEN ONE OF YOU WOULD DIE. EVEN IF IT MEANT MY LIFE!
SAMURAI DEEPER KYO
CHAPTER 42 I BELIEVE

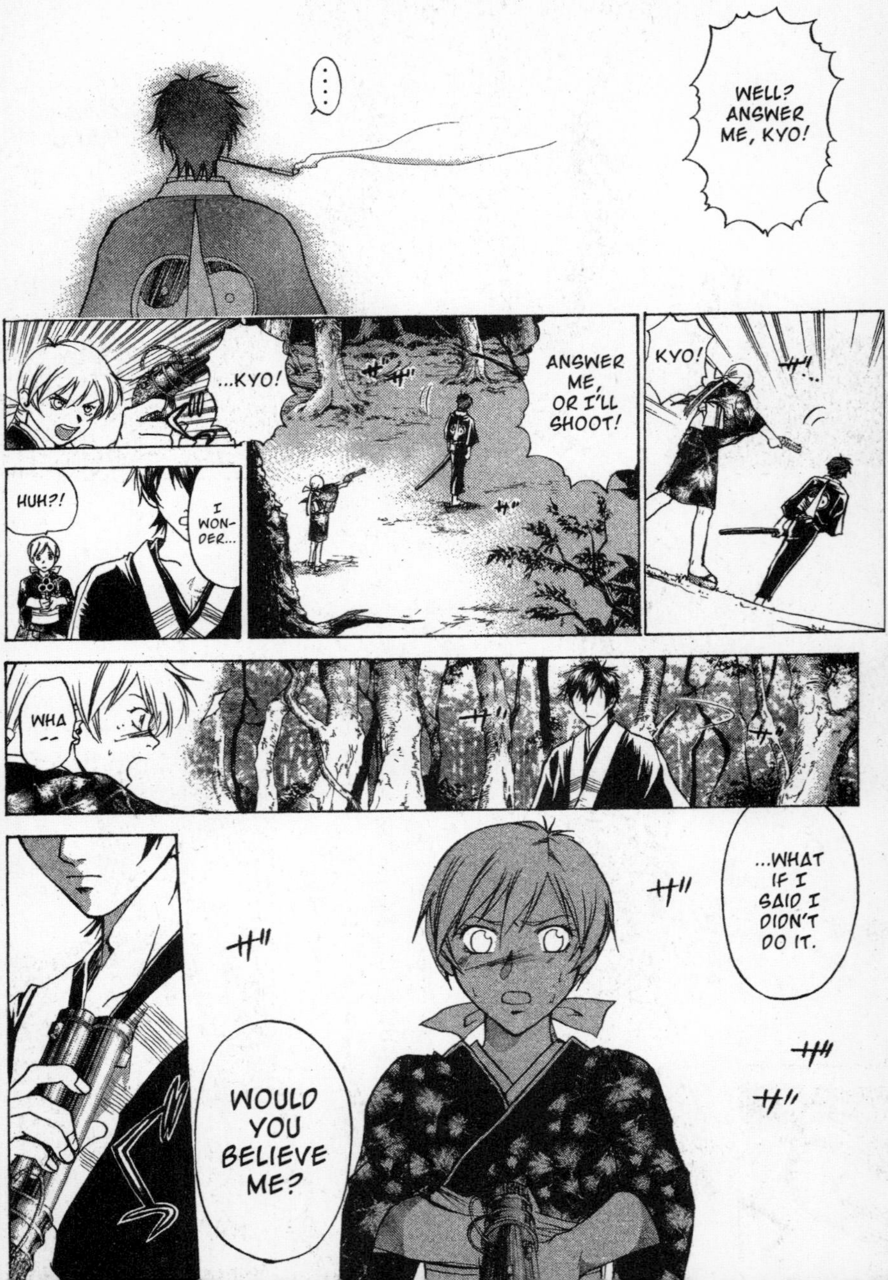
WELL? ANSWER ME, KYO!
...
KYO!
ANSWER ME, OR I'LL SHOOT!
...KYO!
I WONDER...
HUH?!
WHA--
...WHAT IF I SAID I DIDN'T DO IT.
WOULD YOU BELIEVE ME?

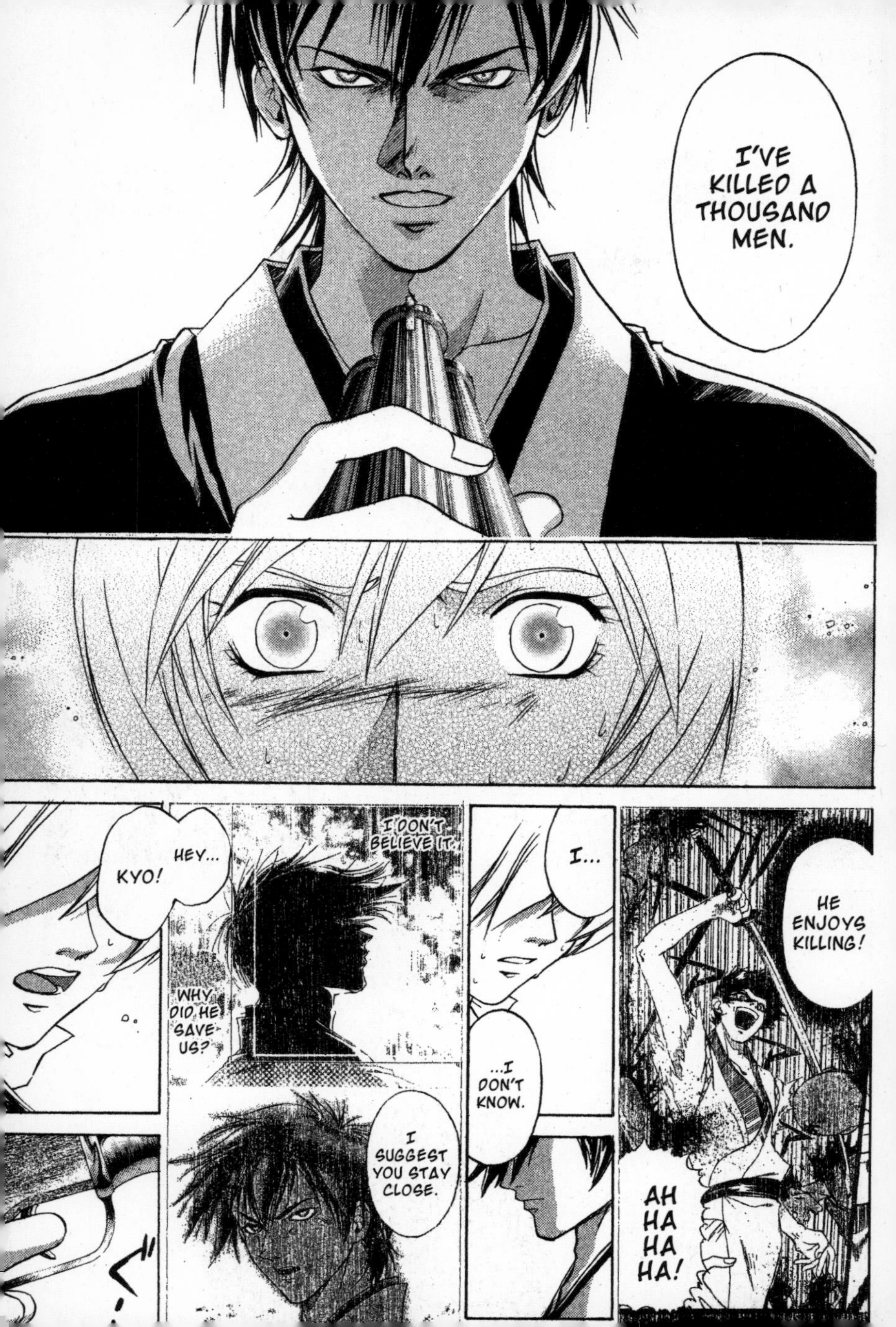
I'VE KILLED A THOUSAND MEN.
HE ENJOYS KILLING!
AH HA HA HA HA!
I...
...I DON'T KNOW.
I DON'T BELIEVE IT.
WHY DID HE SAVE US?
HEY... KYO!
I SUGGEST YOU STAY CLOSE.

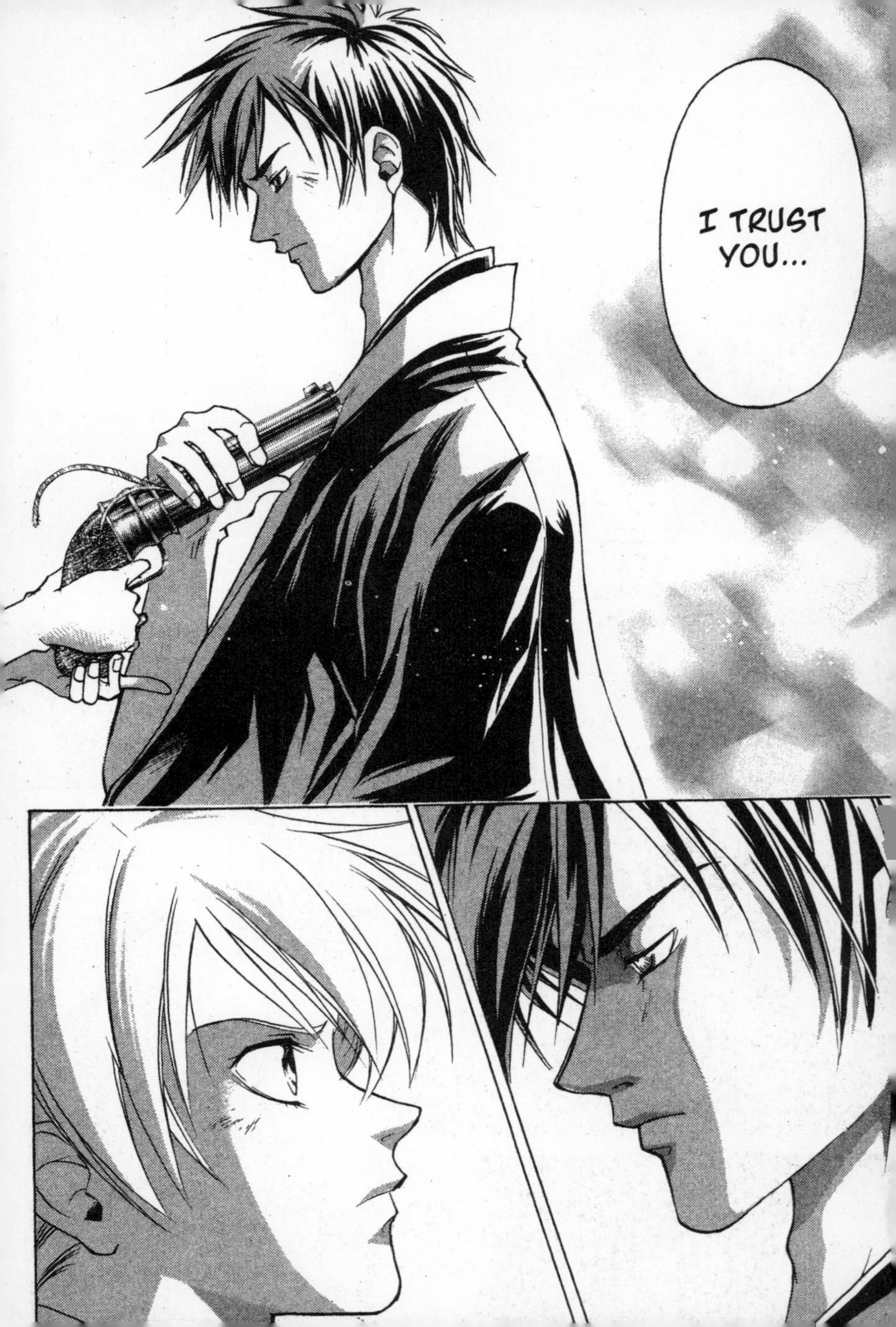
I TRUST YOU...

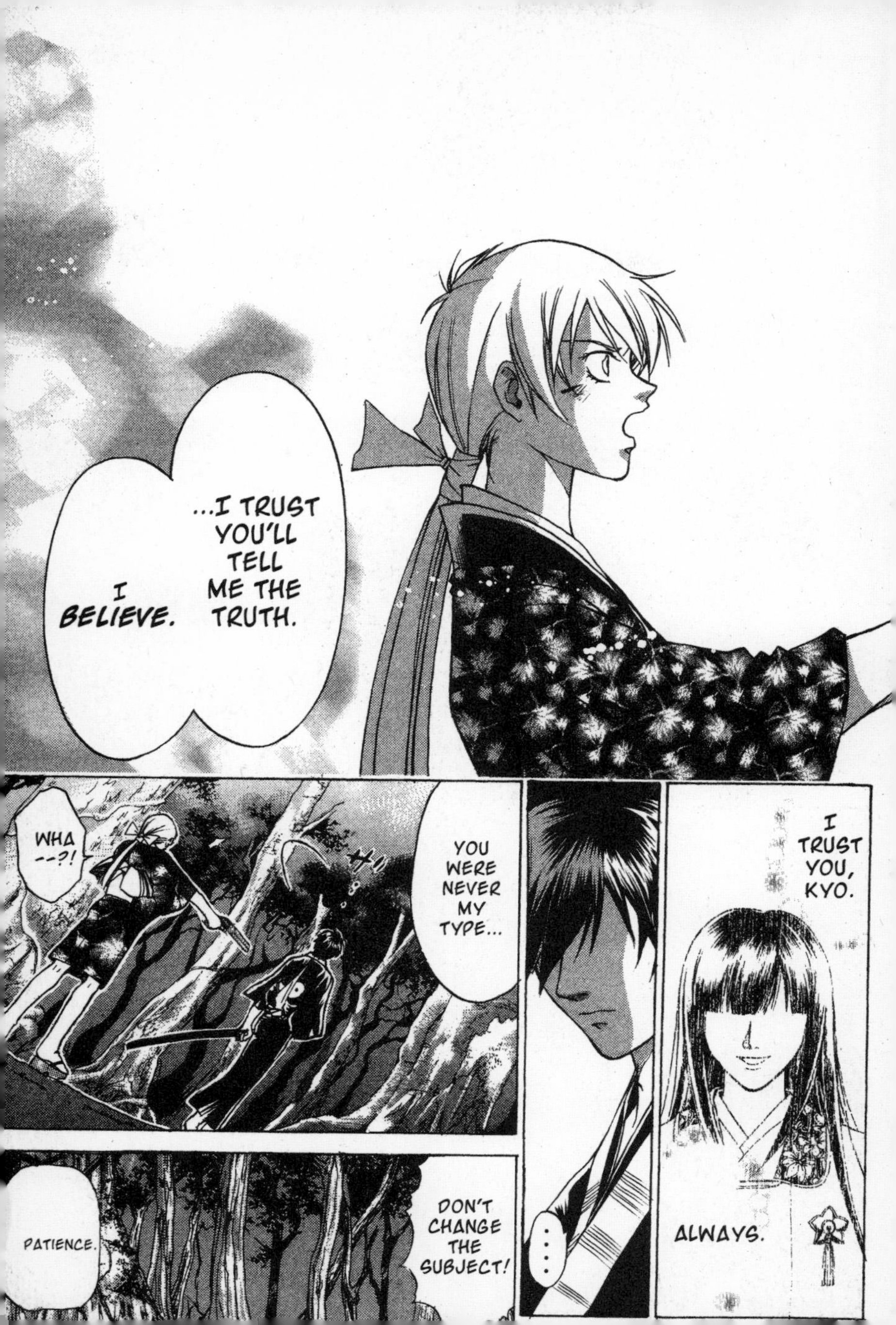
I BELIEVE.
...I TRUST YOU'LL TELL ME THE TRUTH.
I TRUST YOU, KYO.
ALWAYS.
....
YOU WERE NEVER MY TYPE...
WHA--?!
DON'T CHANGE THE SUBJECT!
PATIENCE.

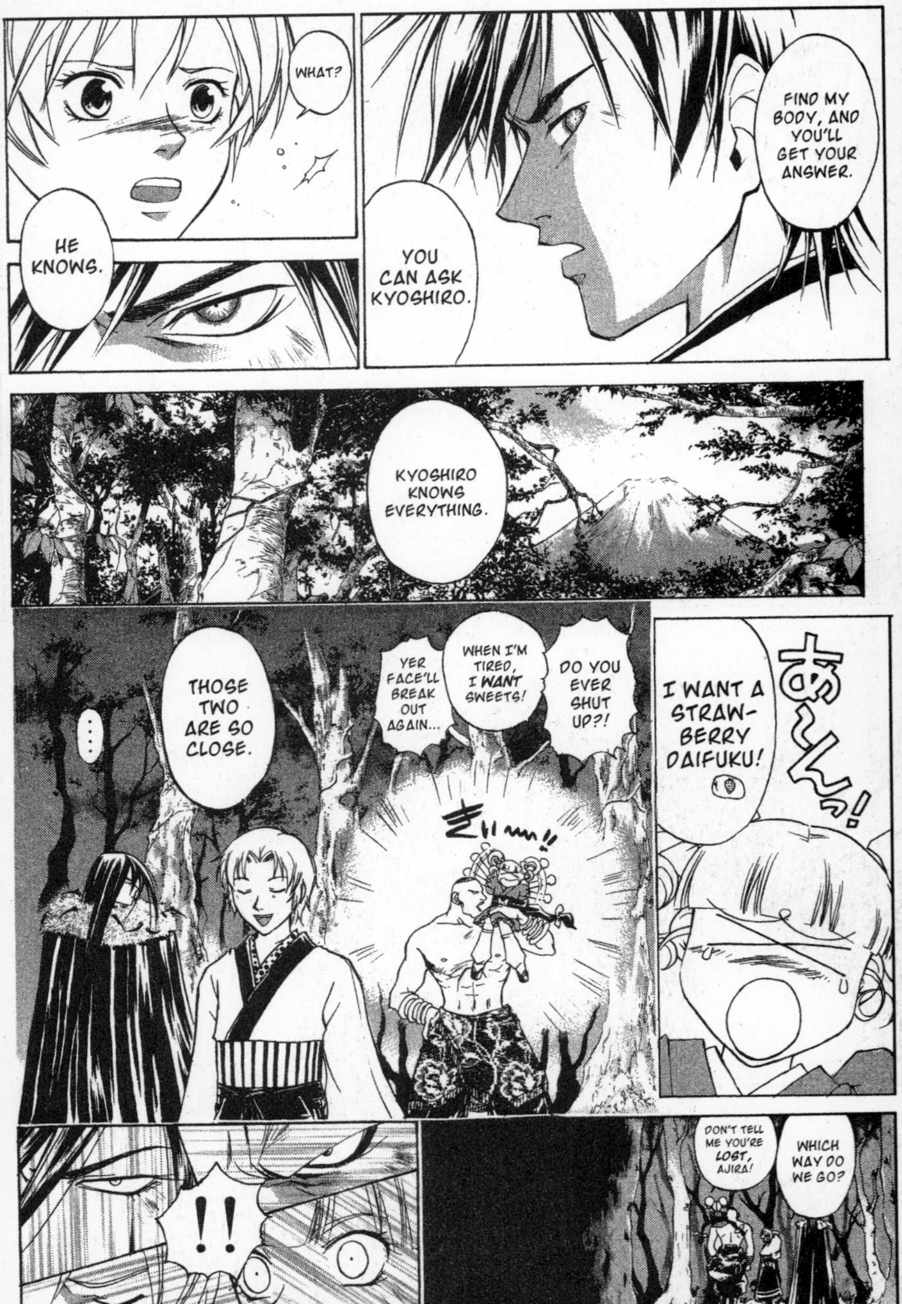
FIND MY BODY, AND YOU'LL GET YOUR ANSWER.
YOU CAN ASK KYOSHIRO.
WHAT?
HE KNOWS.
KYOSHIRO KNOWS EVERYTHING.
あ〜んっ!
I WANT A STRAW-BERRY DAIFUKU!
DO YOU EVER SHUT UP?!
WHEN I'M TIRED, I WANT SWEETS!
YER FACE'LL BREAK OUT AGAIN...
THOSE TWO ARE SO CLOSE.
....
WHICH WAY DO WE GO?
DON'T TELL ME YOU'RE LOST, AJIRA!
!!

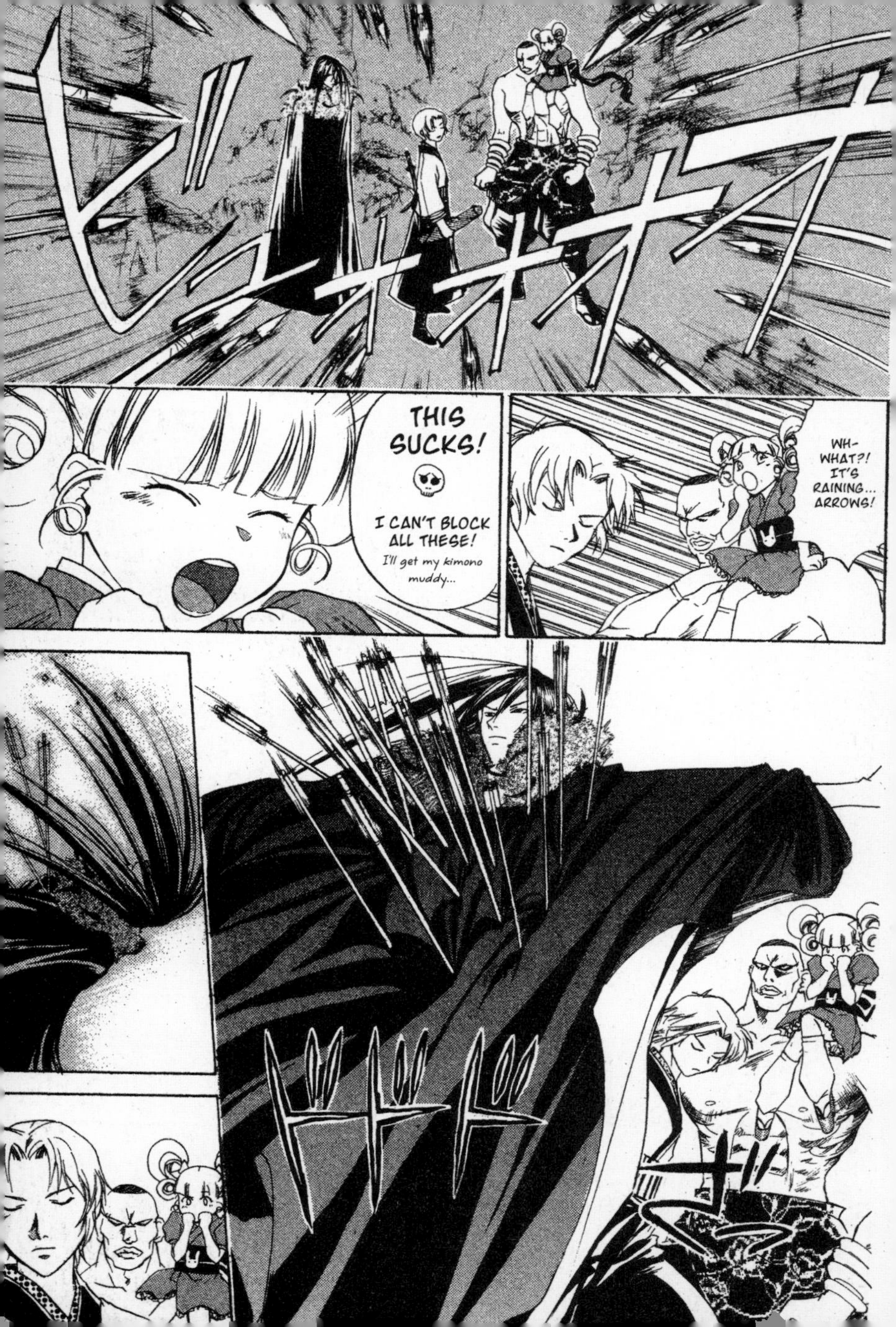
WH-WHAT?! IT'S RAINING... ARROWS!
THIS SUCKS!
I CAN'T BLOCK ALL THESE!
I'll get my kimono muddy...

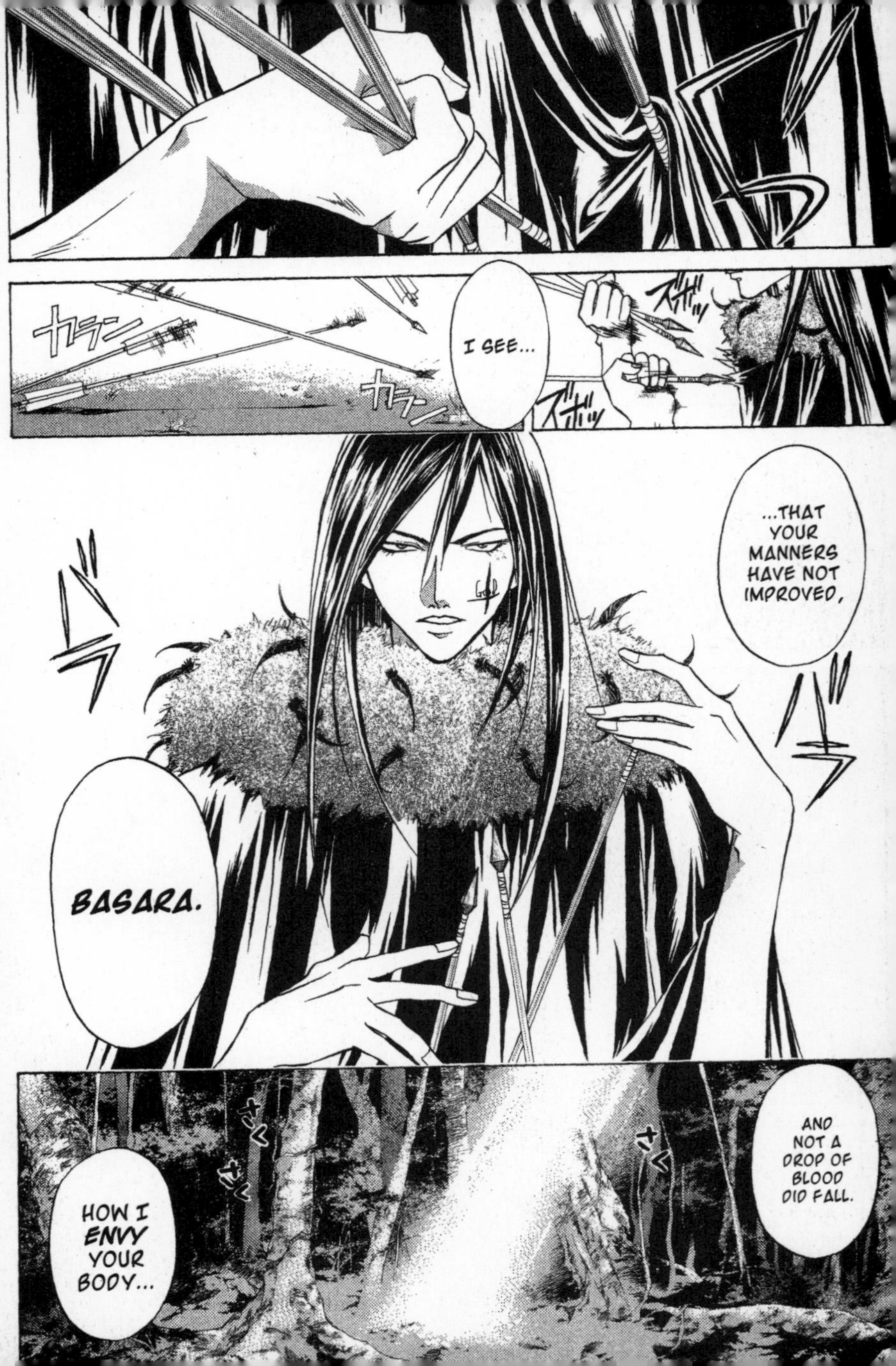

ズボッ
ズボッ
I SEE...
カラン
カラン
...THAT YOUR MANNERS HAVE NOT IMPROVED,
BASARA.
AND NOT A DROP OF BLOOD DID FALL.
HOW I *ENVY* YOUR BODY...

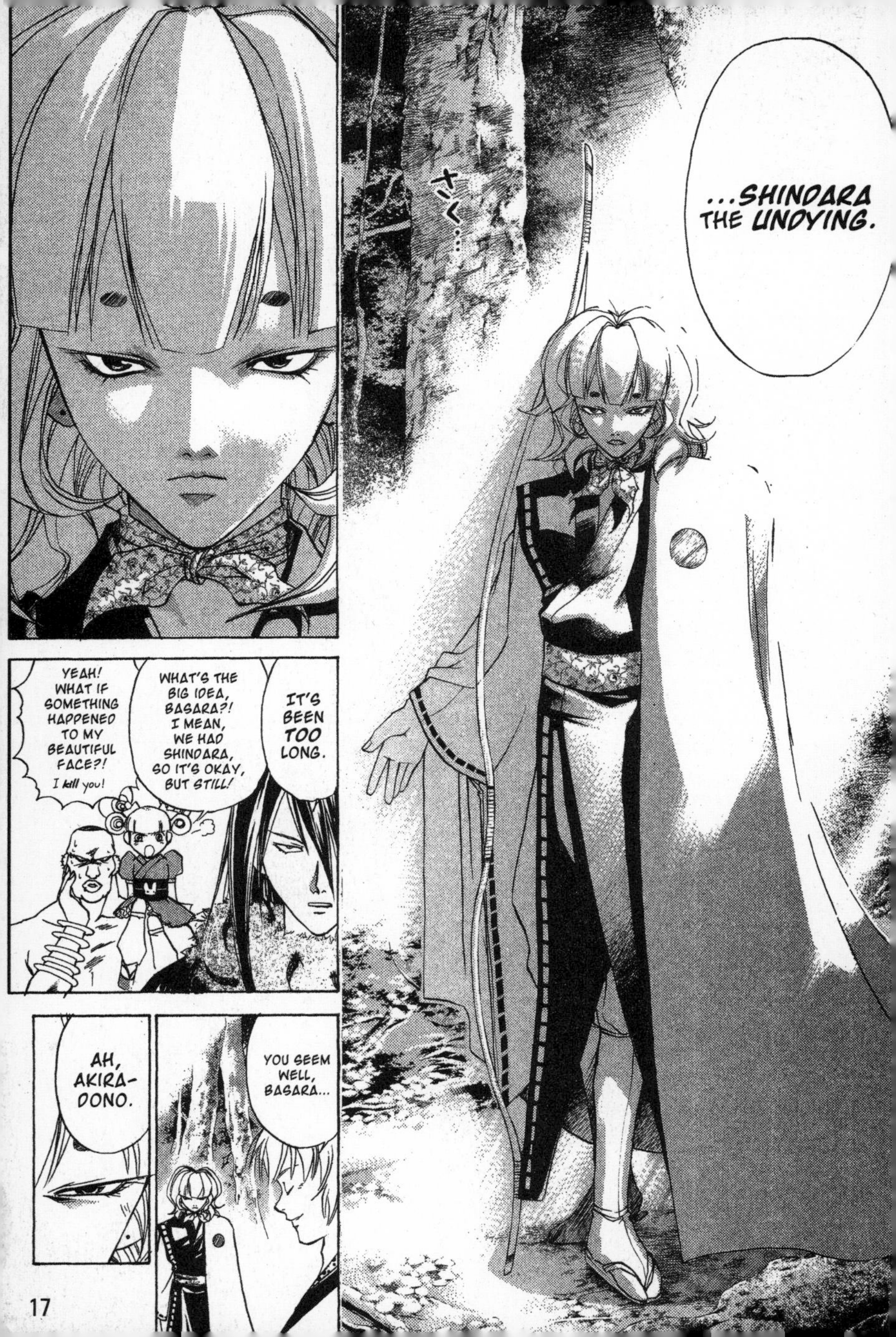
...SHINDARA THE UNDYING.
IT'S BEEN TOO LONG.
WHAT'S THE BIG IDEA, BASARA?! I MEAN, WE HAD SHINDARA, SO IT'S OKAY, BUT STILL!
YEAH! WHAT IF SOMETHING HAPPENED TO MY BEAUTIFUL FACE?!
I kill you!
YOU SEEM WELL, BASARA...
AH, AKIRA-DONO.

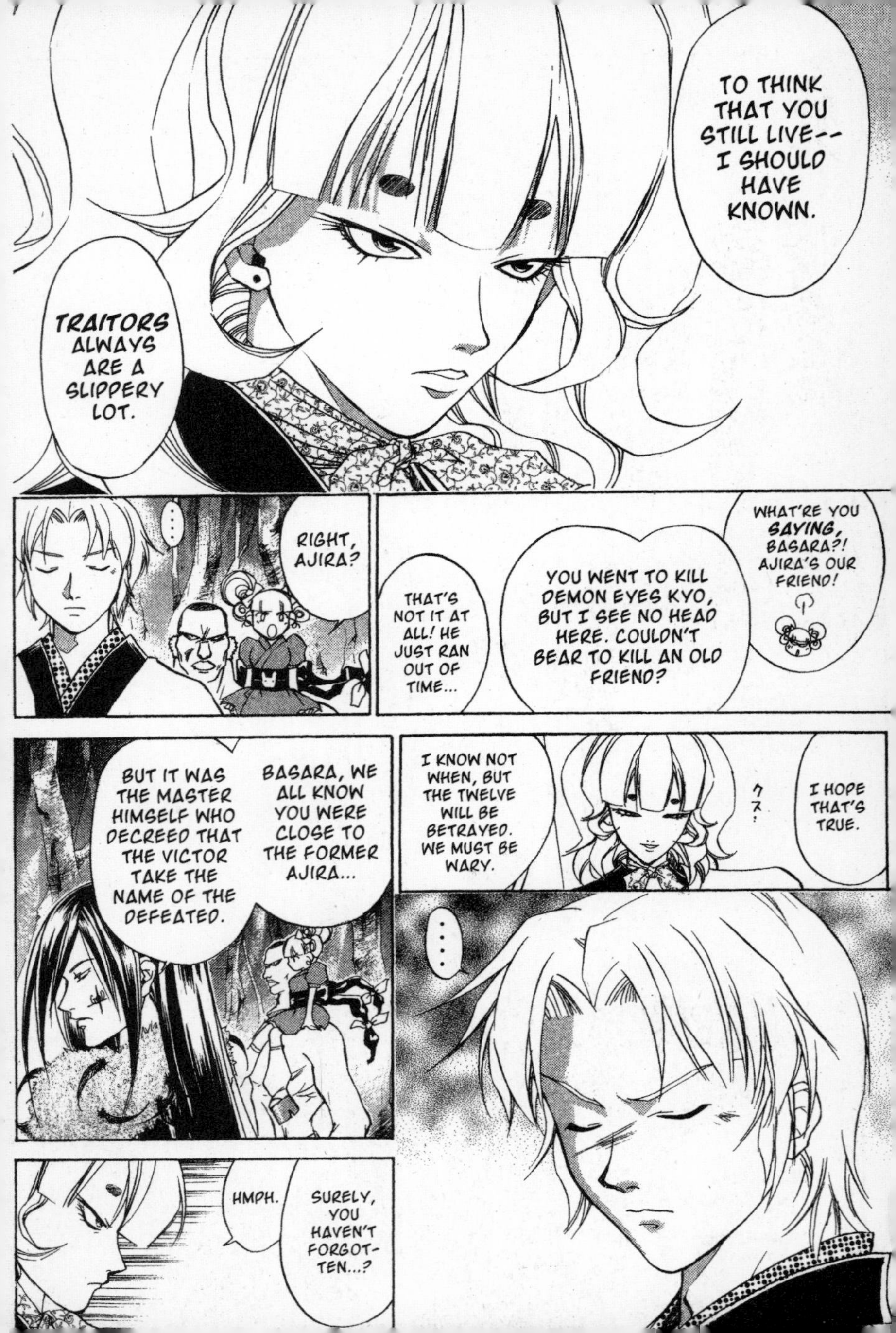

TO THINK THAT YOU STILL LIVE-- I SHOULD HAVE KNOWN.
TRAITORS ALWAYS ARE A SLIPPERY LOT.
WHAT'RE YOU SAYING, BASARA?! AJIRA'S OUR FRIEND!
YOU WENT TO KILL DEMON EYES KYO, BUT I SEE NO HEAD HERE. COULDN'T BEAR TO KILL AN OLD FRIEND?
THAT'S NOT IT AT ALL! HE JUST RAN OUT OF TIME...
RIGHT, AJIRA?
...
I HOPE THAT'S TRUE.
クス!
I KNOW NOT WHEN, BUT THE TWELVE WILL BE BETRAYED. WE MUST BE WARY.
BASARA, WE ALL KNOW YOU WERE CLOSE TO THE FORMER AJIRA...
BUT IT WAS THE MASTER HIMSELF WHO DECREED THAT THE VICTOR TAKE THE NAME OF THE DEFEATED.
...
SURELY, YOU HAVEN'T FORGOTTEN...?
HMPH.

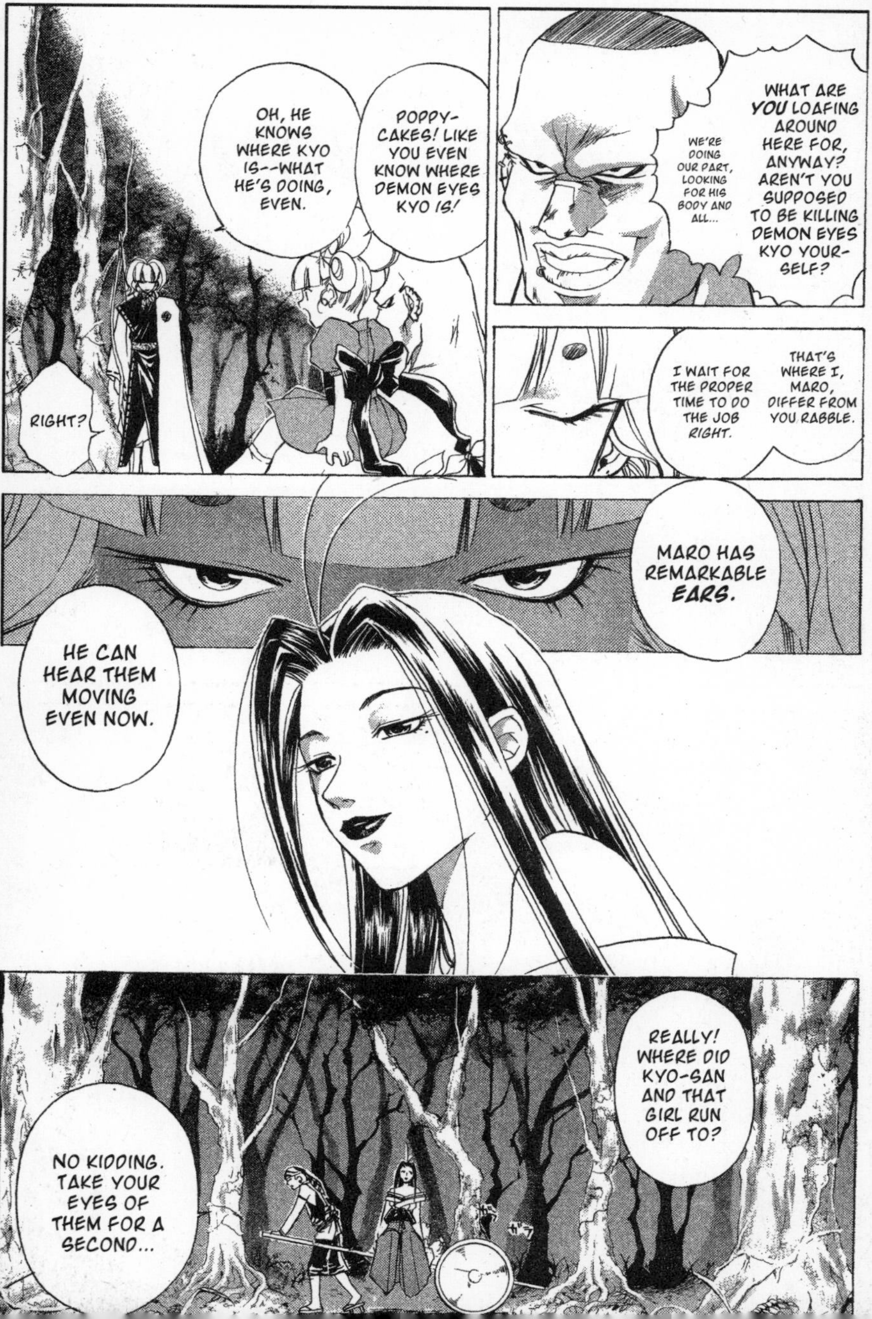
WHAT ARE YOU LOAFING AROUND HERE FOR, ANYWAY? AREN'T YOU SUPPOSED TO BE KILLING DEMON EYES KYO YOURSELF?
WE'RE DOING OUR PART, LOOKING FOR HIS BODY AND ALL...
THAT'S WHERE I, MARO, DIFFER FROM YOU RABBLE.
I WAIT FOR THE PROPER TIME TO DO THE JOB RIGHT.
POPPYCAKES! LIKE YOU EVEN KNOW WHERE DEMON EYES KYO IS!
OH, HE KNOWS WHERE KYO IS--WHAT HE'S DOING, EVEN.
RIGHT?
MARO HAS REMARKABLE EARS.
HE CAN HEAR THEM MOVING EVEN NOW.
REALLY! WHERE DID KYO-SAN AND THAT GIRL RUN OFF TO?
NO KIDDING. TAKE YOUR EYES OF THEM FOR A SECOND...

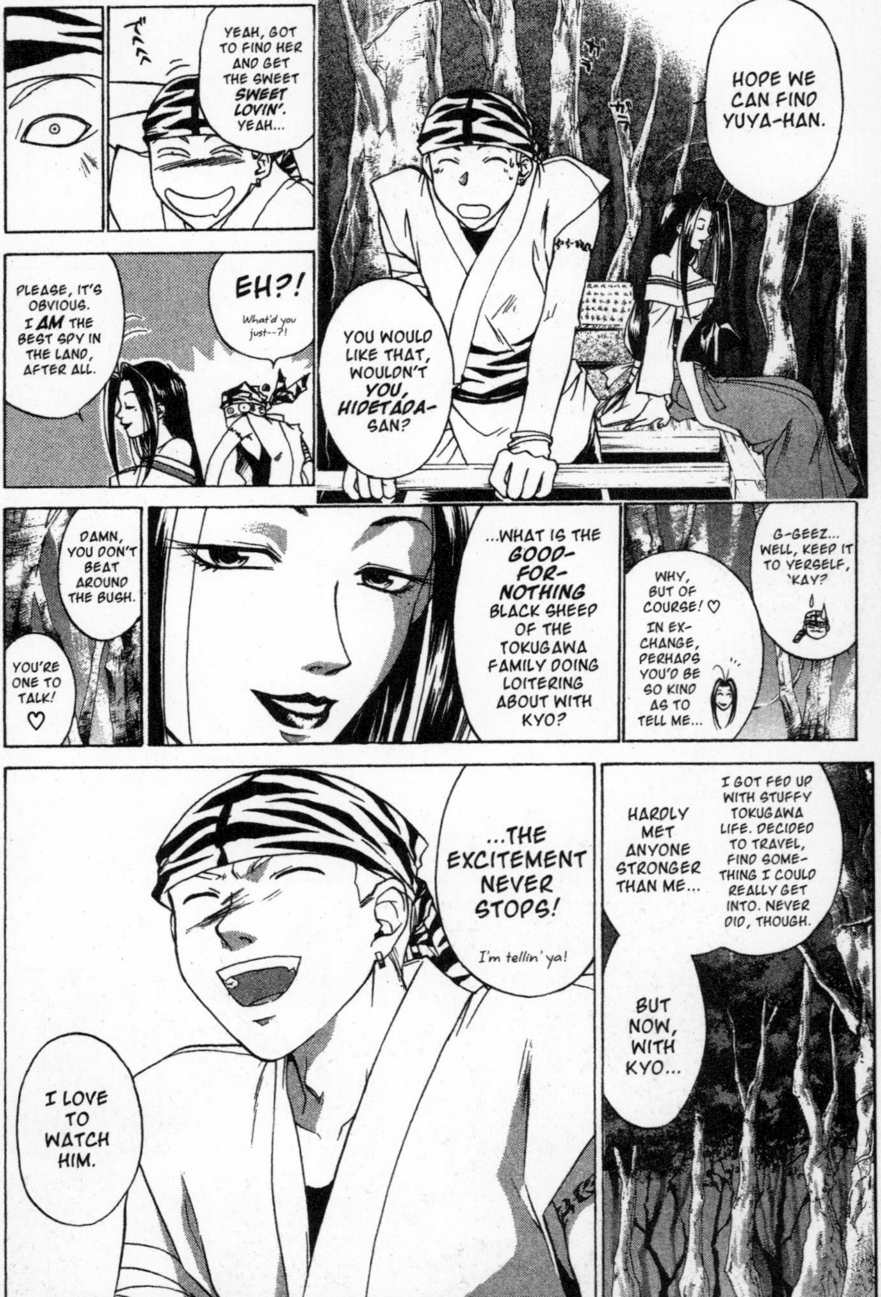
HOPE WE CAN FIND YUYA-HAN.
YOU WOULD LIKE THAT, WOULDN'T YOU, HIDETADA-SAN?
YEAH, GOT TO FIND HER AND GET THE SWEET SWEET LOVIN'. YEAH...
EH?!
What'd you just--?!
PLEASE, IT'S OBVIOUS. I AM THE BEST SPY IN THE LAND, AFTER ALL.
G-GEEZ... WELL, KEEP IT TO YERSELF, 'KAY?
WHY, BUT OF COURSE! ♡
IN EXCHANGE, PERHAPS YOU'D BE SO KIND AS TO TELL ME...
...WHAT IS THE GOOD-FOR-NOTHING BLACK SHEEP OF THE TOKUGAWA FAMILY DOING LOITERING ABOUT WITH KYO?
DAMN, YOU DON'T BEAT AROUND THE BUSH.
YOU'RE ONE TO TALK! ♡
I GOT FED UP WITH STUFFY TOKUGAWA LIFE. DECIDED TO TRAVEL, FIND SOMETHING I COULD REALLY GET INTO. NEVER DID, THOUGH.
HARDLY MET ANYONE STRONGER THAN ME...
BUT NOW, WITH KYO...
...THE EXCITEMENT NEVER STOPS!
I'm tellin' ya!
I LOVE TO WATCH HIM.

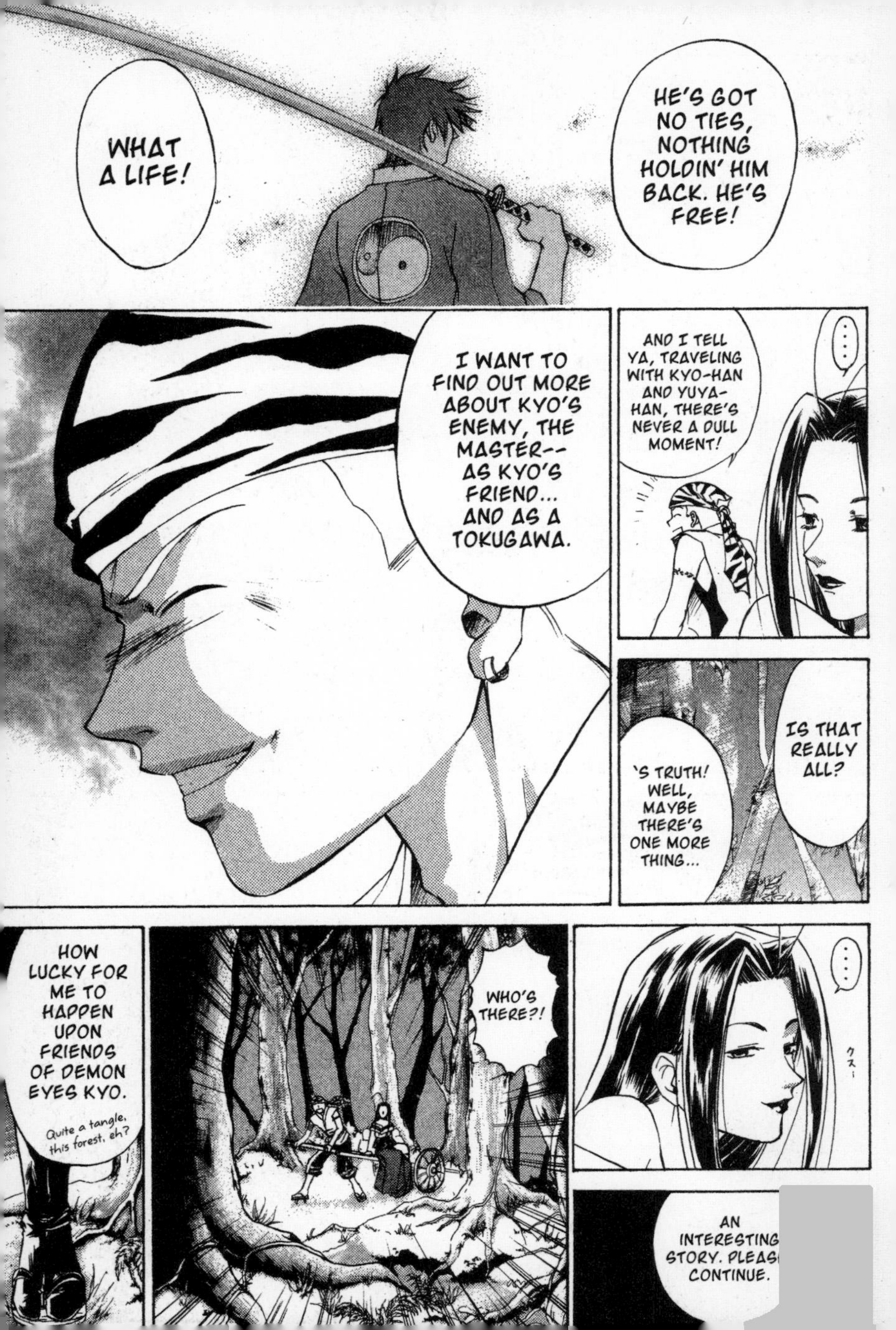
HE'S GOT NO TIES, NOTHING HOLDIN' HIM BACK. HE'S FREE!
WHAT A LIFE!
...
AND I TELL YA, TRAVELING WITH KYO-HAN AND YUYA-HAN, THERE'S NEVER A DULL MOMENT!
IS THAT REALLY ALL?
'S TRUTH! WELL, MAYBE THERE'S ONE MORE THING...
I WANT TO FIND OUT MORE ABOUT KYO'S ENEMY, THE MASTER-- AS KYO'S FRIEND... AND AS A TOKUGAWA.
...
クスー
AN INTERESTING STORY. PLEAS CONTINUE.
WHO'S THERE?!
HOW LUCKY FOR ME TO HAPPEN UPON FRIENDS OF DEMON EYES KYO.
Quite a tangle, this forest, eh?

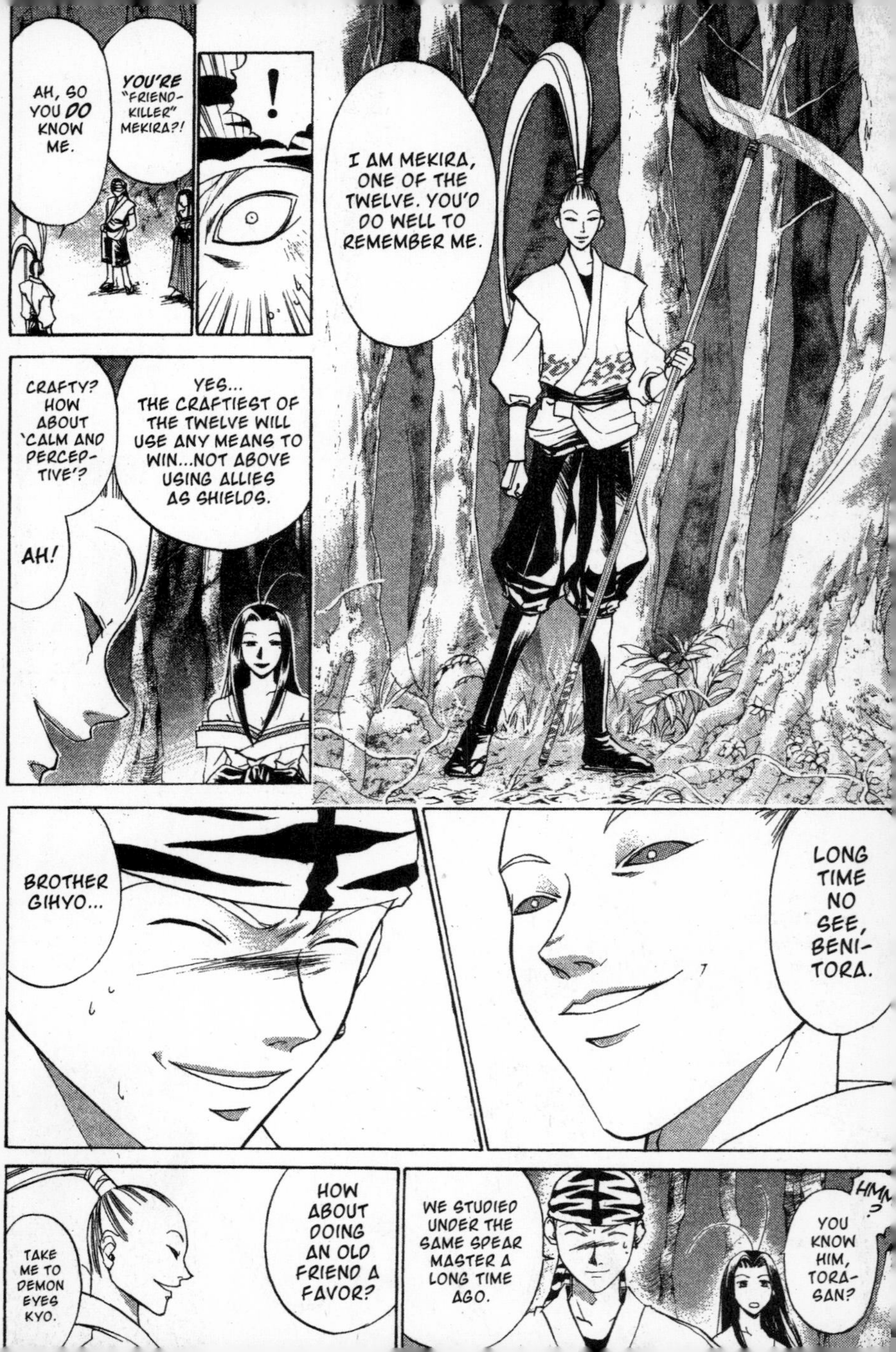
I AM MEKIRA, ONE OF THE TWELVE. YOU'D DO WELL TO REMEMBER ME.
!
YOU'RE "FRIEND-KILLER" MEKIRA?!
AH, SO YOU DO KNOW ME.
YES... THE CRAFTIEST OF THE TWELVE WILL USE ANY MEANS TO WIN...NOT ABOVE USING ALLIES AS SHIELDS.
CRAFTY? HOW ABOUT 'CALM AND PERCEPTIVE'?
AH!
LONG TIME NO SEE, BENI-TORA.
BROTHER GIHYO...
HMM?
YOU KNOW HIM, TORA-SAN?
WE STUDIED UNDER THE SAME SPEAR MASTER A LONG TIME AGO.
HOW ABOUT DOING AN OLD FRIEND A FAVOR?
TAKE ME TO DEMON EYES KYO.

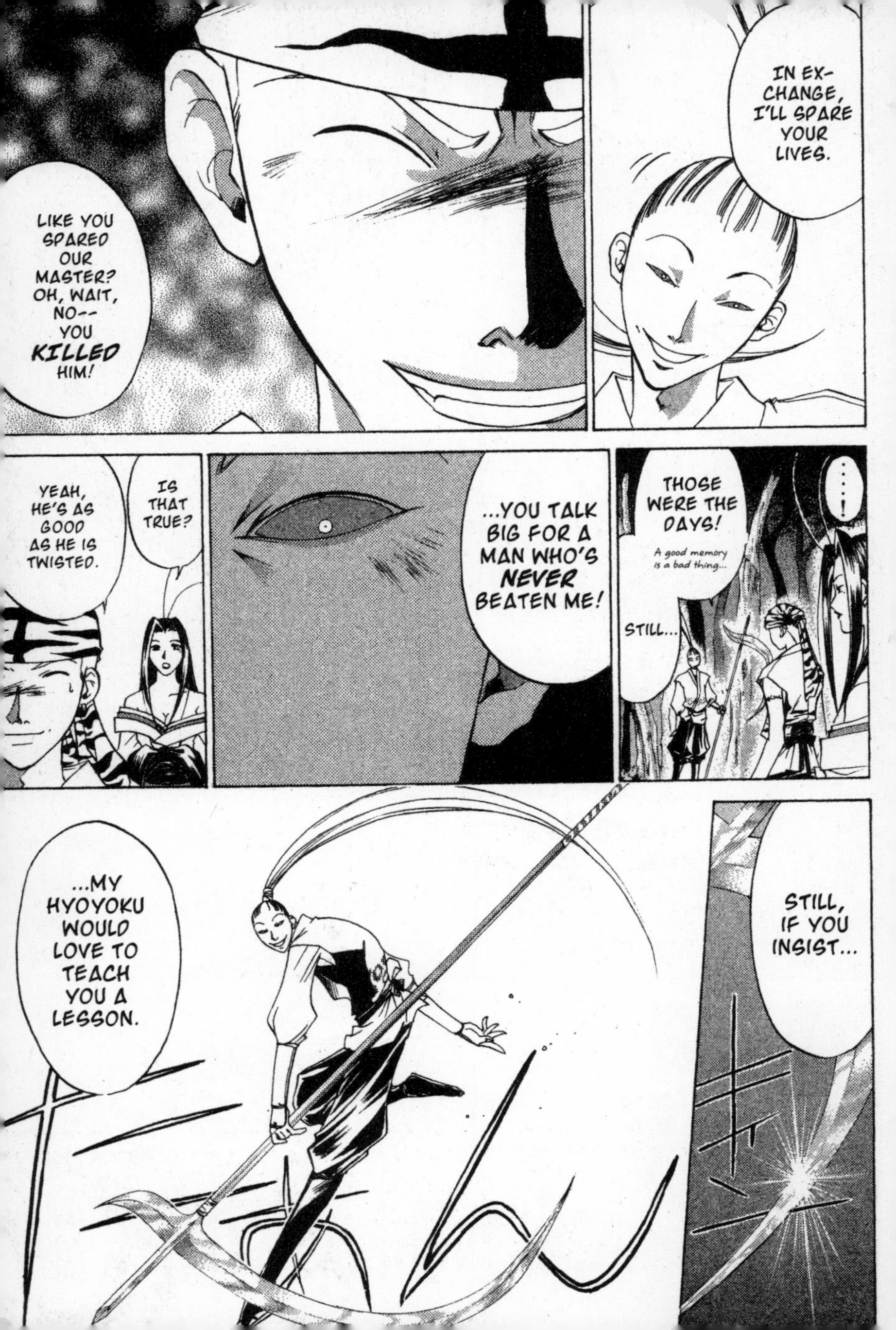
IN EX-CHANGE, I'LL SPARE YOUR LIVES.
LIKE YOU SPARED OUR MASTER? OH, WAIT, NO-- YOU KILLED HIM!
...!
THOSE WERE THE DAYS!
A good memory is a bad thing...
STILL...
...YOU TALK BIG FOR A MAN WHO'S NEVER BEATEN ME!
IS THAT TRUE?
YEAH, HE'S AS GOOD AS HE IS TWISTED.
STILL, IF YOU INSIST...
...MY HYOYOKU WOULD LOVE TO TEACH YOU A LESSON.

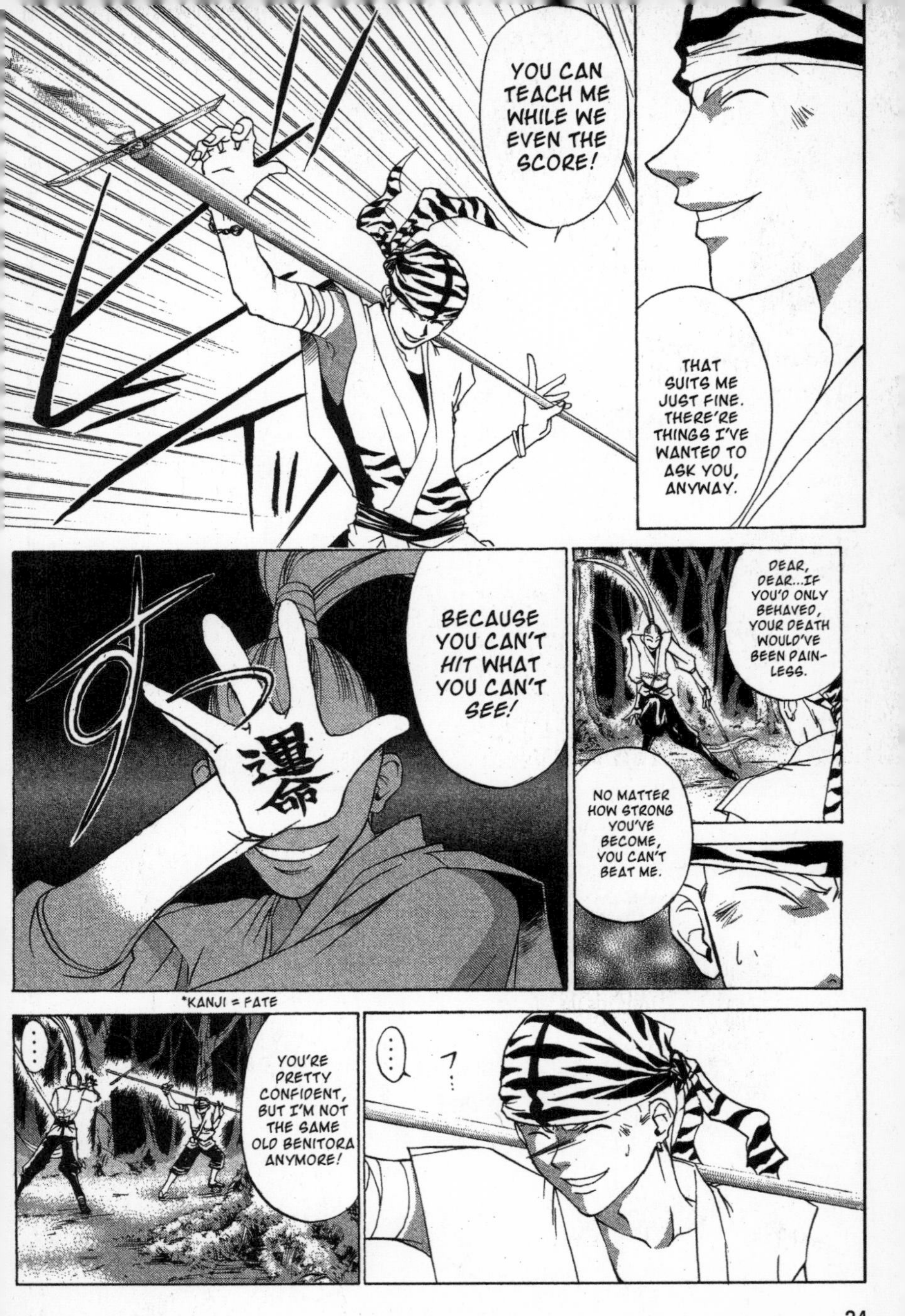
YOU CAN TEACH ME WHILE WE EVEN THE SCORE!
THAT SUITS ME JUST FINE. THERE'RE THINGS I'VE WANTED TO ASK YOU, ANYWAY.
DEAR, DEAR...IF YOU'D ONLY BEHAVED, YOUR DEATH WOULD'VE BEEN PAIN-LESS.
NO MATTER HOW STRONG YOU'VE BECOME, YOU CAN'T BEAT ME.
BECAUSE YOU CAN'T *HIT* WHAT YOU CAN'T *SEE!*
運命
*KANJI = FATE
....?
....
YOU'RE PRETTY CONFIDENT, BUT I'M NOT THE SAME OLD BENITORA ANYMORE!

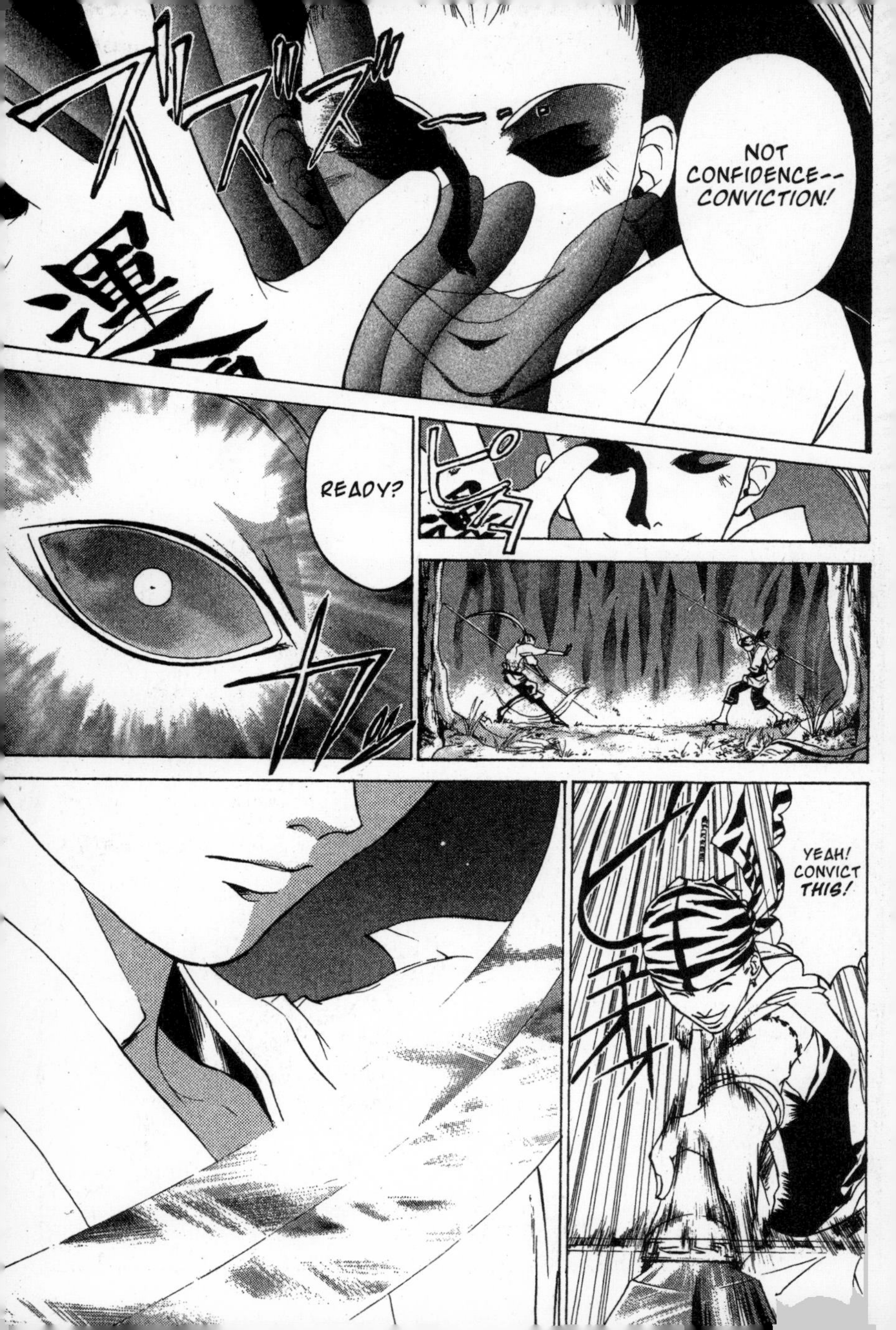
NOT CONFIDENCE-- CONVICTION!
READY?
YEAH! CONVICT THIS!

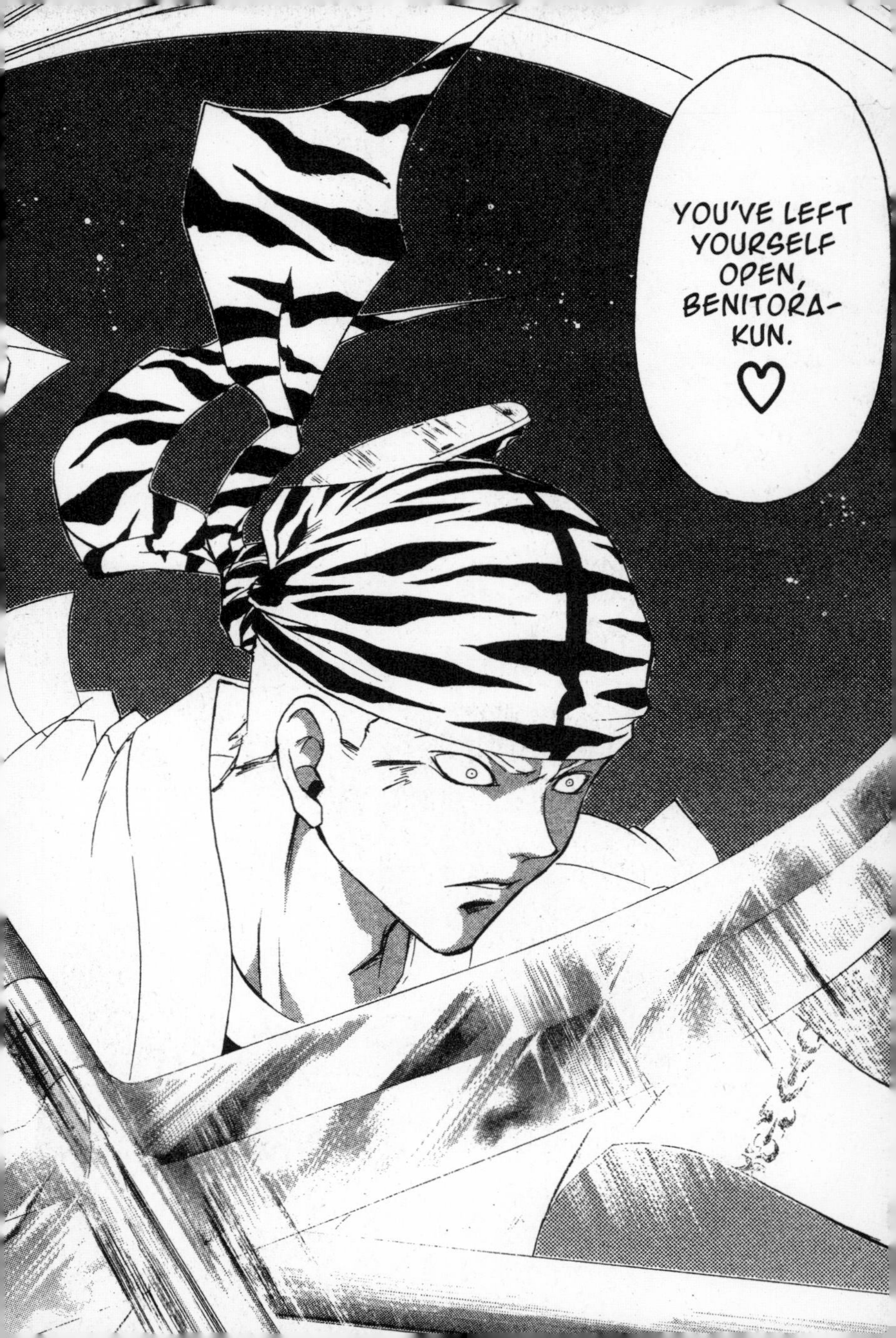
YOU'VE LEFT YOURSELF OPEN, BENITORA-KUN. ♡

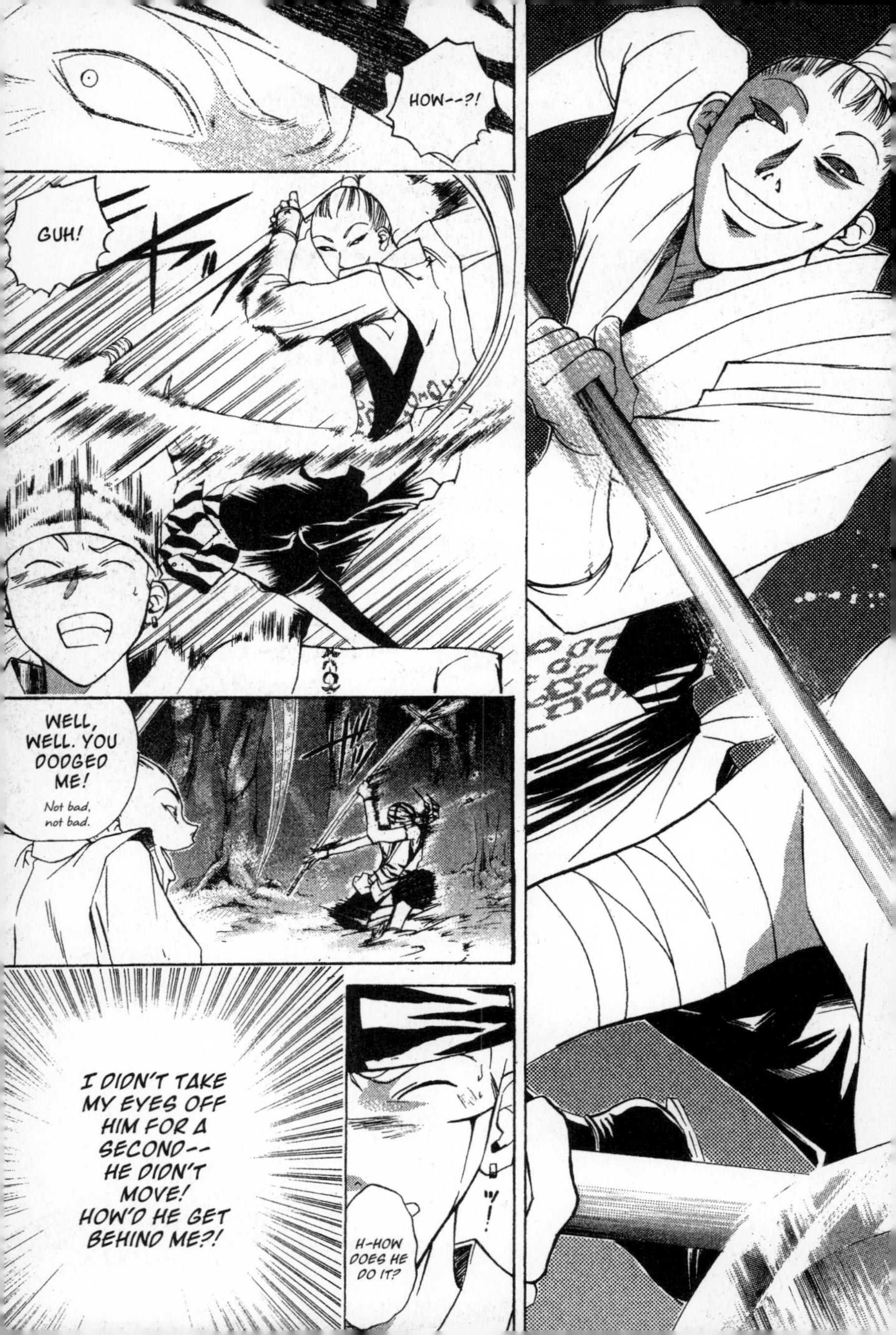
HOW--?!
GUH!
WELL, WELL. YOU DODGED ME!
Not bad, not bad.
H-HOW DOES HE DO IT?
I DIDN'T TAKE MY EYES OFF HIM FOR A SECOND-- HE DIDN'T MOVE! HOW'D HE GET BEHIND ME?!

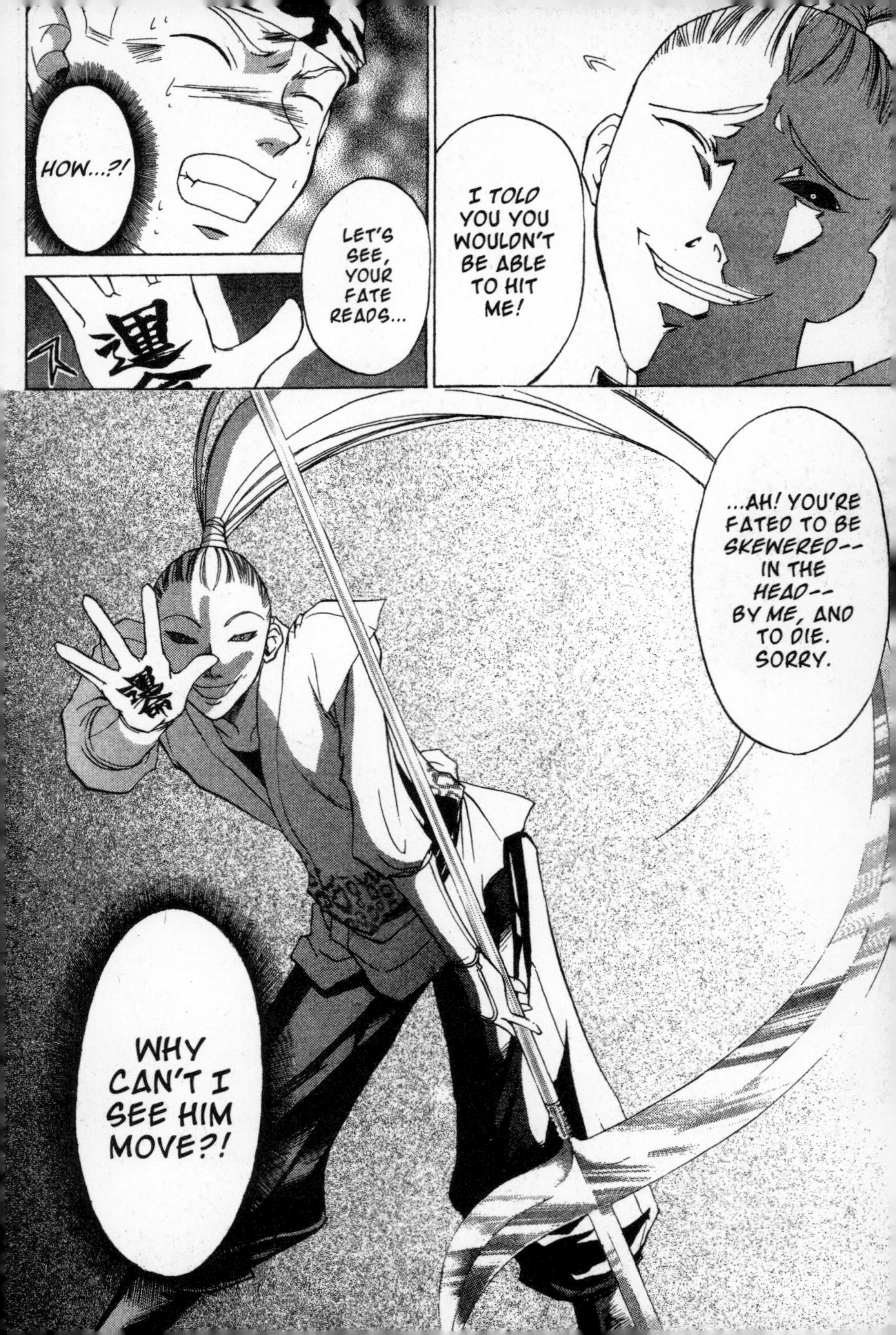
I TOLD YOU YOU WOULDN'T BE ABLE TO HIT ME!
HOW...?!
LET'S SEE, YOUR FATE READS...
...AH! YOU'RE FATED TO BE SKEWERED-- IN THE HEAD-- BY ME, AND TO DIE. SORRY.
WHY CAN'T I SEE HIM MOVE?!

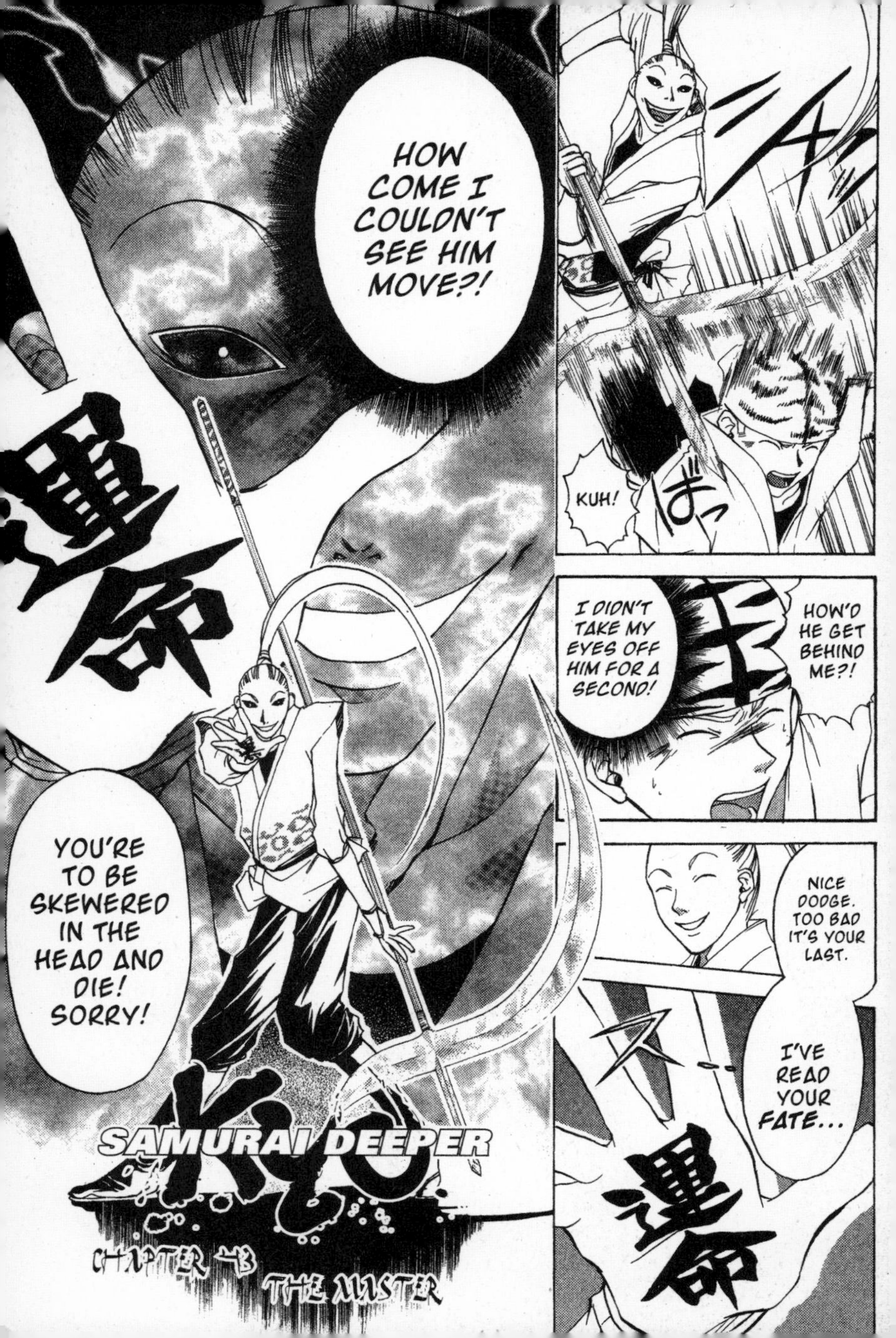
KUH!
ばっ
HOW'D HE GET BEHIND ME?!
I DIDN'T TAKE MY EYES OFF HIM FOR A SECOND!
NICE DODGE. TOO BAD IT'S YOUR LAST.
I'VE READ YOUR FATE...
運命
HOW COME I COULDN'T SEE HIM MOVE?!
運命
YOU'RE TO BE SKEWERED IN THE HEAD AND DIE! SORRY!
SAMURAI DEEPER
KYO
CHAPTER 43 THE MASTER

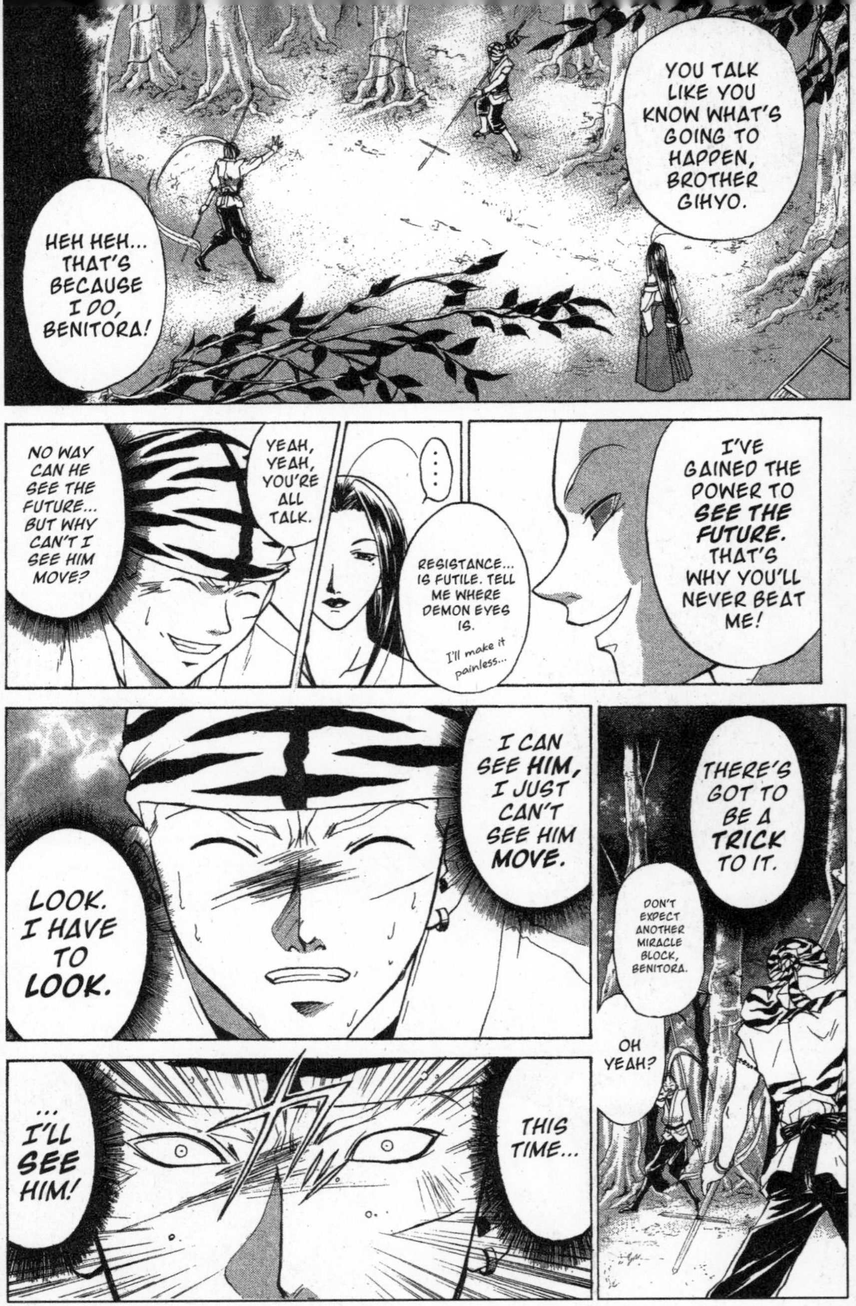
YOU TALK LIKE YOU KNOW WHAT'S GOING TO HAPPEN, BROTHER GIHYO.
HEH HEH... THAT'S BECAUSE I DO, BENITORA!
I'VE GAINED THE POWER TO SEE THE FUTURE. THAT'S WHY YOU'LL NEVER BEAT ME!
...
RESISTANCE... IS FUTILE. TELL ME WHERE DEMON EYES IS.
I'll make it painless...
YEAH, YEAH, YOU'RE ALL TALK.
NO WAY CAN HE SEE THE FUTURE... BUT WHY CAN'T I SEE HIM MOVE?
THERE'S GOT TO BE A TRICK TO IT.
DON'T EXPECT ANOTHER MIRACLE BLOCK, BENITORA.
OH YEAH?
I CAN SEE HIM, I JUST CAN'T SEE HIM MOVE.
LOOK. I HAVE TO LOOK.
THIS TIME...
...I'LL SEE HIM!

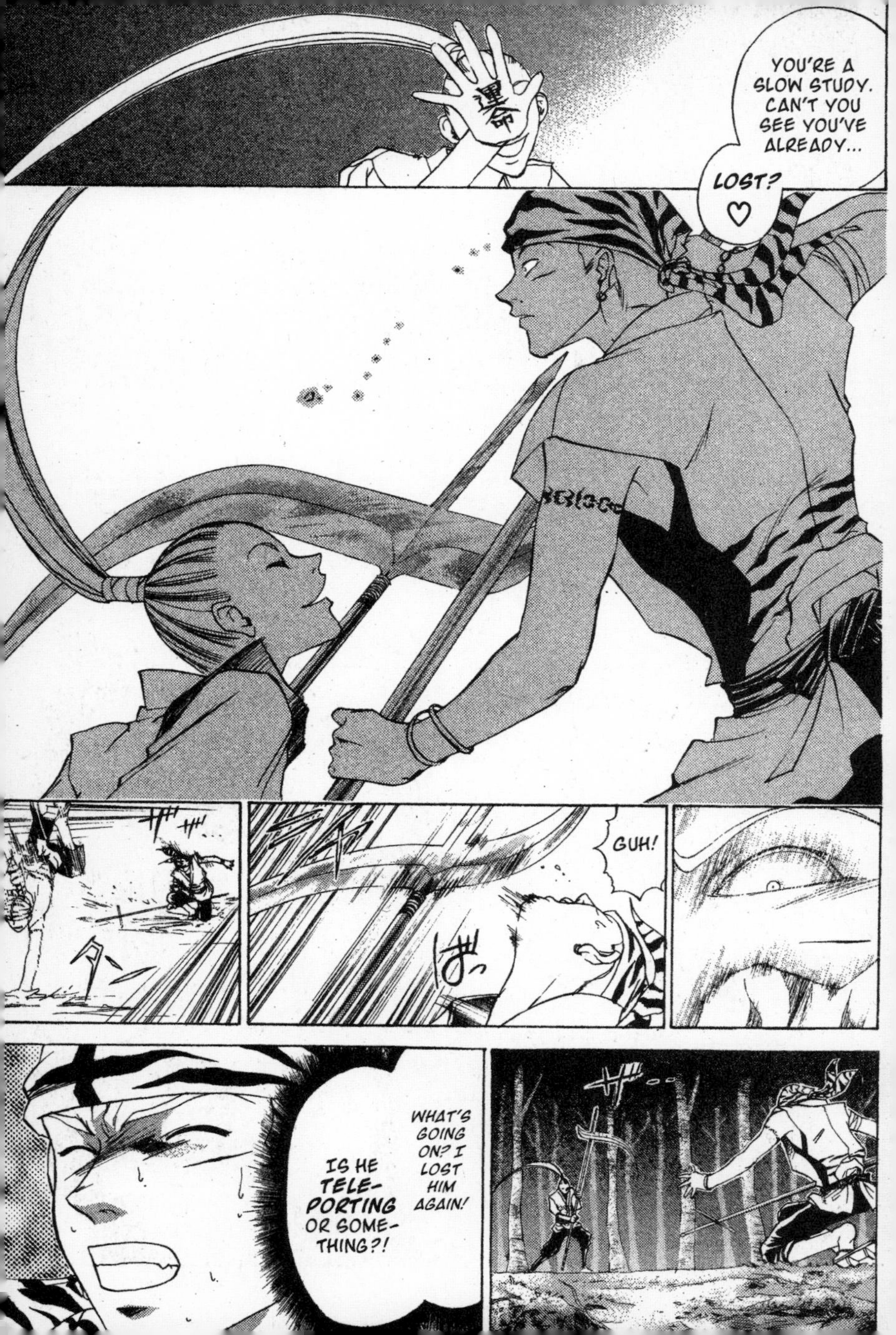

運命
YOU'RE A SLOW STUDY. CAN'T YOU SEE YOU'VE ALREADY...
LOST? ♡
GUH!
WHAT'S GOING ON? I LOST HIM AGAIN!
IS HE **TELE-PORTING** OR SOME-THING?!

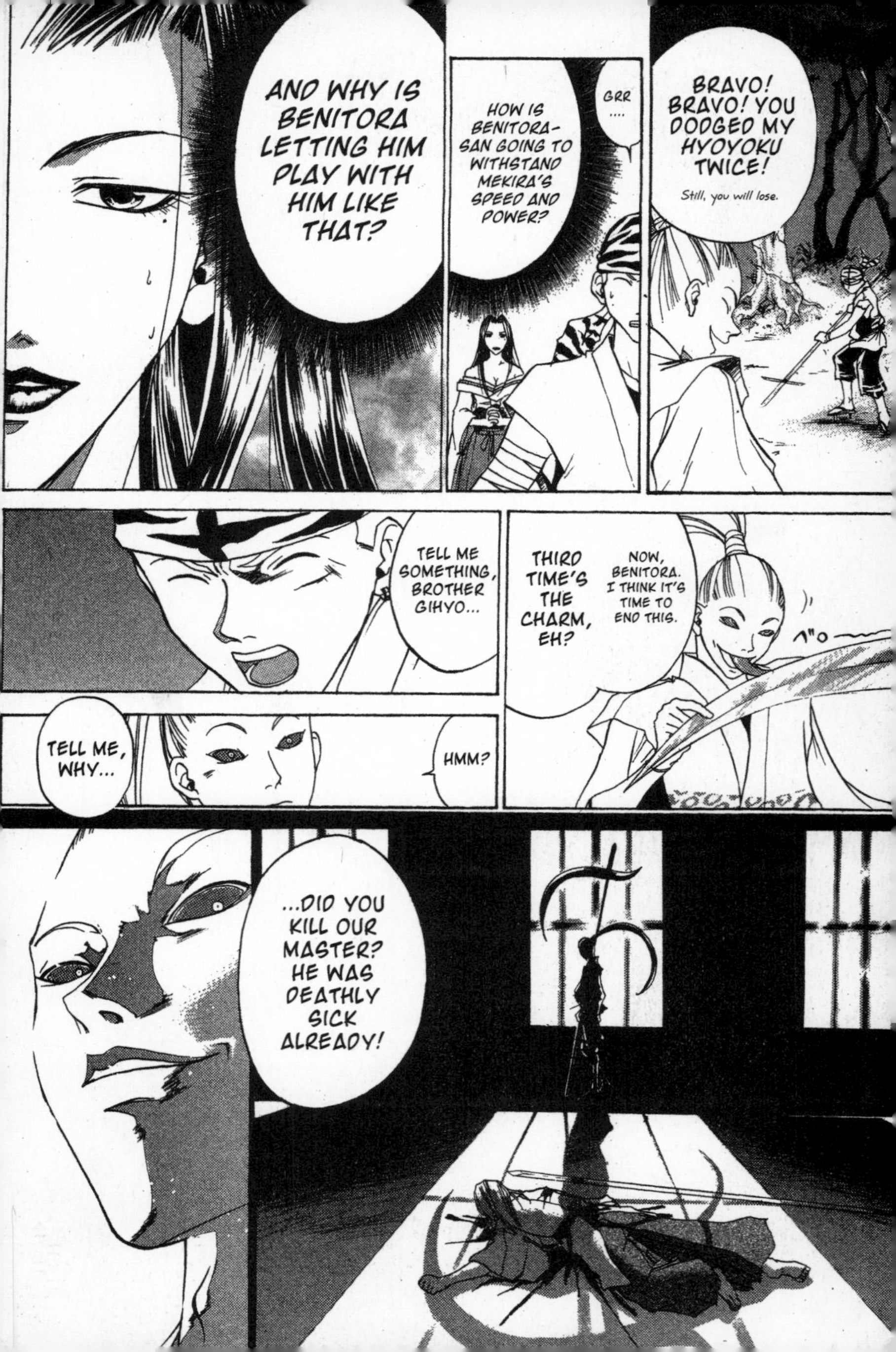
BRAVO! BRAVO! YOU DODGED MY HYOYOKU TWICE!
Still, you will lose.
GRR ....
HOW IS BENITORA-SAN GOING TO WITHSTAND MEKIRA'S SPEED AND POWER?
AND WHY IS BENITORA LETTING HIM PLAY WITH HIM LIKE THAT?
NOW, BENITORA. I THINK IT'S TIME TO END THIS.
THIRD TIME'S THE CHARM, EH?
TELL ME SOMETHING, BROTHER GIHYO...
HMM?
TELL ME, WHY...
...DID YOU KILL OUR MASTER? HE WAS DEATHLY SICK ALREADY!

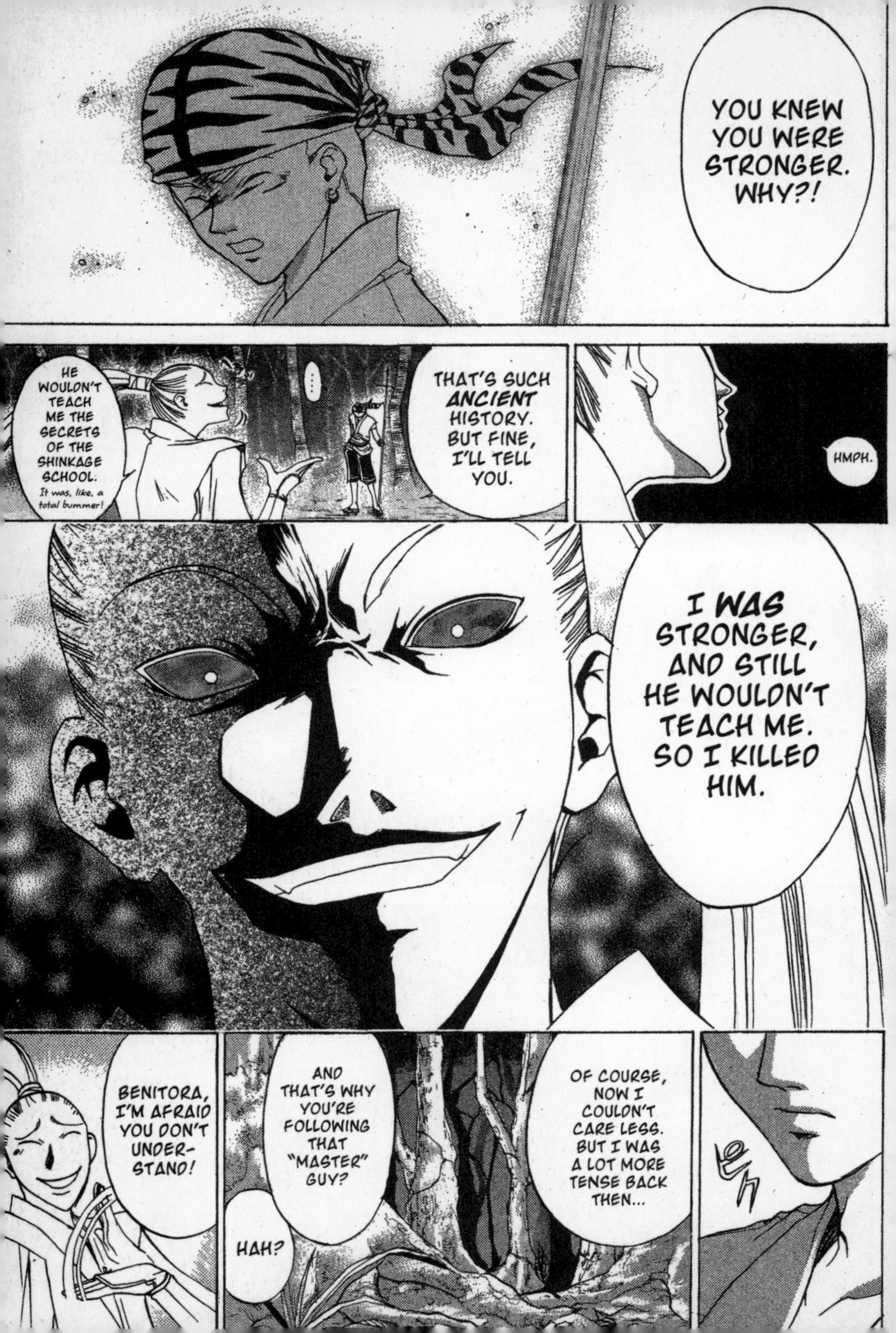
YOU KNEW YOU WERE STRONGER. WHY?!
HMPH.
THAT'S SUCH ANCIENT HISTORY. BUT FINE, I'LL TELL YOU.
....
HE WOULDN'T TEACH ME THE SECRETS OF THE SHINKAGE SCHOOL.
It was, like, a total bummer!
I WAS STRONGER, AND STILL HE WOULDN'T TEACH ME. SO I KILLED HIM.
OF COURSE, NOW I COULDN'T CARE LESS. BUT I WAS A LOT MORE TENSE BACK THEN...
AND THAT'S WHY YOU'RE FOLLOWING THAT "MASTER" GUY?
HAH?
BENITORA, I'M AFRAID YOU DON'T UNDER-STAND!

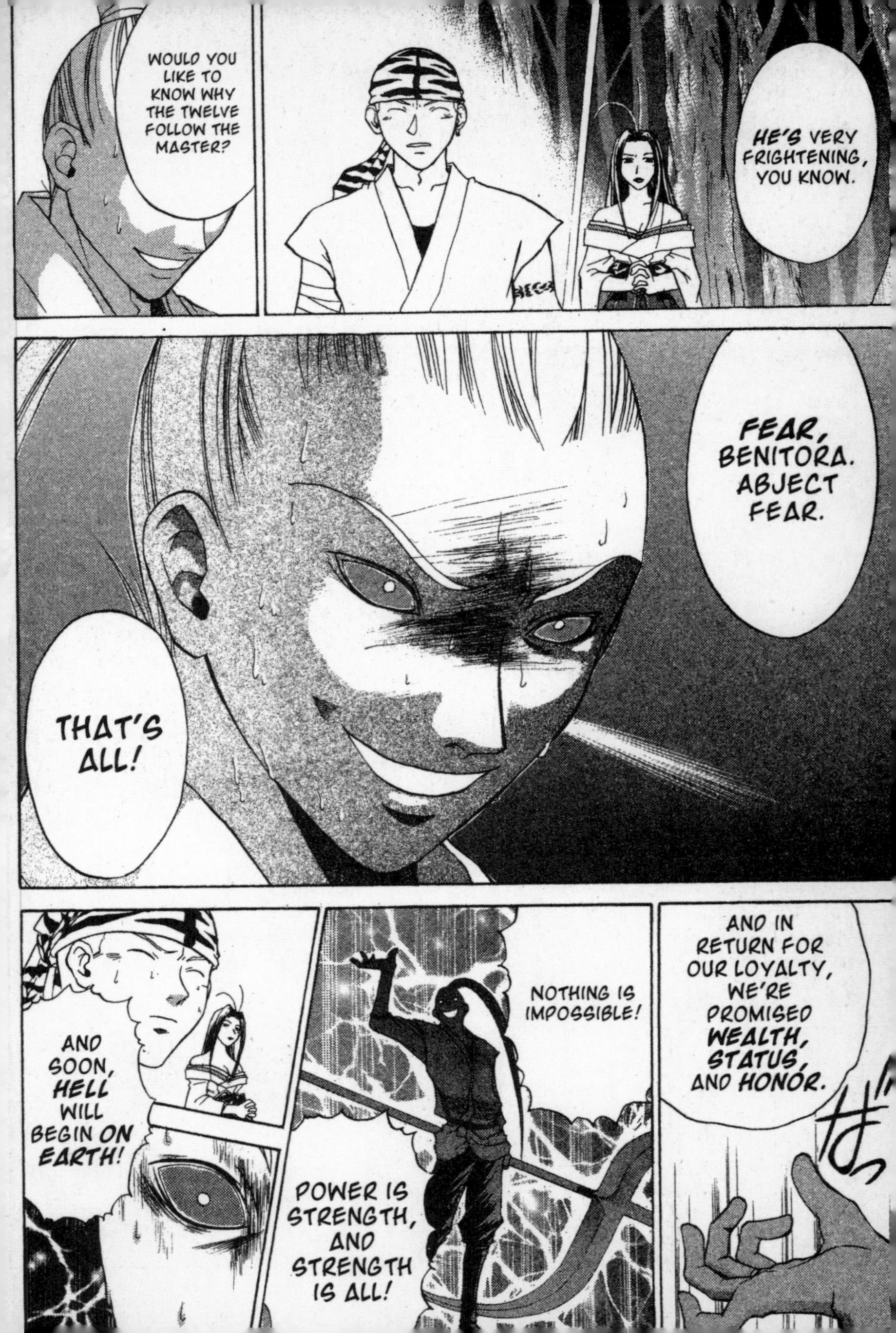
HE'S VERY FRIGHTENING, YOU KNOW.
WOULD YOU LIKE TO KNOW WHY THE TWELVE FOLLOW THE MASTER?
FEAR, BENITORA. ABJECT FEAR.
THAT'S ALL!
AND IN RETURN FOR OUR LOYALTY, WE'RE PROMISED WEALTH, STATUS, AND HONOR.
NOTHING IS IMPOSSIBLE!
POWER IS STRENGTH, AND STRENGTH IS ALL!
AND SOON, HELL WILL BEGIN ON EARTH!

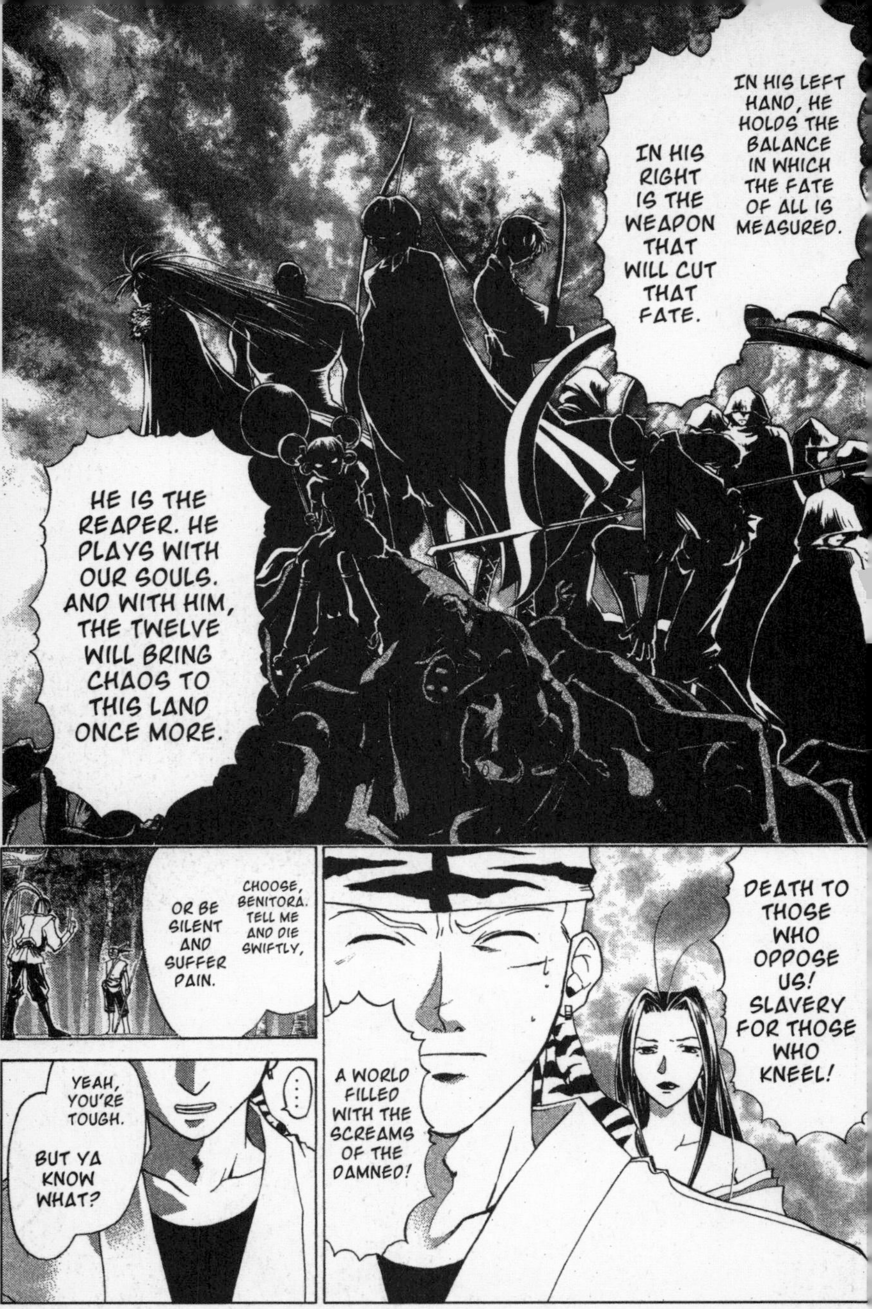
IN HIS LEFT HAND, HE HOLDS THE BALANCE IN WHICH THE FATE OF ALL IS MEASURED.
IN HIS RIGHT IS THE WEAPON THAT WILL CUT THAT FATE.
HE IS THE REAPER. HE PLAYS WITH OUR SOULS. AND WITH HIM, THE TWELVE WILL BRING CHAOS TO THIS LAND ONCE MORE.
DEATH TO THOSE WHO OPPOSE US! SLAVERY FOR THOSE WHO KNEEL!
A WORLD FILLED WITH THE SCREAMS OF THE DAMNED!
CHOOSE, BENITORA. TELL ME AND DIE SWIFTLY,
OR BE SILENT AND SUFFER PAIN.
...
YEAH, YOU'RE TOUGH.
BUT YA KNOW WHAT?

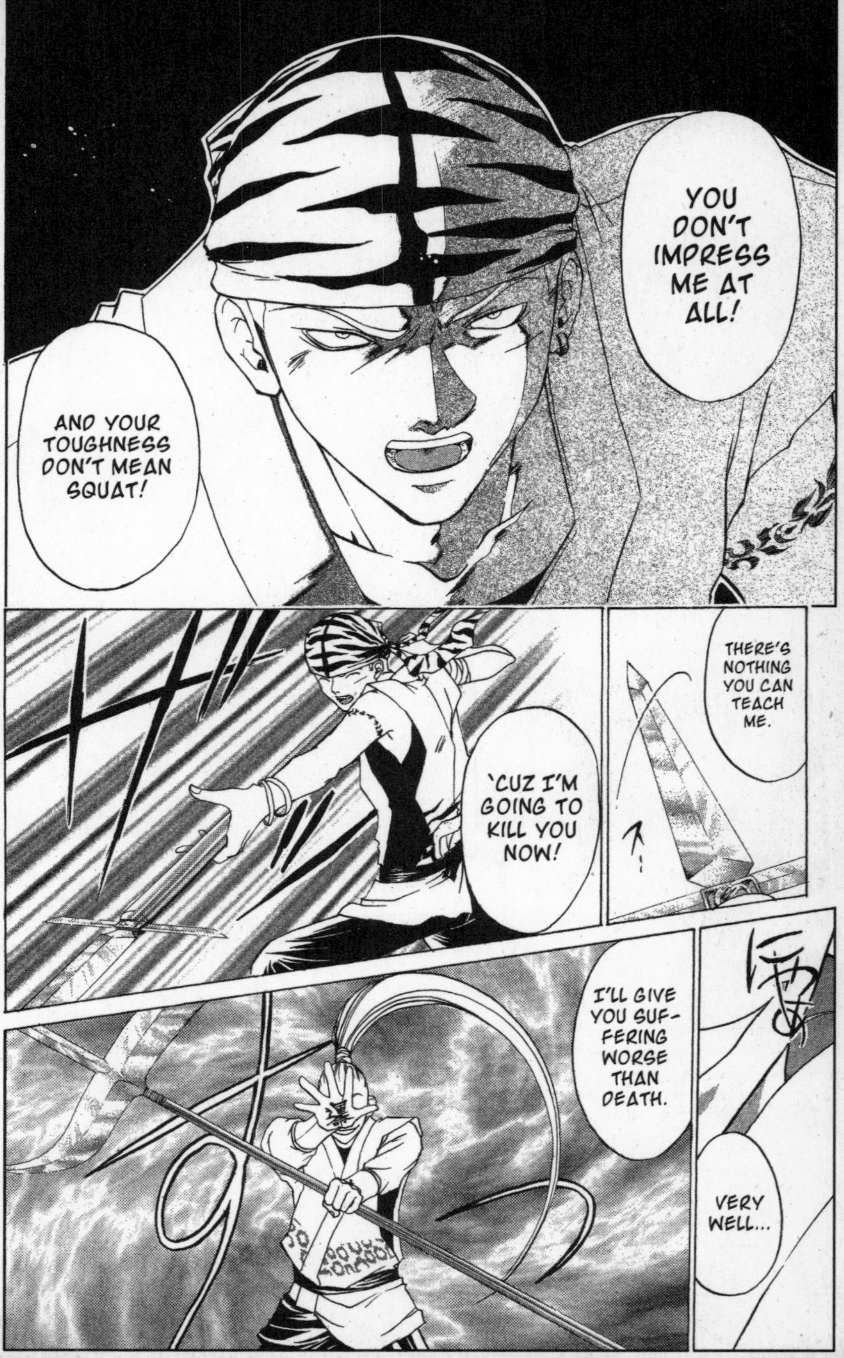
YOU DON'T IMPRESS ME AT ALL!
AND YOUR TOUGHNESS DON'T MEAN SQUAT!
THERE'S NOTHING YOU CAN TEACH ME.
`CUZ I'M GOING TO KILL YOU NOW!
VERY WELL...
I'LL GIVE YOU SUF-FERING WORSE THAN DEATH.

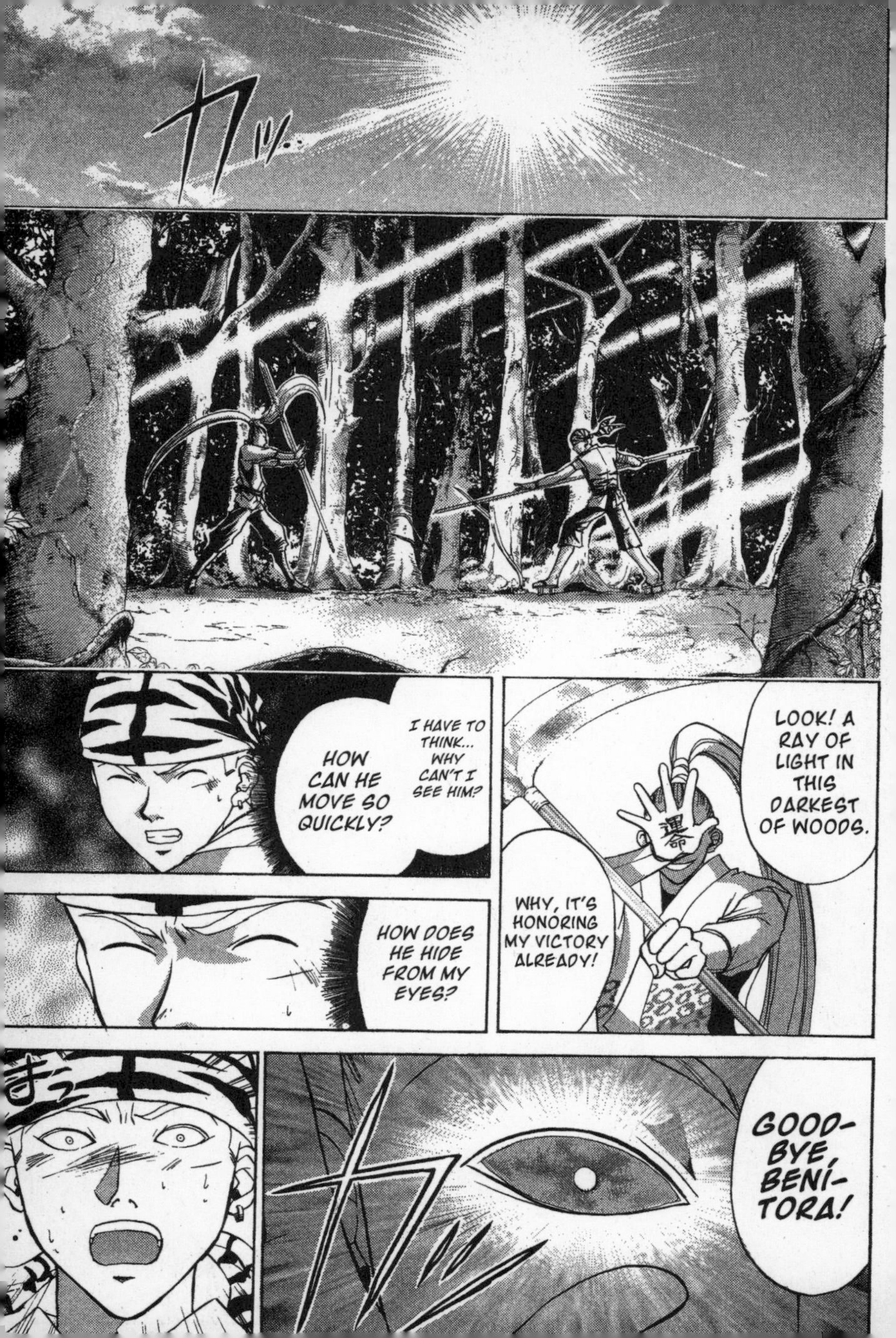
カッ…
運命
LOOK! A RAY OF LIGHT IN THIS DARKEST OF WOODS.
WHY, IT'S HONORING MY VICTORY ALREADY!
I HAVE TO THINK... WHY CAN'T I SEE HIM?
HOW CAN HE MOVE SO QUICKLY?
HOW DOES HE HIDE FROM MY EYES?
GOOD-BYE, BENÍTORA!
カッ
まっ

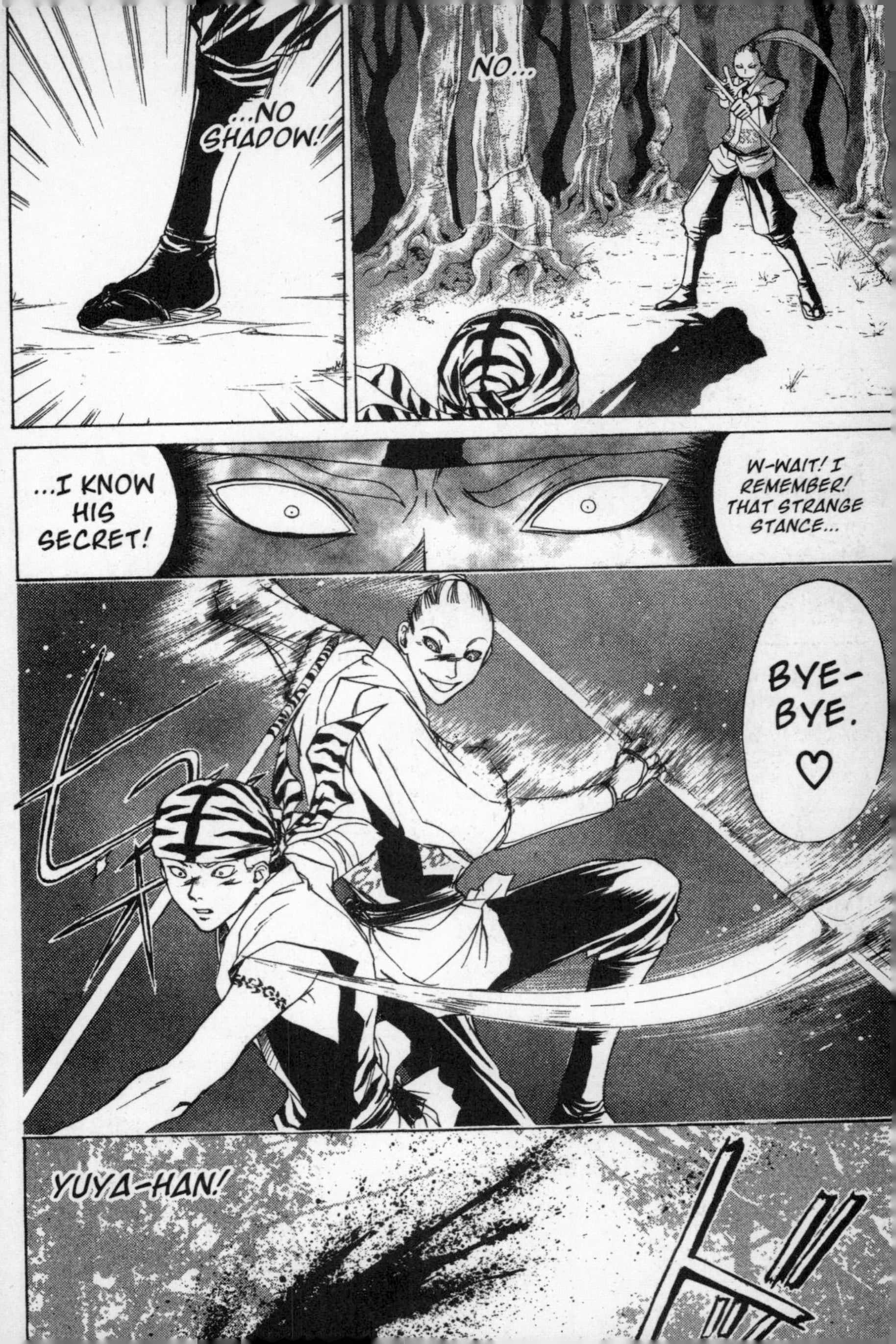
NO...
...NO SHADOW!
W-WAIT! I REMEMBER! THAT STRANGE STANCE...
...I KNOW HIS SECRET!
BYE-BYE. ♡
YUYA-HAN!

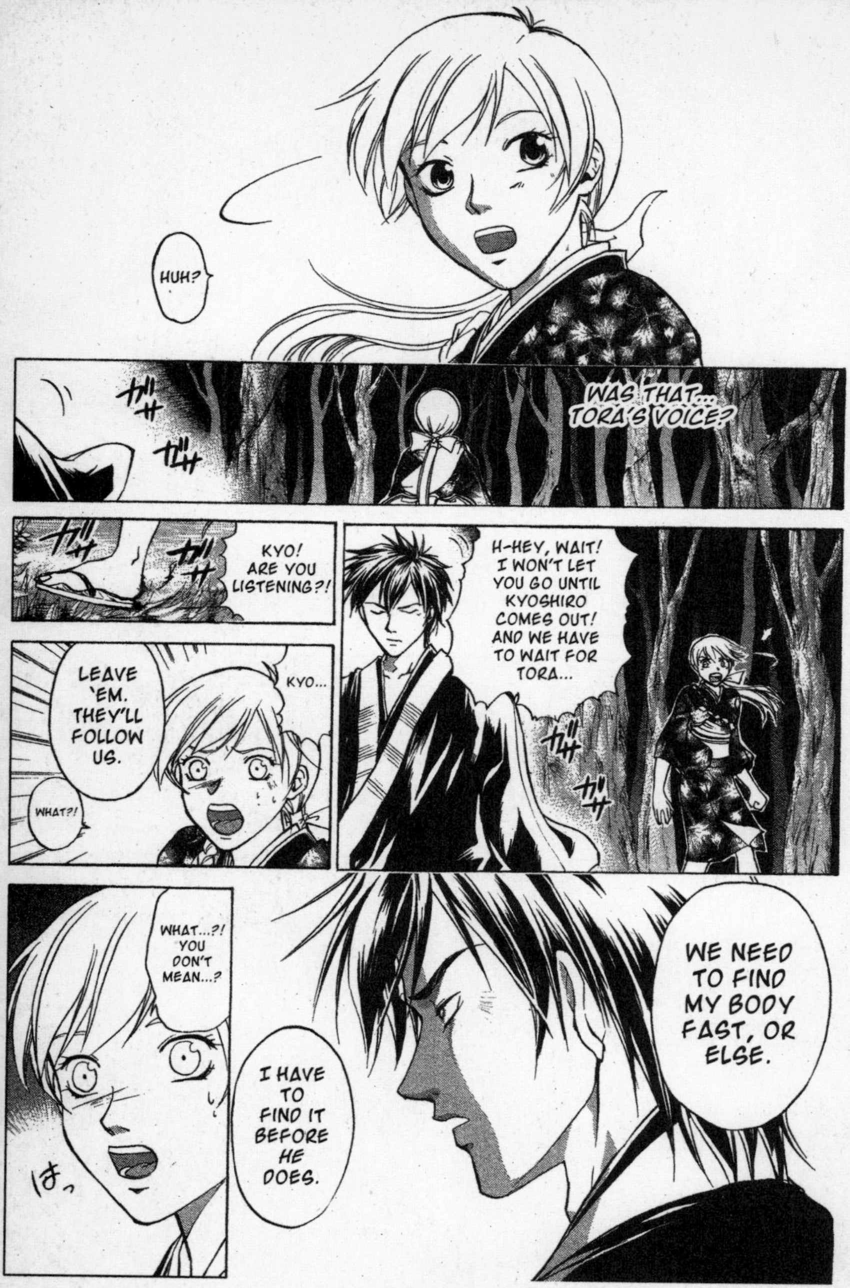
HUH?
WAS THAT... TORA'S VOICE?
H-HEY, WAIT! I WON'T LET YOU GO UNTIL KYOSHIRO COMES OUT! AND WE HAVE TO WAIT FOR TORA...
KYO! ARE YOU LISTENING?!
KYO...
LEAVE 'EM. THEY'LL FOLLOW US.
WHAT?!
WE NEED TO FIND MY BODY FAST, OR ELSE.
I HAVE TO FIND IT BEFORE HE DOES.
WHAT...?! YOU DON'T MEAN...?
はっ

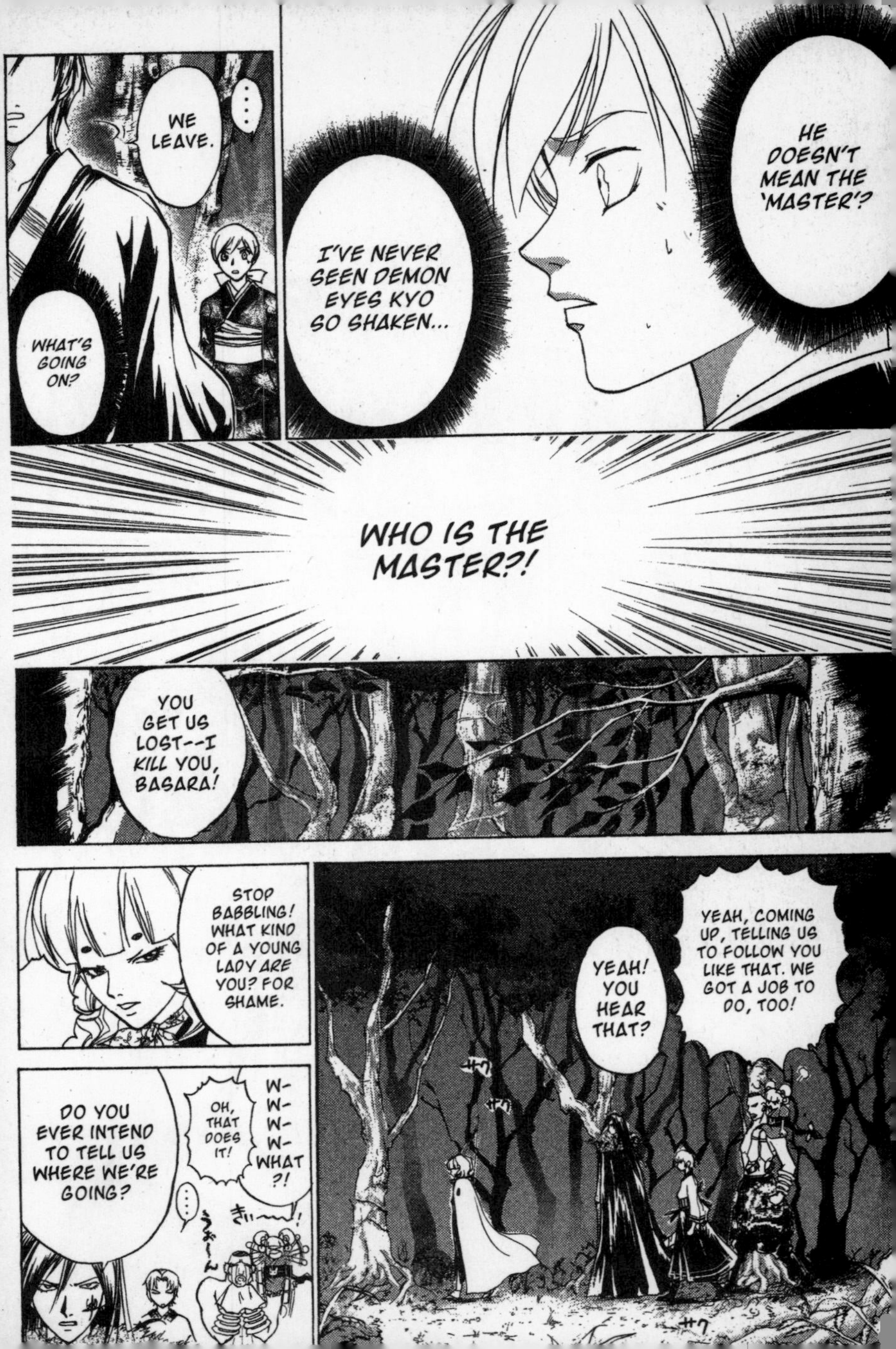
HE DOESN'T MEAN THE 'MASTER'?
I'VE NEVER SEEN DEMON EYES KYO SO SHAKEN...
...
WE LEAVE.
WHAT'S GOING ON?
WHO IS THE MASTER?!
YOU GET US LOST--I KILL YOU, BASARA!
YEAH, COMING UP, TELLING US TO FOLLOW YOU LIKE THAT. WE GOT A JOB TO DO, TOO!
YEAH! YOU HEAR THAT?
STOP BABBLING! WHAT KIND OF A YOUNG LADY ARE YOU? FOR SHAME.
W-W-W-W-WHAT?!
OH, THAT DOES IT!
DO YOU EVER INTEND TO TELL US WHERE WE'RE GOING?
...

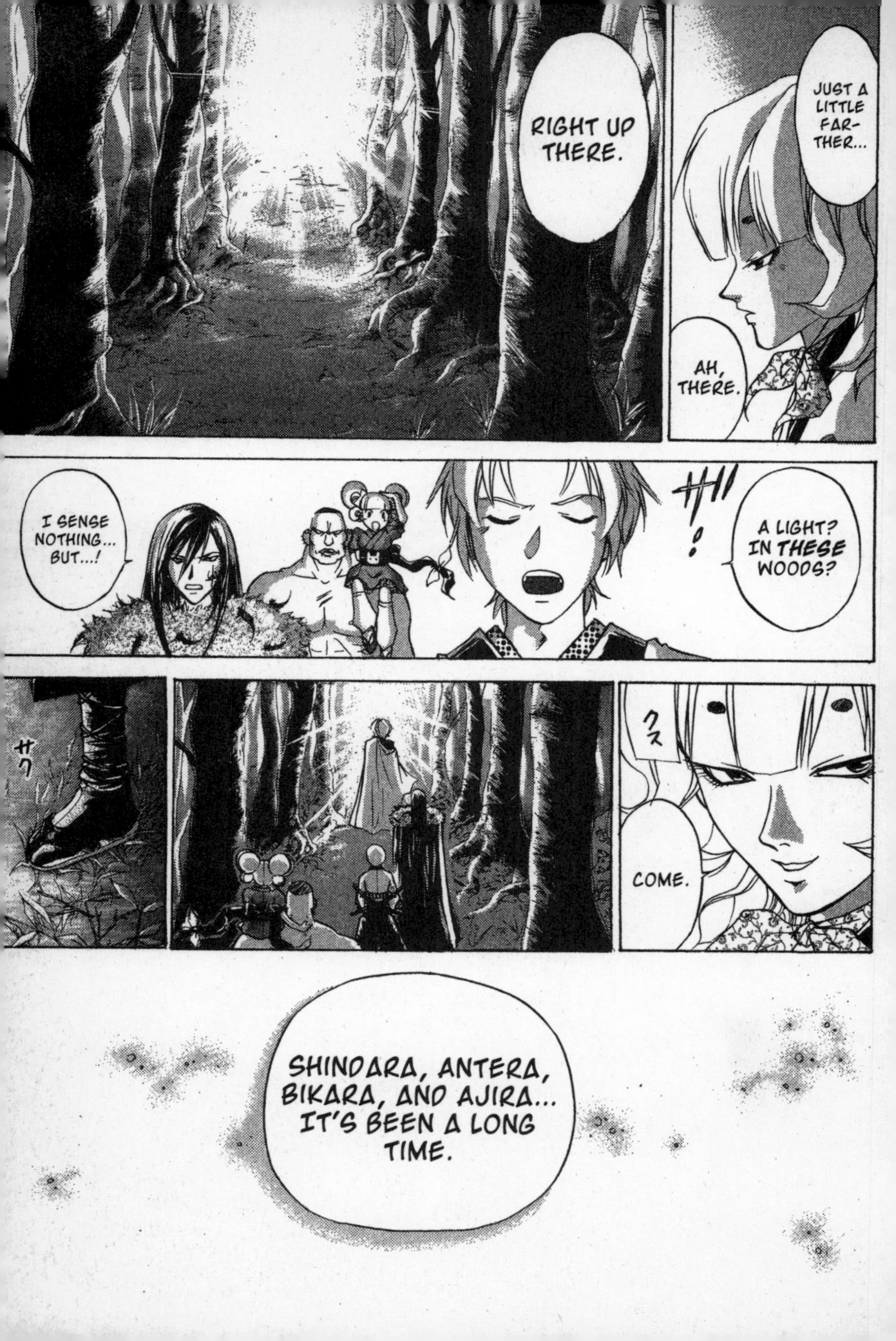
JUST A LITTLE FAR-THER...
AH, THERE.
RIGHT UP THERE.
A LIGHT? IN THESE WOODS?
I SENSE NOTHING... BUT...!
クス
COME.
サク
SHINDARA, ANTERA, BIKARA, AND AJIRA... IT'S BEEN A LONG TIME.

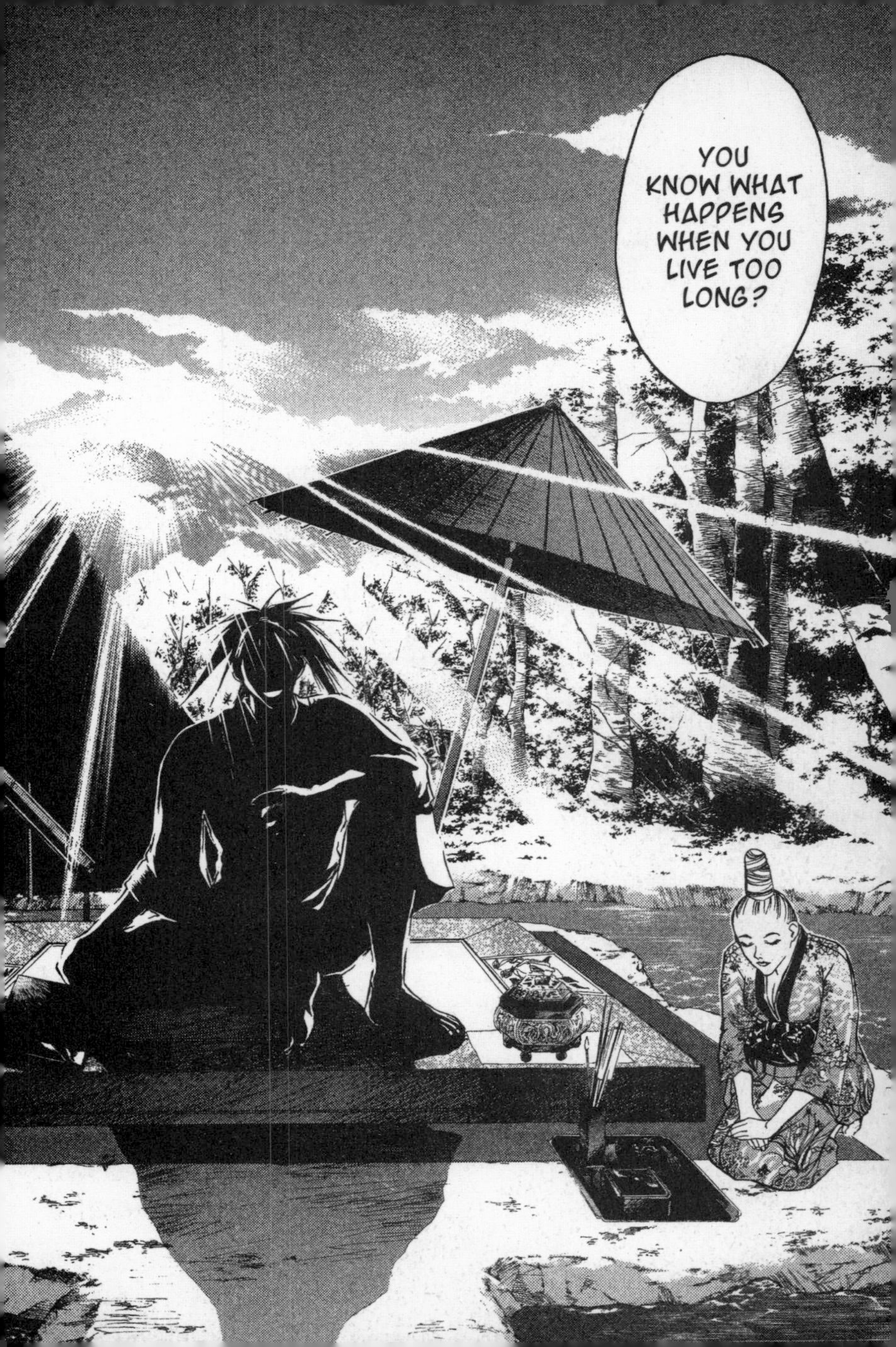
YOU KNOW WHAT HAPPENS WHEN YOU LIVE TOO LONG?

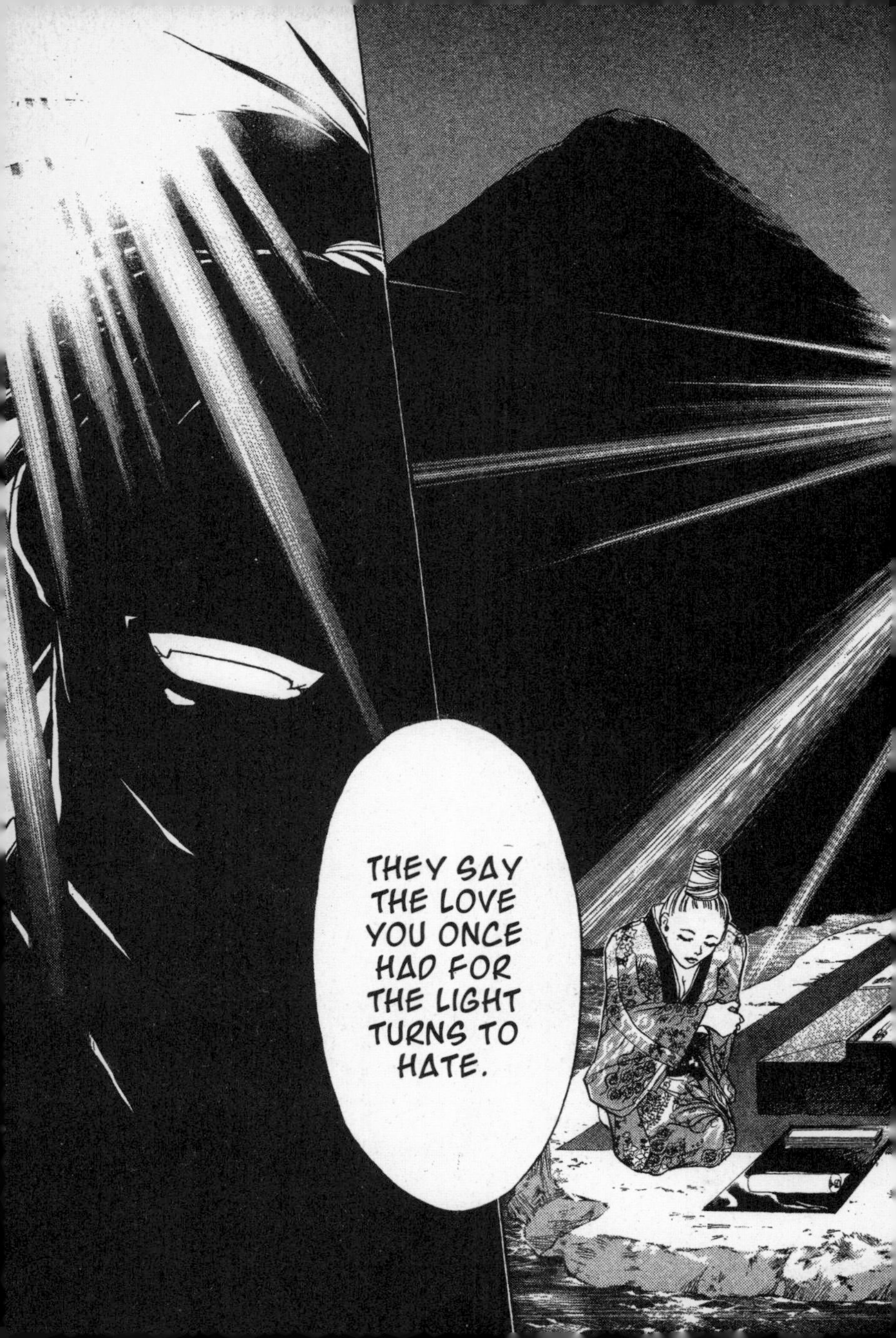
THEY SAY THE LOVE YOU ONCE HAD FOR THE LIGHT TURNS TO HATE.

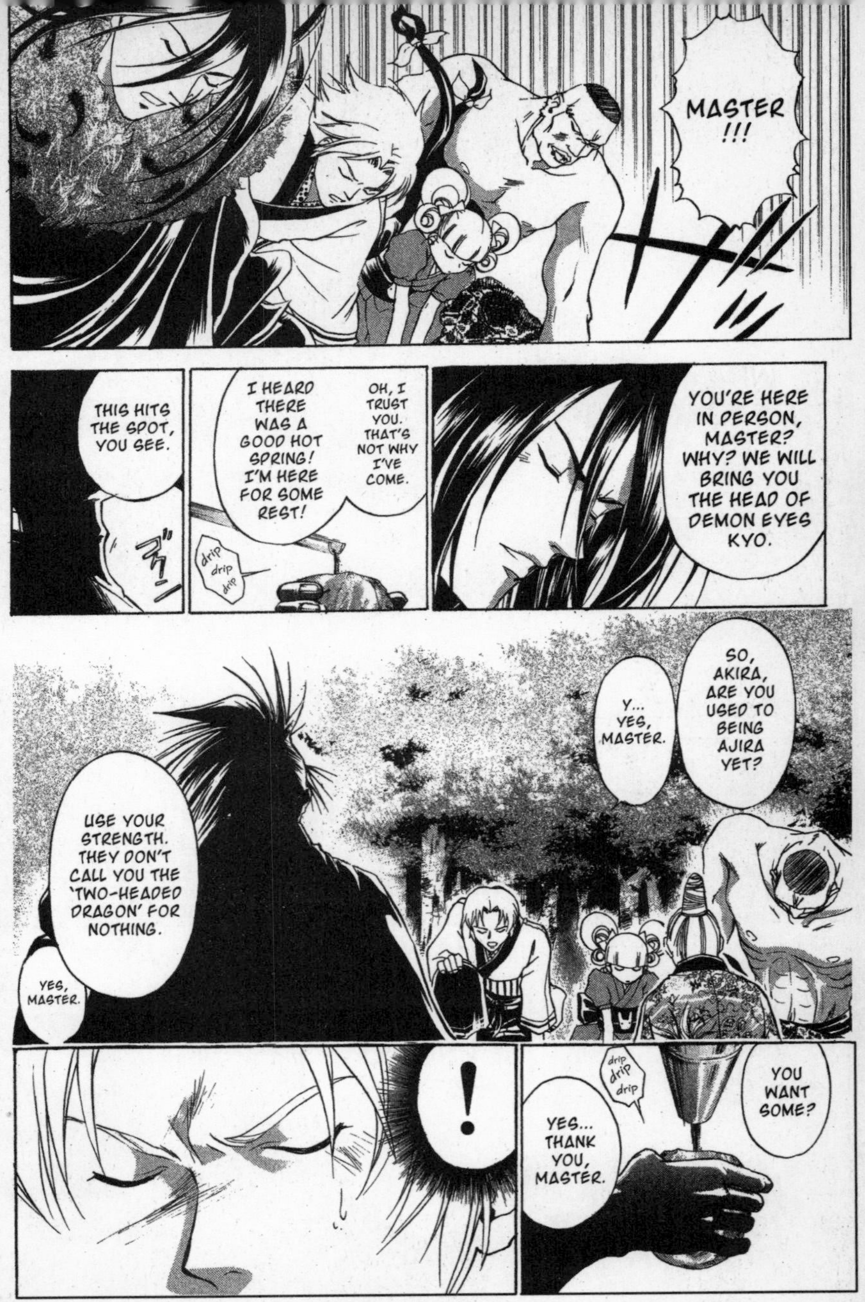
MASTER !!!
YOU'RE HERE IN PERSON, MASTER? WHY? WE WILL BRING YOU THE HEAD OF DEMON EYES KYO.
OH, I TRUST YOU. THAT'S NOT WHY I'VE COME.
I HEARD THERE WAS A GOOD HOT SPRING! I'M HERE FOR SOME REST!
drip drip drip
THIS HITS THE SPOT, YOU SEE.
SO, AKIRA, ARE YOU USED TO BEING AJIRA YET?
Y... YES, MASTER.
USE YOUR STRENGTH. THEY DON'T CALL YOU THE 'TWO-HEADED DRAGON' FOR NOTHING.
YES, MASTER.
drip drip drip
YOU WANT SOME?
YES... THANK YOU, MASTER.
!

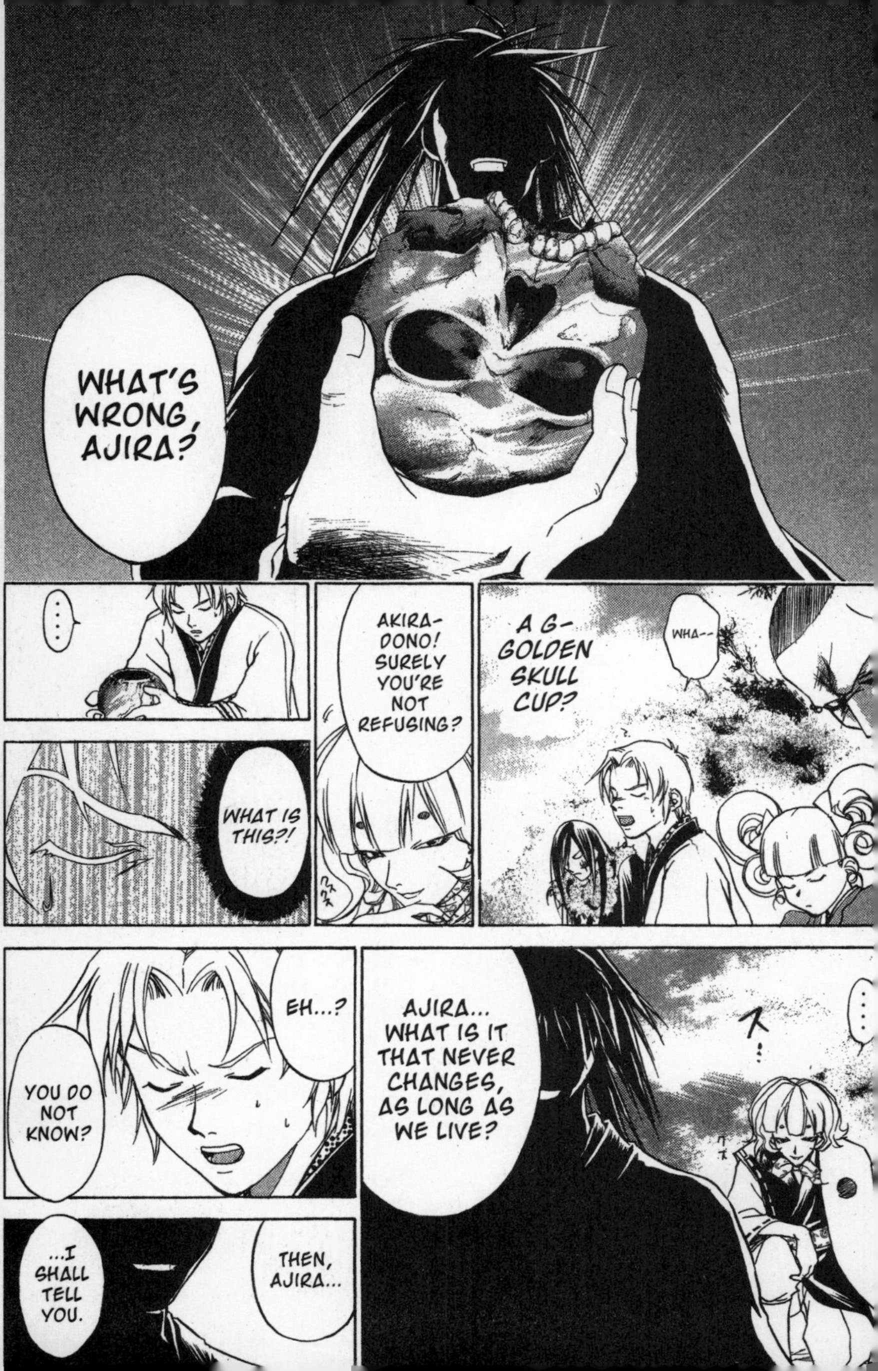
WHAT'S WRONG, AJIRA?
WHA--
A G-GOLDEN SKULL CUP?
AKIRA-DONO! SURELY YOU'RE NOT REFUSING?
...
WHAT IS THIS?!
...
AJIRA... WHAT IS IT THAT NEVER CHANGES, AS LONG AS WE LIVE?
EH...?
YOU DO NOT KNOW?
THEN, AJIRA...
...I SHALL TELL YOU.

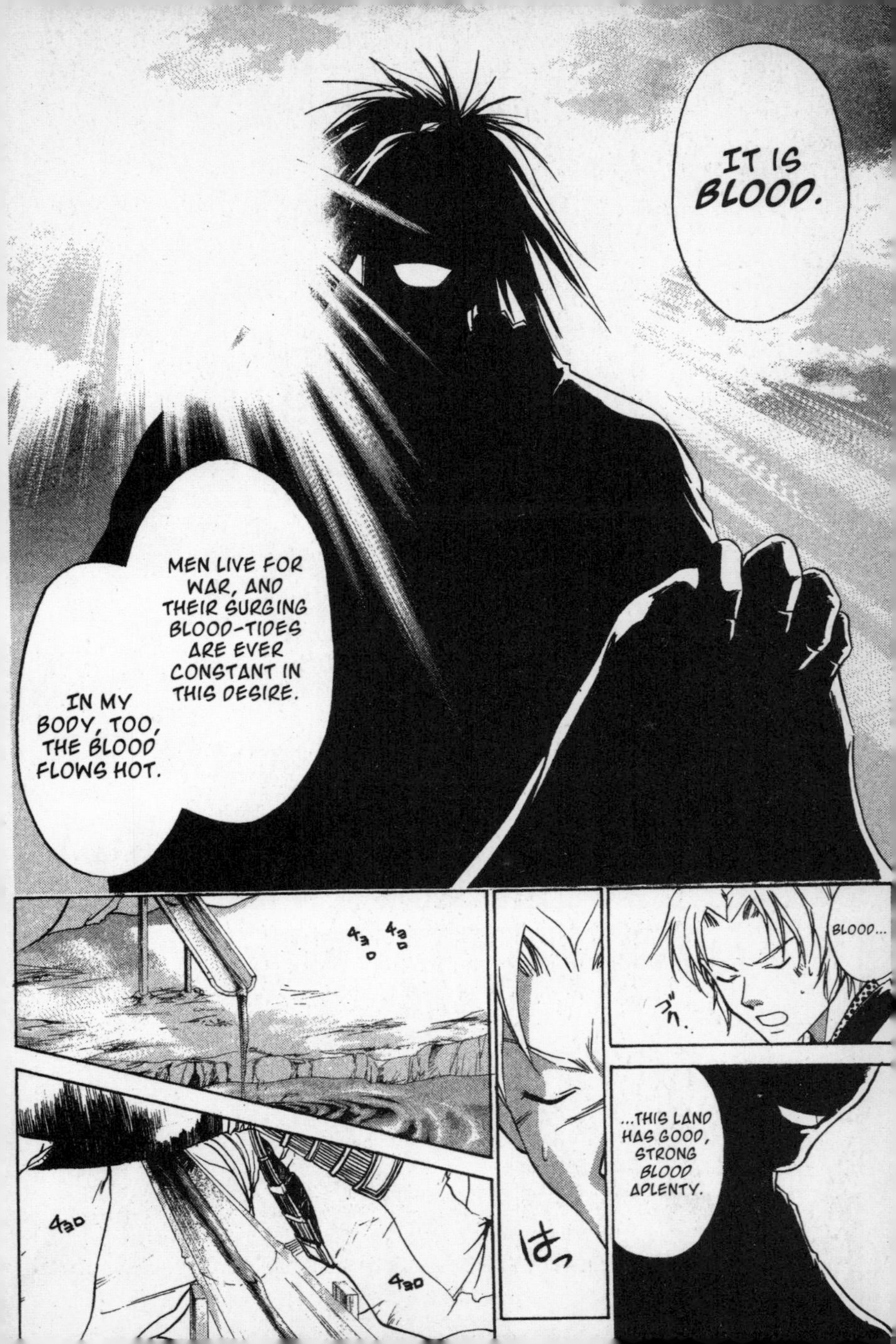
IT IS BLOOD.
MEN LIVE FOR WAR, AND THEIR SURGING BLOOD-TIDES ARE EVER CONSTANT IN THIS DESIRE.
IN MY BODY, TOO, THE BLOOD FLOWS HOT.
BLOOD...
...THIS LAND HAS GOOD, STRONG BLOOD APLENTY.
はっ

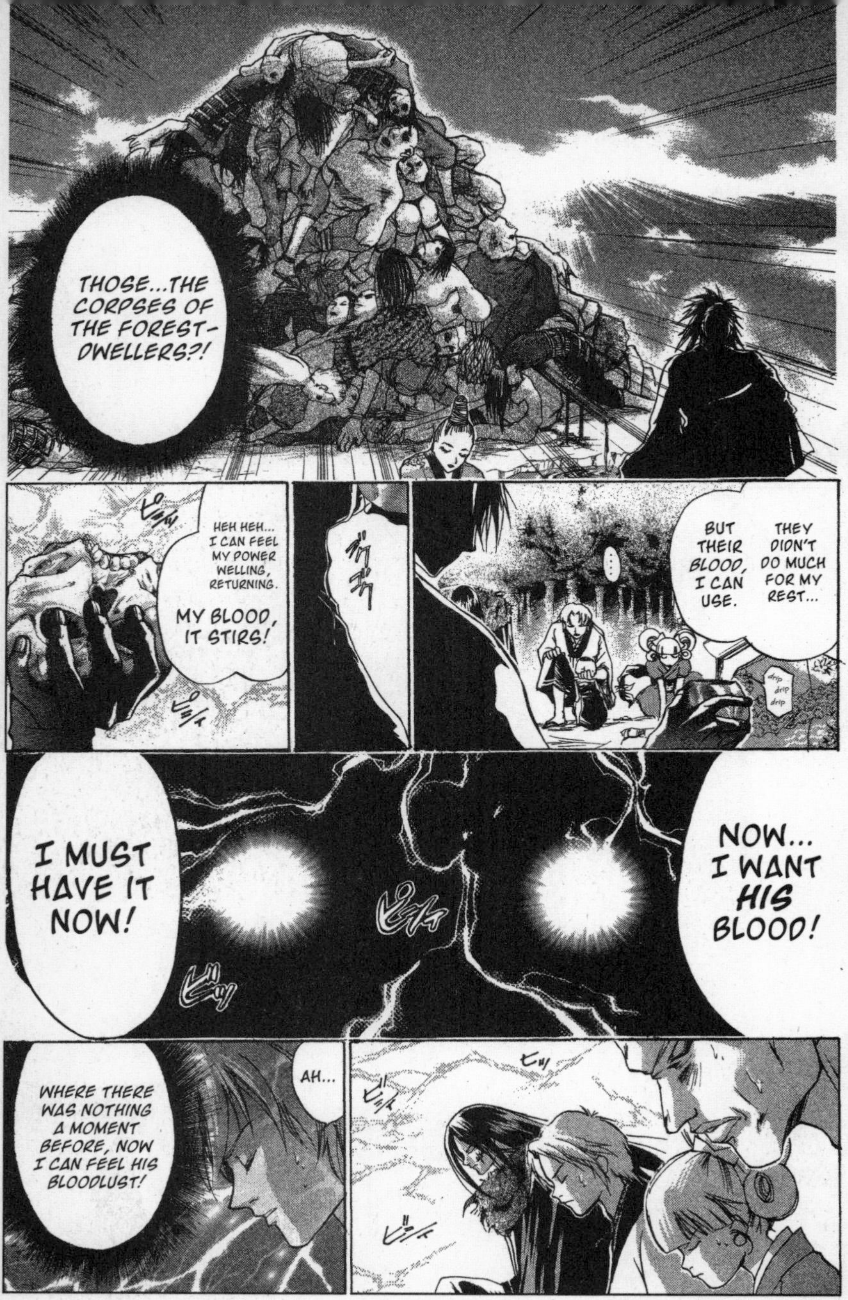
THOSE...THE CORPSES OF THE FOREST-DWELLERS?!
THEY DIDN'T DO MUCH FOR MY REST...
BUT THEIR BLOOD, I CAN USE.
...
drip drip drip
HEH HEH... I CAN FEEL MY POWER WELLING, RETURNING.
MY BLOOD, IT STIRS!
NOW... I WANT HIS BLOOD!
I MUST HAVE IT NOW!
AH...
WHERE THERE WAS NOTHING A MOMENT BEFORE, NOW I CAN FEEL HIS BLOODLUST!

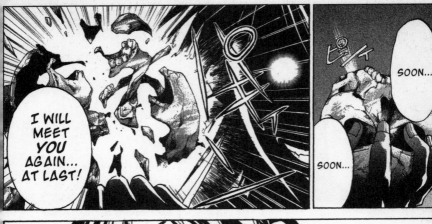

I WILL MEET *YOU* AGAIN... AT LAST!

SOON...

SOON...

DEMON EYES KYO!

STAFF

Yuzu Haruno (The Chief)
Hazuki Asami
Ken'ichi Suetake
Takaya Nagao
Akatsuki Soma (from chapter 42 on)

w/ Special Help from: Takiko Kamiya (chapter 48)

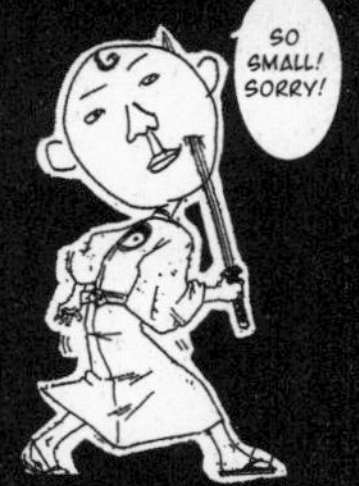
SO SMALL! SORRY!

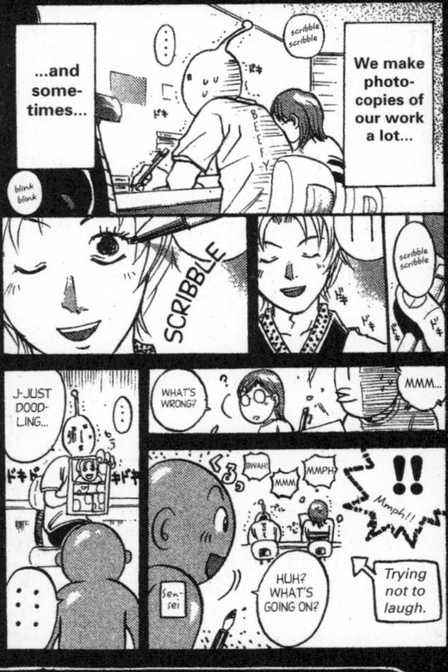
We make photocopies of our work a lot...
scribble scribble
...and sometimes...
blink blink
scribble scribble
SCRIBBLE
MMM...
WHAT'S WRONG?
J-JUST DOODLING...
!!
Mmph!!
Trying not to laugh.
BWAH!
MMPH
MMM
HUH? WHAT'S GOING ON?
Sen-sei

Yuzu Haruno

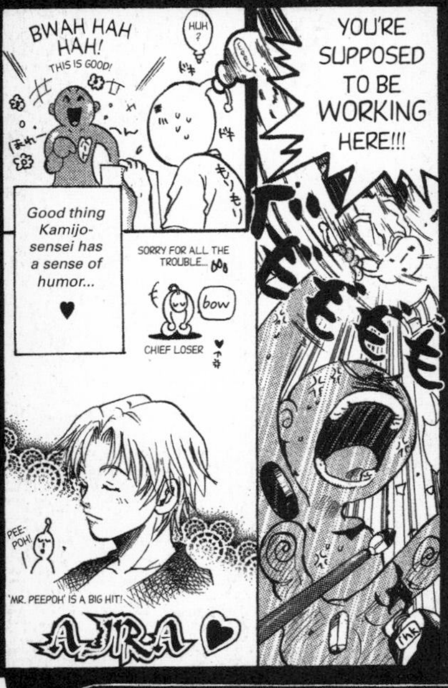
YOU'RE SUPPOSED TO BE WORKING HERE!!!
BWAH HAH HAH!
THIS IS GOOD!
HUH?
Good thing Kamijo-sensei has a sense of humor... ♥
SORRY FOR ALL THE TROUBLE...
bow
CHIEF LOSER
PEE-POH!
'MR. PEEPOH' IS A BIG HIT!
AJIRA ♥

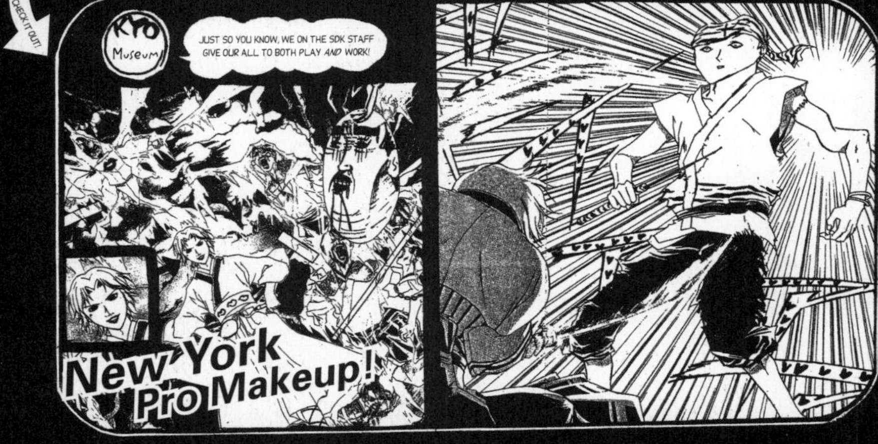
CHECK IT OUT!
KYO Museum
JUST SO YOU KNOW, WE ON THE SDK STAFF GIVE OUR ALL TO BOTH PLAY AND WORK!
New York Pro Makeup!

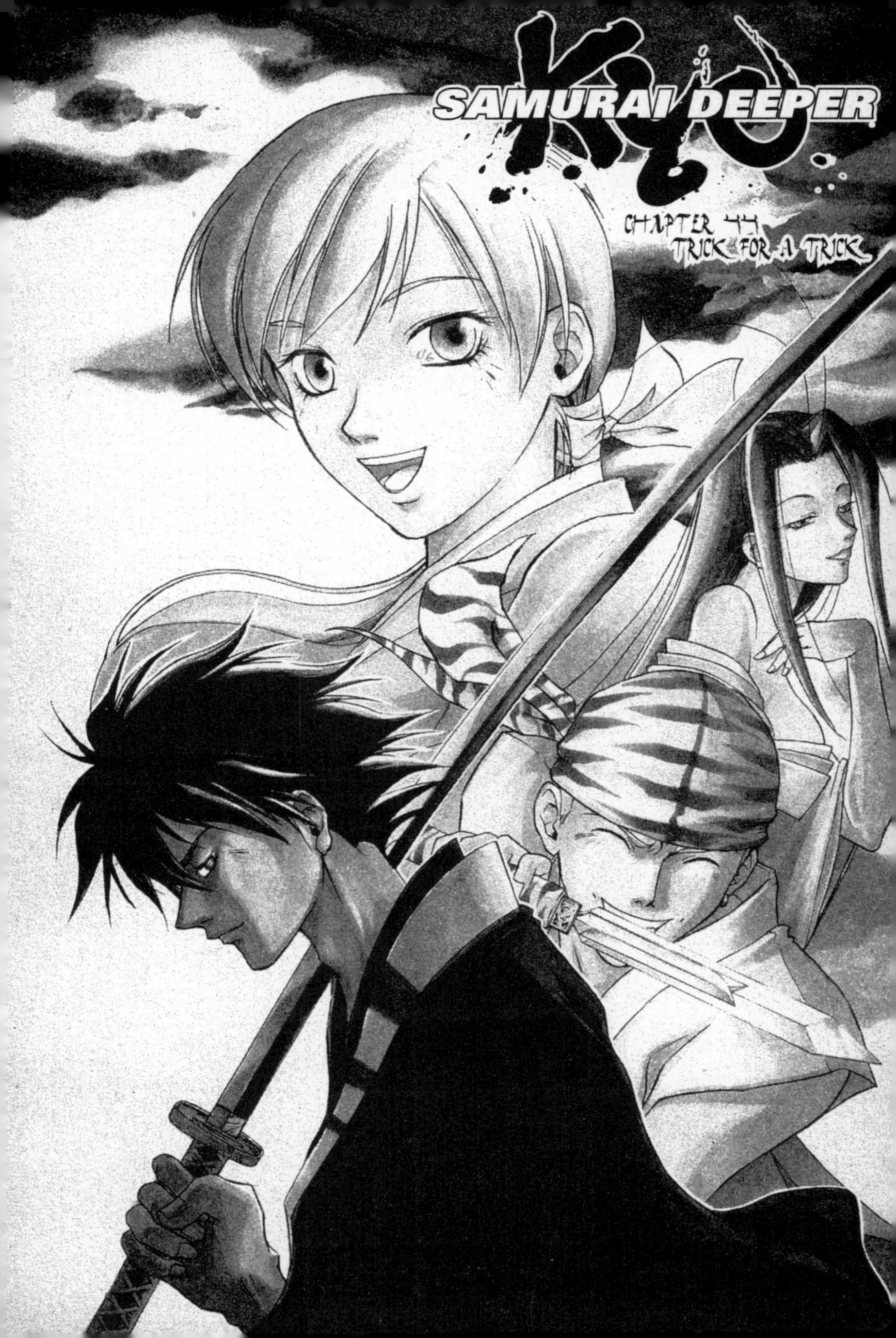
SAMURAI DEEPER
KYO
CHAPTER 44
TRICK FOR A TRICK

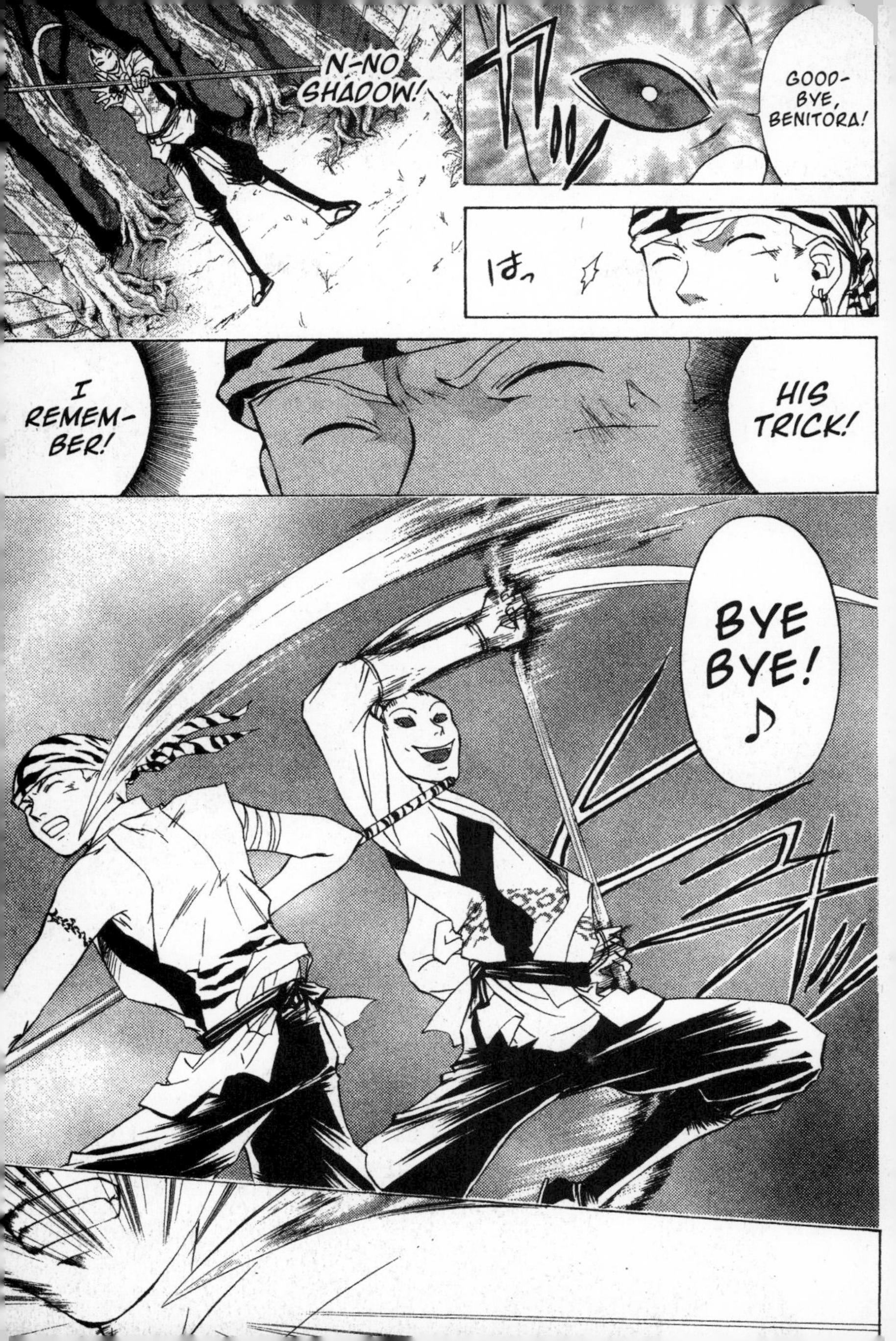
GOOD-BYE, BENITORA!
カッ
はっ
N-NO SHADOW!
HIS TRICK!
I REMEMBER!
BYE BYE! ♪

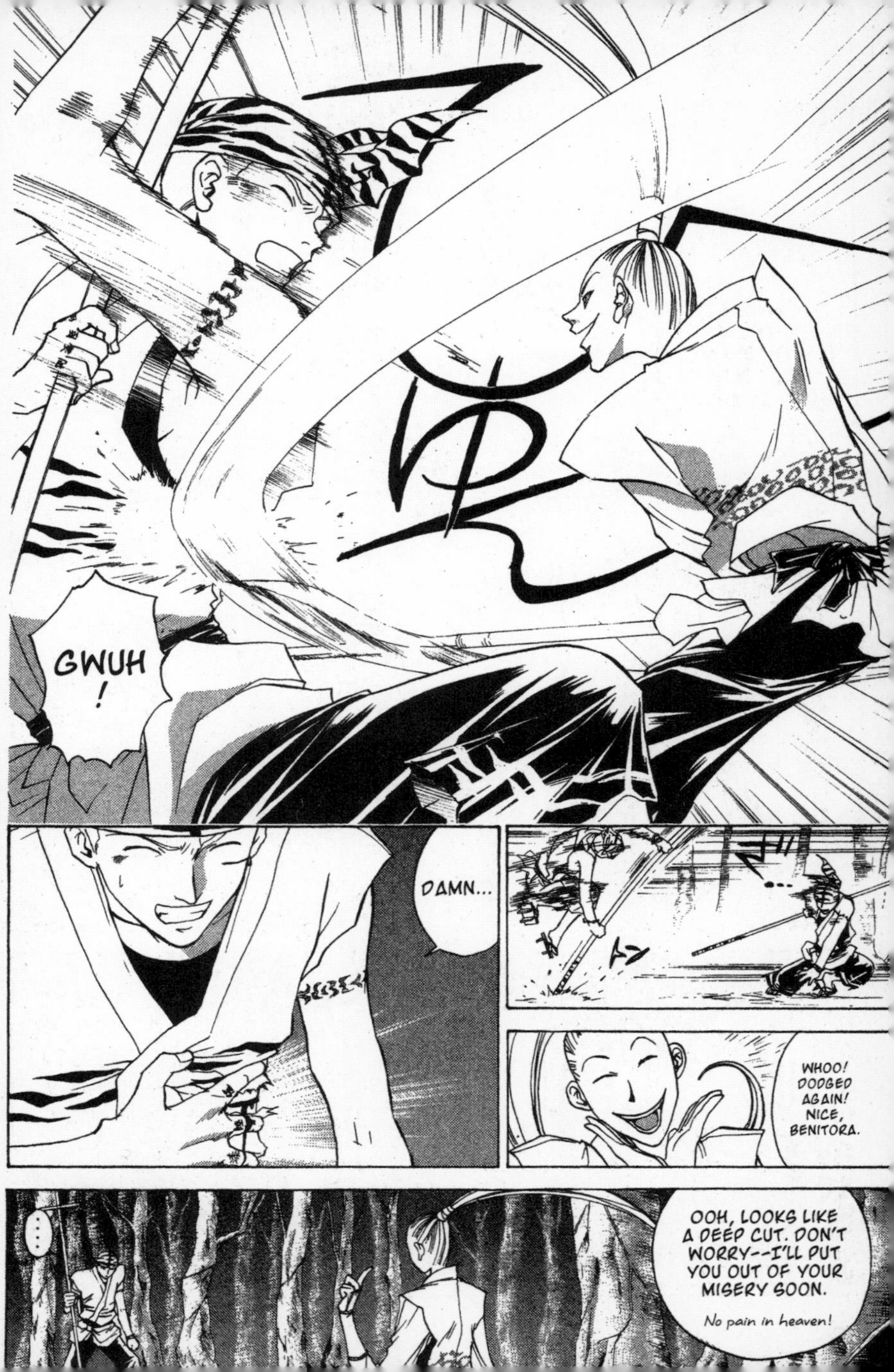

GWUH!
...
WHOO! DODGED AGAIN! NICE, BENITORA.
DAMN...
OOH, LOOKS LIKE A DEEP CUT. DON'T WORRY--I'LL PUT YOU OUT OF YOUR MISERY SOON.
No pain in heaven!
....

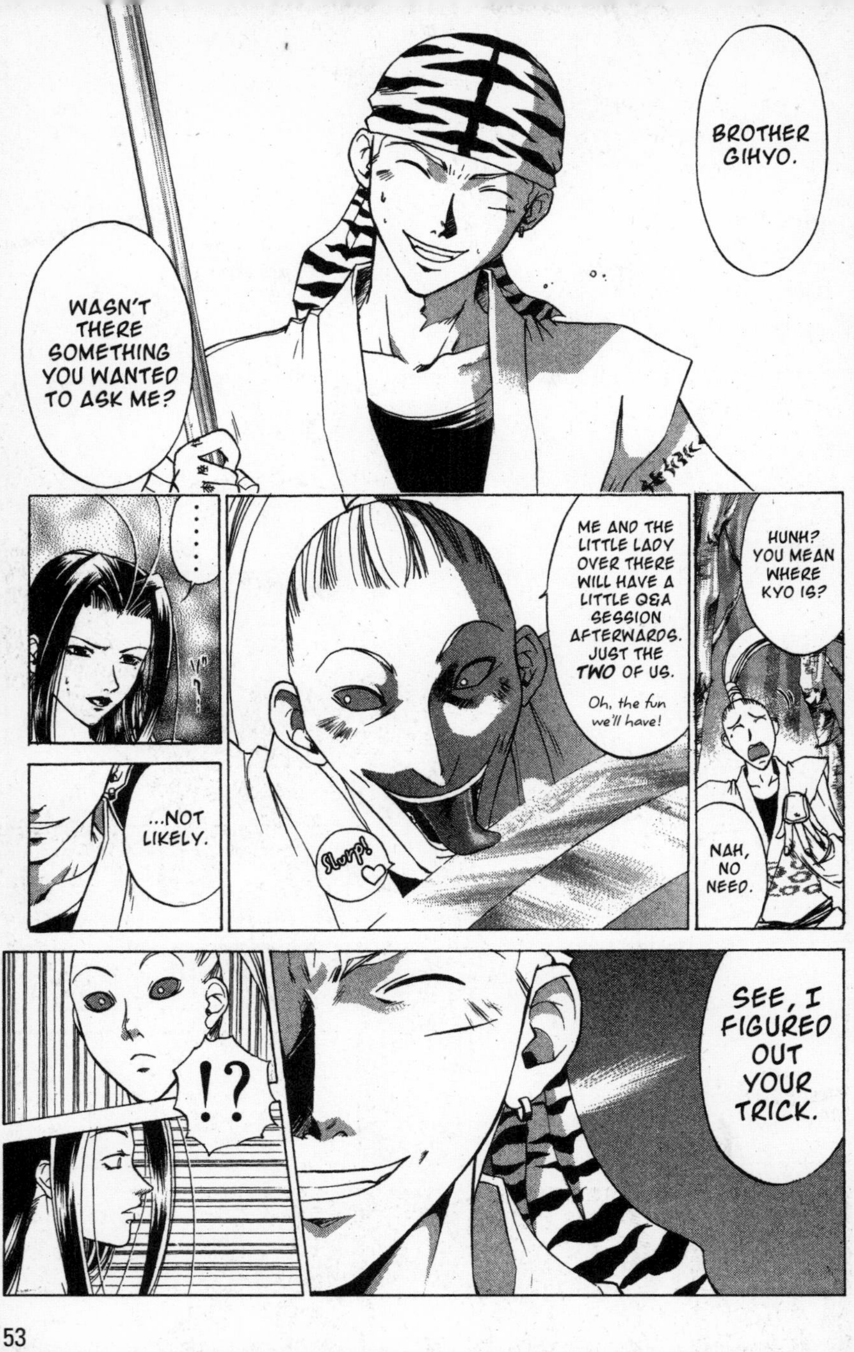

BROTHER GIHYO.
WASN'T THERE SOMETHING YOU WANTED TO ASK ME?
HUNH? YOU MEAN WHERE KYO IS?
NAH, NO NEED.
ME AND THE LITTLE LADY OVER THERE WILL HAVE A LITTLE Q&A SESSION AFTERWARDS. JUST THE **TWO** OF US.
Oh, the fun we'll have!
Slurp! ♡
......
...NOT LIKELY.
SEE, I FIGURED OUT YOUR TRICK.
!?

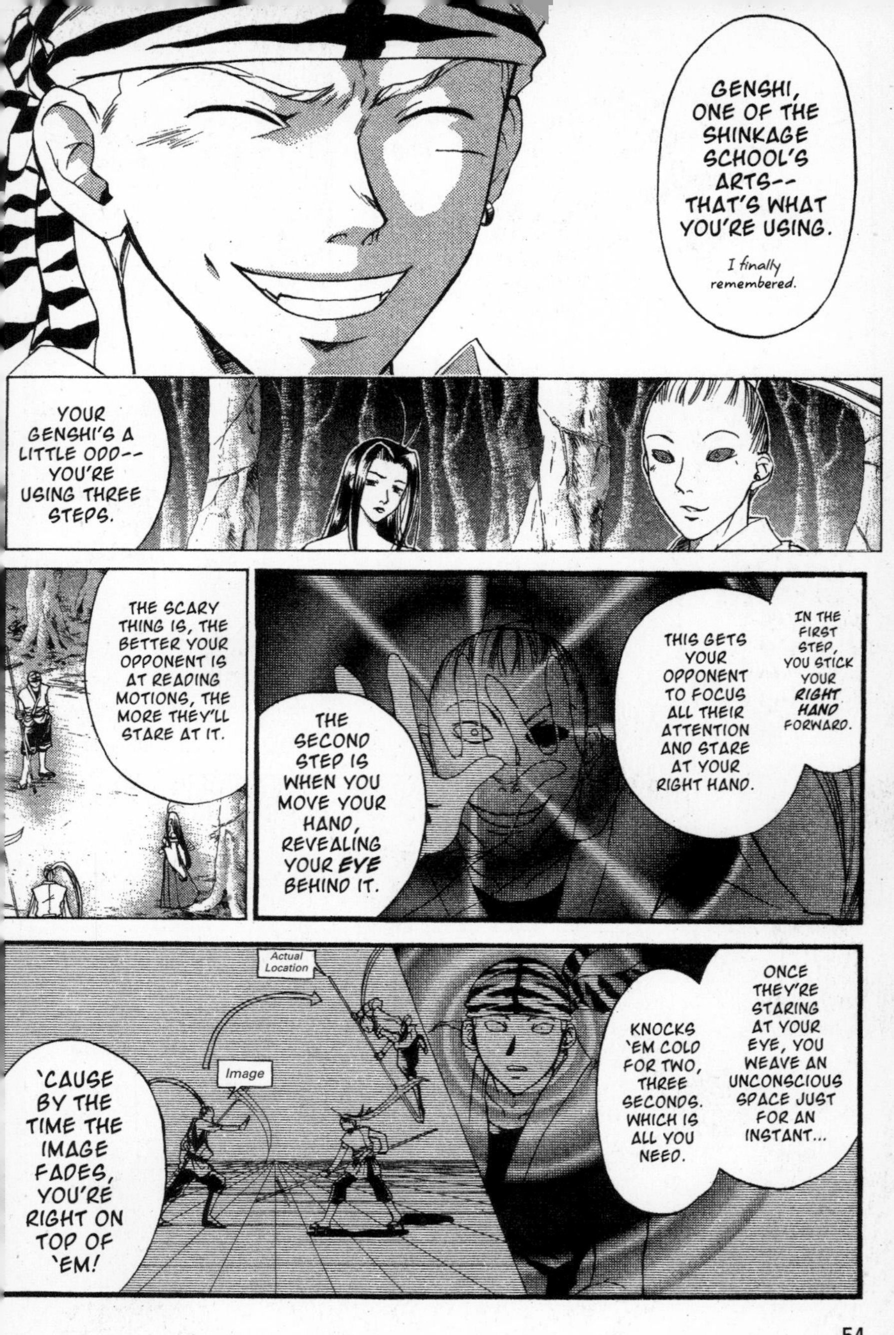
GENSHI, ONE OF THE SHINKAGE SCHOOL'S ARTS-- THAT'S WHAT YOU'RE USING.
I finally remembered.
YOUR GENSHI'S A LITTLE ODD-- YOU'RE USING THREE STEPS.
IN THE FIRST STEP, YOU STICK YOUR **RIGHT HAND** FORWARD.
THIS GETS YOUR OPPONENT TO FOCUS ALL THEIR ATTENTION AND STARE AT YOUR RIGHT HAND.
THE SECOND STEP IS WHEN YOU MOVE YOUR HAND, REVEALING YOUR **EYE** BEHIND IT.
THE SCARY THING IS, THE BETTER YOUR OPPONENT IS AT READING MOTIONS, THE MORE THEY'LL STARE AT IT.
ONCE THEY'RE STARING AT YOUR EYE, YOU WEAVE AN UNCONSCIOUS SPACE JUST FOR AN INSTANT...
KNOCKS 'EM COLD FOR TWO, THREE SECONDS. WHICH IS ALL YOU NEED.
Actual Location
Image
'CAUSE BY THE TIME THE IMAGE FADES, YOU'RE RIGHT ON TOP OF 'EM!

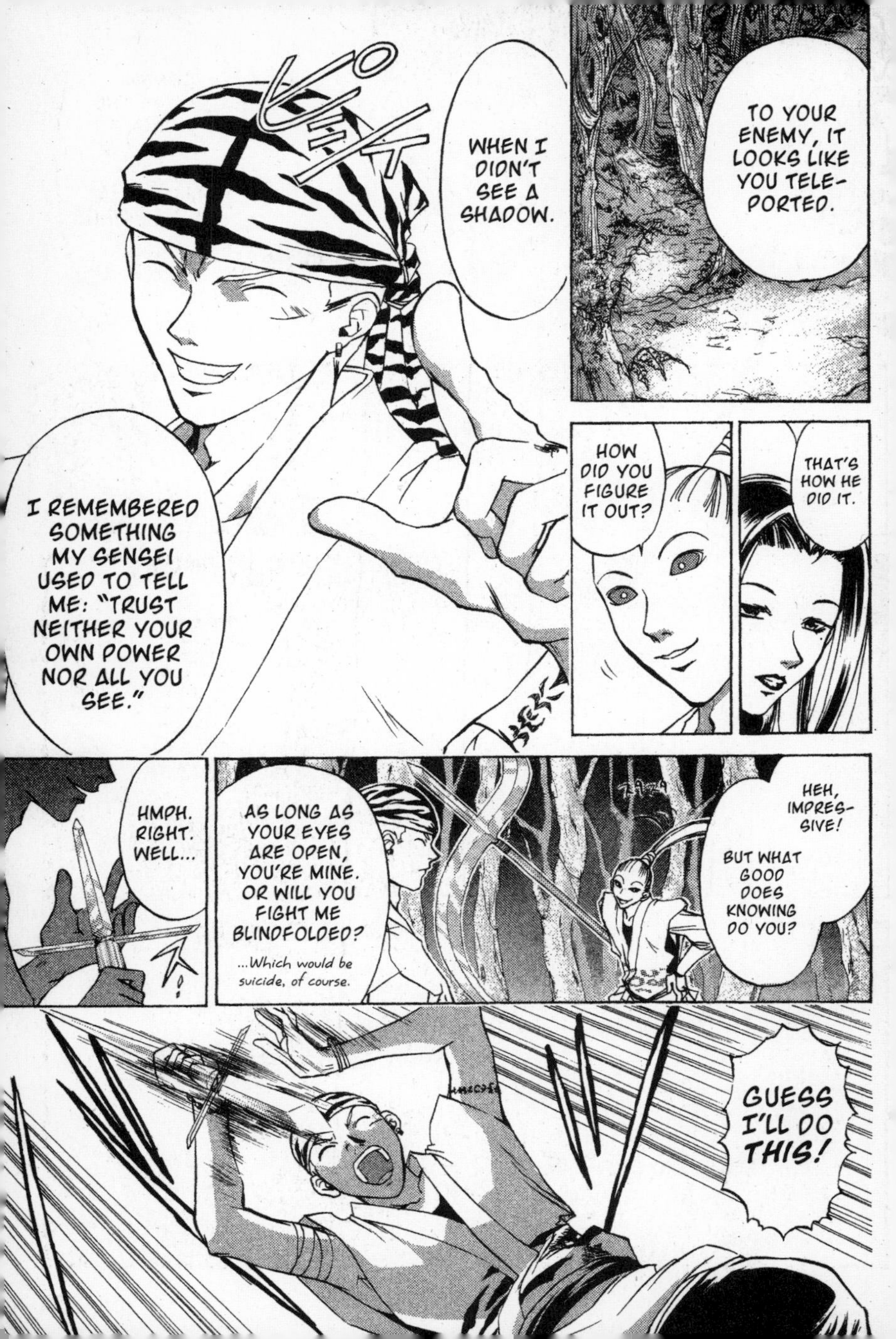
TO YOUR ENEMY, IT LOOKS LIKE YOU TELE-PORTED.
THAT'S HOW HE DID IT.
HOW DID YOU FIGURE IT OUT?
WHEN I DIDN'T SEE A SHADOW.
I REMEMBERED SOMETHING MY SENSEI USED TO TELL ME: "TRUST NEITHER YOUR OWN POWER NOR ALL YOU SEE."
HEH, IMPRES-SIVE!
BUT WHAT GOOD DOES KNOWING DO YOU?
AS LONG AS YOUR EYES ARE OPEN, YOU'RE MINE. OR WILL YOU FIGHT ME BLINDFOLDED?
...Which would be suicide, of course.
HMPH. RIGHT. WELL...
GUESS I'LL DO THIS!

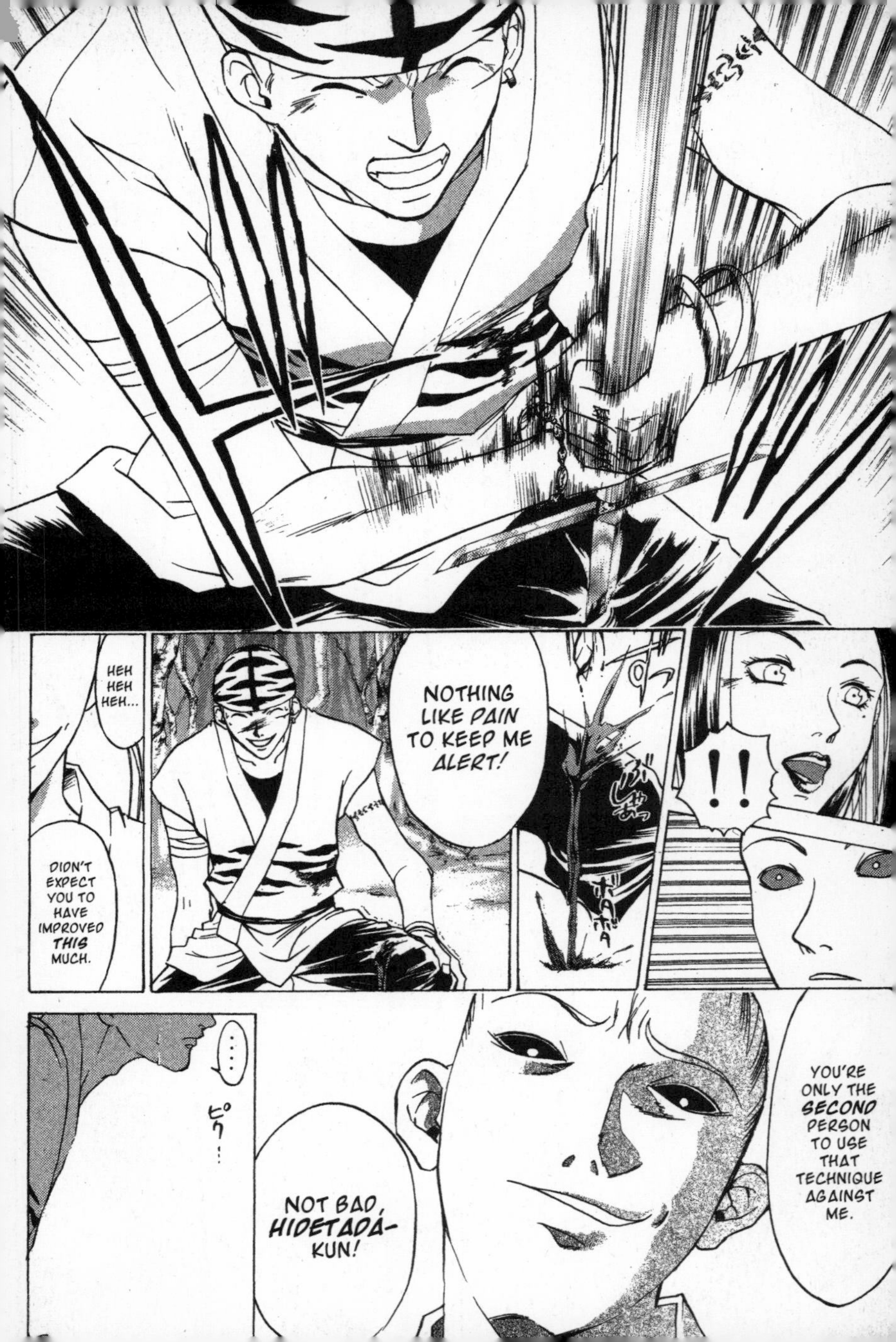
!!
NOTHING LIKE PAIN TO KEEP ME ALERT!
HEH HEH HEH...
DIDN'T EXPECT YOU TO HAVE IMPROVED THIS MUCH.
YOU'RE ONLY THE SECOND PERSON TO USE THAT TECHNIQUE AGAINST ME.
NOT BAD, HIDETADA-KUN!
....
ピク…

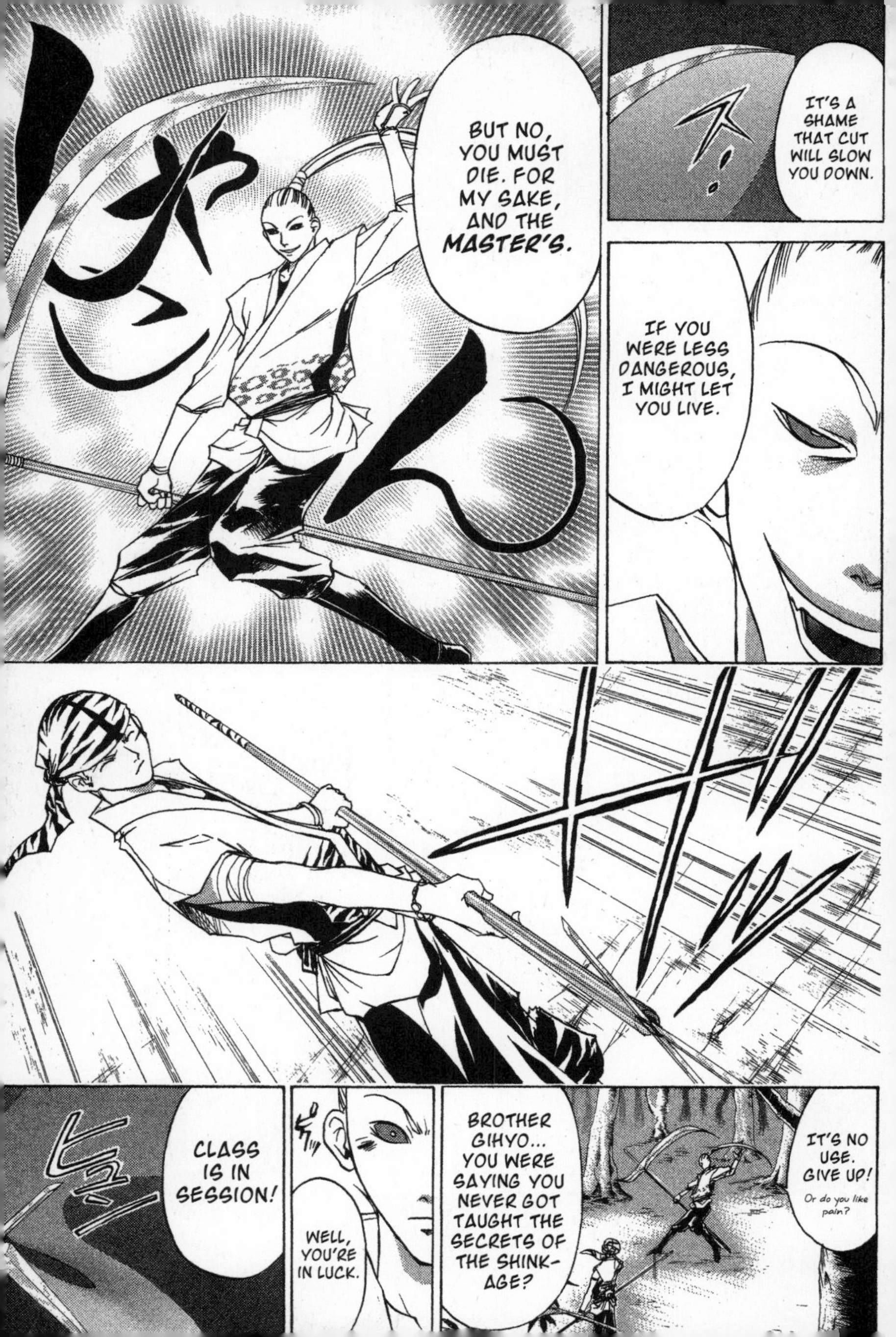
IT'S A SHAME THAT CUT WILL SLOW YOU DOWN.
IF YOU WERE LESS DANGEROUS, I MIGHT LET YOU LIVE.
BUT NO, YOU MUST DIE. FOR MY SAKE, AND THE MASTER'S.
IT'S NO USE. GIVE UP!
Or do you like pain?
BROTHER GIHYO... YOU WERE SAYING YOU NEVER GOT TAUGHT THE SECRETS OF THE SHINK-AGE?
WELL, YOU'RE IN LUCK.
CLASS IS IN SESSION!

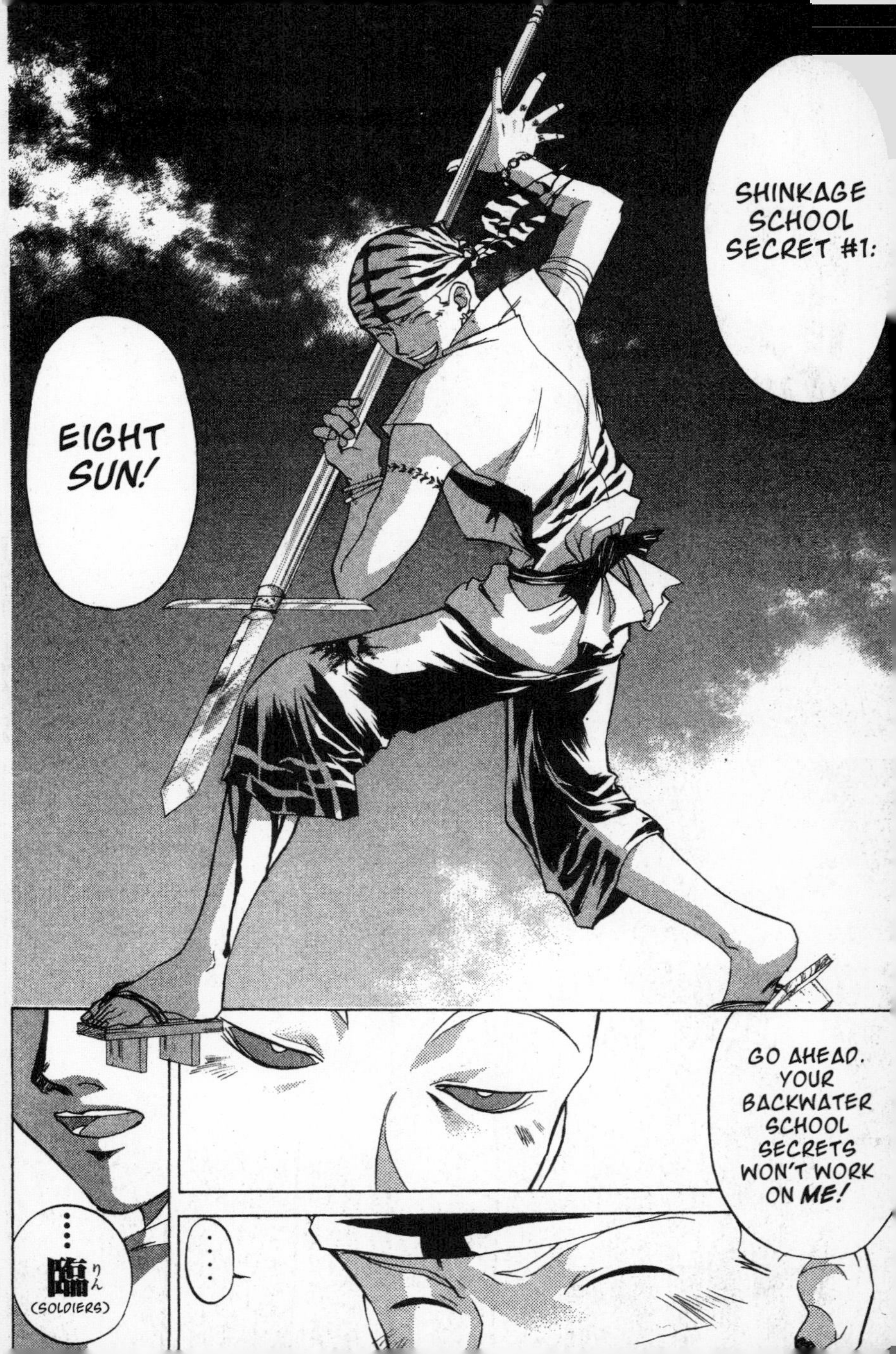
SHINKAGE SCHOOL SECRET #1:
EIGHT SUN!
GO AHEAD. YOUR BACKWATER SCHOOL SECRETS WON'T WORK ON ME!
...
... 臨 りん
(SOLDIERS)

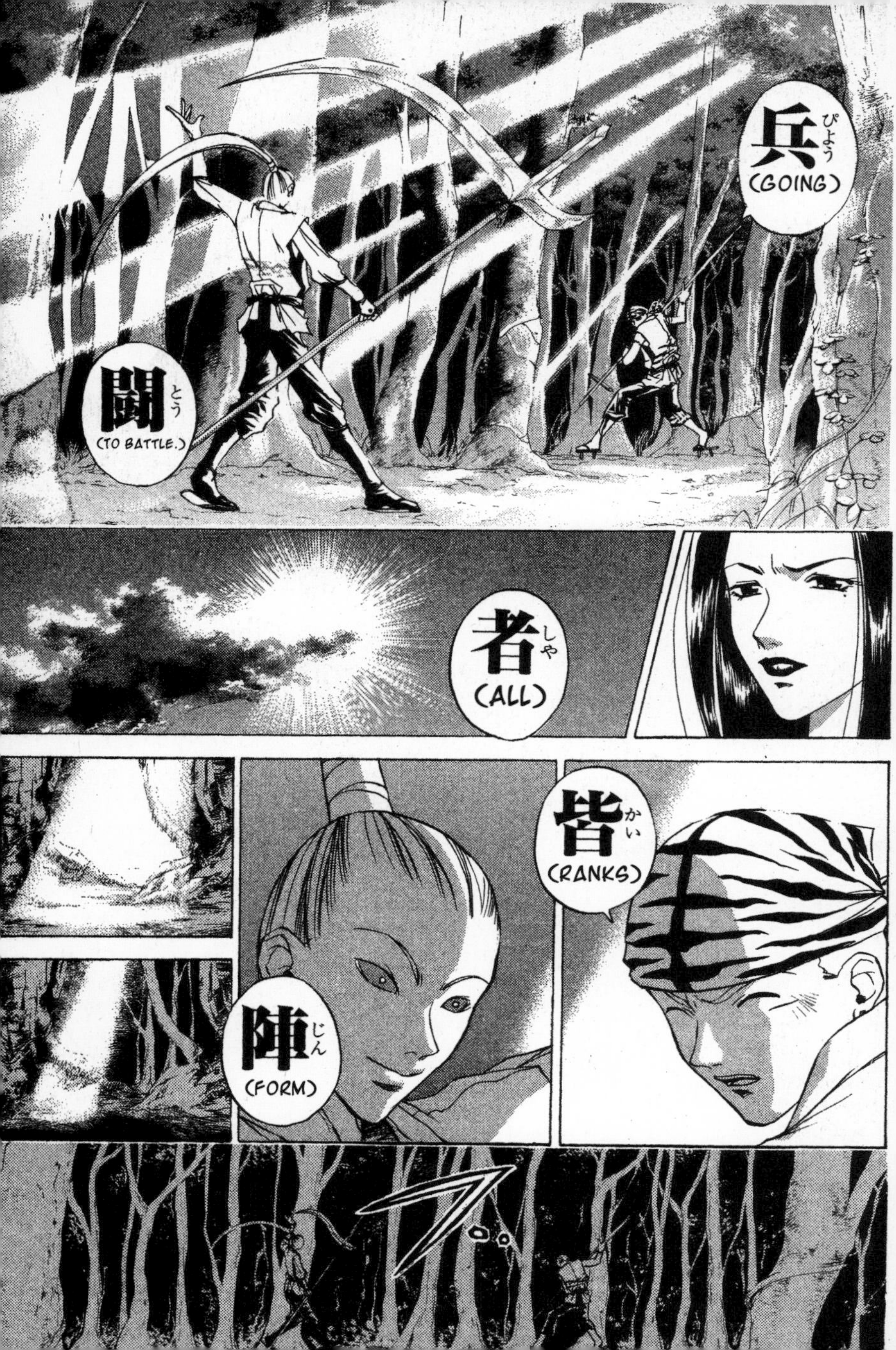
兵 ぴょう (GOING)
闘 とう (TO BATTLE.)
者 しゃ (ALL)
皆 かい (RANKS)
陣 じん (FORM)

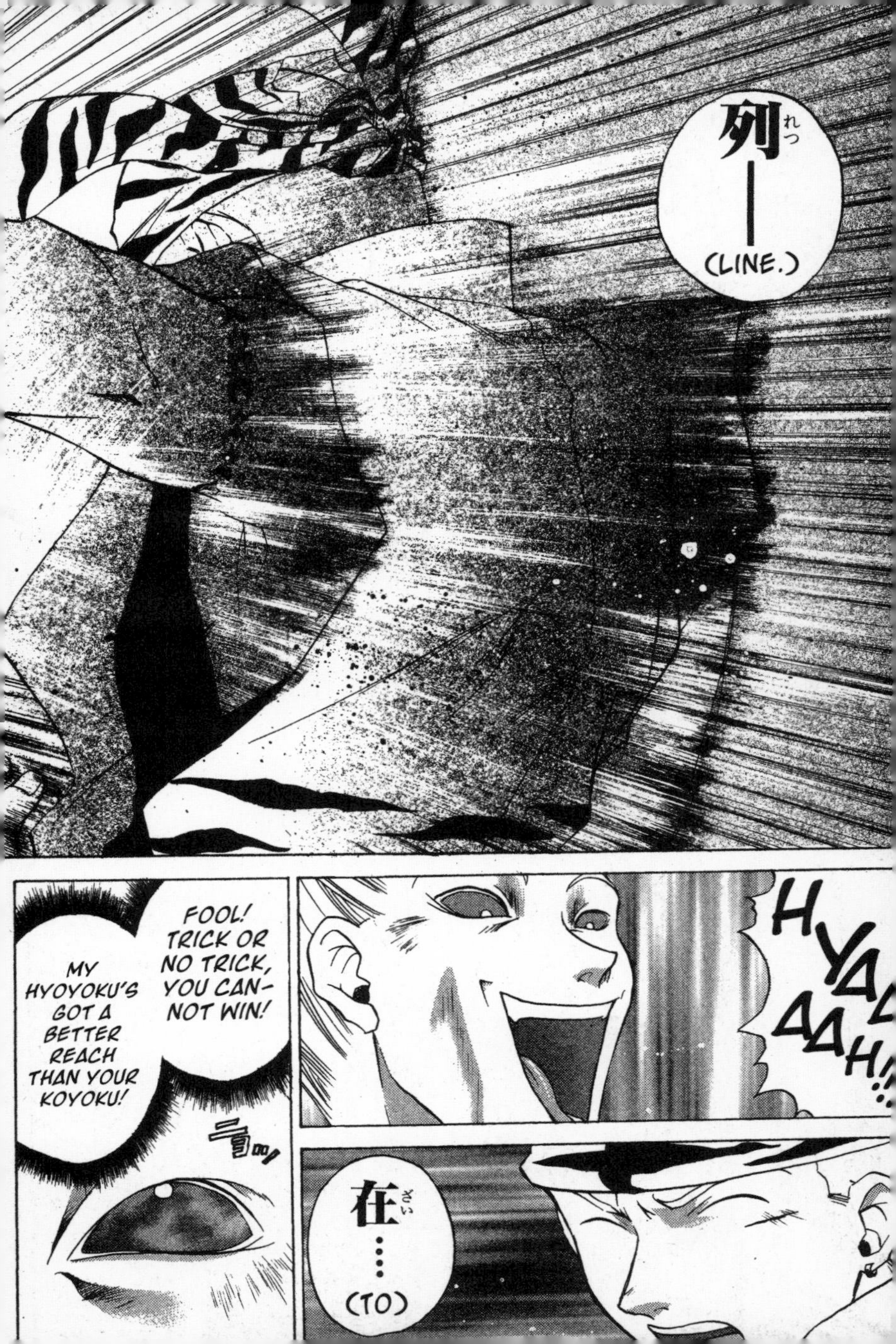

列れつ——
(LINE.)
HYAAAAH!!!
在さい……
(TO)
FOOL! TRICK OR NO TRICK, YOU CAN-NOT WIN!
MY HYOYOKU'S GOT A BETTER REACH THAN YOUR KOYOKU!

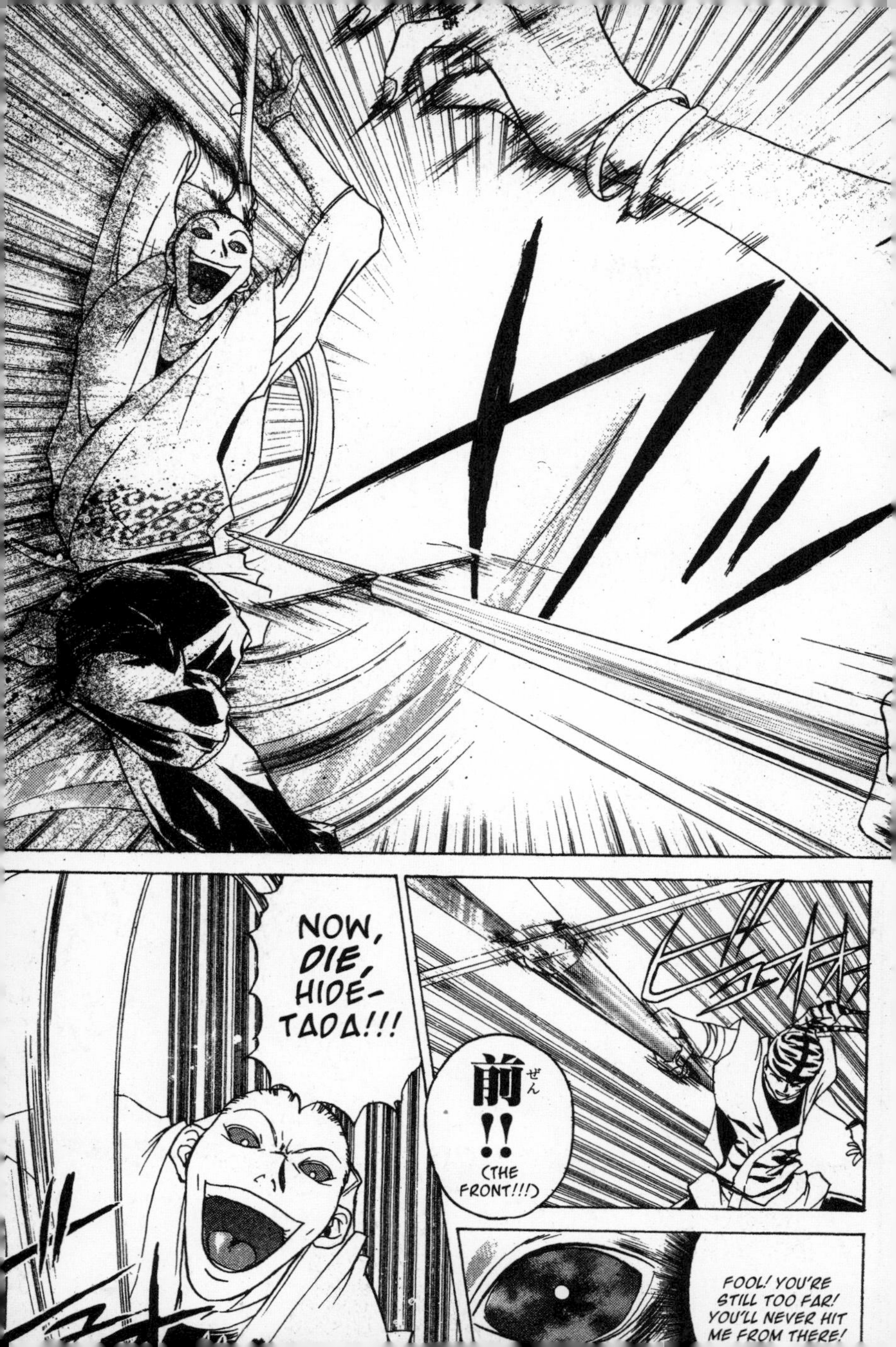
前!!
(THE FRONT!!!)
FOOL! YOU'RE STILL TOO FAR! YOU'LL NEVER HIT ME FROM THERE!
NOW, DIE, HIDE-TADA!!!

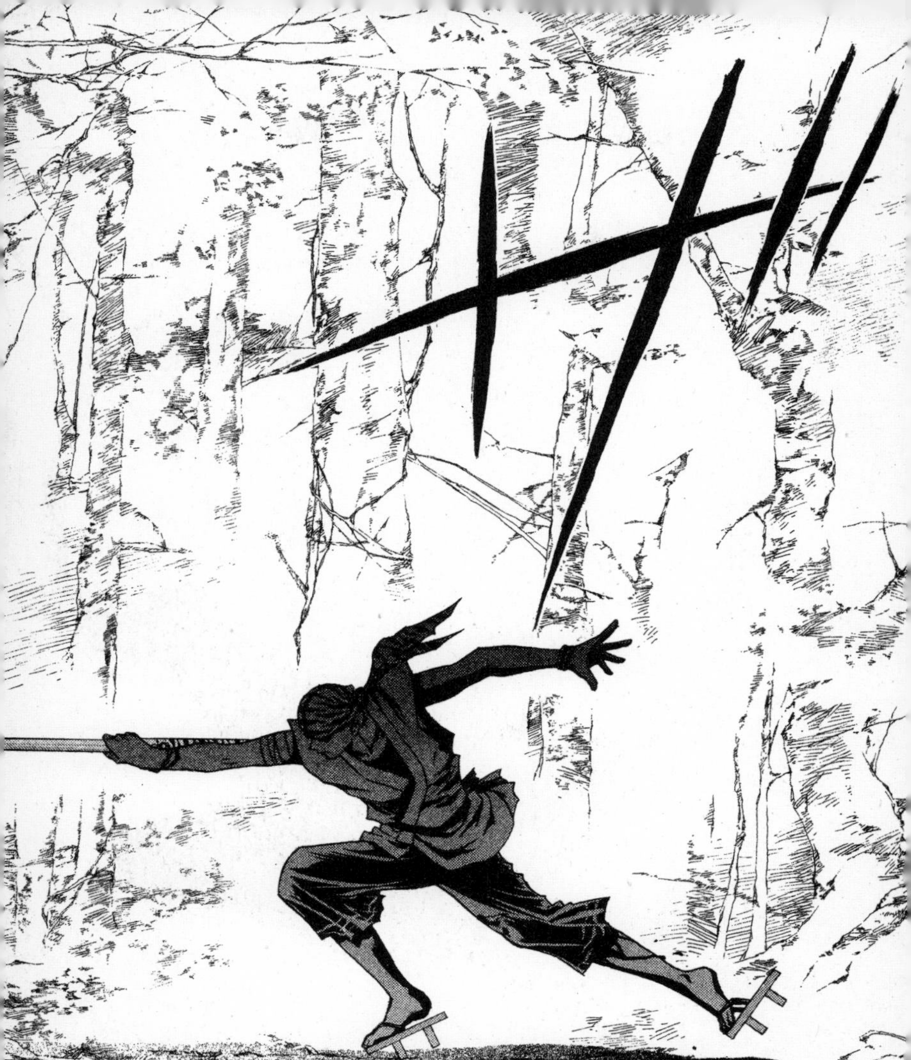

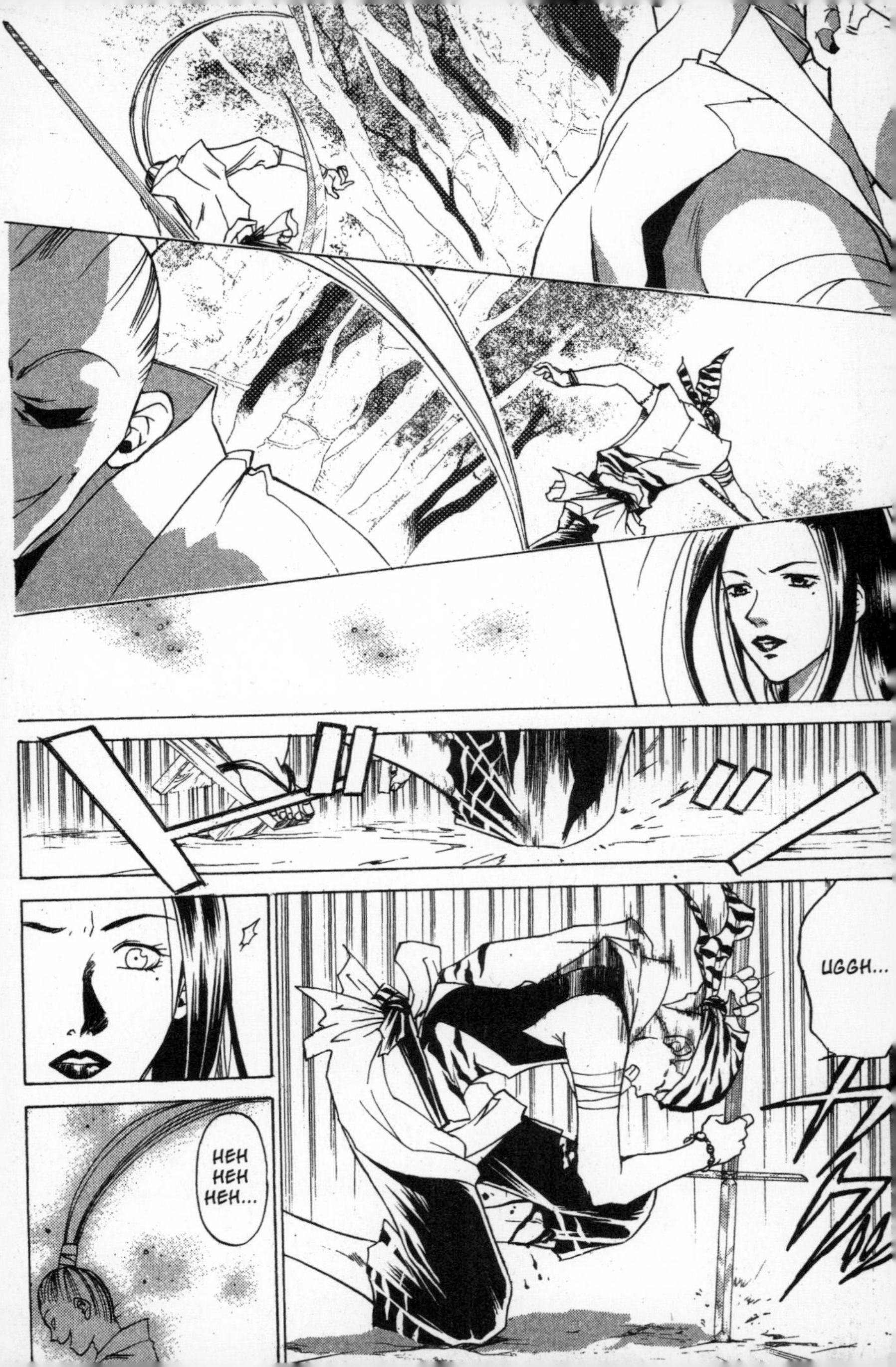
UGGH...
HEH HEH HEH...

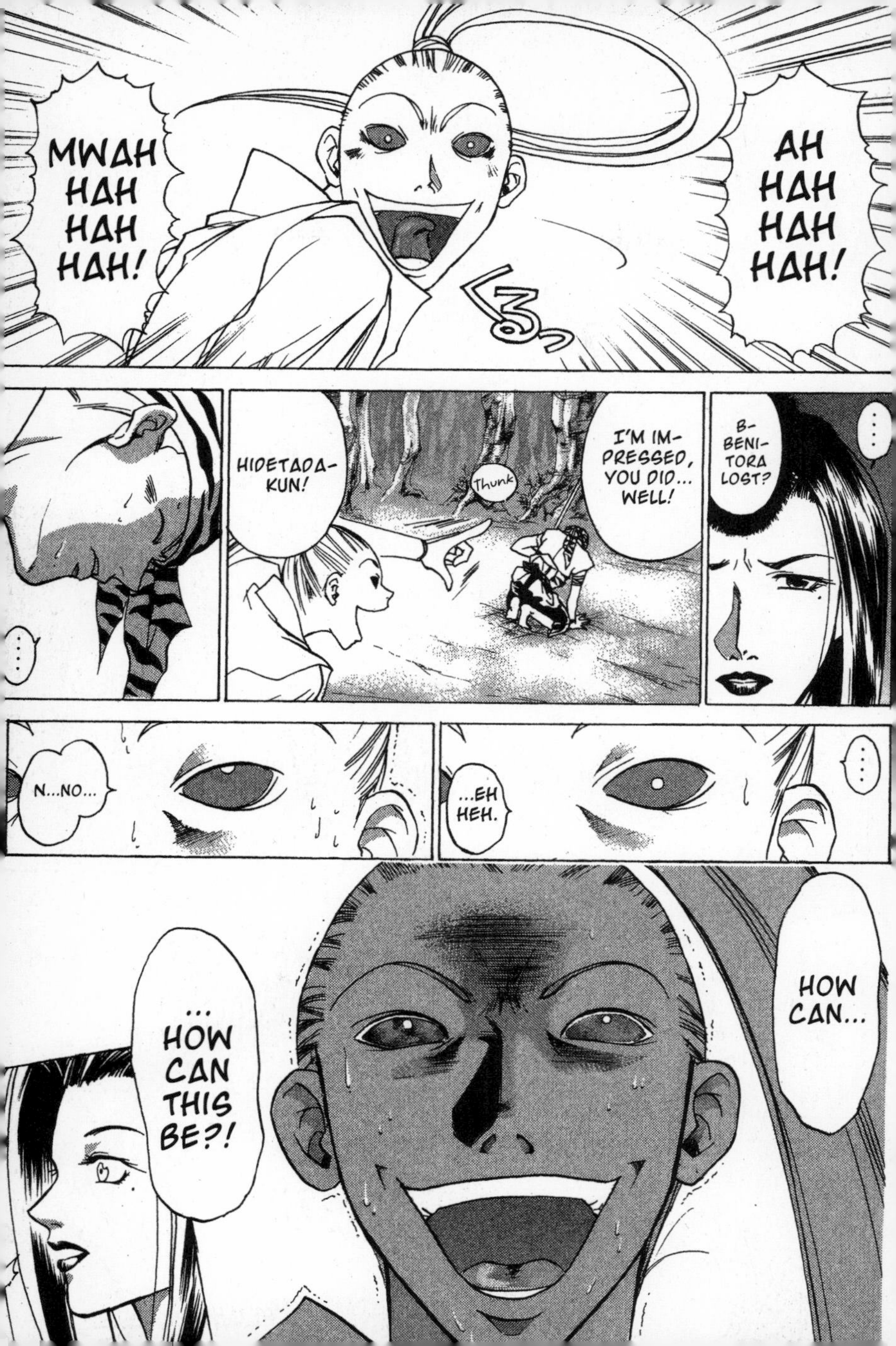
AH HAH HAH HAH!
MWAH HAH HAH HAH!
くるっ
...
B-BENI-TORA LOST?
I'M IM-PRESSED, YOU DID... WELL!
Thunk
HIDETADA-KUN!
...
...
...EH HEH.
N...NO...
HOW CAN...
... HOW CAN THIS BE?!

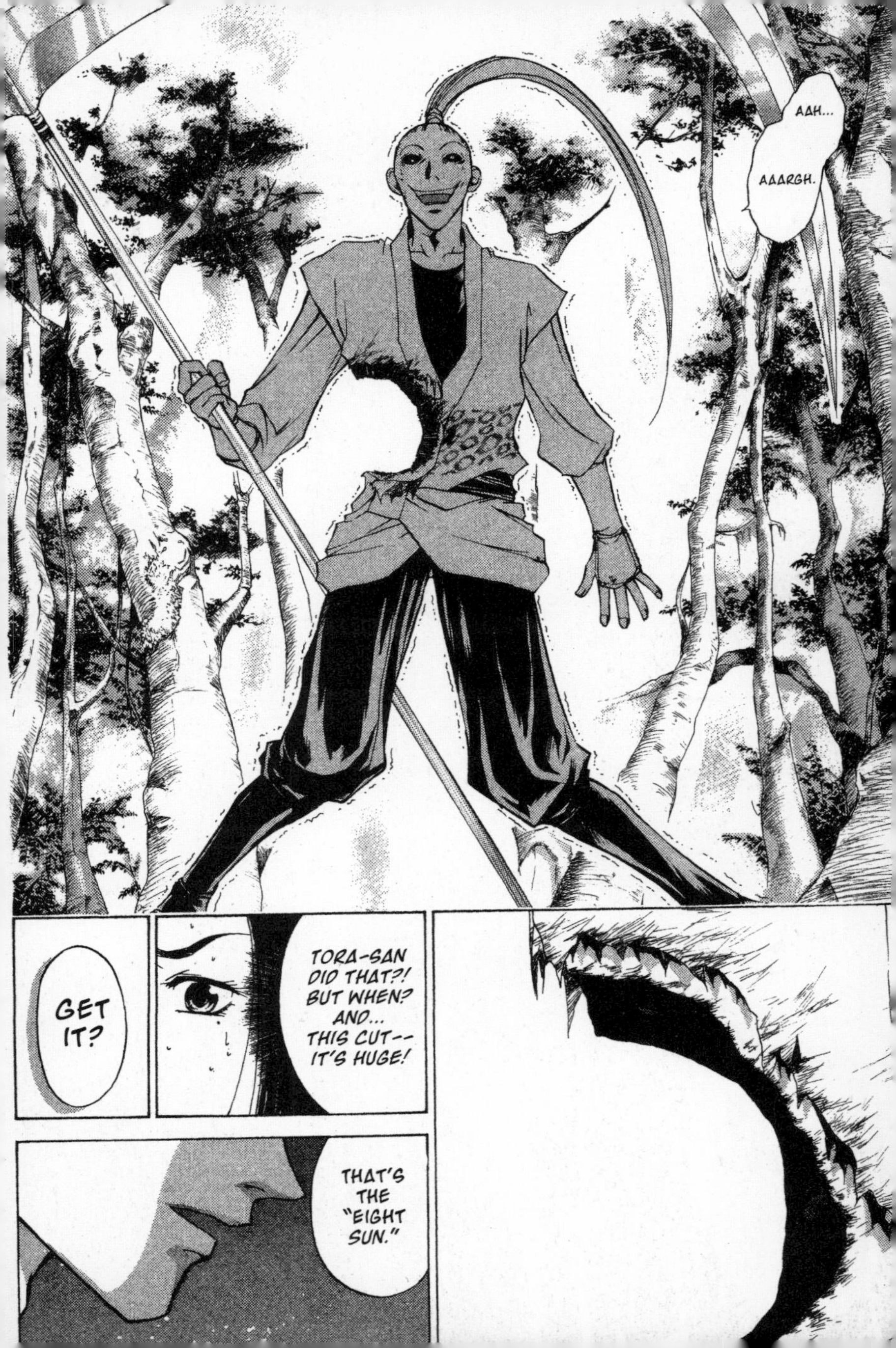
AAH...
AAARGH.
TORA-SAN DID THAT?! BUT WHEN? AND... THIS CUT-- IT'S HUGE!
GET IT?
THAT'S THE "EIGHT SUN."

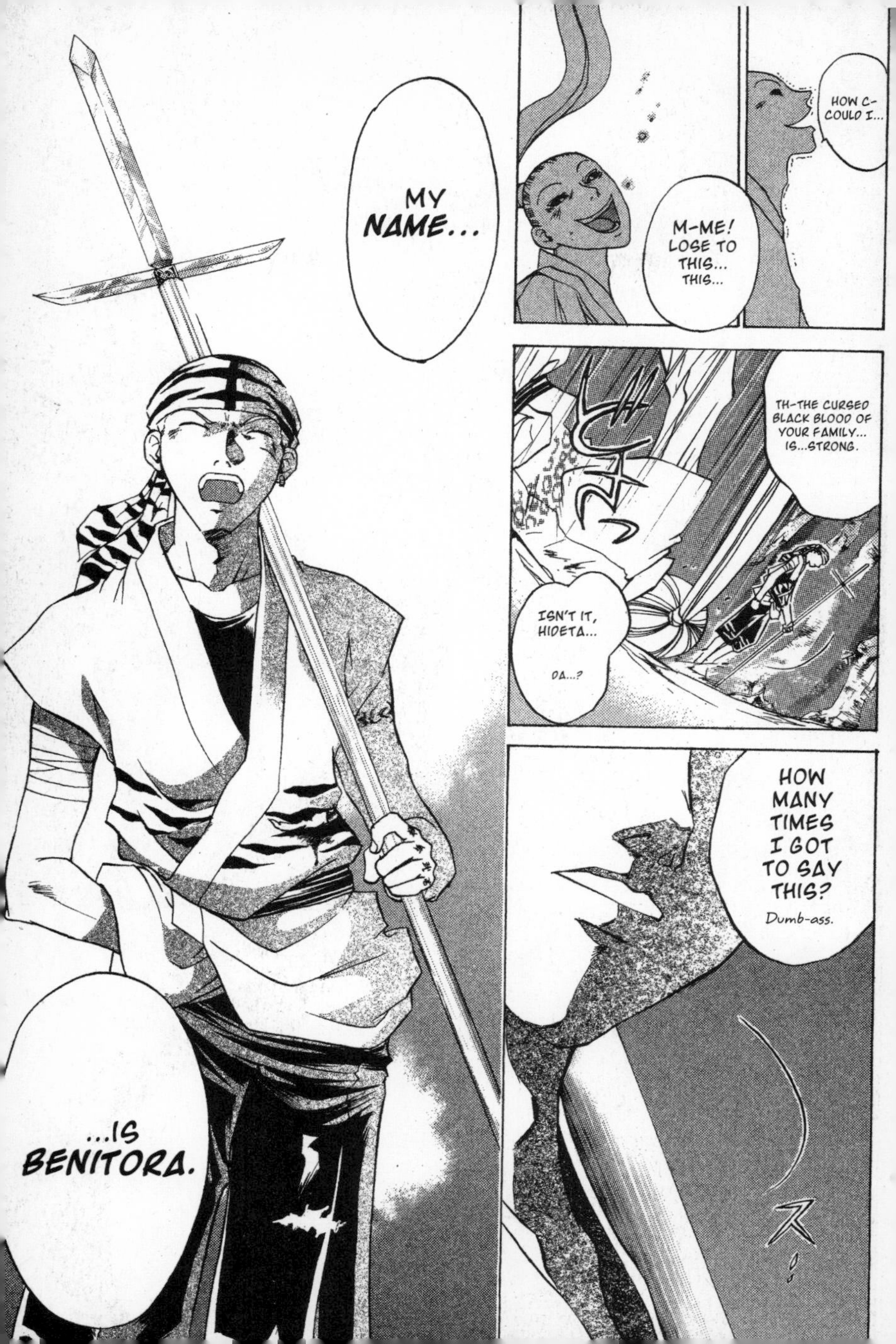
HOW C-COULD I...
M-ME! LOSE TO THIS... THIS...
TH-THE CURSED BLACK BLOOD OF YOUR FAMILY... IS...STRONG.
ISN'T IT, HIDETA...
DA...?
HOW MANY TIMES I GOT TO SAY THIS?
Dumb-ass.
MY NAME...
...IS BENITORA.

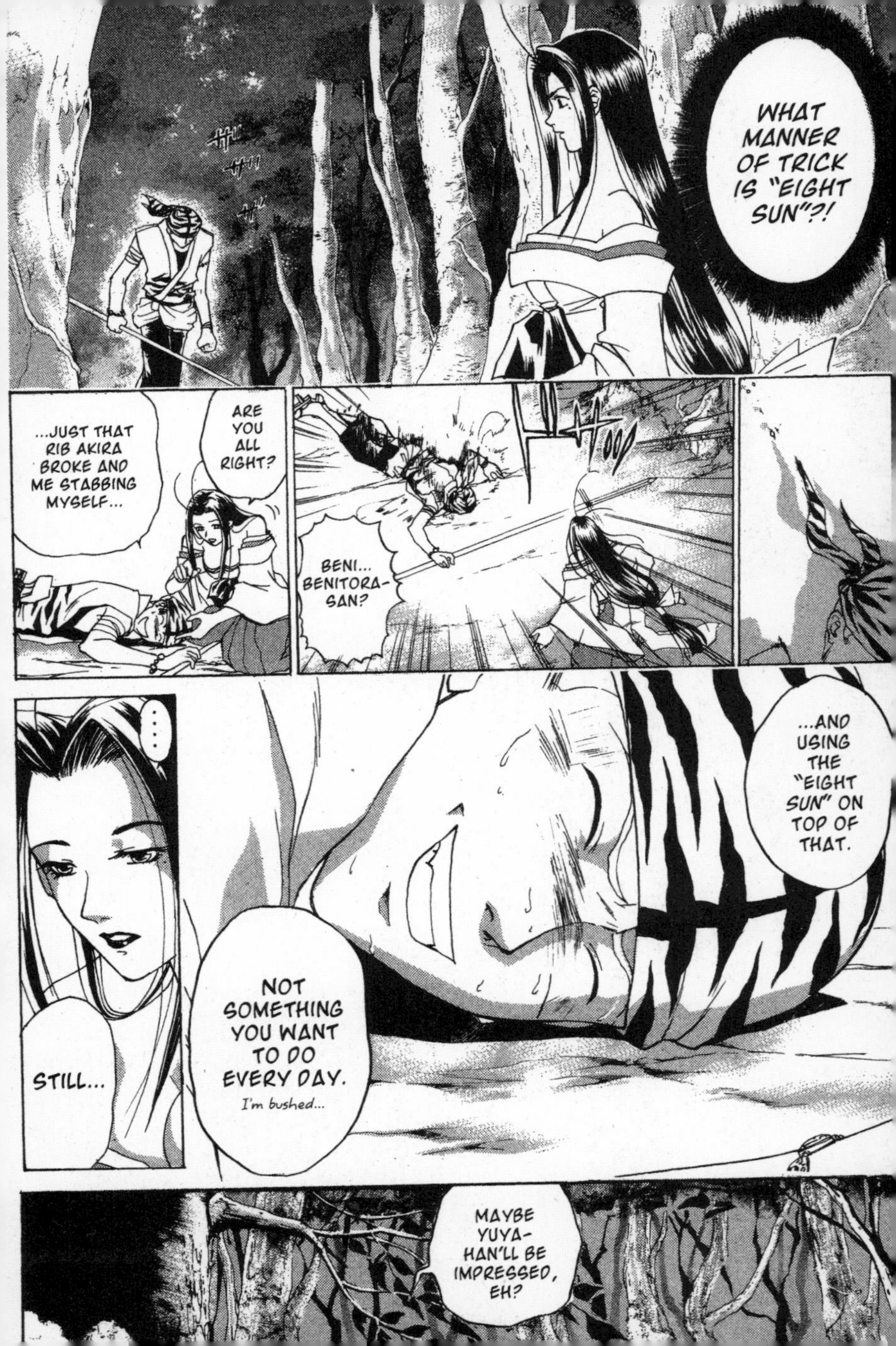
WHAT MANNER OF TRICK IS "EIGHT SUN"?!
BENI... BENITORA-SAN?
ARE YOU ALL RIGHT?
...JUST THAT RIB AKIRA BROKE AND ME STABBING MYSELF...
...AND USING THE "EIGHT SUN" ON TOP OF THAT.
NOT SOMETHING YOU WANT TO DO EVERY DAY.
I'm bushed...
...
STILL...
MAYBE YUYA-HAN'LL BE IMPRESSED, EH?

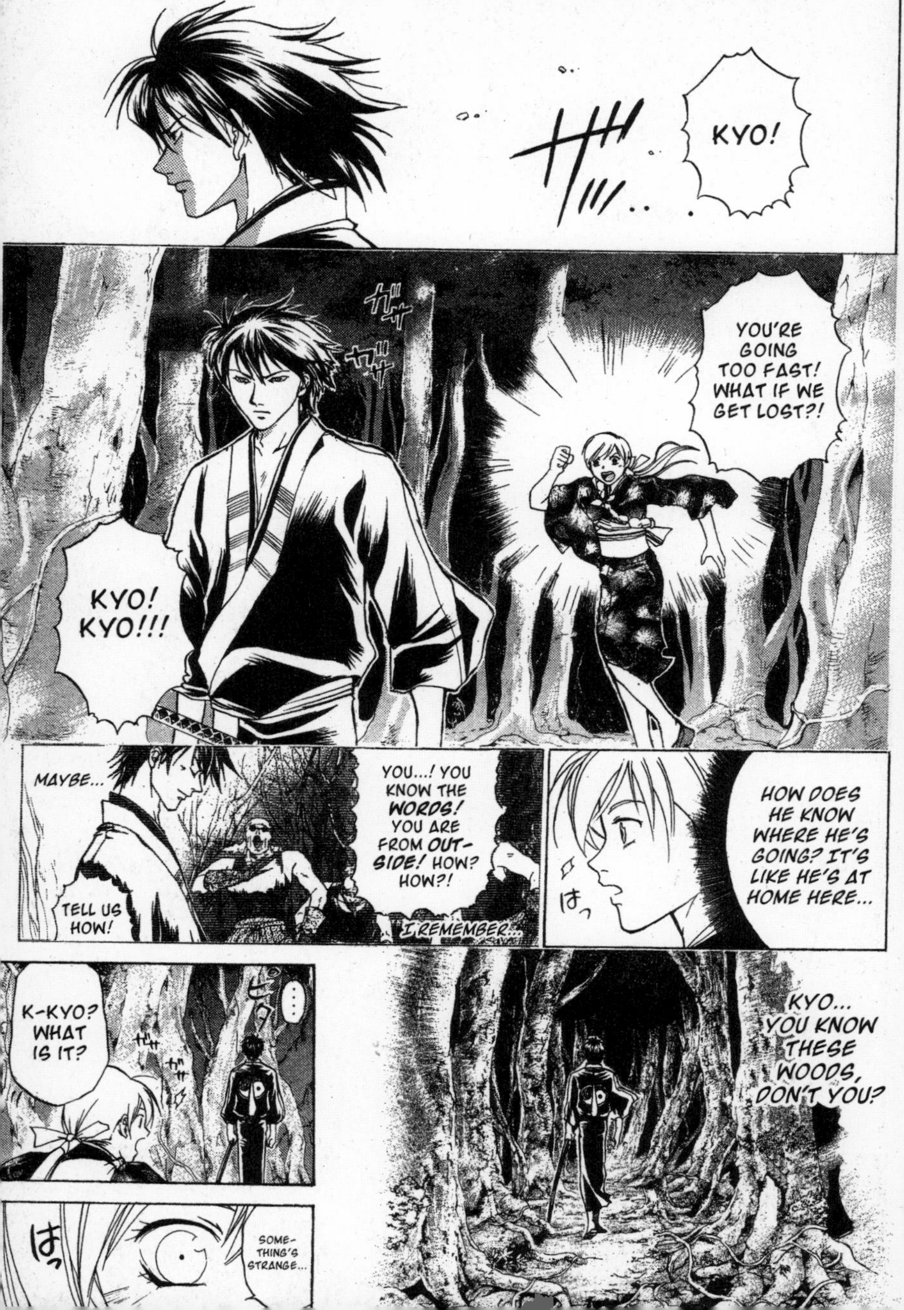
KYO!
YOU'RE GOING TOO FAST! WHAT IF WE GET LOST?!
KYO! KYO!!!
HOW DOES HE KNOW WHERE HE'S GOING? IT'S LIKE HE'S AT HOME HERE...
はっ
YOU...! YOU KNOW THE WORDS! YOU ARE FROM OUT-SIDE! HOW? HOW?!
MAYBE...
TELL US HOW!
I REMEMBER...
KYO... YOU KNOW THESE WOODS, DON'T YOU?
K-KYO? WHAT IS IT?
...
はっ
SOME-THING'S STRANGE...

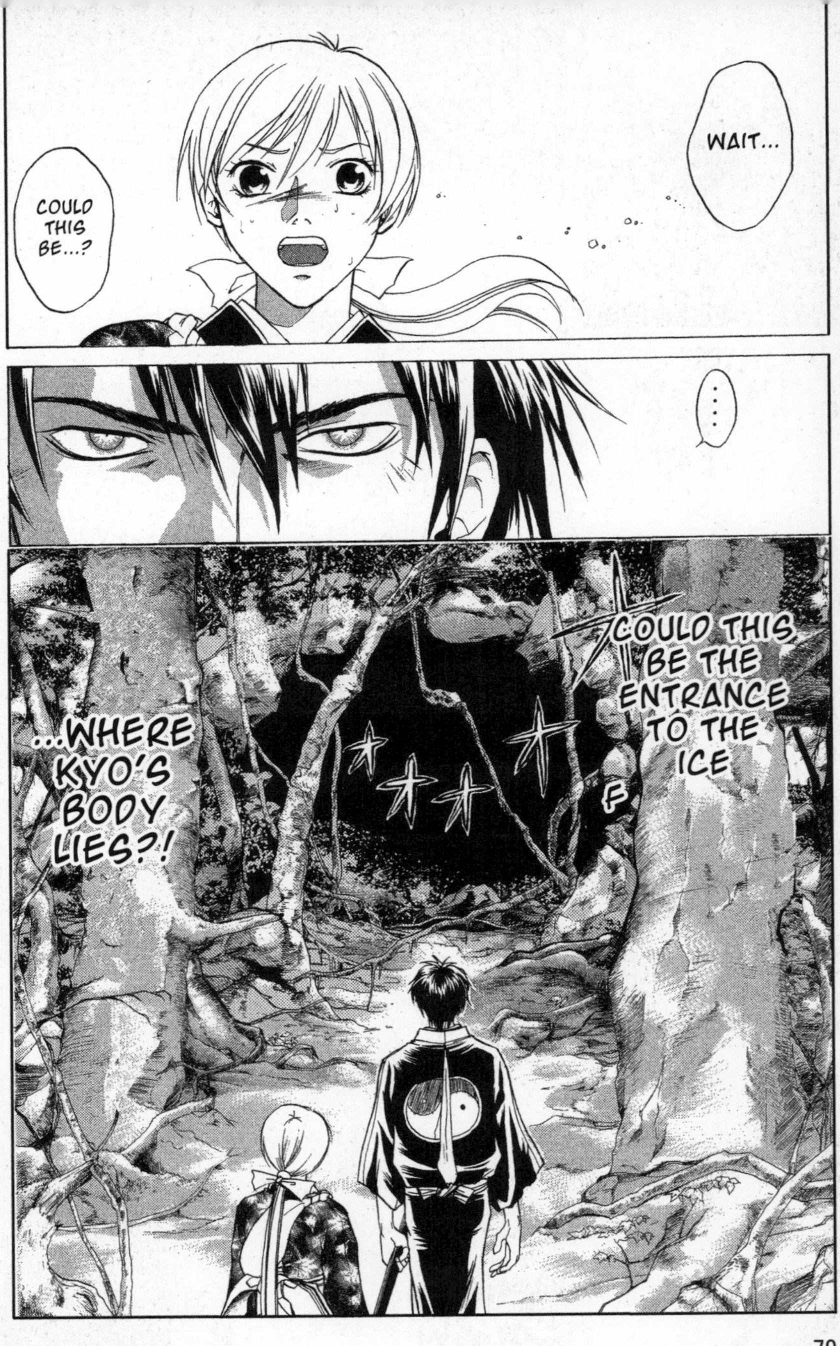
WAIT...
COULD THIS BE...?
......
COULD THIS BE THE ENTRANCE TO THE ICE
F
...WHERE KYO'S BODY LIES?!

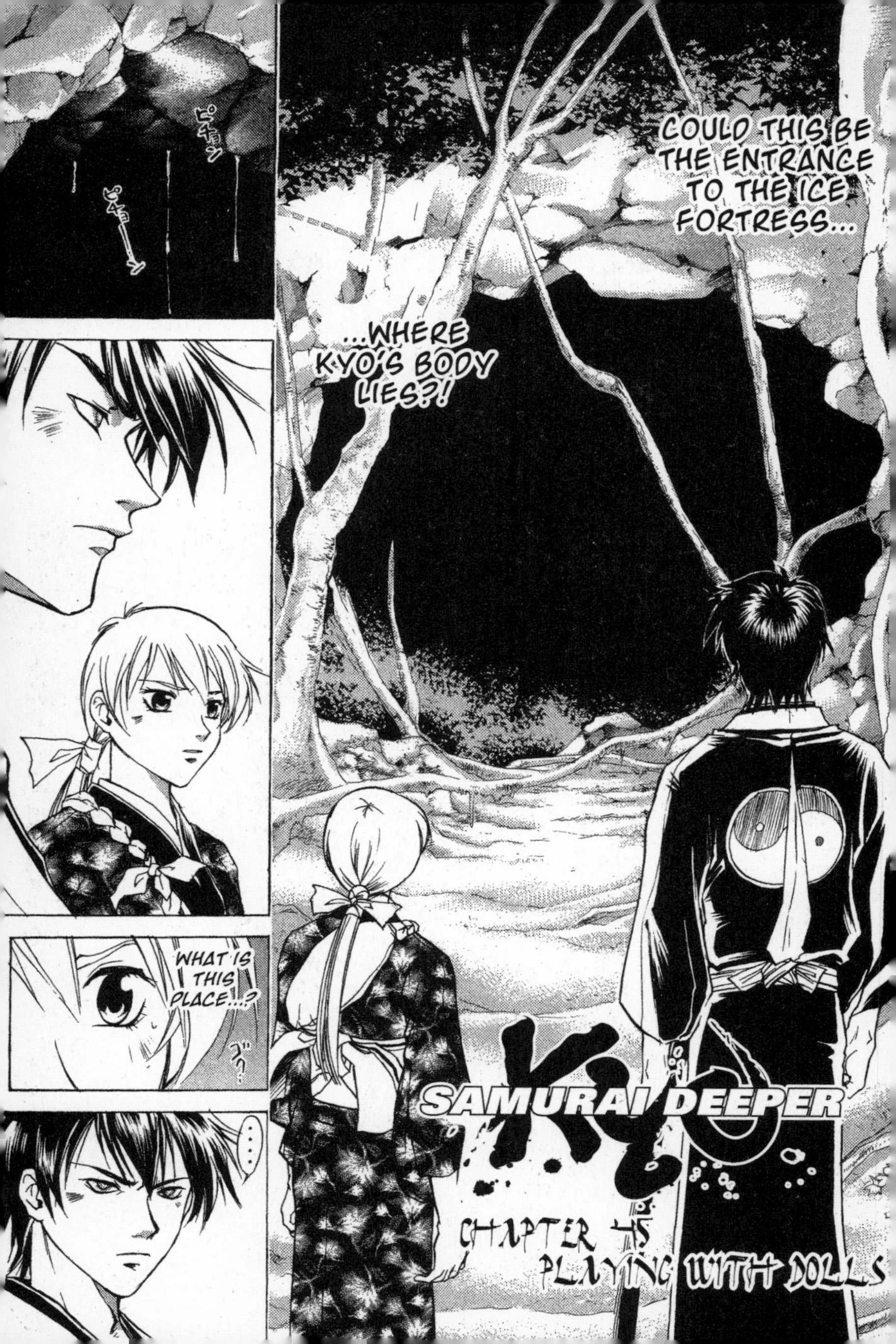
COULD THIS BE THE ENTRANCE TO THE ICE FORTRESS...
...WHERE KYO'S BODY LIES?!
SAMURAI DEEPER KYO
CHAPTER 45
PLAYING WITH DOLLS
ピチョン
WHAT IS THIS PLACE...?
...

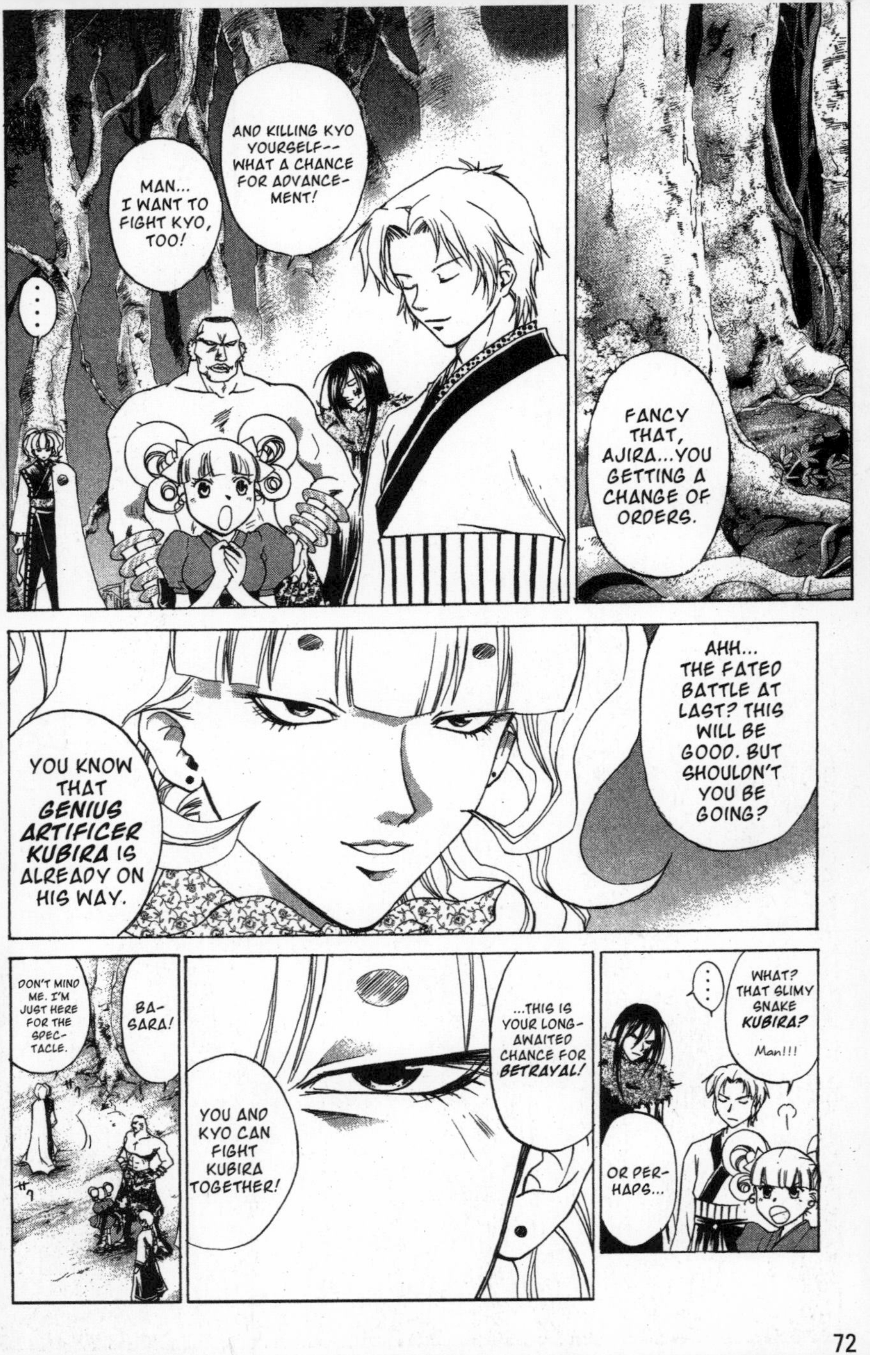
FANCY THAT, AJIRA...YOU GETTING A CHANGE OF ORDERS.
AND KILLING KYO YOURSELF--WHAT A CHANCE FOR ADVANCEMENT!
MAN... I WANT TO FIGHT KYO, TOO!
...
AHH... THE FATED BATTLE AT LAST? THIS WILL BE GOOD. BUT SHOULDN'T YOU BE GOING?
YOU KNOW THAT **GENIUS ARTIFICER KUBIRA** IS ALREADY ON HIS WAY.
WHAT? THAT SLIMY SNAKE **KUBIRA?**
Man!!!
...
OR PERHAPS...
...THIS IS YOUR LONG-AWAITED CHANCE FOR **BETRAYAL!**
YOU AND KYO CAN FIGHT KUBIRA TOGETHER!
BASARA!
DON'T MIND ME. I'M JUST HERE FOR THE SPECTACLE.

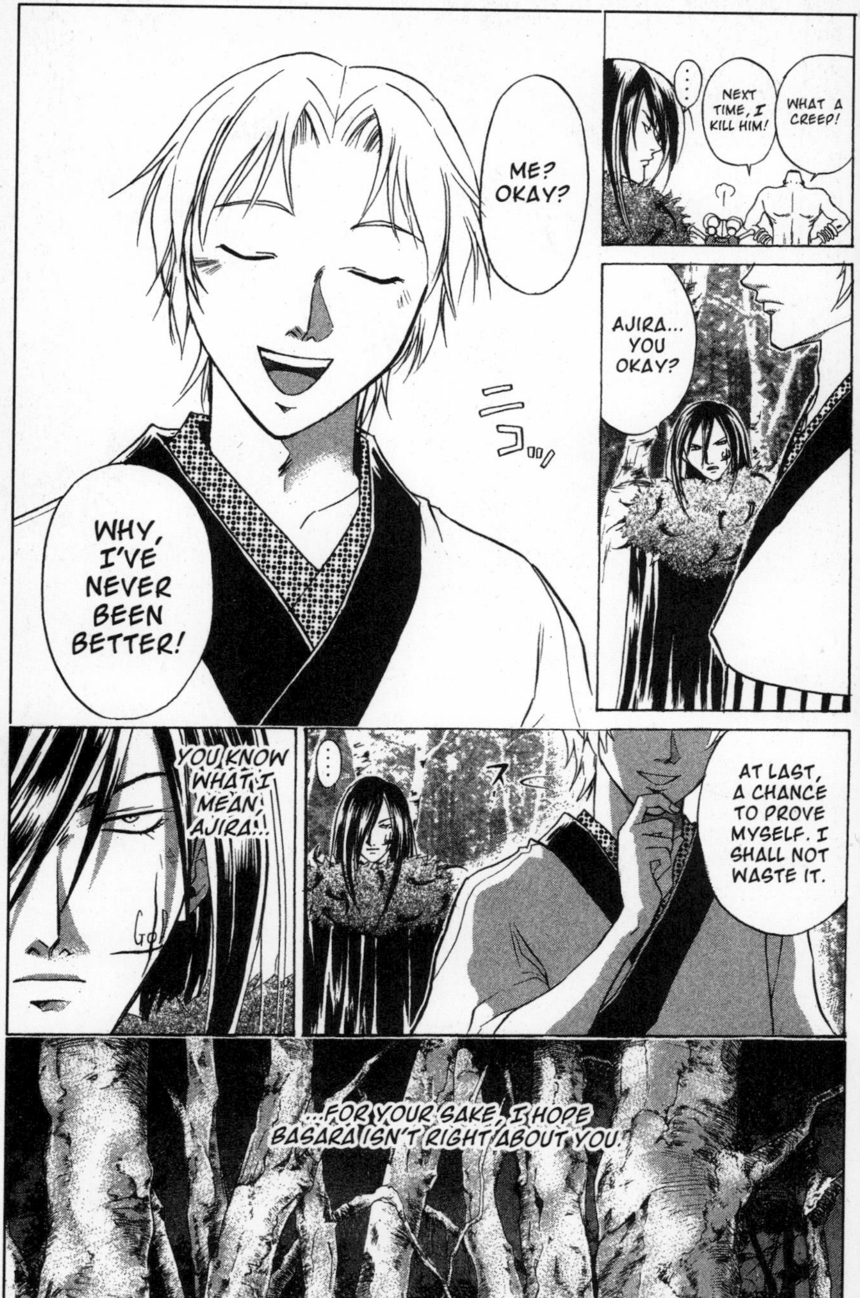
WHAT A CREEP!
NEXT TIME, I KILL HIM!
...
AJIRA... YOU OKAY?
ME? OKAY?
ニコッ
WHY, I'VE NEVER BEEN BETTER!
AT LAST, A CHANCE TO PROVE MYSELF. I SHALL NOT WASTE IT.
...
YOU KNOW WHAT I MEAN, AJIRA...
...FOR YOUR SAKE, I HOPE BASARA ISN'T RIGHT ABOUT YOU.

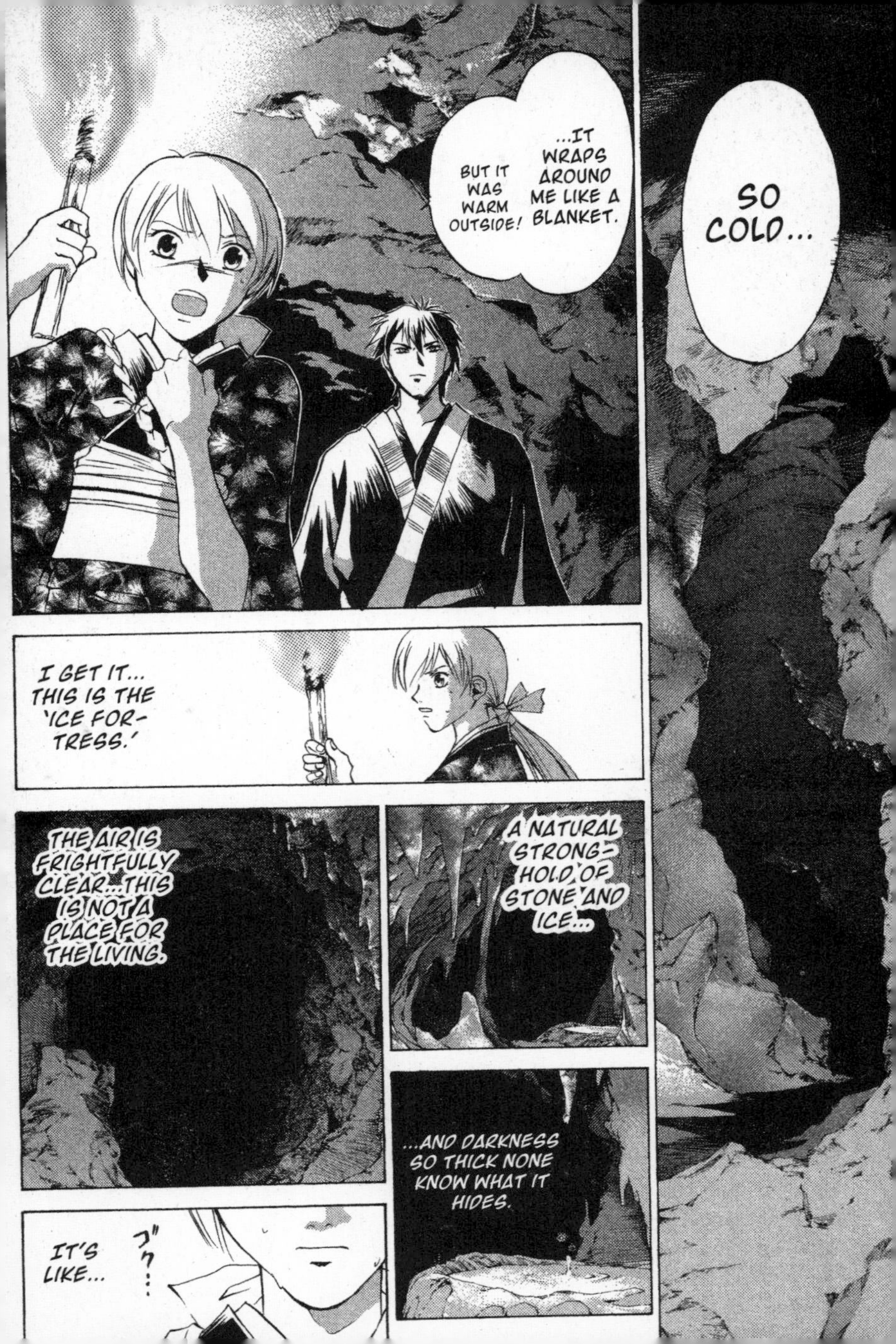
SO COLD...
...IT WRAPS AROUND ME LIKE A BLANKET.
BUT IT WAS WARM OUTSIDE!
I GET IT... THIS IS THE 'ICE FORTRESS.'
A NATURAL STRONGHOLD OF STONE AND ICE...
...AND DARKNESS SO THICK NONE KNOW WHAT IT HIDES.
THE AIR IS FRIGHTFULLY CLEAR...THIS IS NOT A PLACE FOR THE LIVING.
IT'S LIKE...
ゴク…

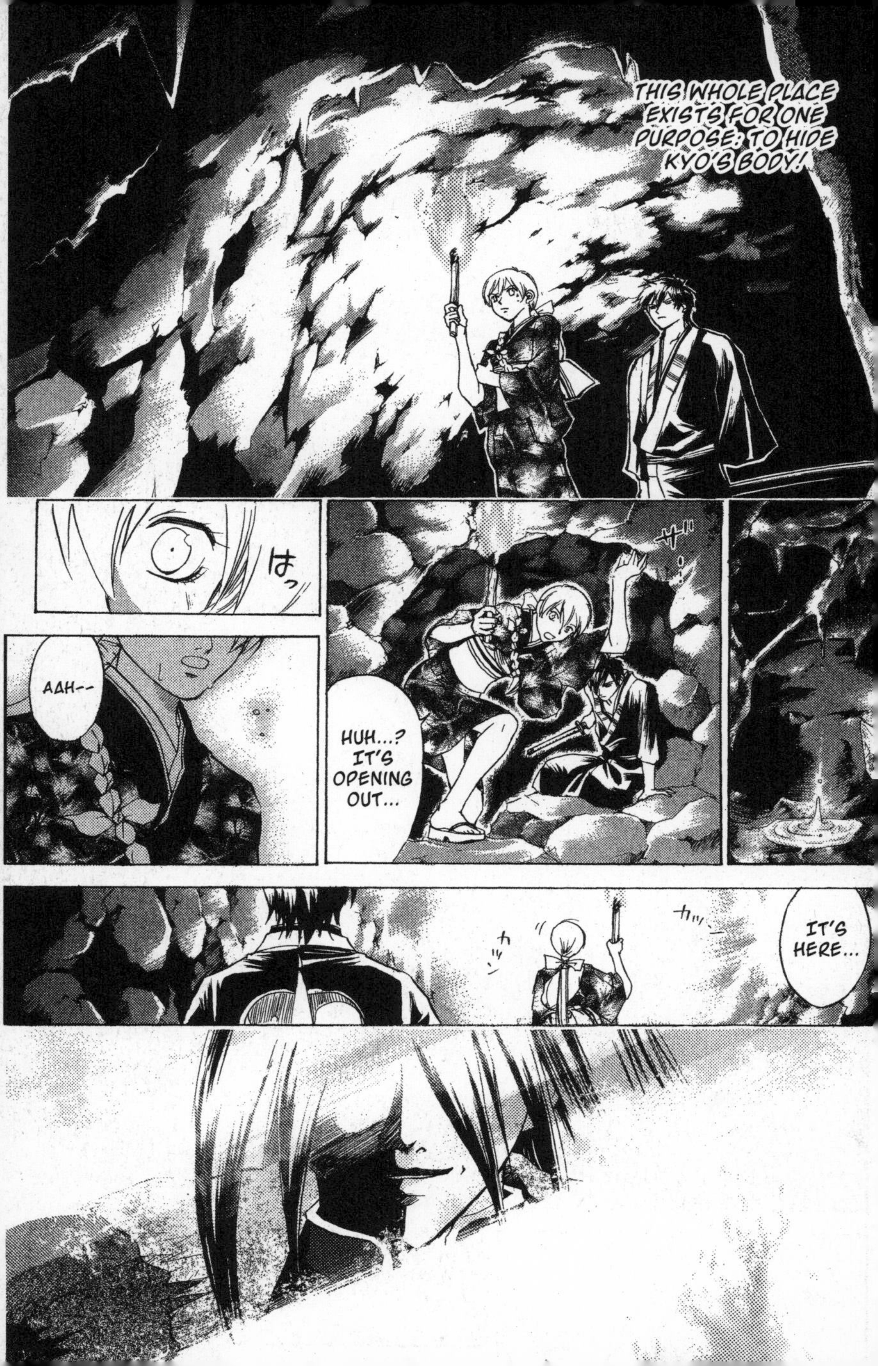
THIS WHOLE PLACE EXISTS FOR ONE PURPOSE: TO HIDE KYO'S BODY!
HUH...? IT'S OPENING OUT...
はっ
AAH--
IT'S HERE...
カッ
カッ

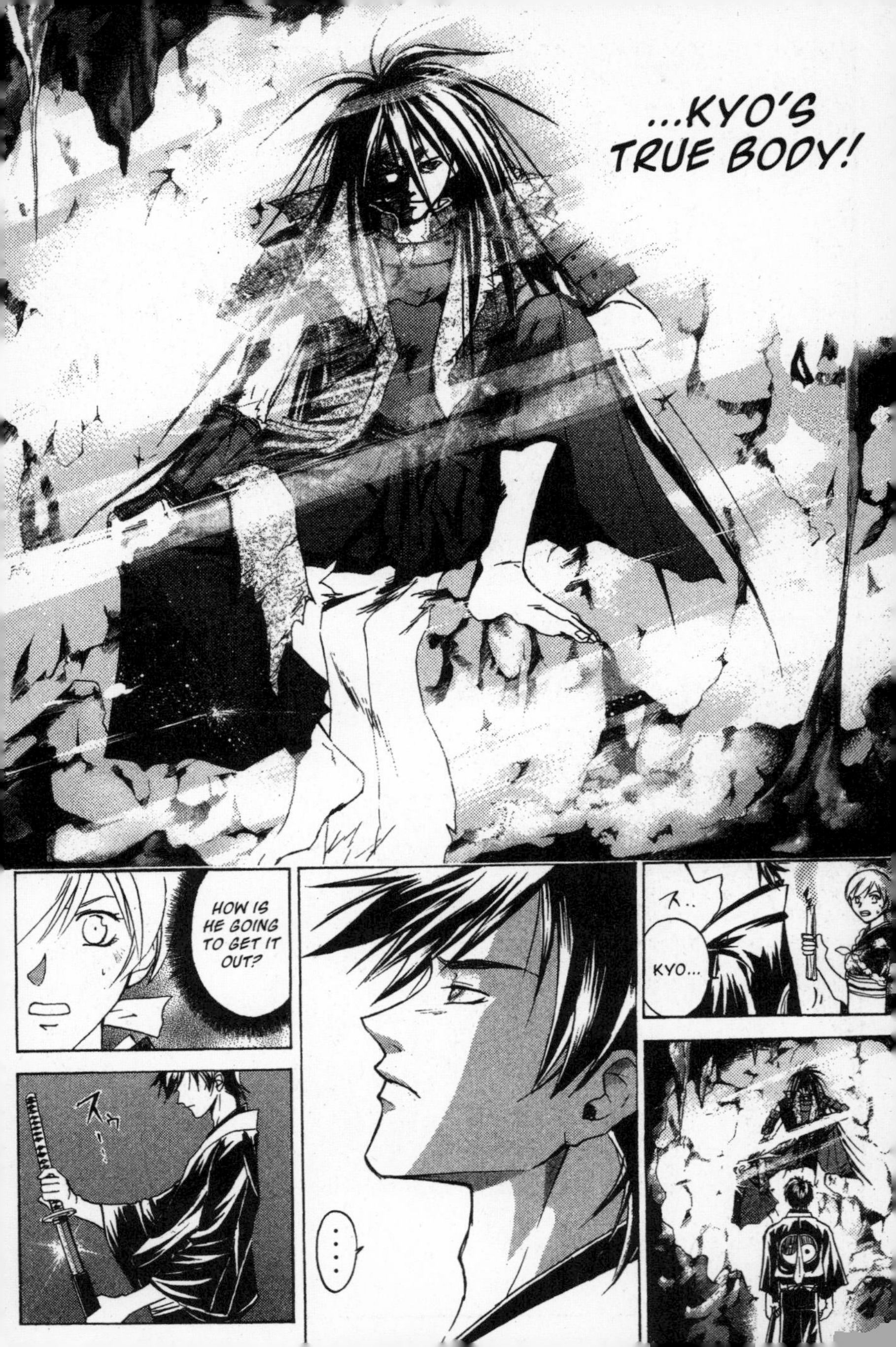
...KYO'S TRUE BODY!
ス..
KYO...
....
HOW IS HE GOING TO GET IT OUT?

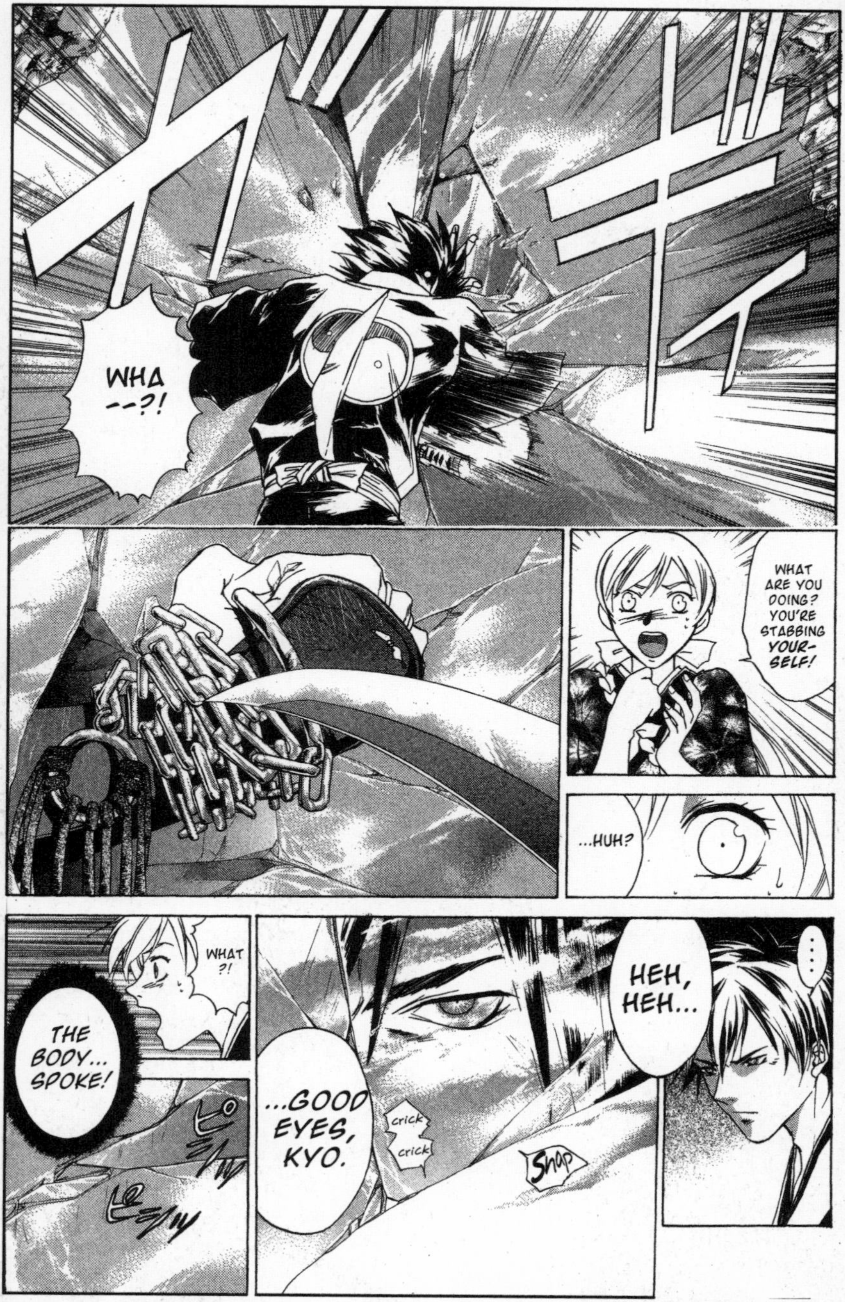
WHA --?!
WHAT ARE YOU DOING? YOU'RE STABBING YOURSELF!
...HUH?
...
HEH, HEH...
...GOOD EYES, KYO.
crick crick
Snap
WHAT ?!
THE BODY... SPOKE!

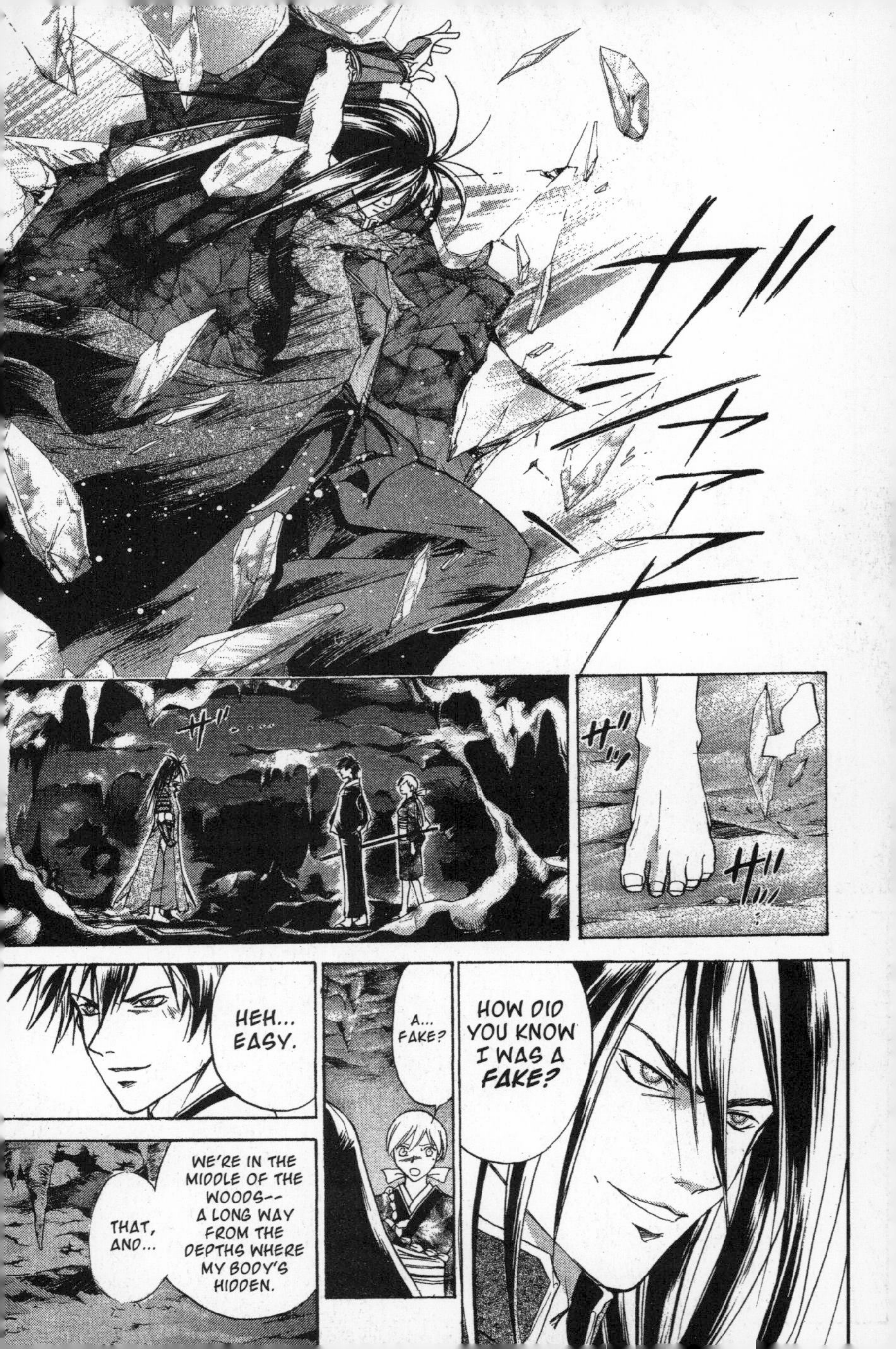

HOW DID YOU KNOW I WAS A FAKE?
A... FAKE?
HEH... EASY.
THAT, AND...
WE'RE IN THE MIDDLE OF THE WOODS-- A LONG WAY FROM THE DEPTHS WHERE MY BODY'S HIDDEN.

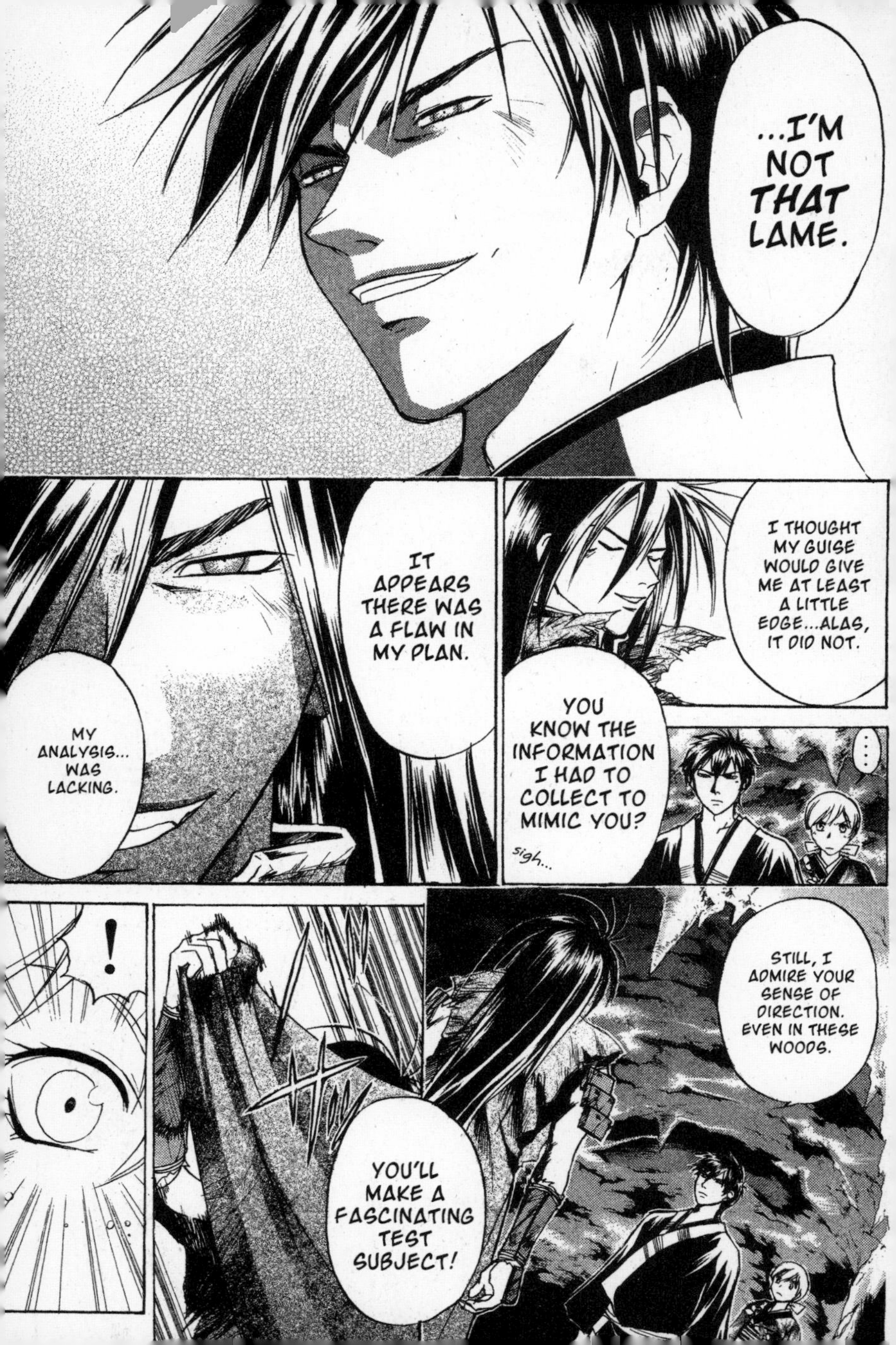

...I'M NOT THAT LAME.
I THOUGHT MY GUISE WOULD GIVE ME AT LEAST A LITTLE EDGE...ALAS, IT DID NOT.
YOU KNOW THE INFORMATION I HAD TO COLLECT TO MIMIC YOU?
...
sigh...
IT APPEARS THERE WAS A FLAW IN MY PLAN.
MY ANALYSIS... WAS LACKING.
STILL, I ADMIRE YOUR SENSE OF DIRECTION. EVEN IN THESE WOODS.
YOU'LL MAKE A FASCINATING TEST SUBJECT!
!

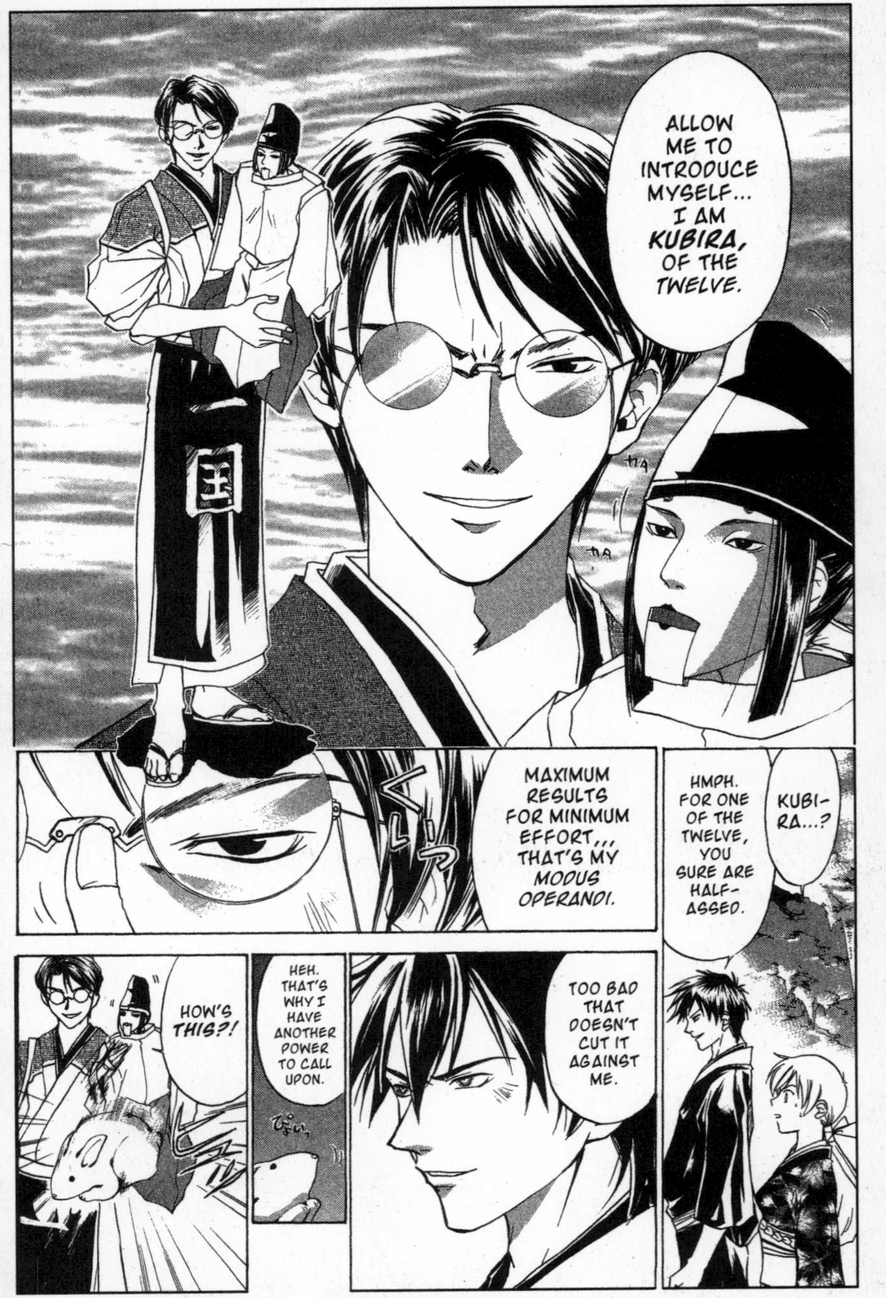
ALLOW ME TO INTRODUCE MYSELF... I AM KUBIRA, OF THE TWELVE.
HA
HA
KUBI-RA...?
HMPH. FOR ONE OF THE TWELVE, YOU SURE ARE HALF-ASSED.
MAXIMUM RESULTS FOR MINIMUM EFFORT,,, THAT'S MY MODUS OPERANDI.
TOO BAD THAT DOESN'T CUT IT AGAINST ME.
HEH. THAT'S WHY I HAVE ANOTHER POWER TO CALL UPON.
HOW'S THIS?!

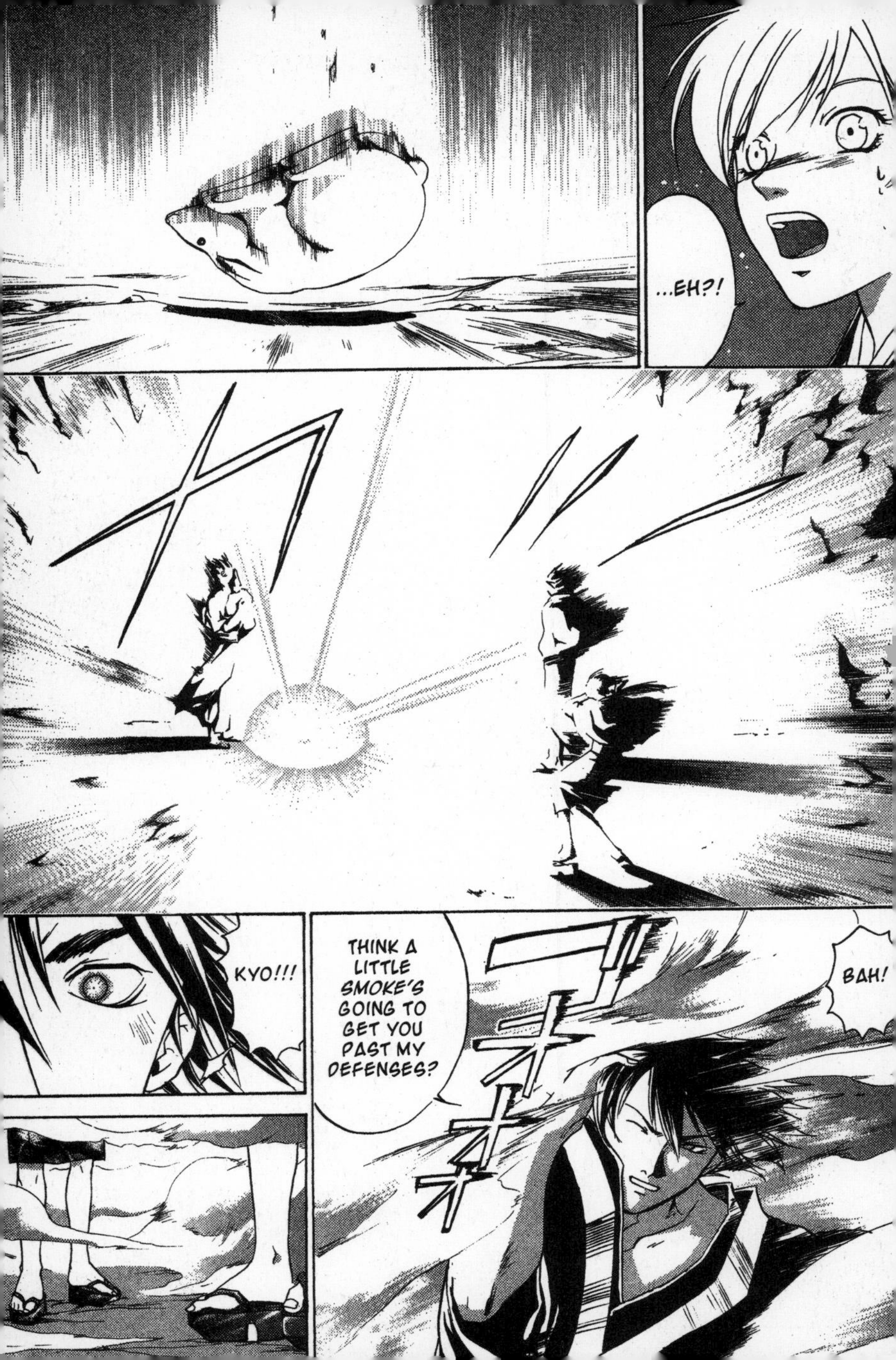
...EH?!
BAH!
THINK A LITTLE SMOKE'S GOING TO GET YOU PAST MY DEFENSES?
KYO!!!

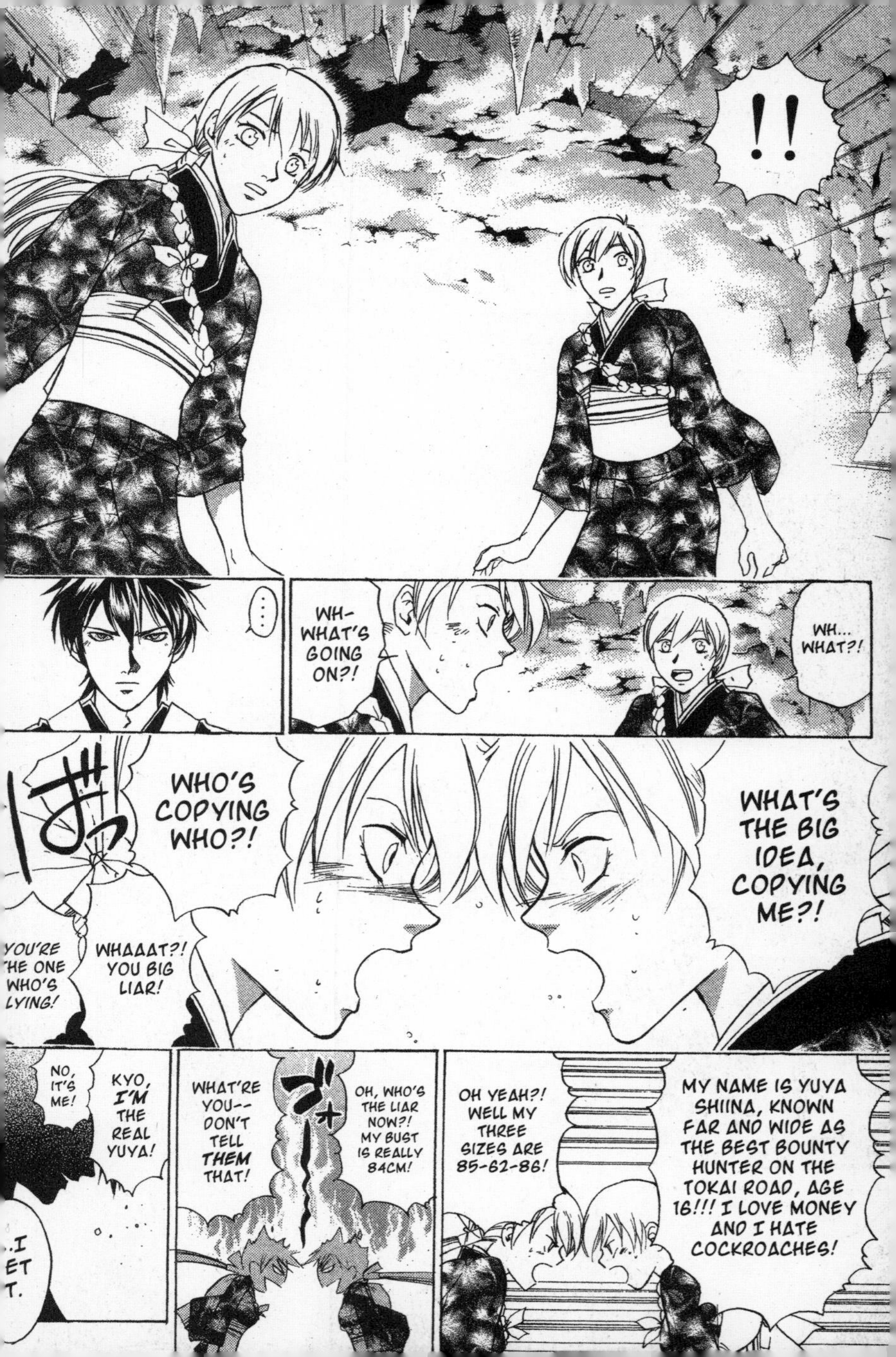
!!
WH... WHAT?!
WH- WHAT'S GOING ON?!
...
WHAT'S THE BIG IDEA, COPYING ME?!
WHO'S COPYING WHO?!
ばっ
WHAAAT?! YOU BIG LIAR!
YOU'RE THE ONE WHO'S LYING!
MY NAME IS YUYA SHIINA, KNOWN FAR AND WIDE AS THE BEST BOUNTY HUNTER ON THE TOKAI ROAD, AGE 16!!! I LOVE MONEY AND I HATE COCKROACHES!
OH YEAH?! WELL MY THREE SIZES ARE 85-62-86!
OH, WHO'S THE LIAR NOW?! MY BUST IS REALLY 84CM!
ゴォー
WHAT'RE YOU-- DON'T TELL THEM THAT!
KYO, I'M THE REAL YUYA!
NO, IT'S ME!

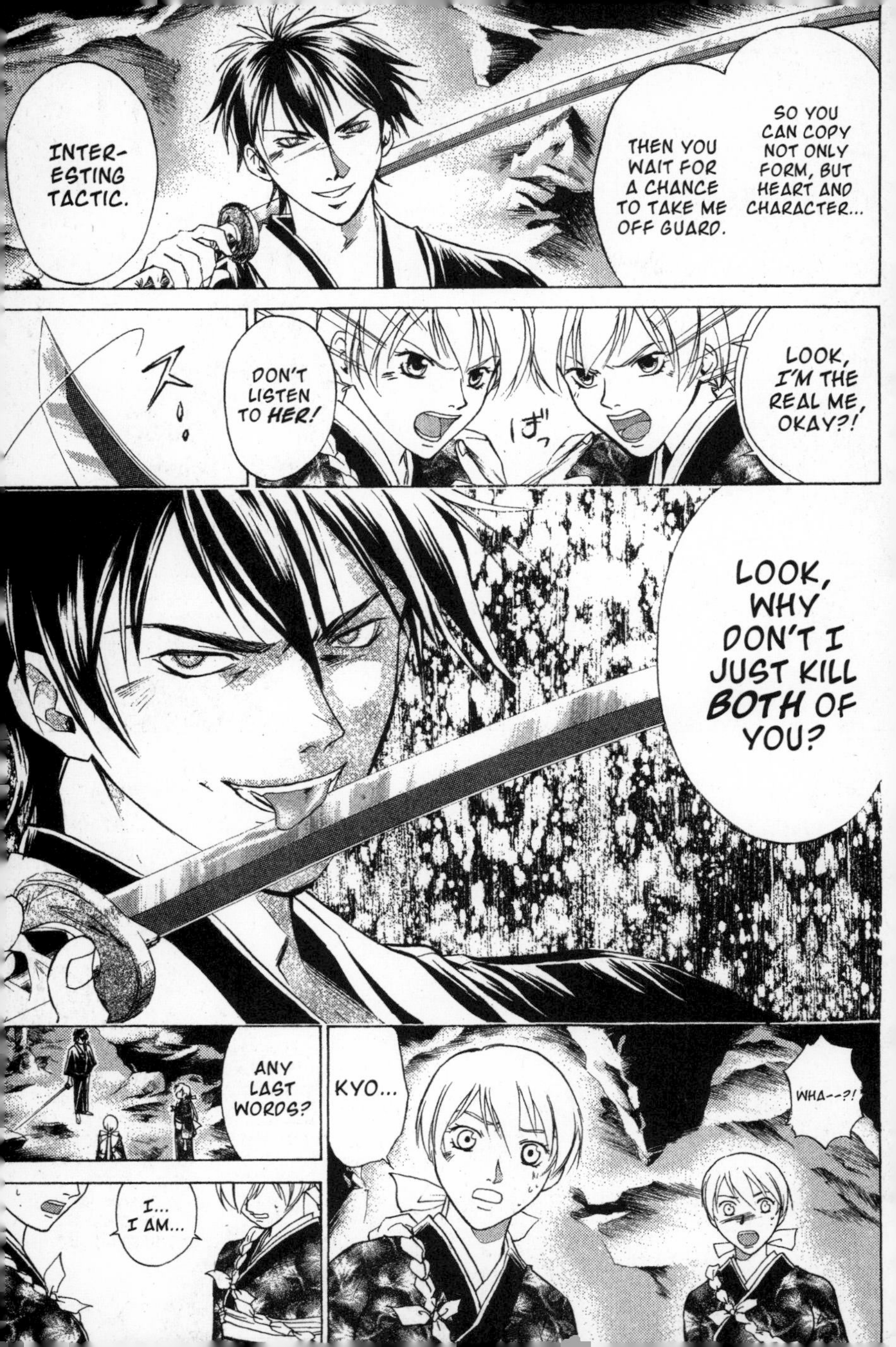
SO YOU CAN COPY NOT ONLY FORM, BUT HEART AND CHARACTER...
THEN YOU WAIT FOR A CHANCE TO TAKE ME OFF GUARD.
INTER-ESTING TACTIC.
LOOK, I'M THE REAL ME, OKAY?!
ばっ
DON'T LISTEN TO HER!
ス
LOOK, WHY DON'T I JUST KILL BOTH OF YOU?
WHA--?!
KYO...
ANY LAST WORDS?
I... I AM...

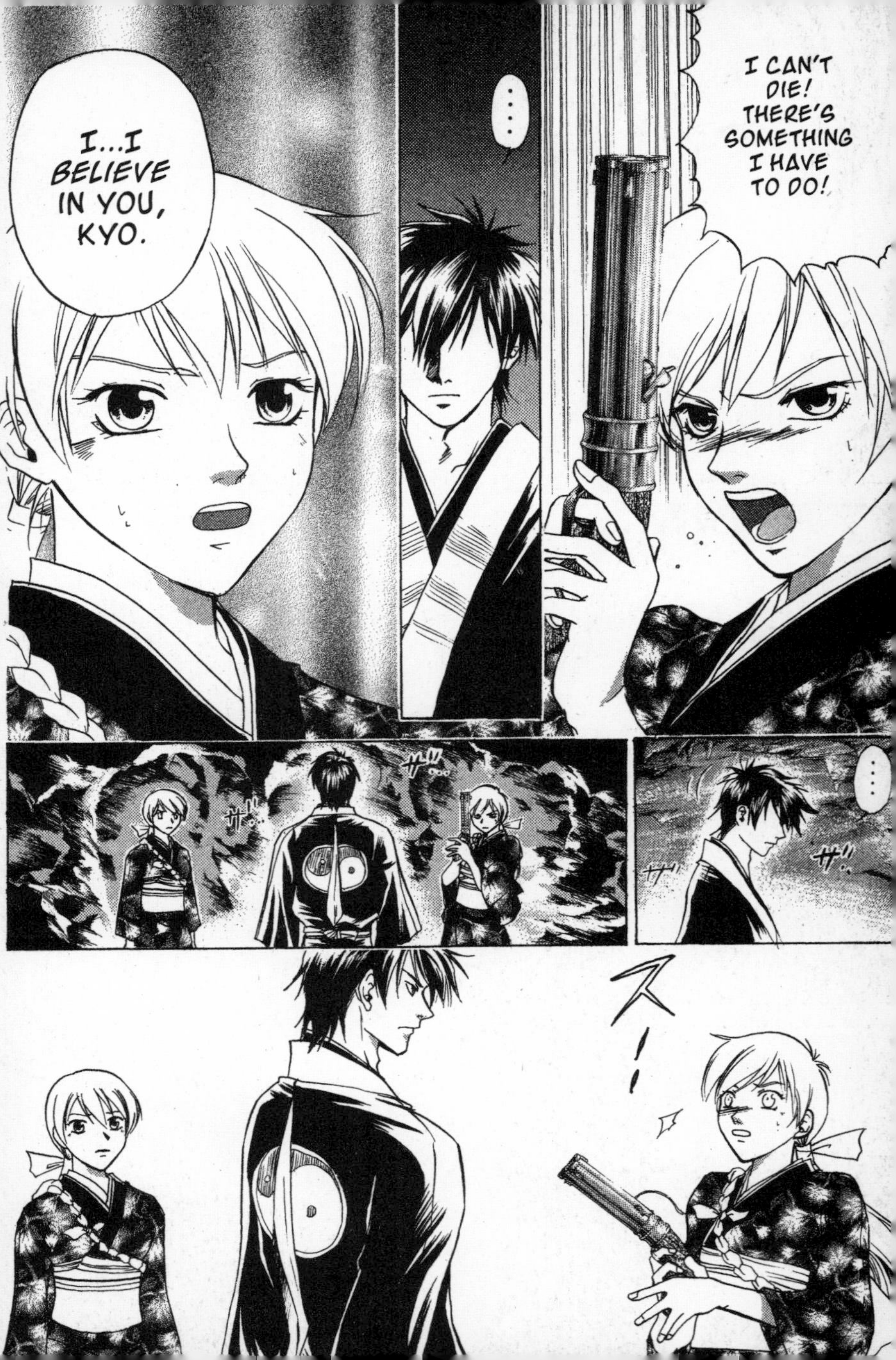
I CAN'T DIE! THERE'S SOMETHING I HAVE TO DO!
...
I...I BELIEVE IN YOU, KYO.
...
ス

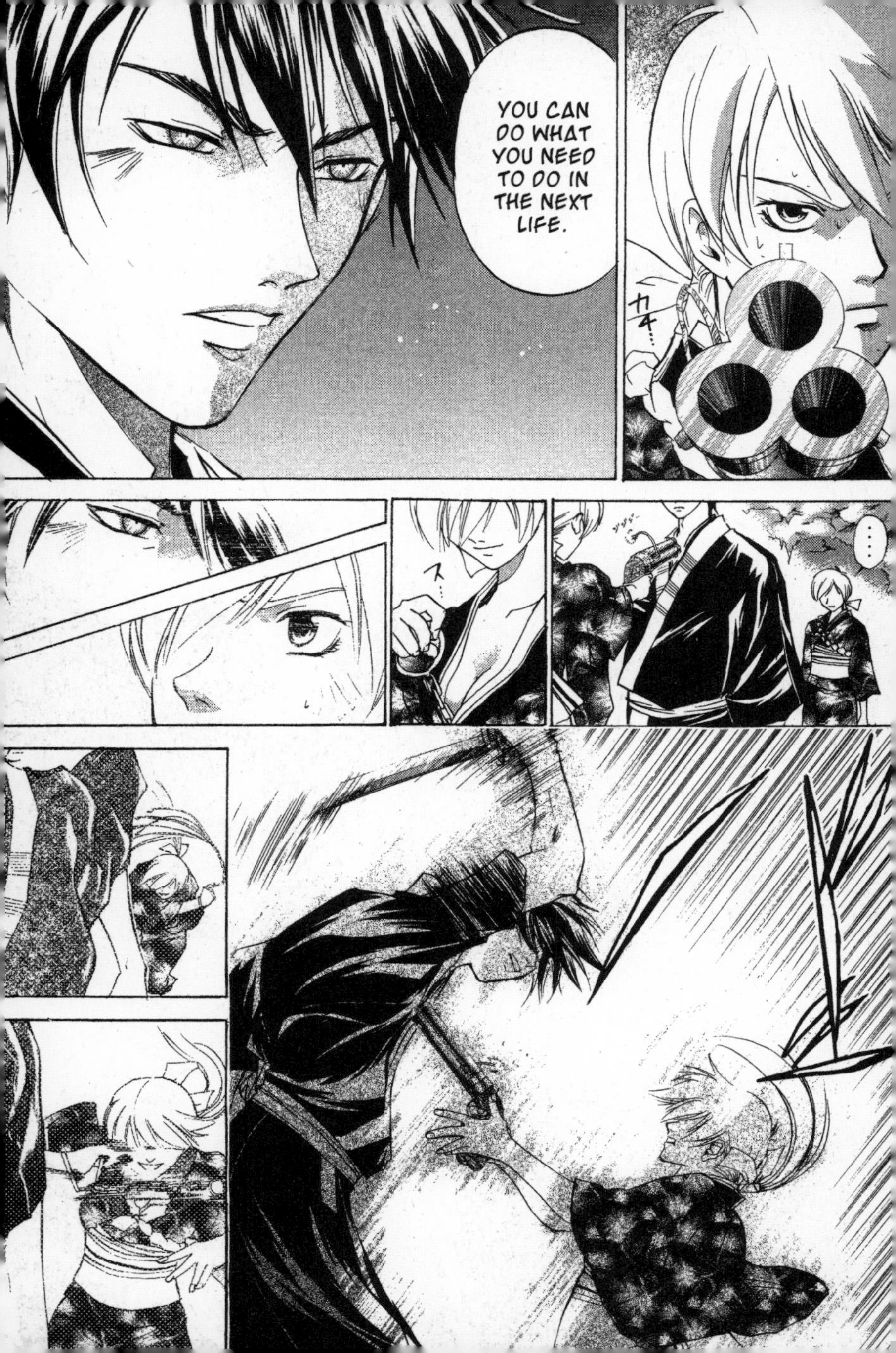
カチ…
YOU CAN DO WHAT YOU NEED TO DO IN THE NEXT LIFE.
…
ス…

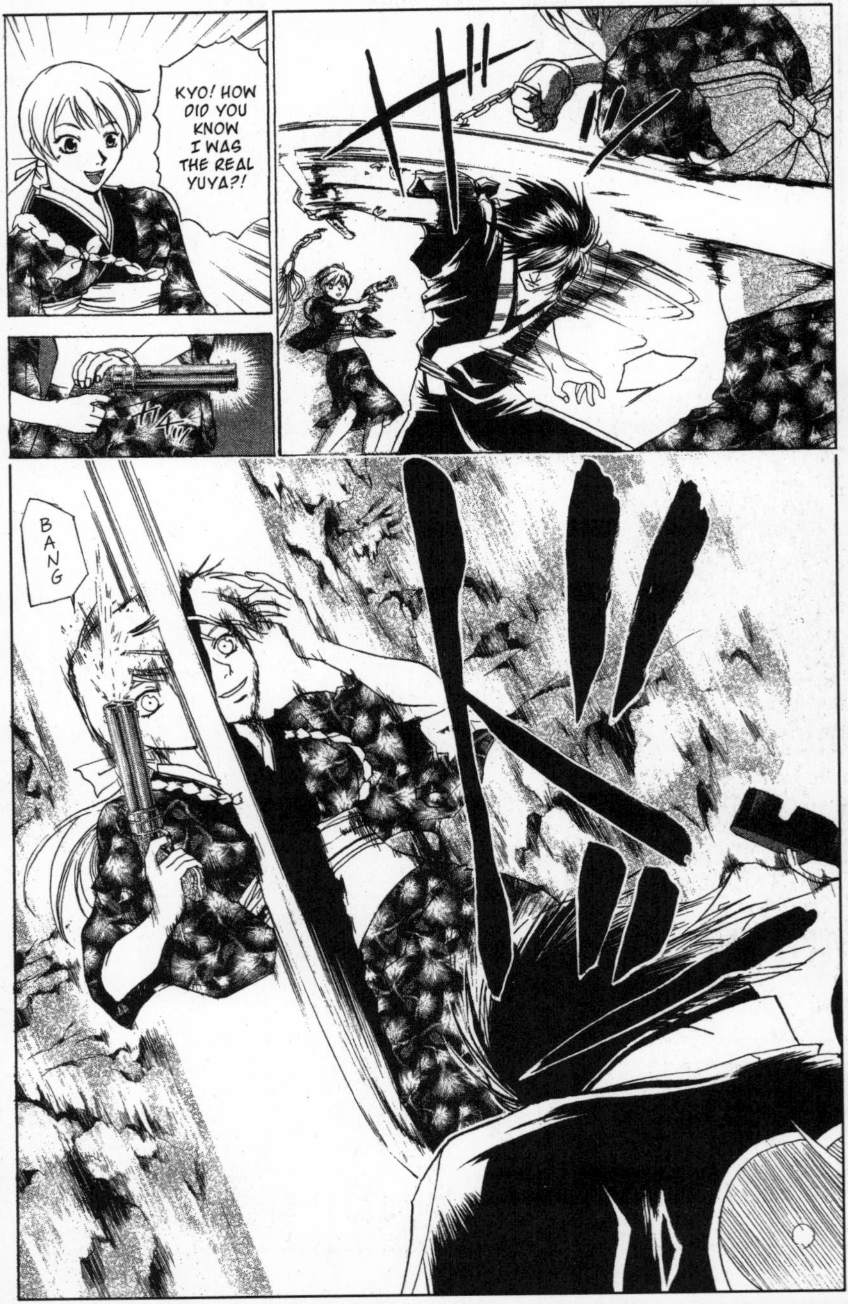
KYO! HOW DID YOU KNOW I WAS THE REAL YUYA?!
BANG

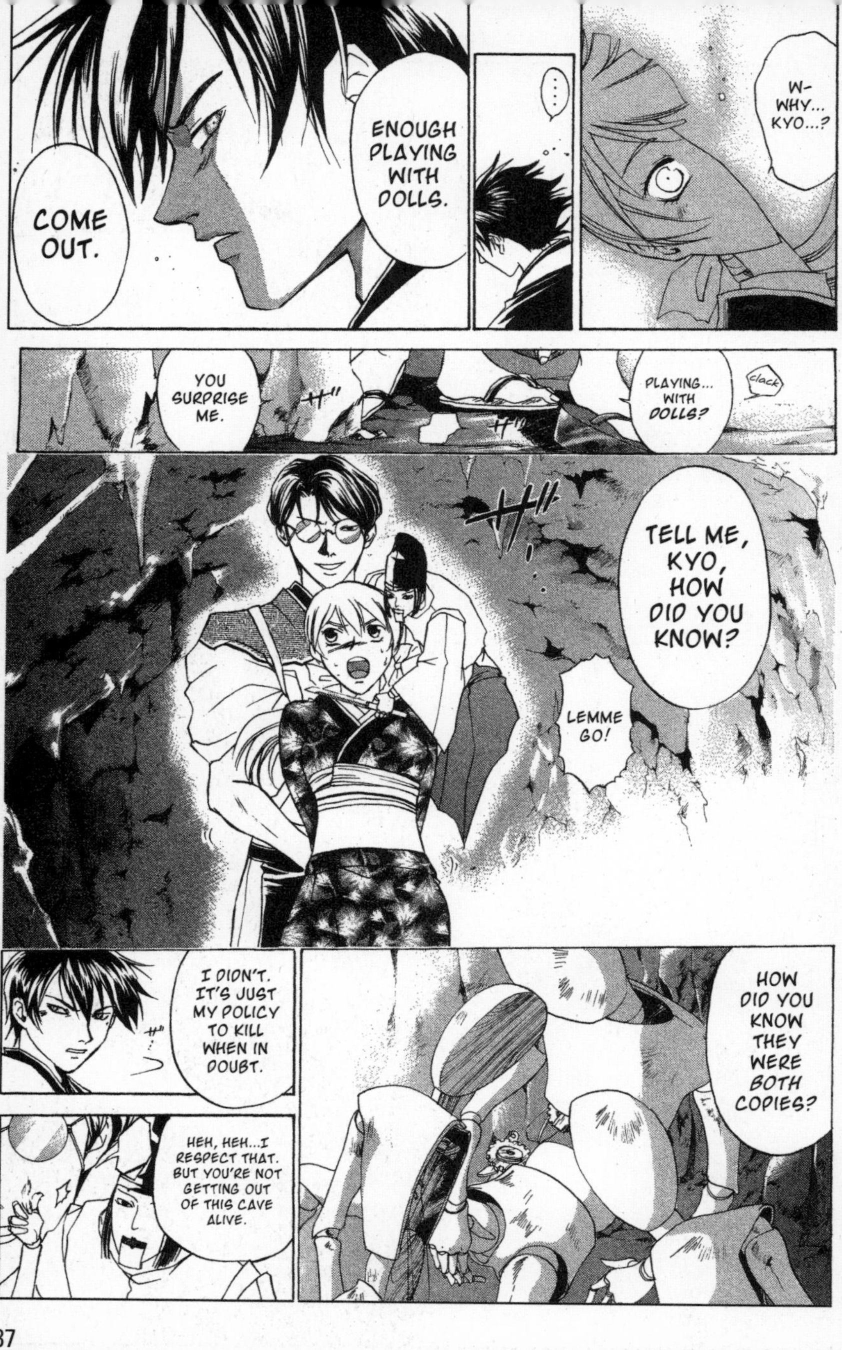
W-WHY... KYO...?
...
ENOUGH PLAYING WITH DOLLS.
COME OUT.
clack
PLAYING... WITH DOLLS?
YOU SURPRISE ME.
TELL ME, KYO, HOW DID YOU KNOW?
LEMME GO!
HOW DID YOU KNOW THEY WERE BOTH COPIES?
I DIDN'T. IT'S JUST MY POLICY TO KILL WHEN IN DOUBT.
HEH, HEH...I RESPECT THAT. BUT YOU'RE NOT GETTING OUT OF THIS CAVE ALIVE.

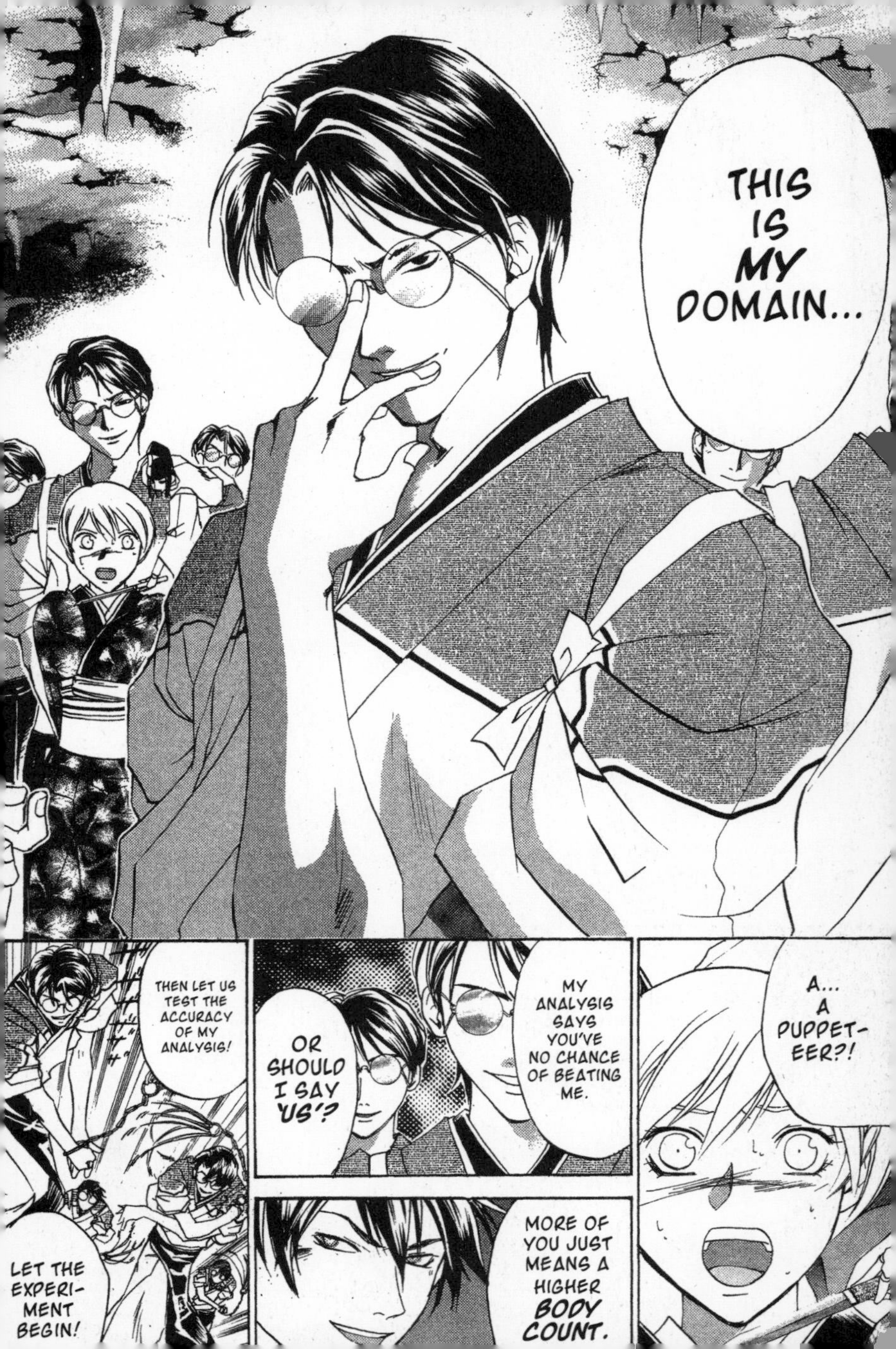
THIS IS MY DOMAIN...
A... A PUPPETEER?!
MY ANALYSIS SAYS YOU'VE NO CHANCE OF BEATING ME.
OR SHOULD I SAY 'US'?
MORE OF YOU JUST MEANS A HIGHER BODY COUNT.
THEN LET US TEST THE ACCURACY OF MY ANALYSIS!
LET THE EXPERIMENT BEGIN!

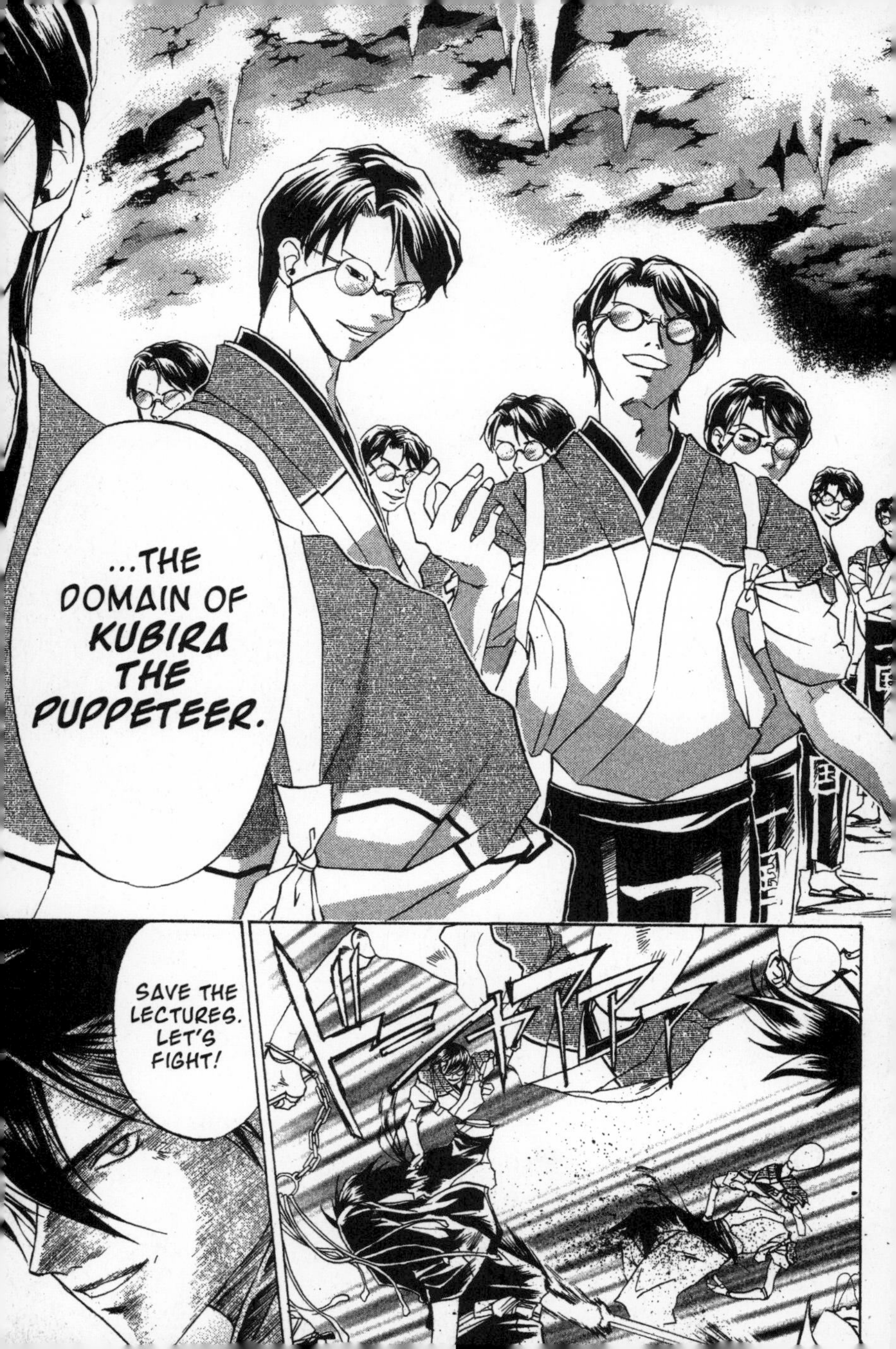
...THE DOMAIN OF KUBIRA THE PUPPETEER.
SAVE THE LECTURES. LET'S FIGHT!

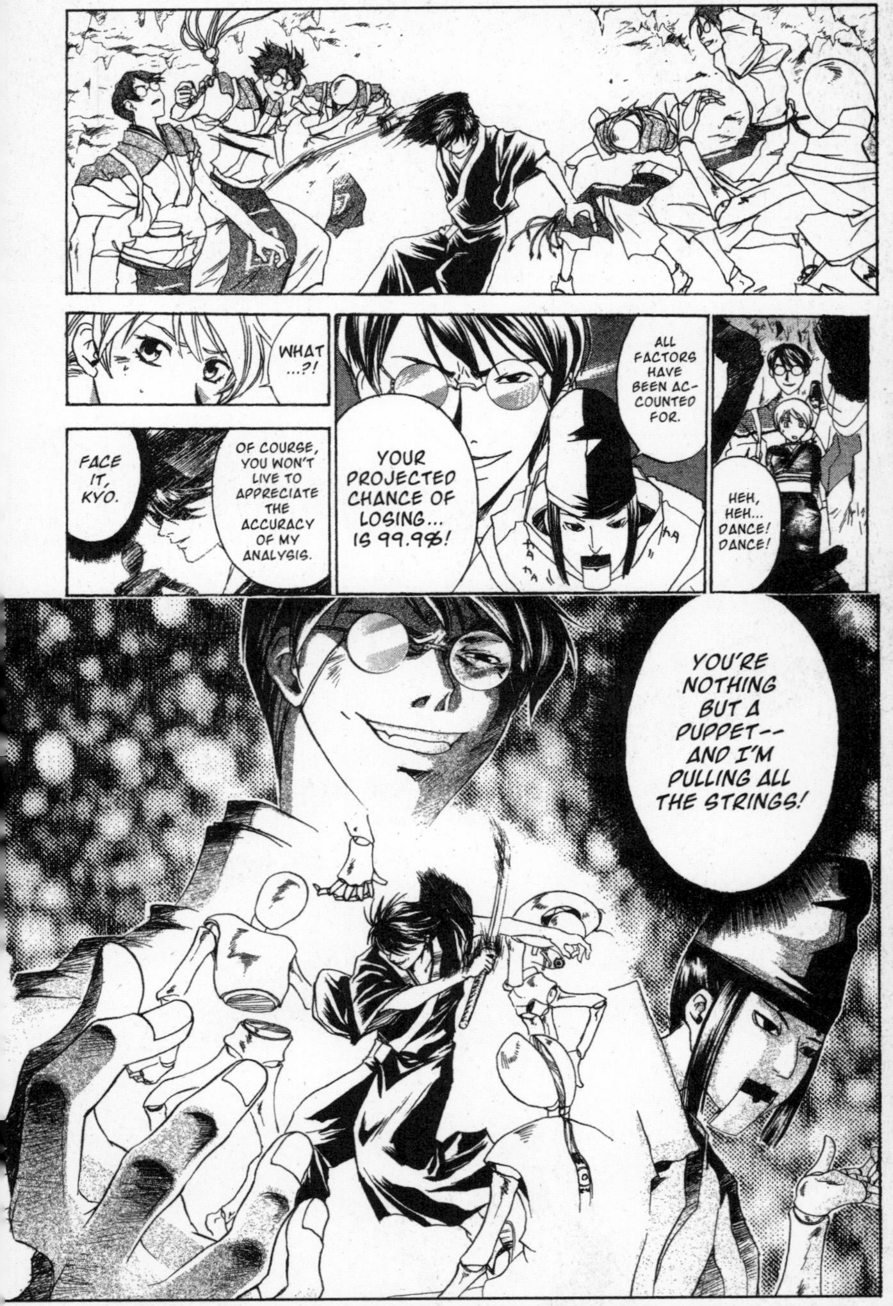
HEH, HEH... DANCE! DANCE!
ALL FACTORS HAVE BEEN AC-COUNTED FOR.
YOUR PROJECTED CHANCE OF LOSING... IS 99.9%!
HA HA HA
WHAT ...?!
OF COURSE, YOU WON'T LIVE TO APPRECIATE THE ACCURACY OF MY ANALYSIS.
FACE IT, KYO.
YOU'RE NOTHING BUT A PUPPET-- AND I'M PULLING ALL THE STRINGS!

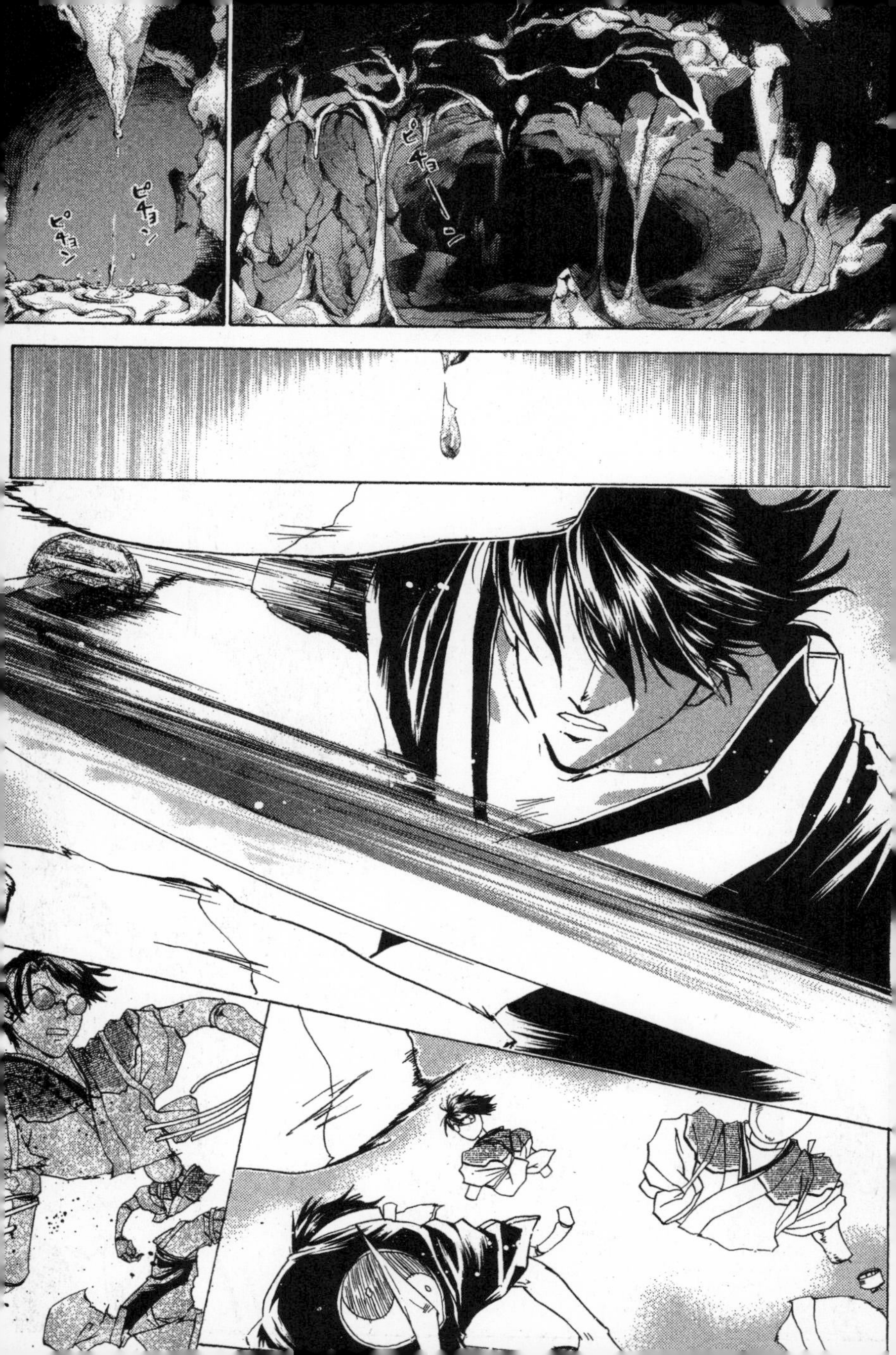
ピチョーーン
ピチョン
ピチョン

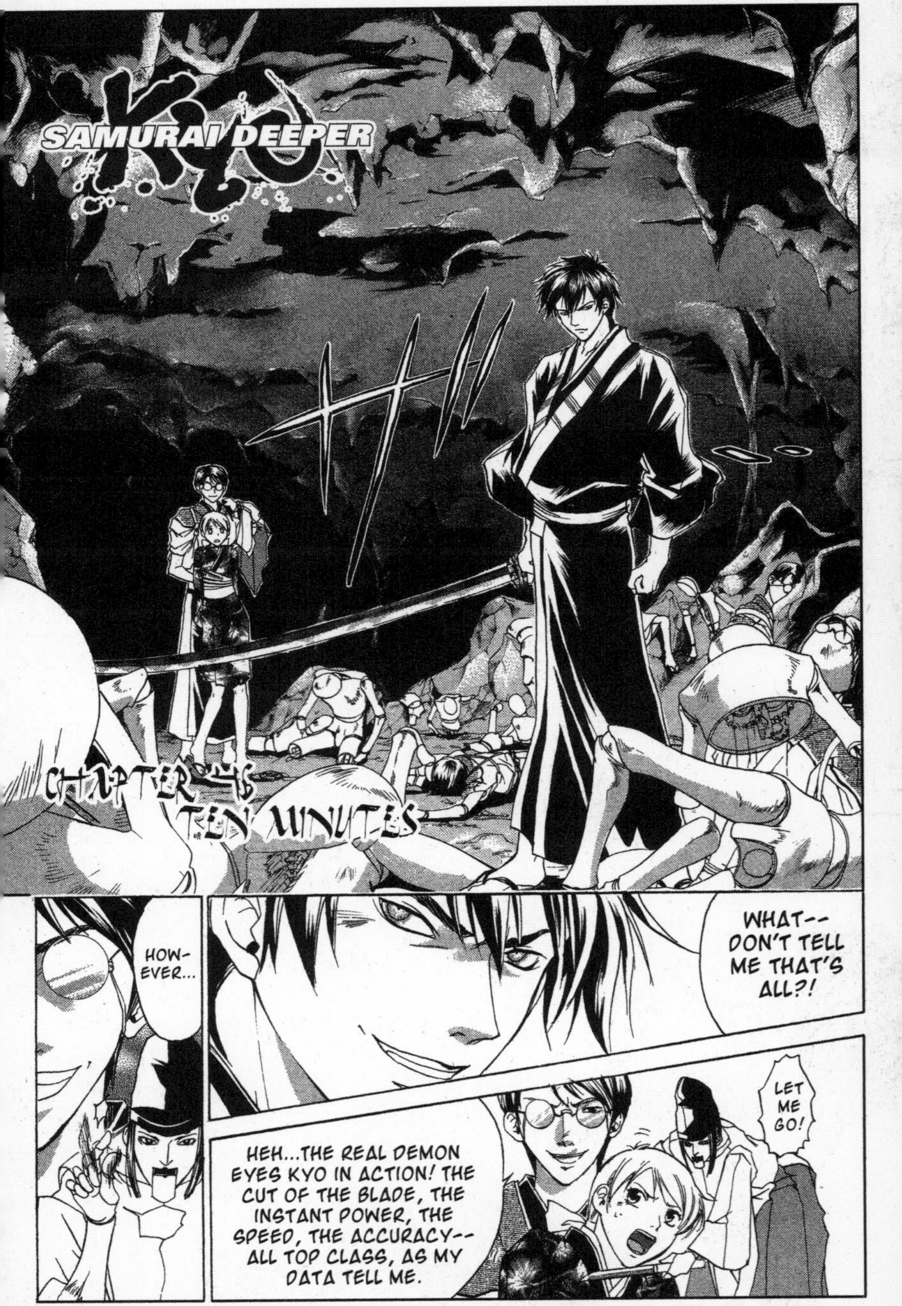
SAMURAI DEEPER KYO
CHAPTER 45
TEN MINUTES
WHAT--DON'T TELL ME THAT'S ALL?!
HOW-EVER...
LET ME GO!
HEH...THE REAL DEMON EYES KYO IN ACTION! THE CUT OF THE BLADE, THE INSTANT POWER, THE SPEED, THE ACCURACY--ALL TOP CLASS, AS MY DATA TELL ME.

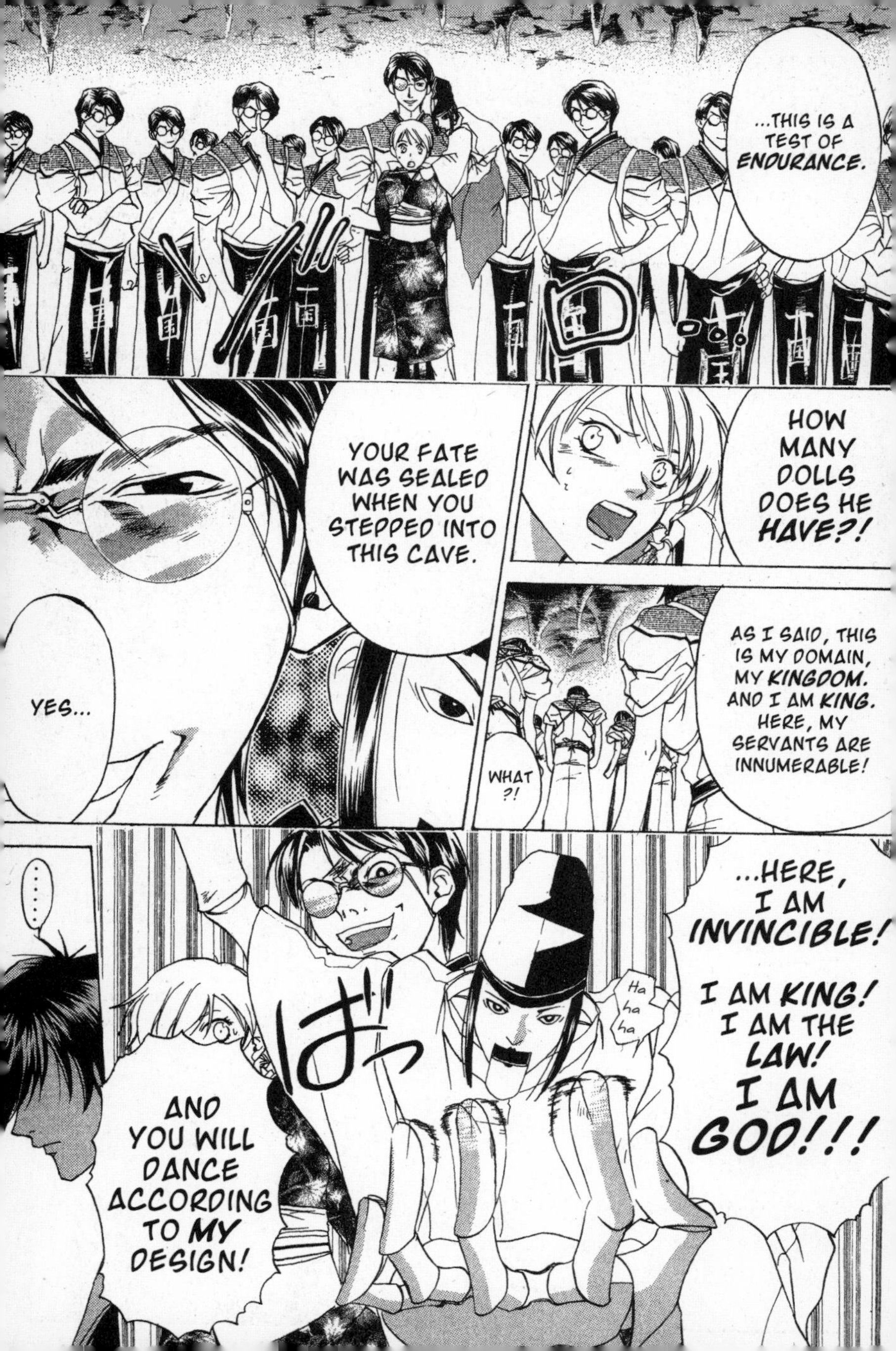
...THIS IS A TEST OF ENDURANCE.
HOW MANY DOLLS DOES HE HAVE?!
AS I SAID, THIS IS MY DOMAIN, MY KINGDOM. AND I AM KING. HERE, MY SERVANTS ARE INNUMERABLE!
WHAT ?!
YOUR FATE WAS SEALED WHEN YOU STEPPED INTO THIS CAVE.
YES...
...HERE, I AM INVINCIBLE!
I AM KING! I AM THE LAW! I AM GOD!!!
Ha ha ha
ばっ
AND YOU WILL DANCE ACCORDING TO MY DESIGN!
......

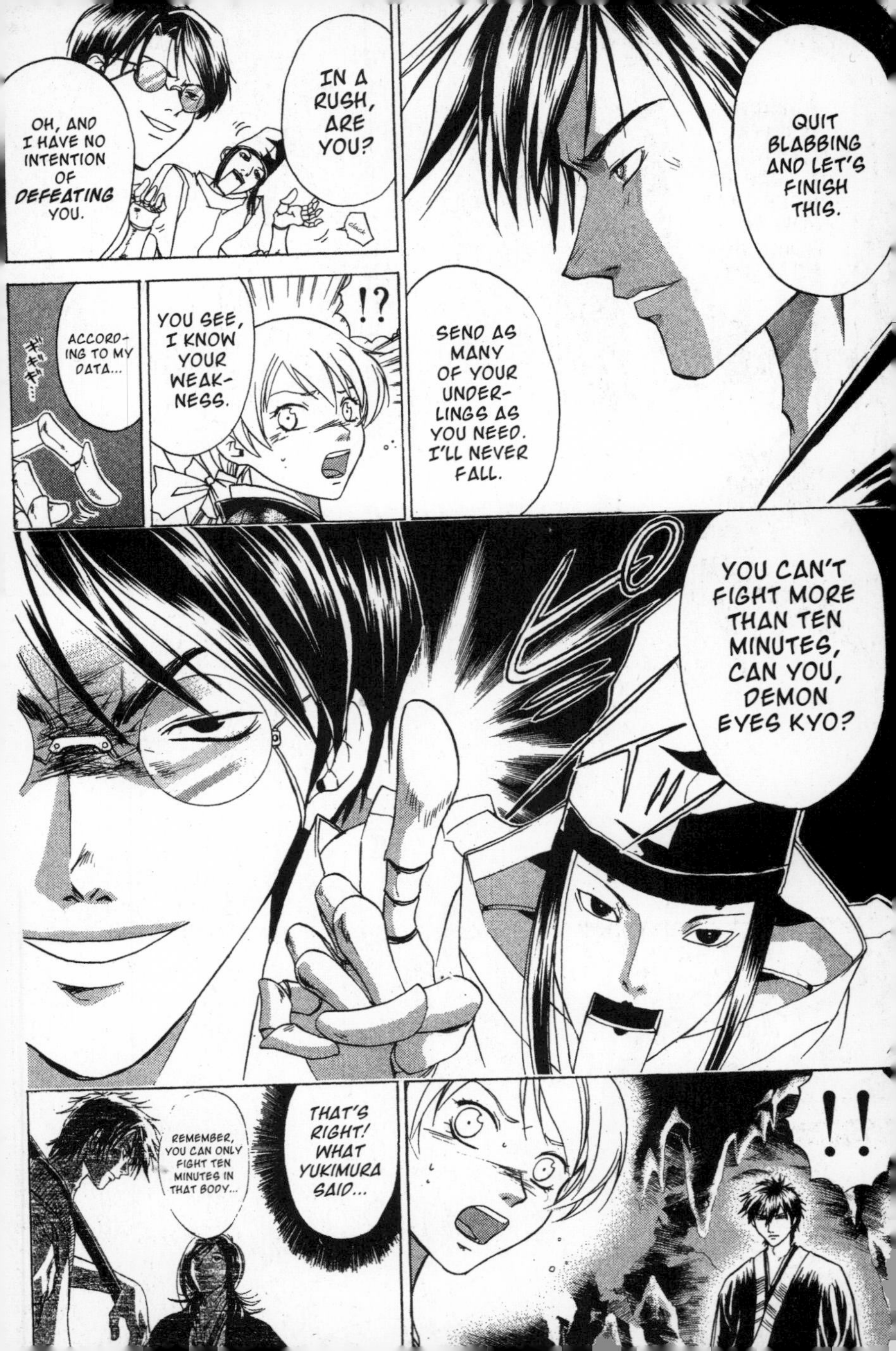
QUIT BLABBING AND LET'S FINISH THIS.
SEND AS MANY OF YOUR UNDER-LINGS AS YOU NEED. I'LL NEVER FALL.
IN A RUSH, ARE YOU?
OH, AND I HAVE NO INTENTION OF DEFEATING YOU.
clack
!?
YOU SEE, I KNOW YOUR WEAK-NESS.
ACCORD-ING TO MY DATA...
YOU CAN'T FIGHT MORE THAN TEN MINUTES, CAN YOU, DEMON EYES KYO?
!!
THAT'S RIGHT! WHAT YUKIMURA SAID...
REMEMBER, YOU CAN ONLY FIGHT TEN MINUTES IN THAT BODY...

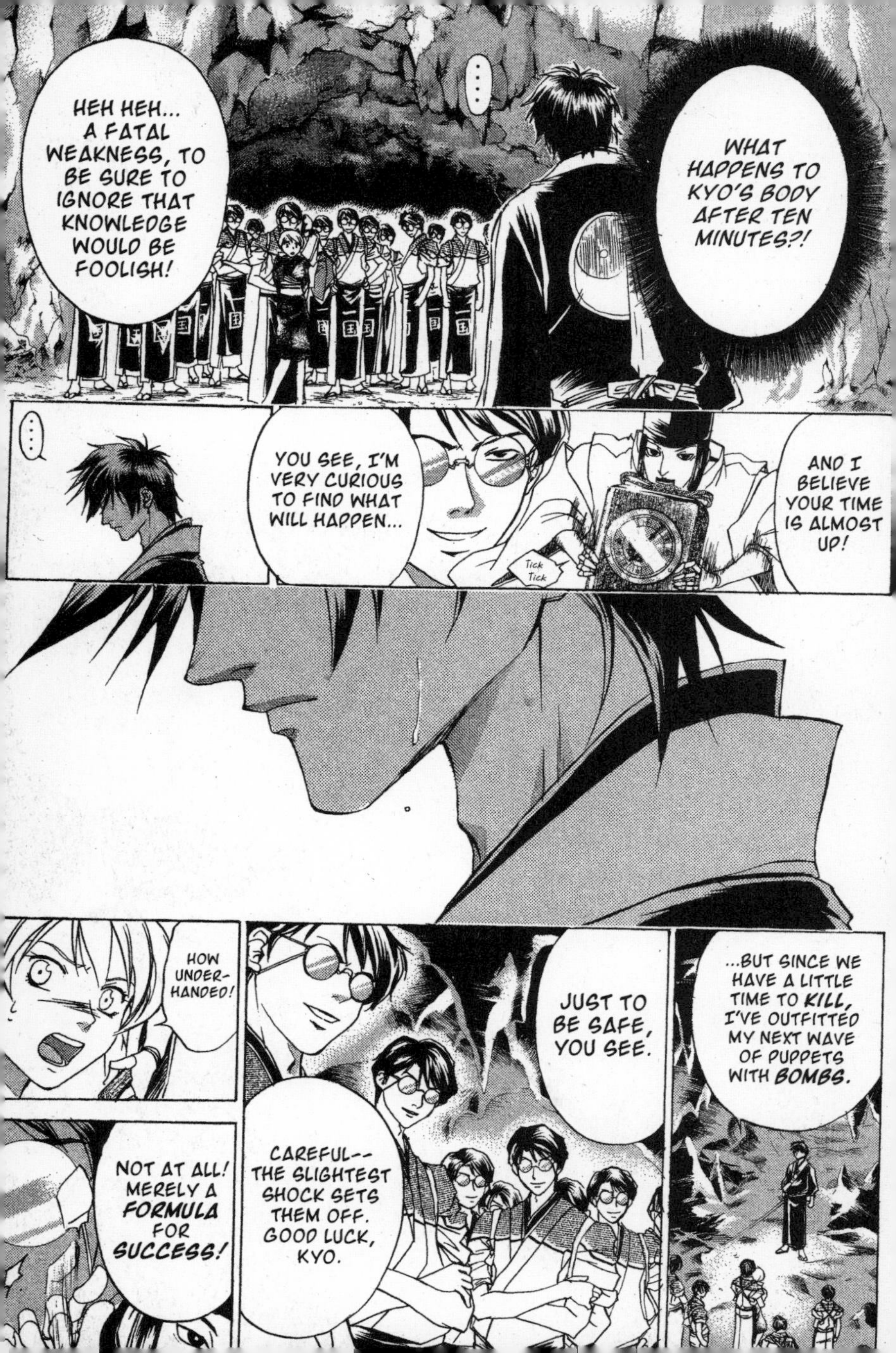
WHAT HAPPENS TO KYO'S BODY AFTER TEN MINUTES?!
...
HEH HEH... A FATAL WEAKNESS, TO BE SURE TO IGNORE THAT KNOWLEDGE WOULD BE FOOLISH!
AND I BELIEVE YOUR TIME IS ALMOST UP!
Tick Tick
YOU SEE, I'M VERY CURIOUS TO FIND WHAT WILL HAPPEN...
...
...BUT SINCE WE HAVE A LITTLE TIME TO KILL, I'VE OUTFITTED MY NEXT WAVE OF PUPPETS WITH BOMBS.
JUST TO BE SAFE, YOU SEE.
CAREFUL-- THE SLIGHTEST SHOCK SETS THEM OFF. GOOD LUCK, KYO.
HOW UNDER-HANDED!
NOT AT ALL! MERELY A FORMULA FOR SUCCESS!

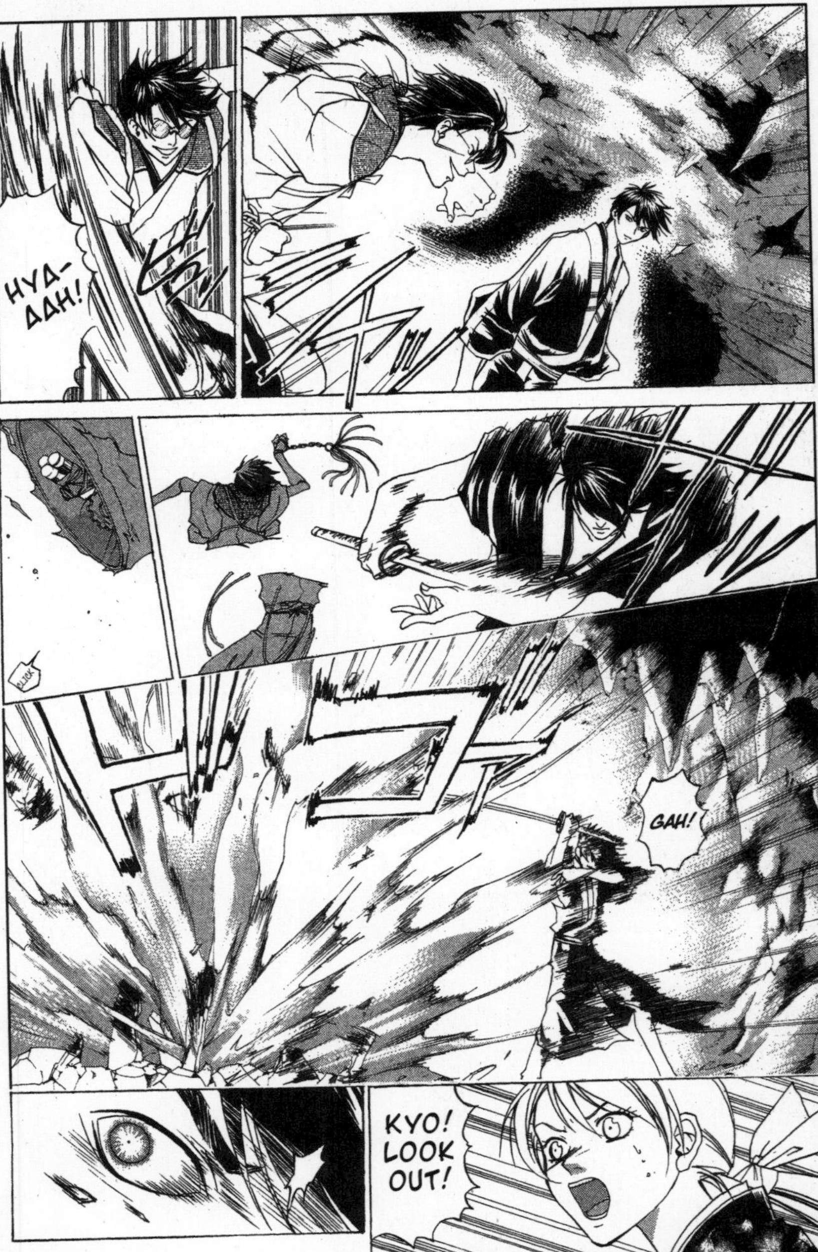
HYA-AAH!
CLICK
GAH!
KYO! LOOK OUT!

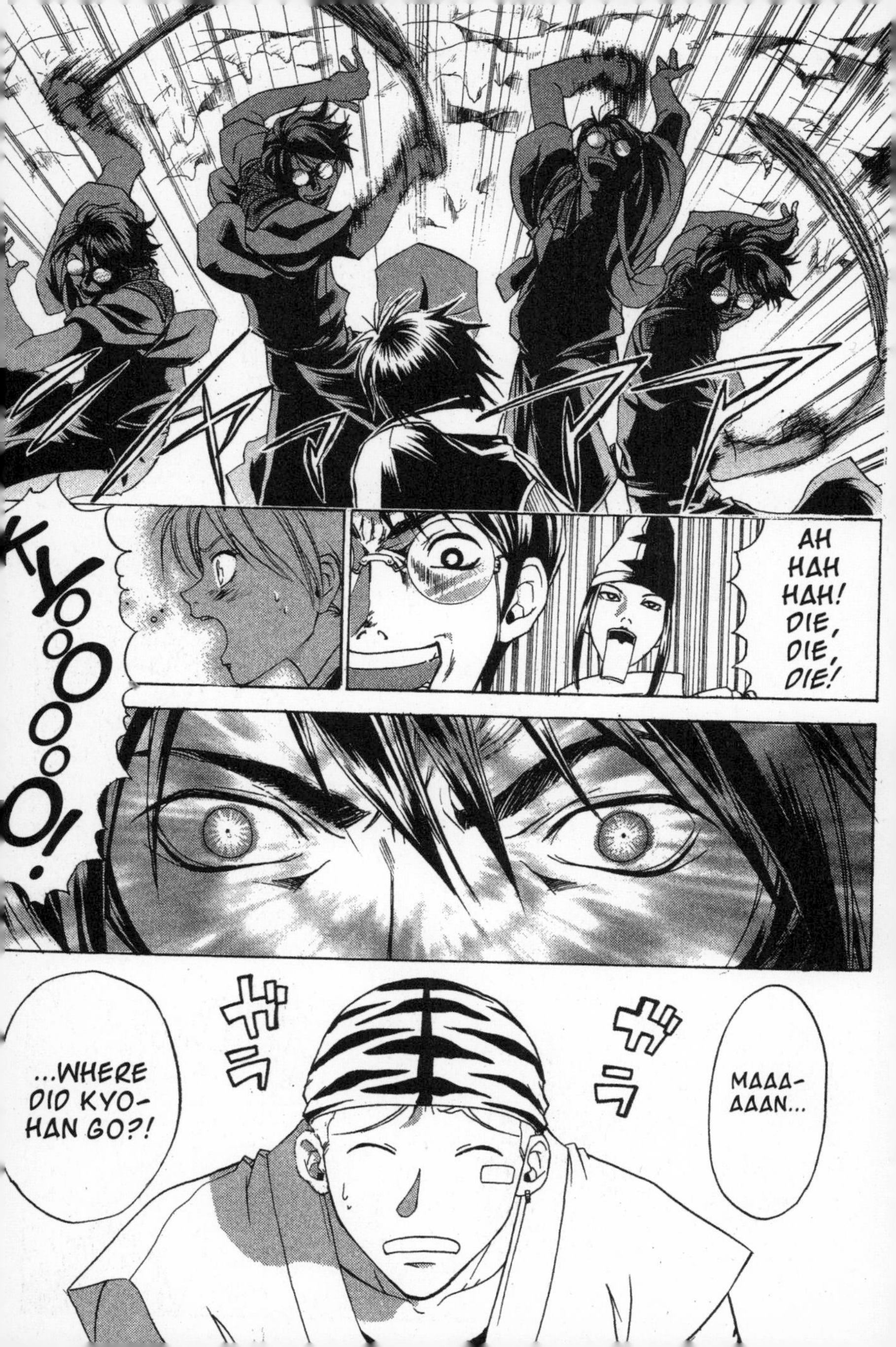
AH HAH HAH! DIE, DIE, DIE!
KYOOOOOO!
ガラ
MAAA-AAAN...
ガラ
...WHERE DID KYO-HAN GO?!

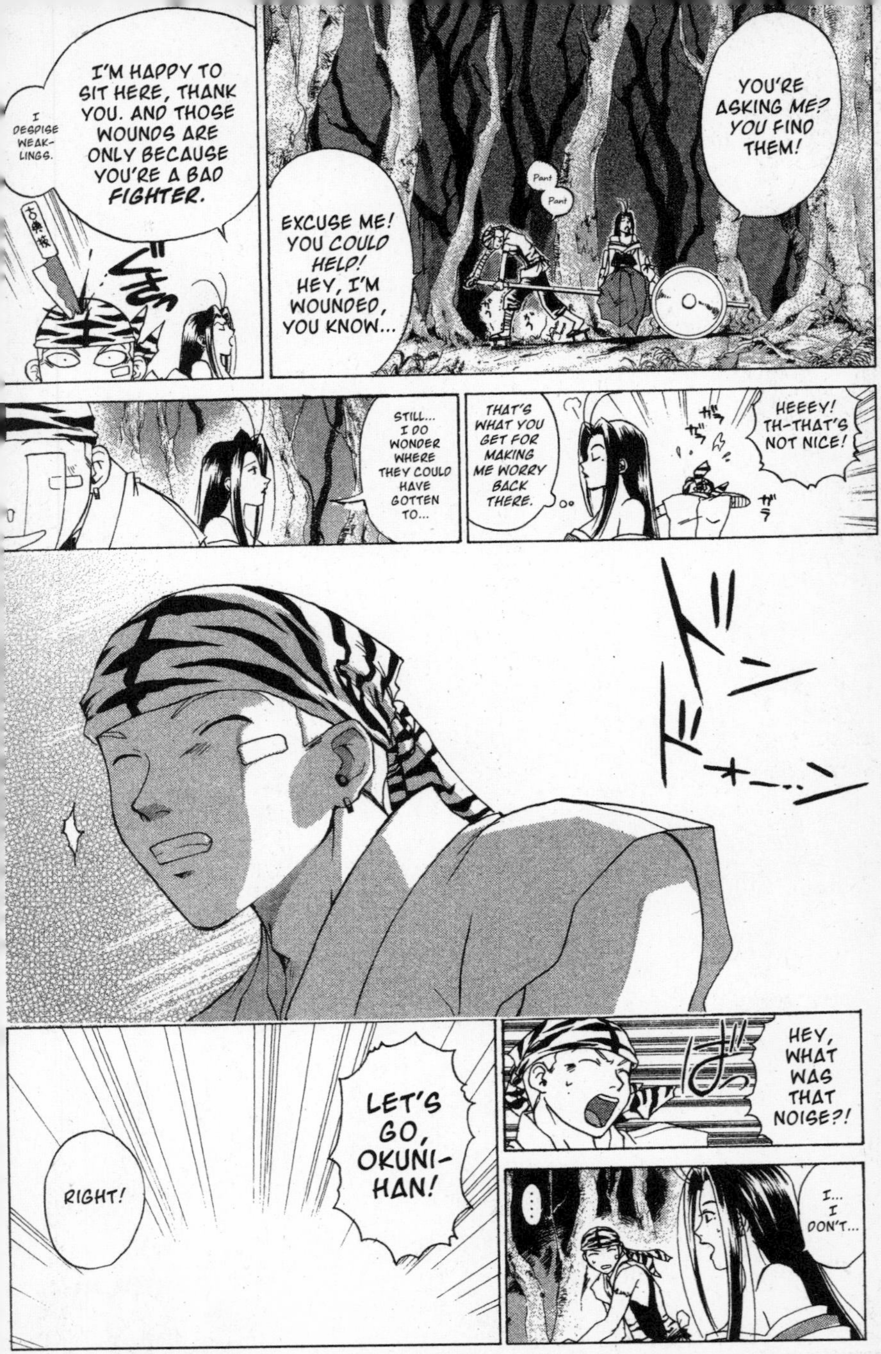
YOU'RE ASKING ME? YOU FIND THEM!
Pant
Pant
EXCUSE ME! YOU COULD HELP! HEY, I'M WOUNDED, YOU KNOW...
I'M HAPPY TO SIT HERE, THANK YOU. AND THOSE WOUNDS ARE ONLY BECAUSE YOU'RE A BAD FIGHTER.
I DESPISE WEAK-LINGS.
HEEEY! TH-THAT'S NOT NICE!
THAT'S WHAT YOU GET FOR MAKING ME WORRY BACK THERE.
STILL... I DO WONDER WHERE THEY COULD HAVE GOTTEN TO...
HEY, WHAT WAS THAT NOISE?!
I... I DON'T...
...
LET'S GO, OKUNI-HAN!
RIGHT!

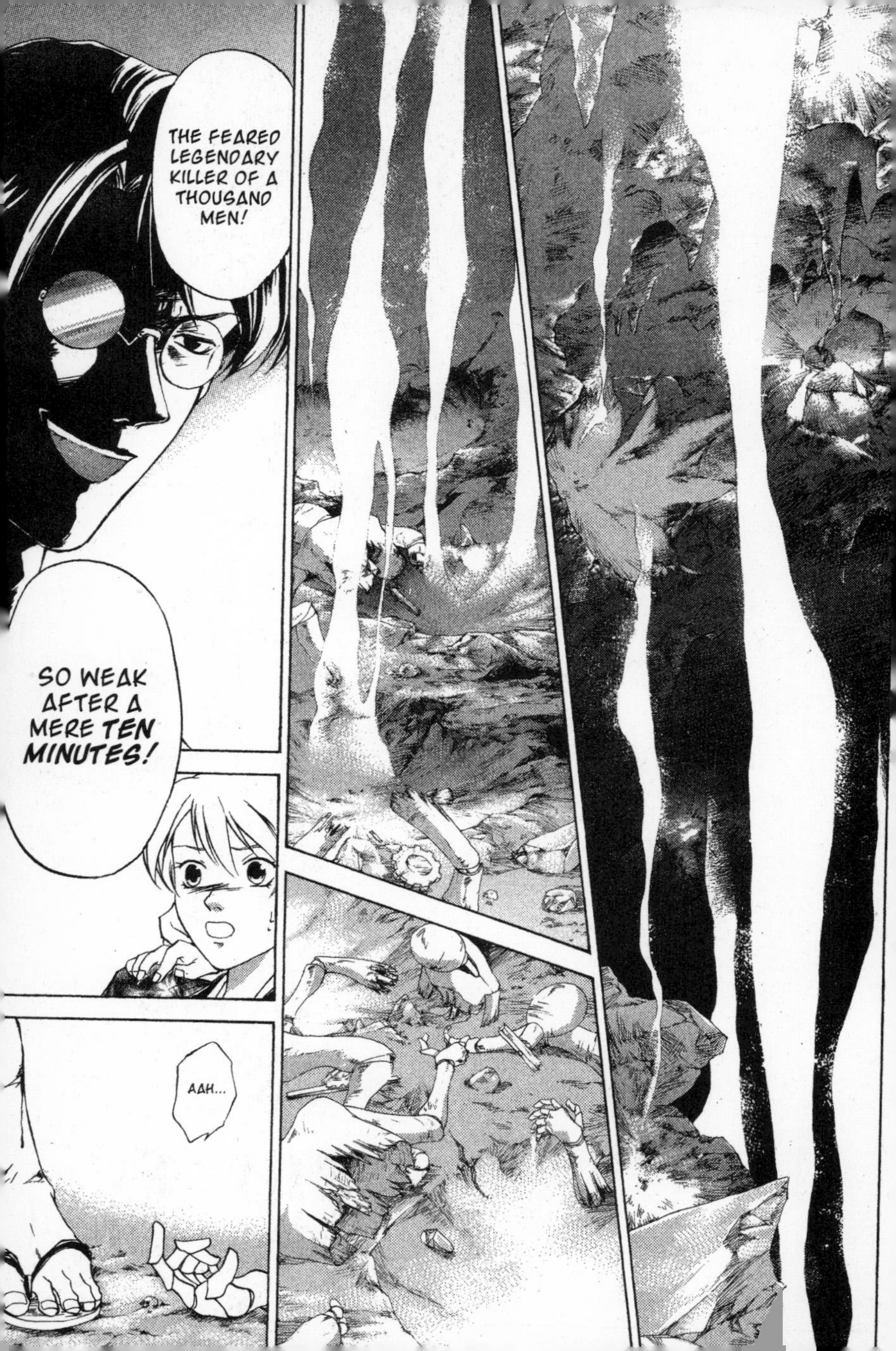
THE FEARED LEGENDARY KILLER OF A THOUSAND MEN!
SO WEAK AFTER A MERE TEN MINUTES!
AAH...

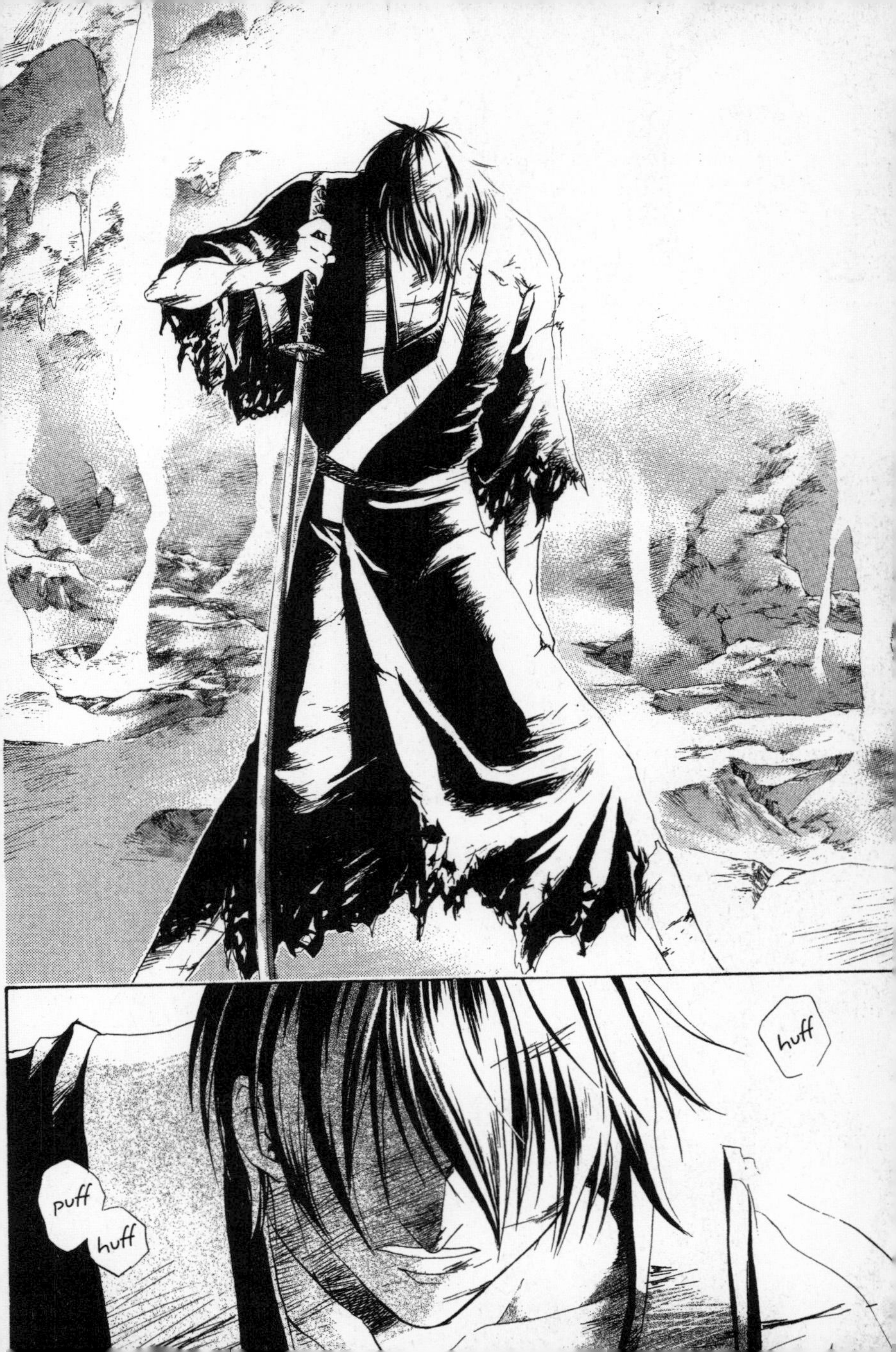
huff
puff
huff

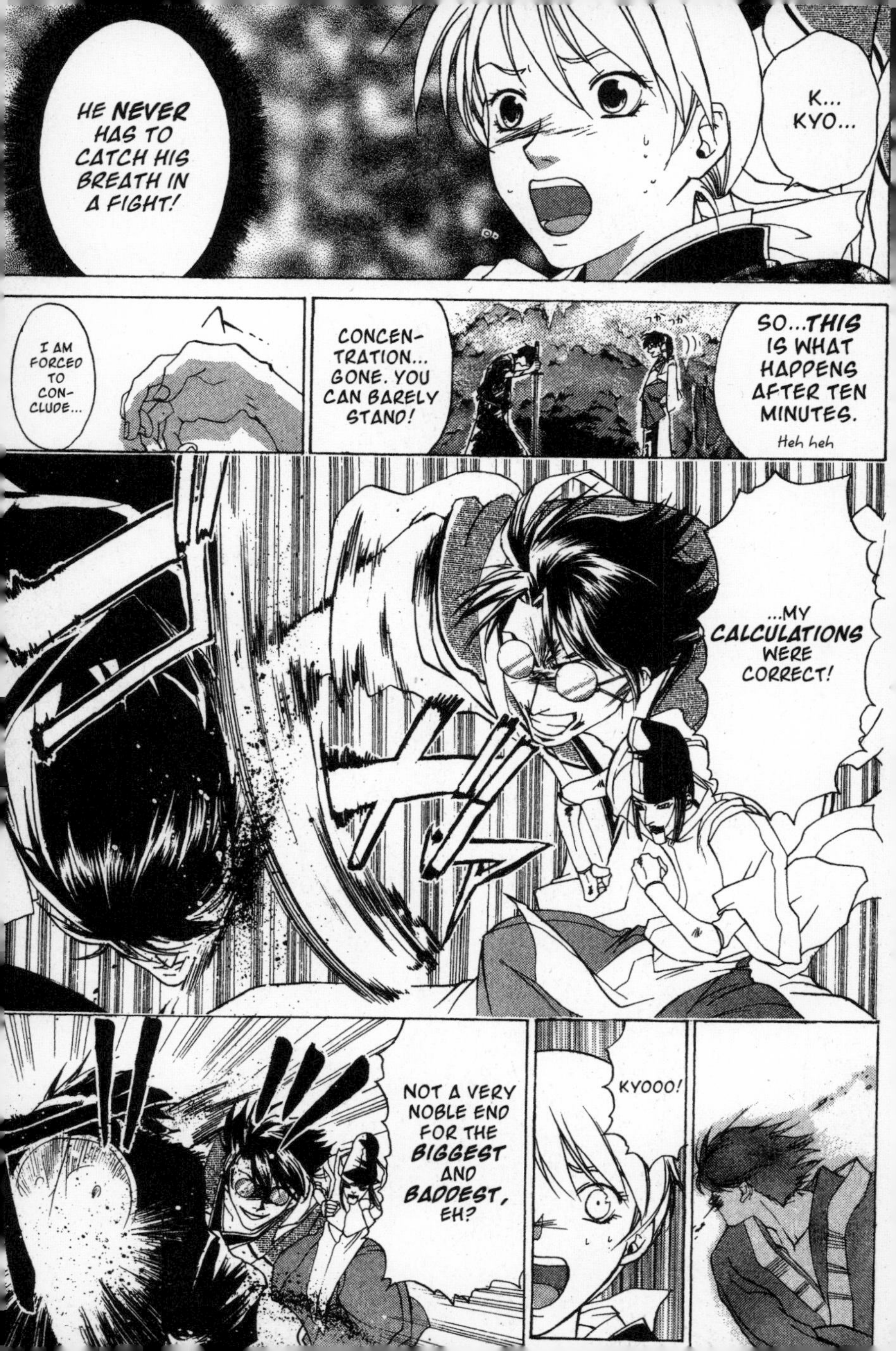
K... KYO...
HE NEVER HAS TO CATCH HIS BREATH IN A FIGHT!
SO...THIS IS WHAT HAPPENS AFTER TEN MINUTES.
Heh heh
CONCEN-TRATION... GONE. YOU CAN BARELY STAND!
I AM FORCED TO CON-CLUDE...
...MY CALCULATIONS WERE CORRECT!
KYOOO!
NOT A VERY NOBLE END FOR THE BIGGEST AND BADDEST, EH?

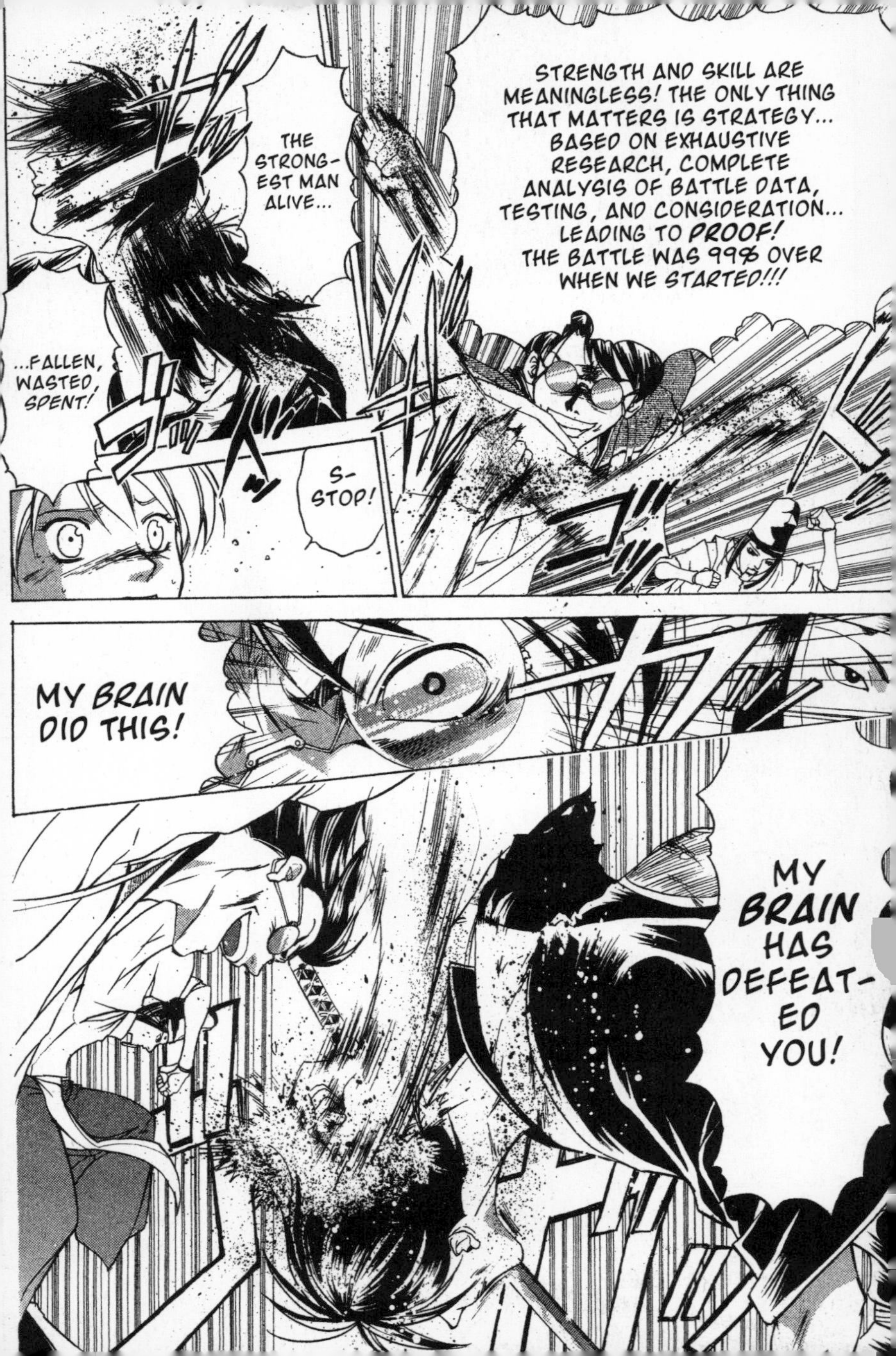
STRENGTH AND SKILL ARE MEANINGLESS! THE ONLY THING THAT MATTERS IS STRATEGY... BASED ON EXHAUSTIVE RESEARCH, COMPLETE ANALYSIS OF BATTLE DATA, TESTING, AND CONSIDERATION... LEADING TO PROOF! THE BATTLE WAS 99% OVER WHEN WE STARTED!!!
THE STRONG-EST MAN ALIVE...
...FALLEN, WASTED, SPENT!
S-STOP!
MY BRAIN DID THIS!
MY BRAIN HAS DEFEAT-ED YOU!

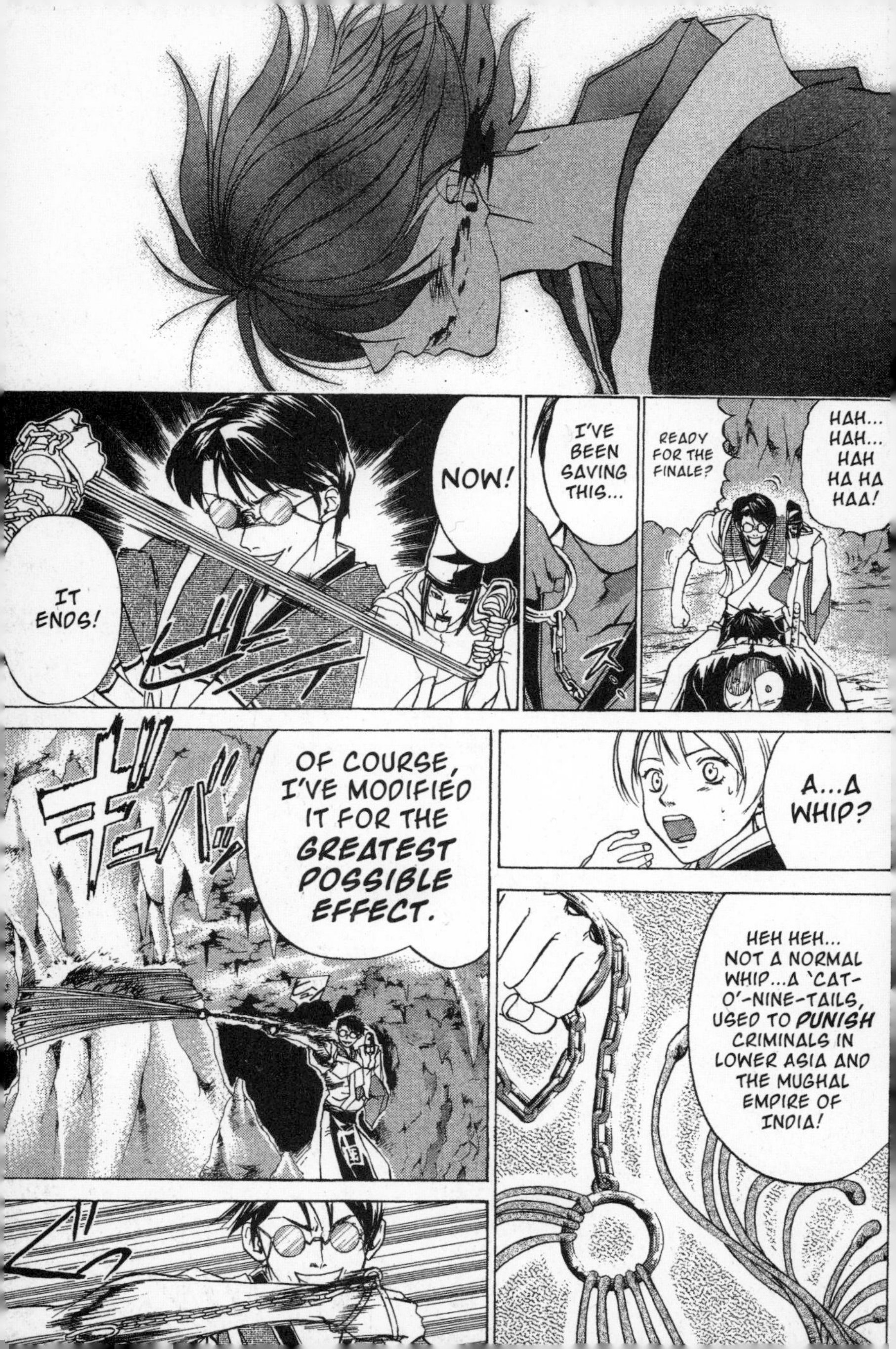

HAH... HAH... HAH HA HA HAA!
READY FOR THE FINALE?
I'VE BEEN SAVING THIS...
NOW!
IT ENDS!
A...A WHIP?
HEH HEH... NOT A NORMAL WHIP...A 'CAT-O'-NINE-TAILS, USED TO PUNISH CRIMINALS IN LOWER ASIA AND THE MUGHAL EMPIRE OF INDIA!
ギュバッ
OF COURSE, I'VE MODIFIED IT FOR THE GREATEST POSSIBLE EFFECT.

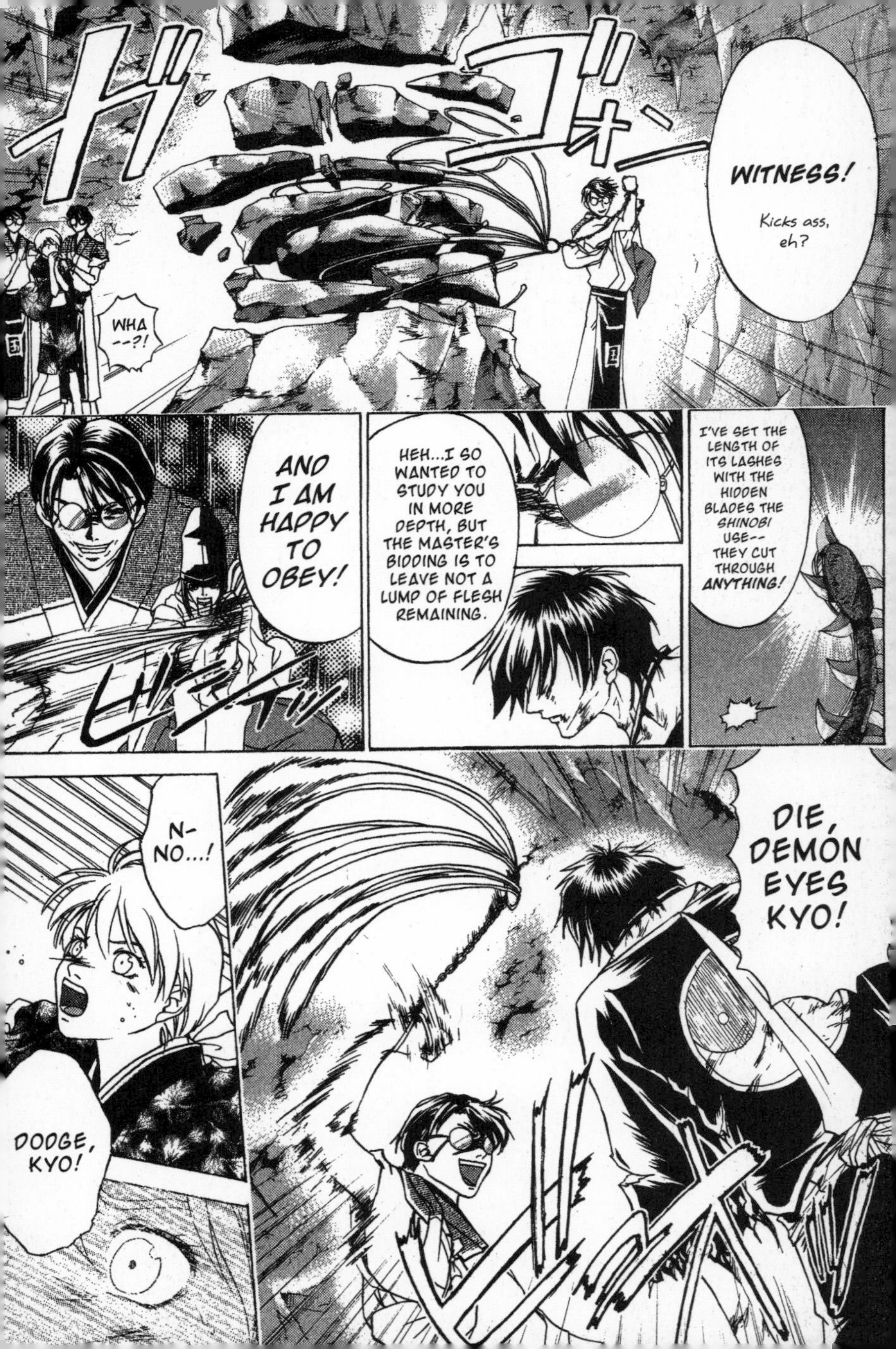
WITNESS!
Kicks ass, eh?
WHA --?!
I'VE SET THE LENGTH OF ITS LASHES WITH THE HIDDEN BLADES THE SHINOBI USE-- THEY CUT THROUGH ANYTHING!
HEH...I SO WANTED TO STUDY YOU IN MORE DEPTH, BUT THE MASTER'S BIDDING IS TO LEAVE NOT A LUMP OF FLESH REMAINING.
AND I AM HAPPY TO OBEY!
DIE, DEMON EYES KYO!
N-NO...!
DODGE, KYO!

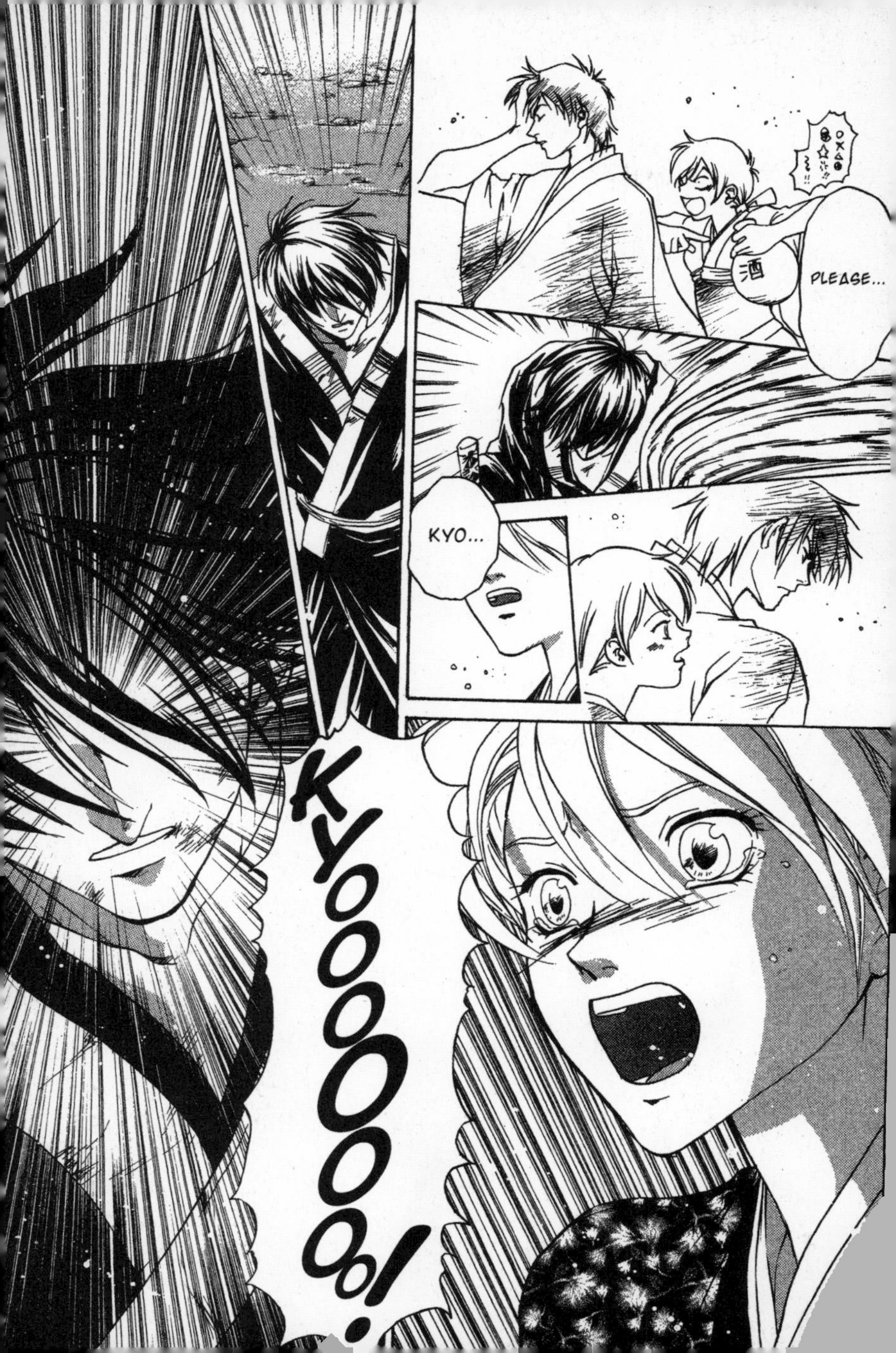
PLEASE...
KYO...
KYOOOOOoo!

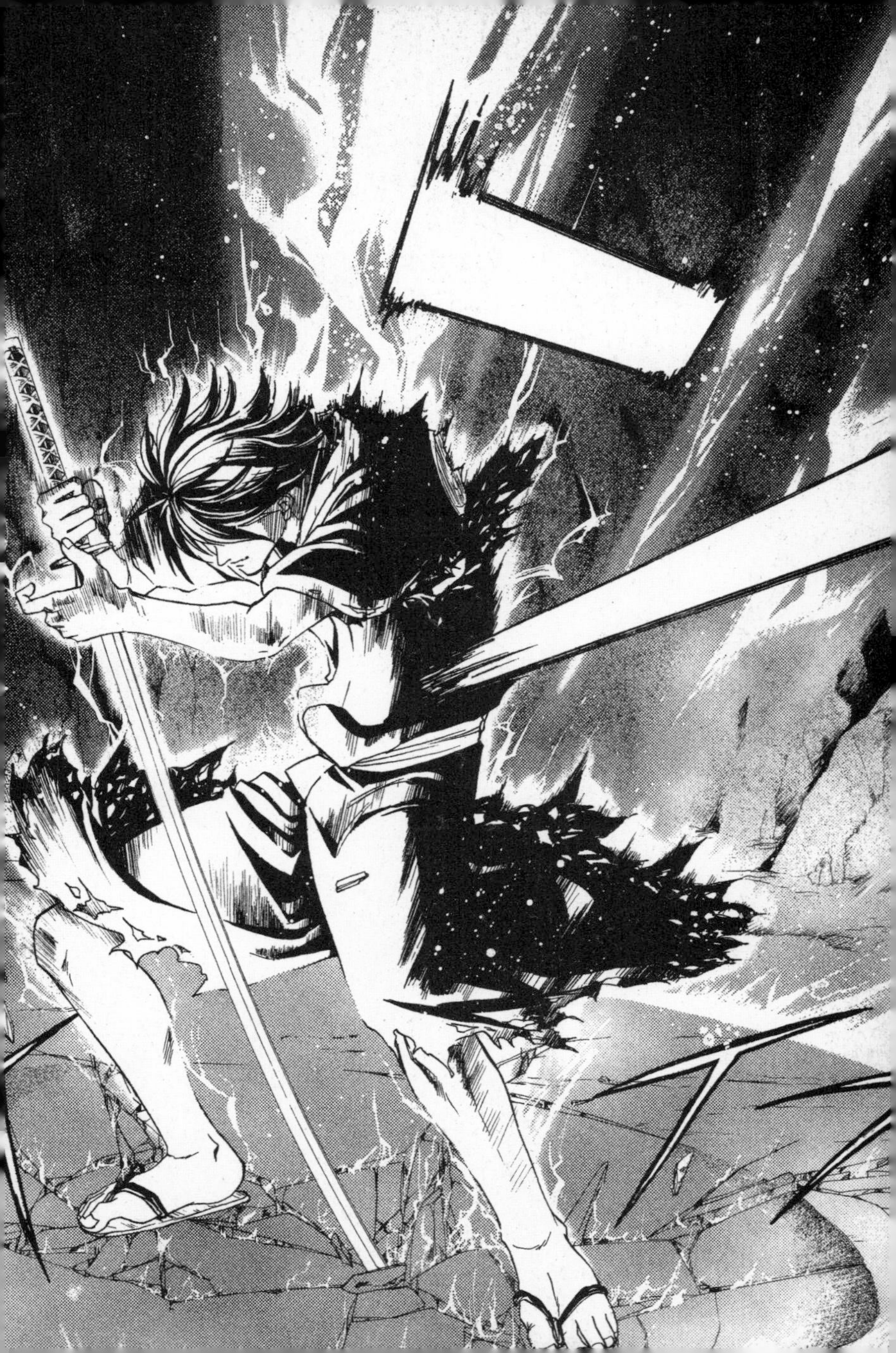

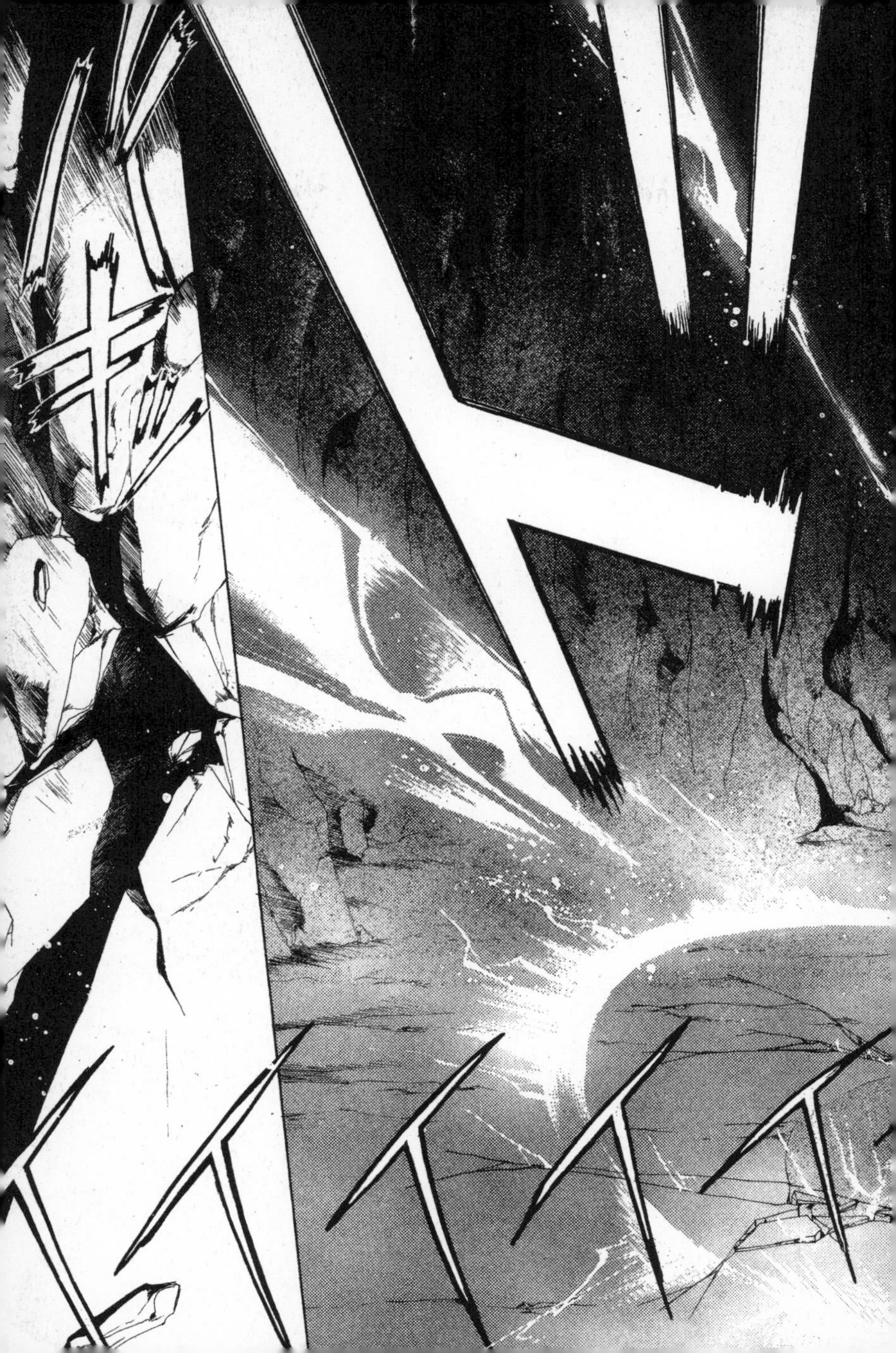

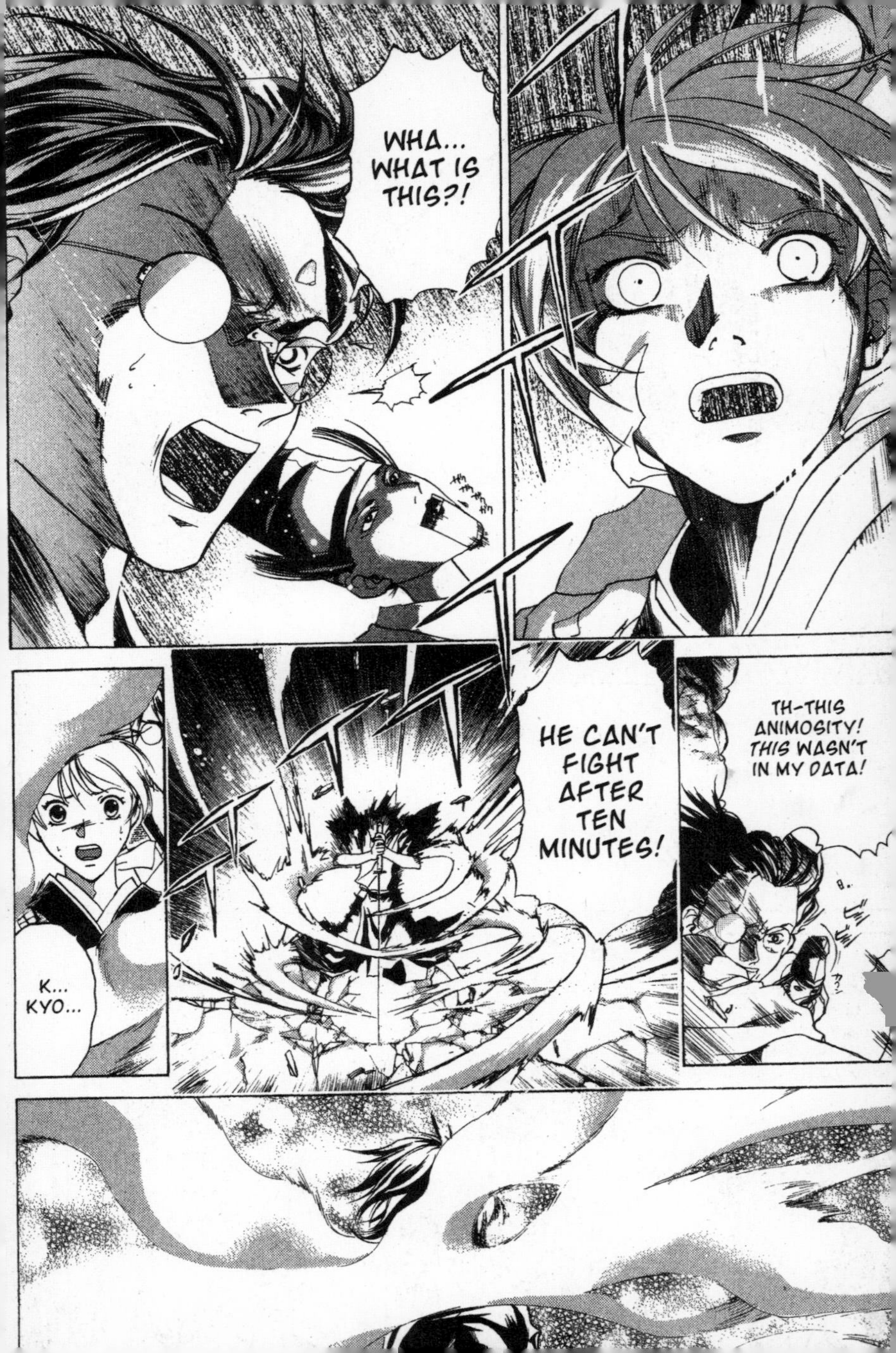
WHA... WHAT IS THIS?!
TH-THIS ANIMOSITY! THIS WASN'T IN MY DATA!
HE CAN'T FIGHT AFTER TEN MINUTES!
K... KYO...

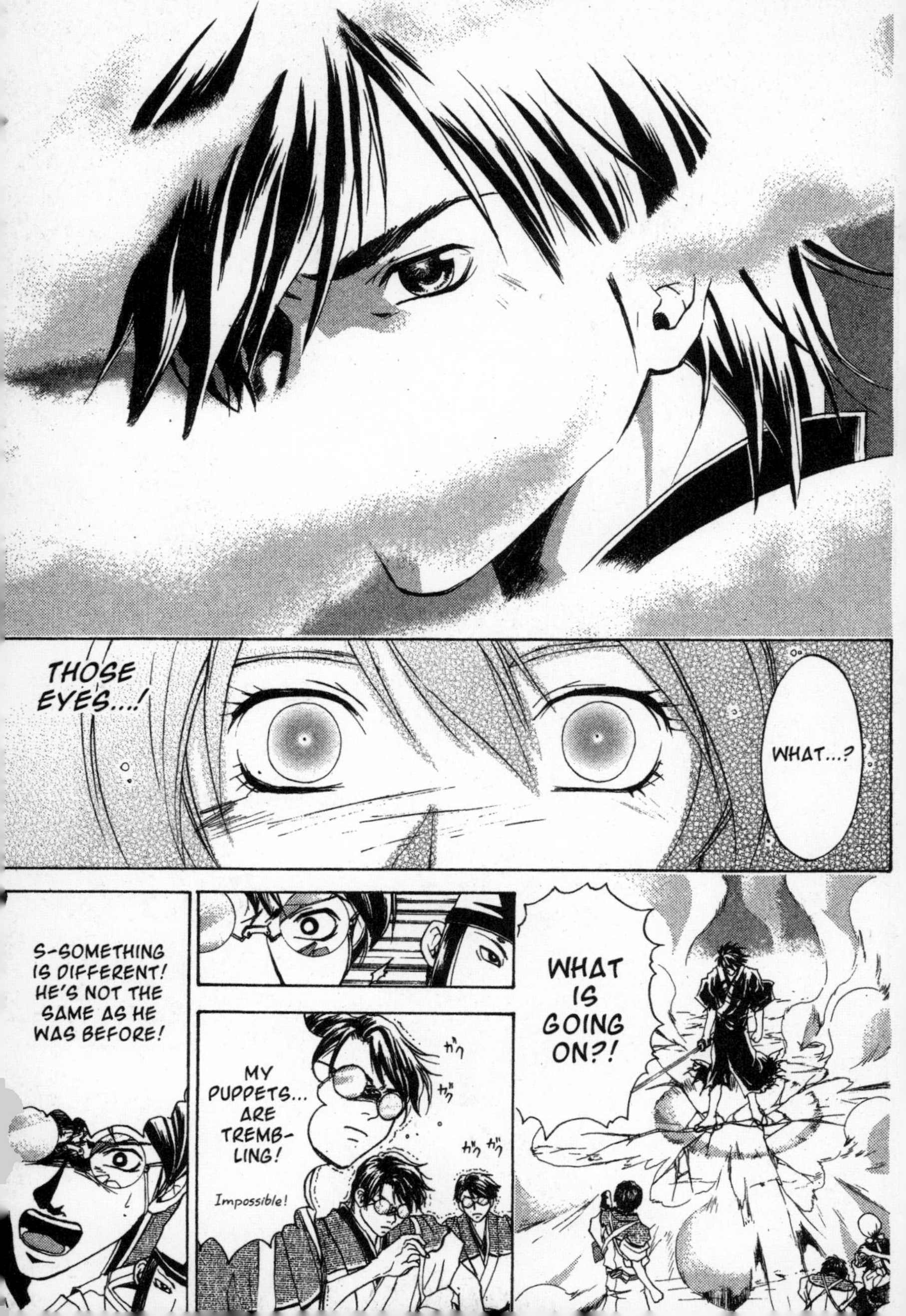
WHAT...?
THOSE EYES...!
WHAT IS GOING ON?!
MY PUPPETS... ARE TREMB-LING!
Impossible!
S-SOMETHING IS DIFFERENT! HE'S NOT THE SAME AS HE WAS BEFORE!

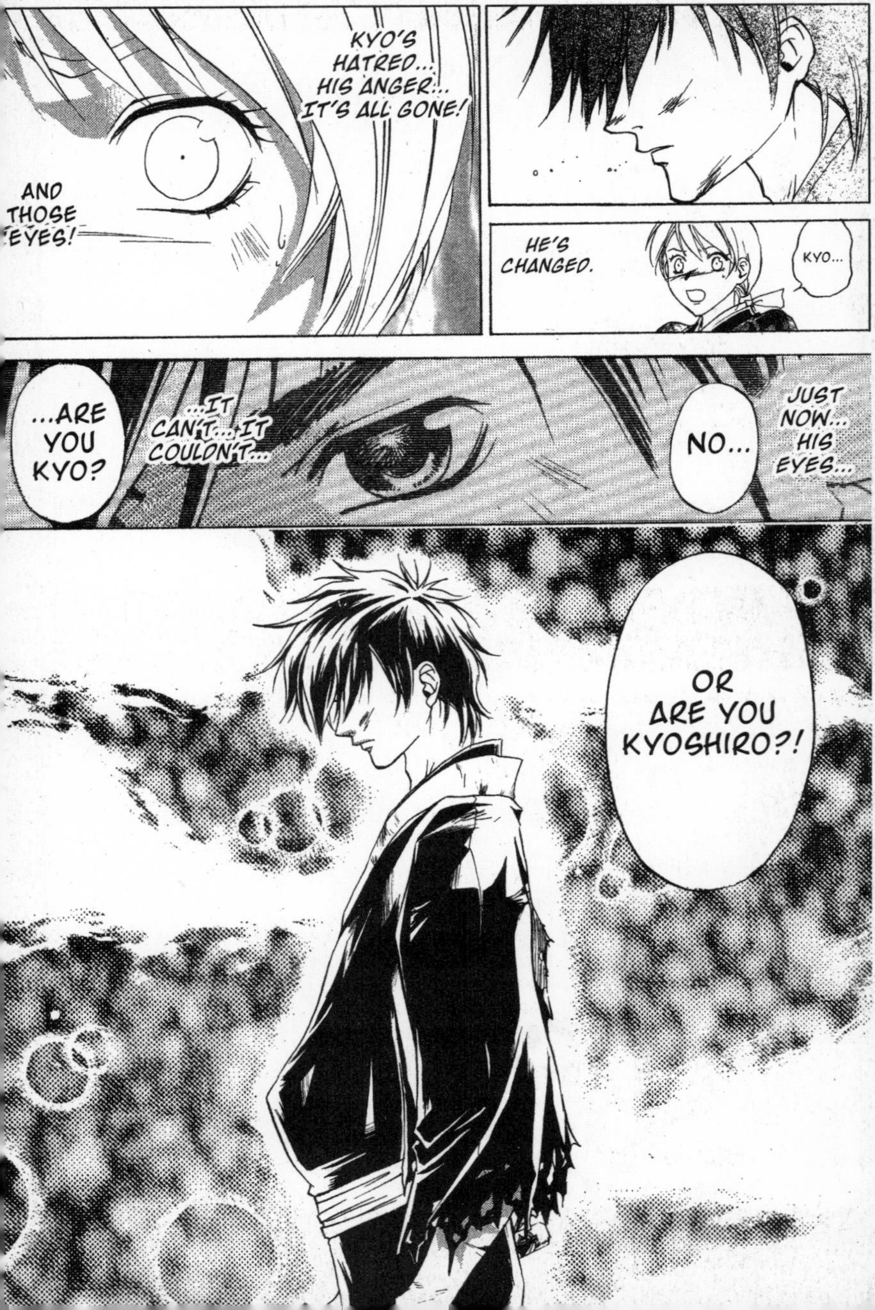
KYO...
HE'S CHANGED.
KYO'S HATRED... HIS ANGER... IT'S ALL GONE!
AND THOSE EYES!
JUST NOW... HIS EYES...
NO...
...IT CAN'T... IT COULDN'T...
...ARE YOU KYO?
OR ARE YOU KYOSHIRO?!

ABOUT **MTB**

(NOT THAT I GO TO THE MOUNTAINS...)

MTBS (MOUNTAIN BIKES) ARE GREAT! I WENT TO THE CYCLE SHOP TO GET A BICYCLE FOR SHOPPING AND SUCH, BUT WHEN I SAW THE MTBS I FELL IN LOVE. THEY'RE GREAT, EVEN IN THE CITY. HILLS ARE NO PROBLEM, AND THE SPEED! MY HIGH REGARD FOR THE BICYCLE HAS BEEN REAFFIRMED. SO, EVERYONE, GET OUT THERE! FUNNY THING THE OTHER DAY--I WAS OUT RIDING AND TWO KIDS ON A SCOOTER SHOUTED OUT "MESSENGER!" GUESS THEY THOUGHT I WAS A BIKE MESSENGER...?

The writer cannot actually perform this trick as shown.
WHOOPIE!
twinkle
Whooo!

(daydreaming)
MESSENGER!

Kamijo-sensei, sorry for always drawing such totally unrelated things. No, I'm really not sorry! heh... <kamijo: you aren't sorry are you! hey!>

↑ ***Ken'ichi Suetake***

↓ ***Hazuki Asami***

■ LOTS OF CATS. LATELY, WHEN I GO HOME, THERE'S STRAY CATS COMING AND GOING, AND WHEN I GO TO MY PARENTS', I PLAY WITH THEIR CAT. YASHIOKA-SAN! KAMIJO-SENSEI! DOGS ARE FINE, BUT I RECOMMEND...CATS! ♡

■ NOT ONLY ARE THERE LETTERS FOR KAMIJYO-SENSEI, THERE'S LETTERS FOR US ASSISTANTS, TOO! THANK YOU! (SOB)

I think Yukimura'd go well with a cat. (I can dream, can't I?)

An Average Day At Work 2

My first day drawing Benitora's bandanna pattern.
Tiger.
DON'T FORGET: TORA = TIGER! ♡
IT'S TOUGHER THAN IT LOOKS...
Master Copy
Our Sensei!
MAYBE... TRY FLICKING YOUR BRUSH A BIT MORE?
AAAH! I'M SORRY! SORRY! I DON'T KNOW HOW!
Whoops.
Utter failure. Of course. ♡
SOME-THING'S VERY WRONG!
...BIG BLAST...
smooth
Hey hey hey!
That's too much flicking!
Dummy!
EH HEH HEH...

<Kamijyo: normally, I draw Tora's bandanna, but that day, I just didn't have time... Asami's bandanna was so wacky, it really brightened my day. Thank

I'm into long baths, self-healing, acupressure, and stretching lately.

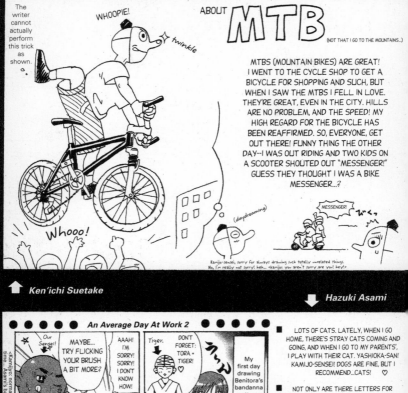

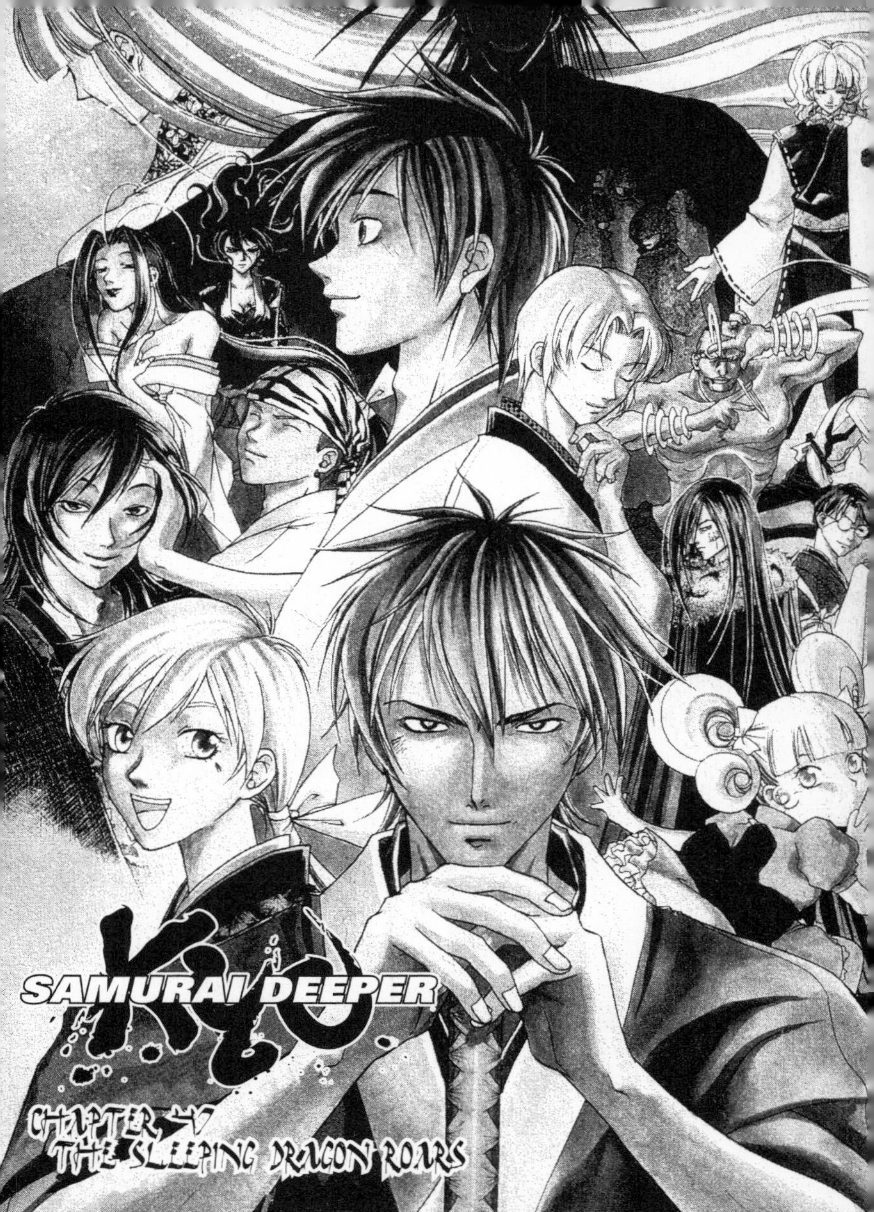
SAMURAI DEEPER KYO
CHAPTER 50
THE SLEEPING DRAGON ROARS

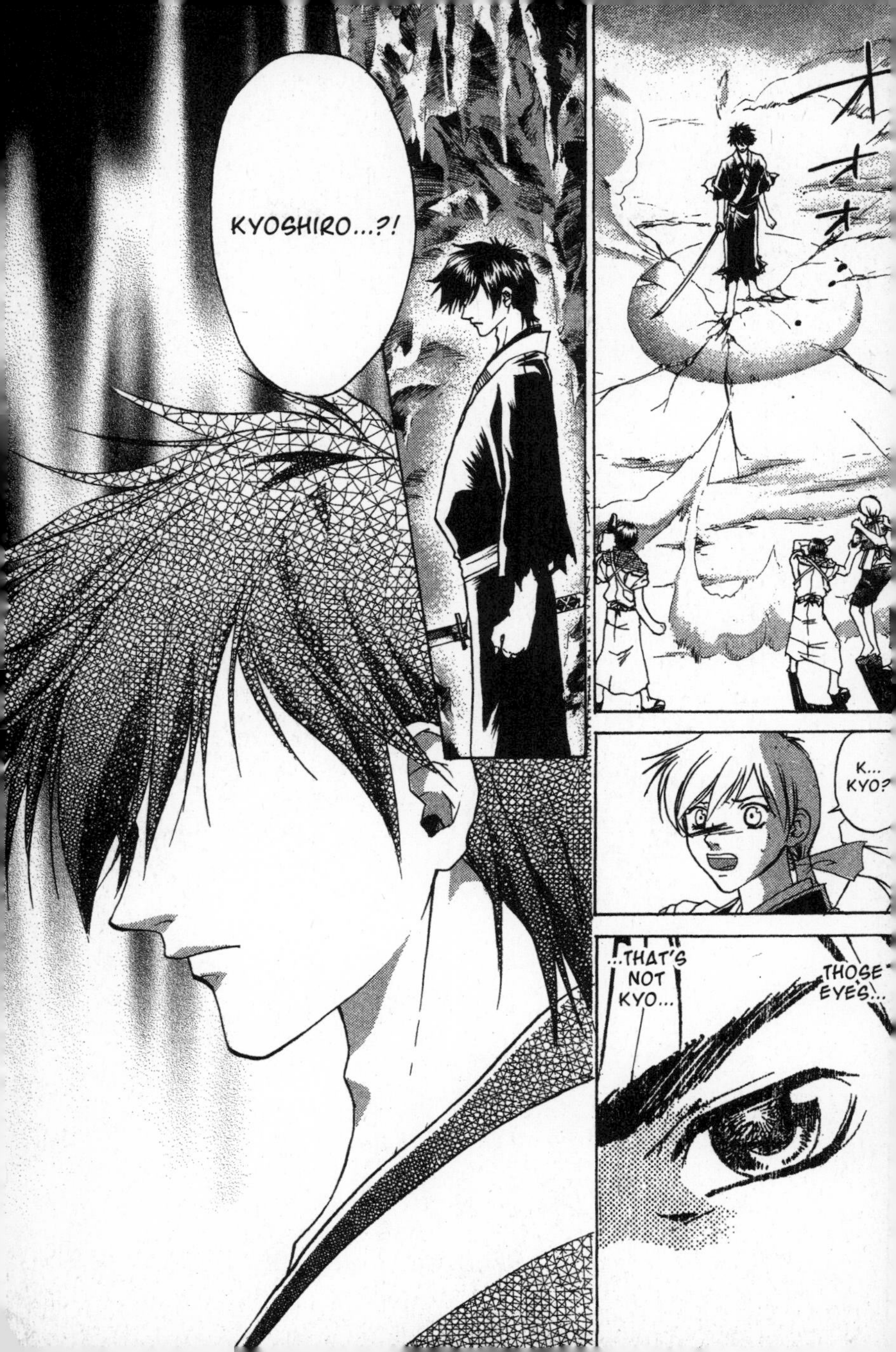
K... KYO?
THOSE EYES...
...THAT'S NOT KYO...
KYOSHIRO...?!

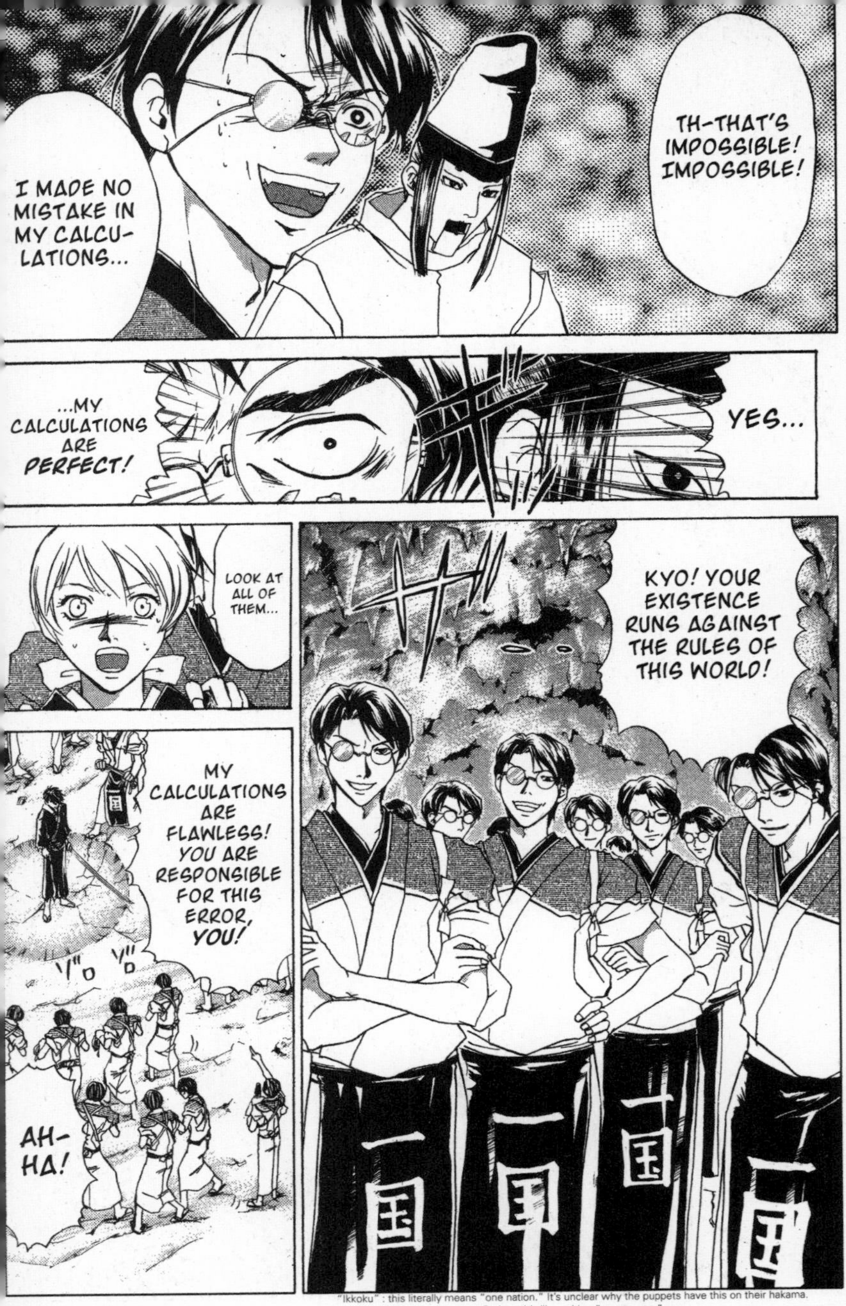
TH-THAT'S IMPOSSIBLE! IMPOSSIBLE!
I MADE NO MISTAKE IN MY CALCULATIONS...
YES...
...MY CALCULATIONS ARE PERFECT!
KYO! YOUR EXISTENCE RUNS AGAINST THE RULES OF THIS WORLD!
LOOK AT ALL OF THEM...
MY CALCULATIONS ARE FLAWLESS! YOU ARE RESPONSIBLE FOR THIS ERROR, YOU!
AH-HA!

"Ikkoku" : this literally means "one nation." It's unclear why the puppets have this on their hakama. Perhaps it's like writing "we are one."

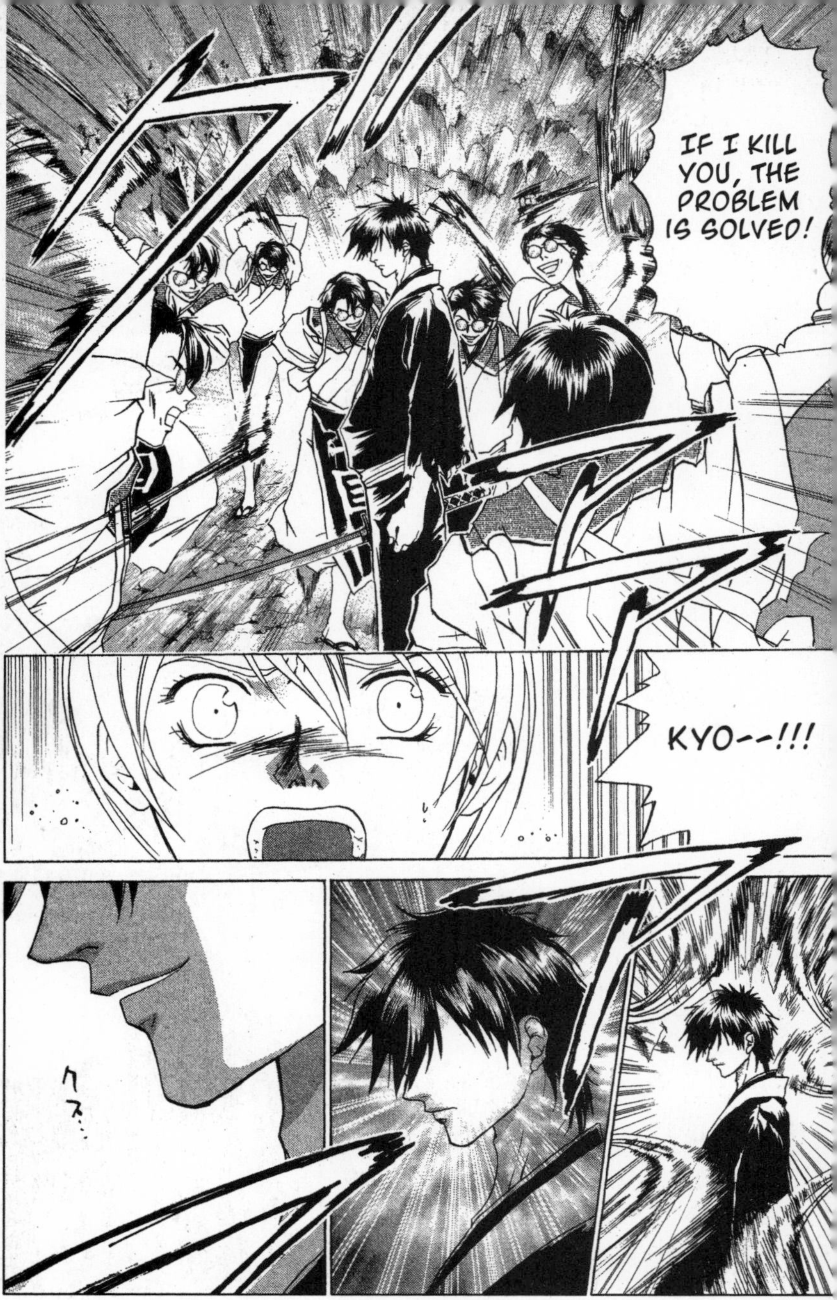
IF I KILL YOU, THE PROBLEM IS SOLVED!
KYO--!!!
クス…

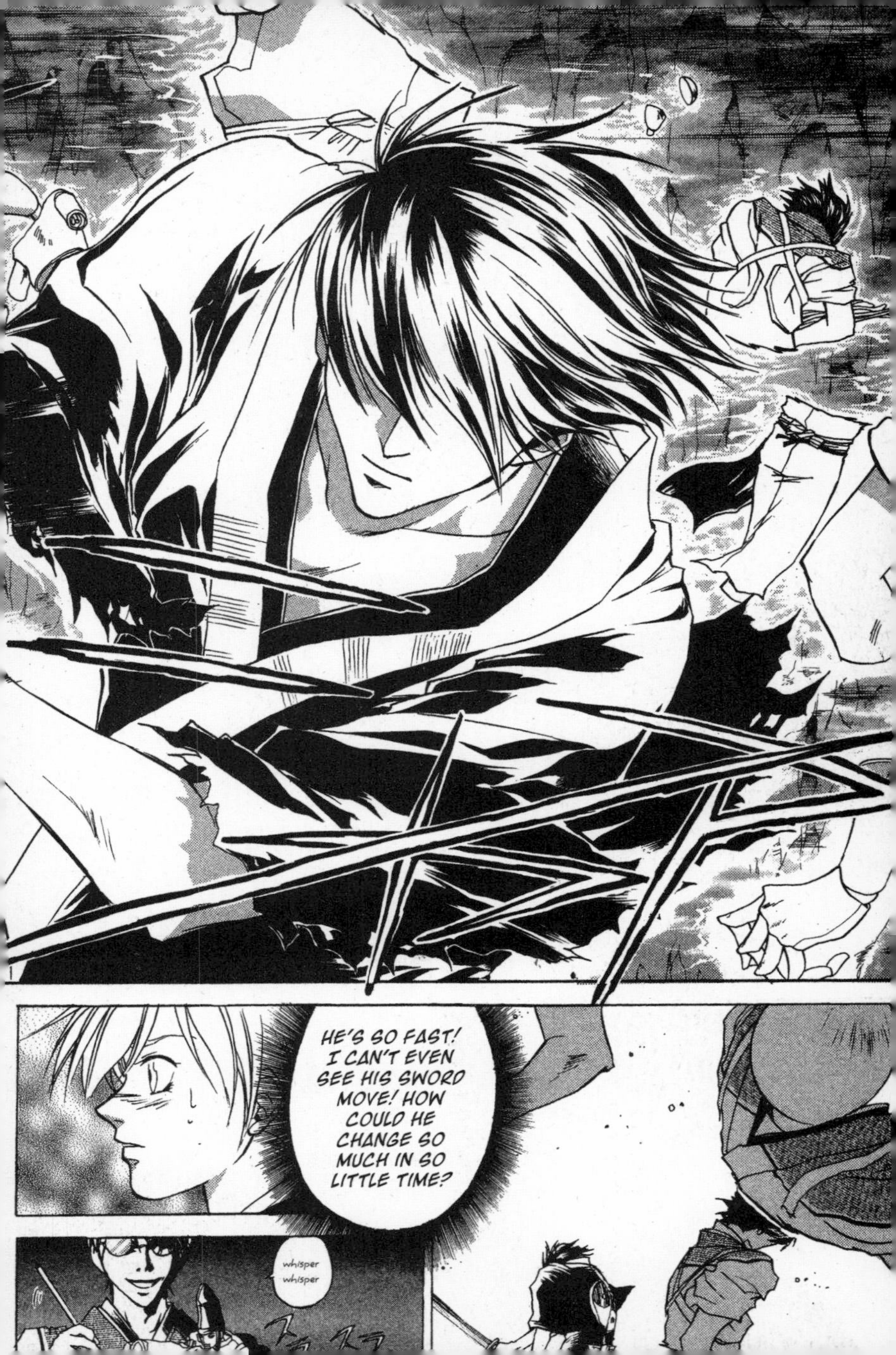
HE'S SO FAST! I CAN'T EVEN SEE HIS SWORD MOVE! HOW COULD HE CHANGE SO MUCH IN SO LITTLE TIME?
whisper
whisper

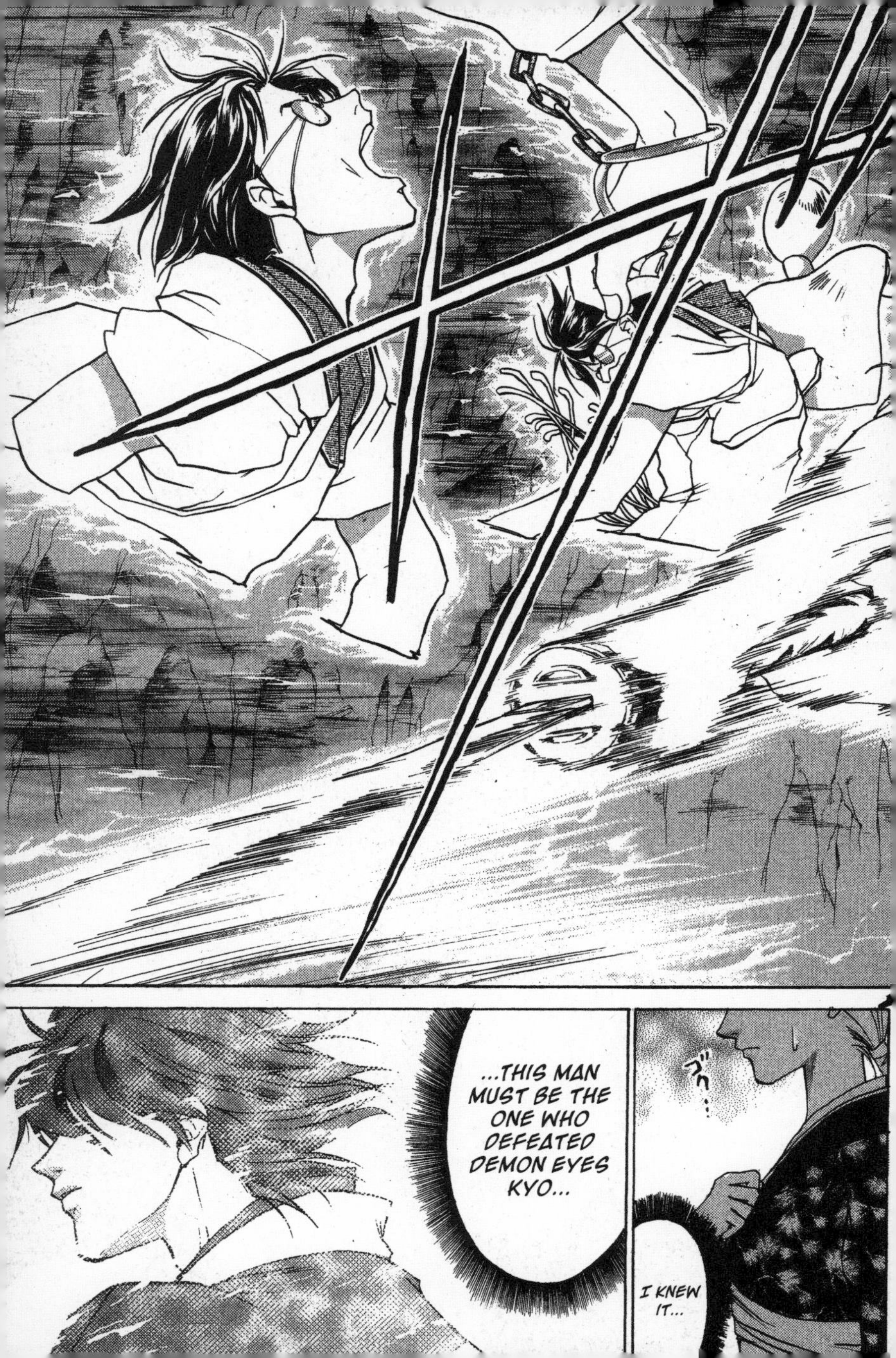
ゴク…
I KNEW IT...
...THIS MAN MUST BE THE ONE WHO DEFEATED DEMON EYES KYO...

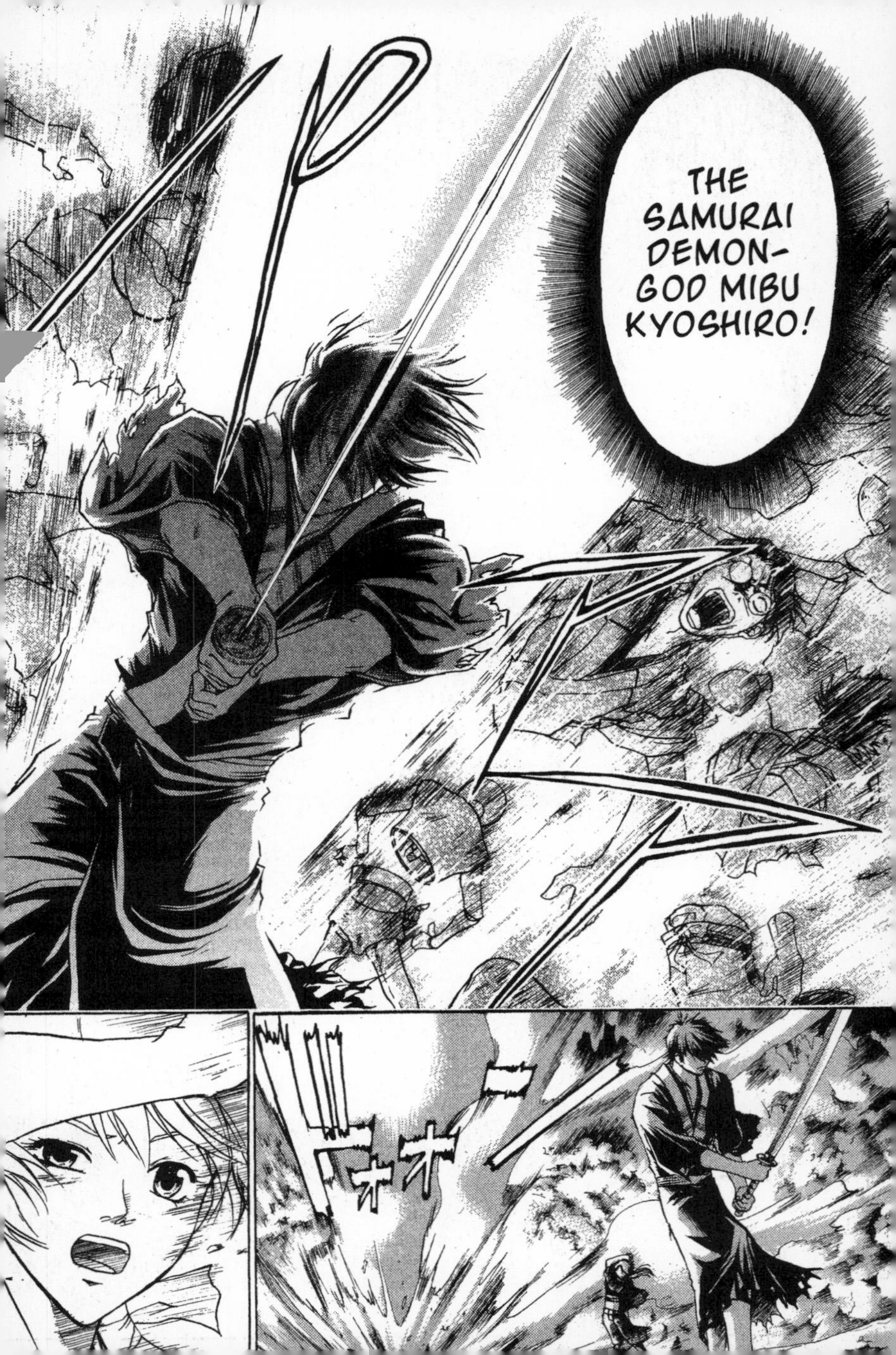
THE SAMURAI DEMON-GOD MIBU KYOSHIRO!

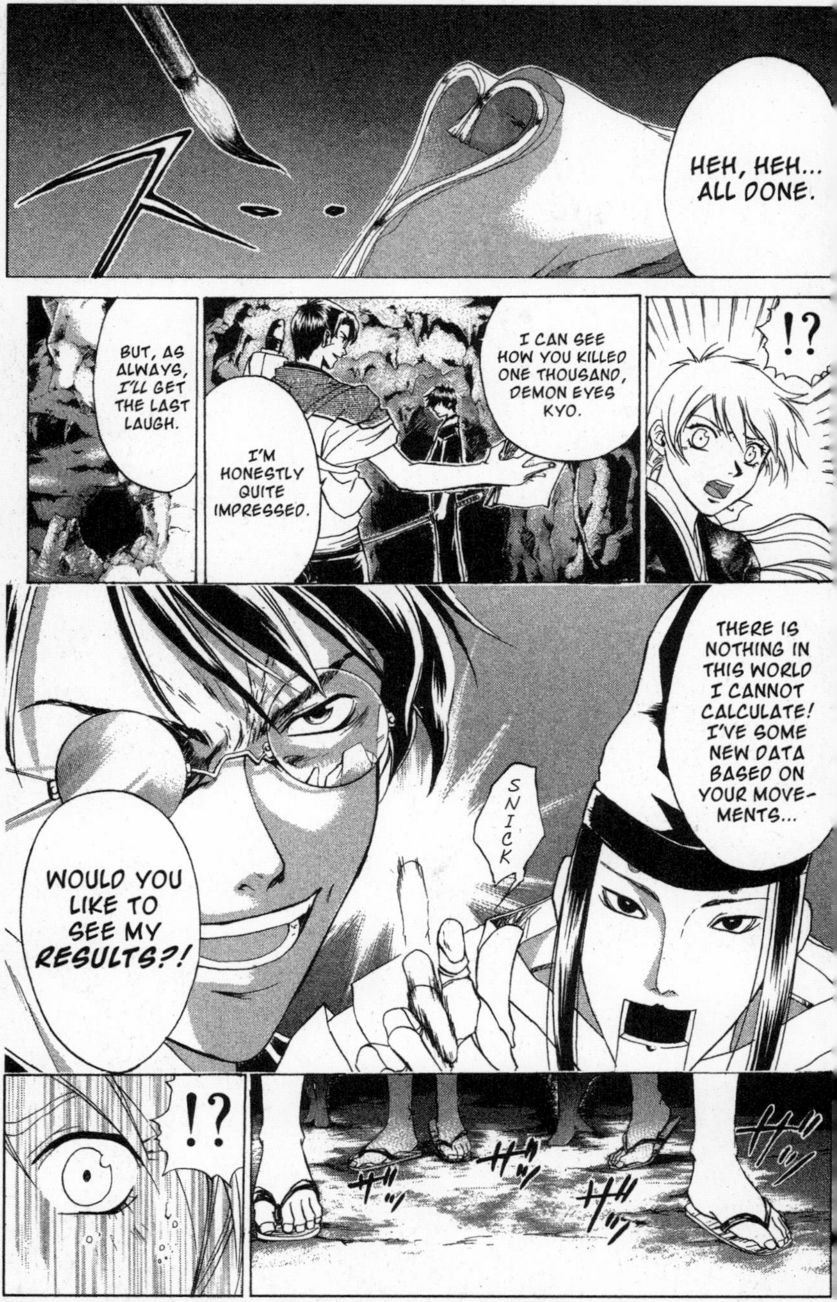

HEH, HEH... ALL DONE.
!?
I CAN SEE HOW YOU KILLED ONE THOUSAND, DEMON EYES KYO.
I'M HONESTLY QUITE IMPRESSED.
BUT, AS ALWAYS, I'LL GET THE LAST LAUGH.
THERE IS NOTHING IN THIS WORLD I CANNOT CALCULATE! I'VE SOME NEW DATA BASED ON YOUR MOVEMENTS...
SNICK
WOULD YOU LIKE TO SEE MY *RESULTS?!*
!?

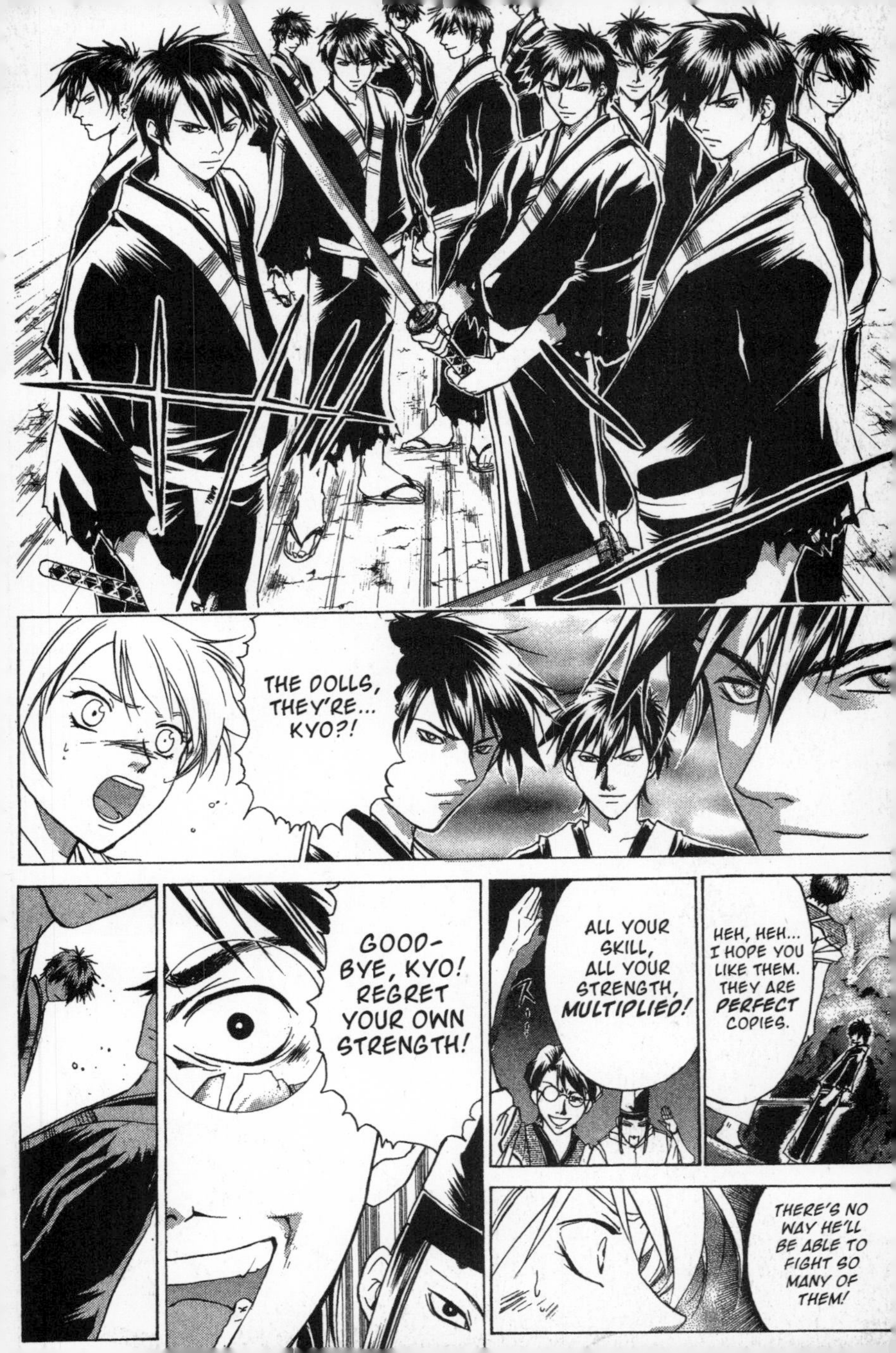

THE DOLLS, THEY'RE... KYO?!
HEH, HEH... I HOPE YOU LIKE THEM. THEY ARE PERFECT COPIES.
ALL YOUR SKILL, ALL YOUR STRENGTH, MULTIPLIED!
THERE'S NO WAY HE'LL BE ABLE TO FIGHT SO MANY OF THEM!
GOOD-BYE, KYO! REGRET YOUR OWN STRENGTH!

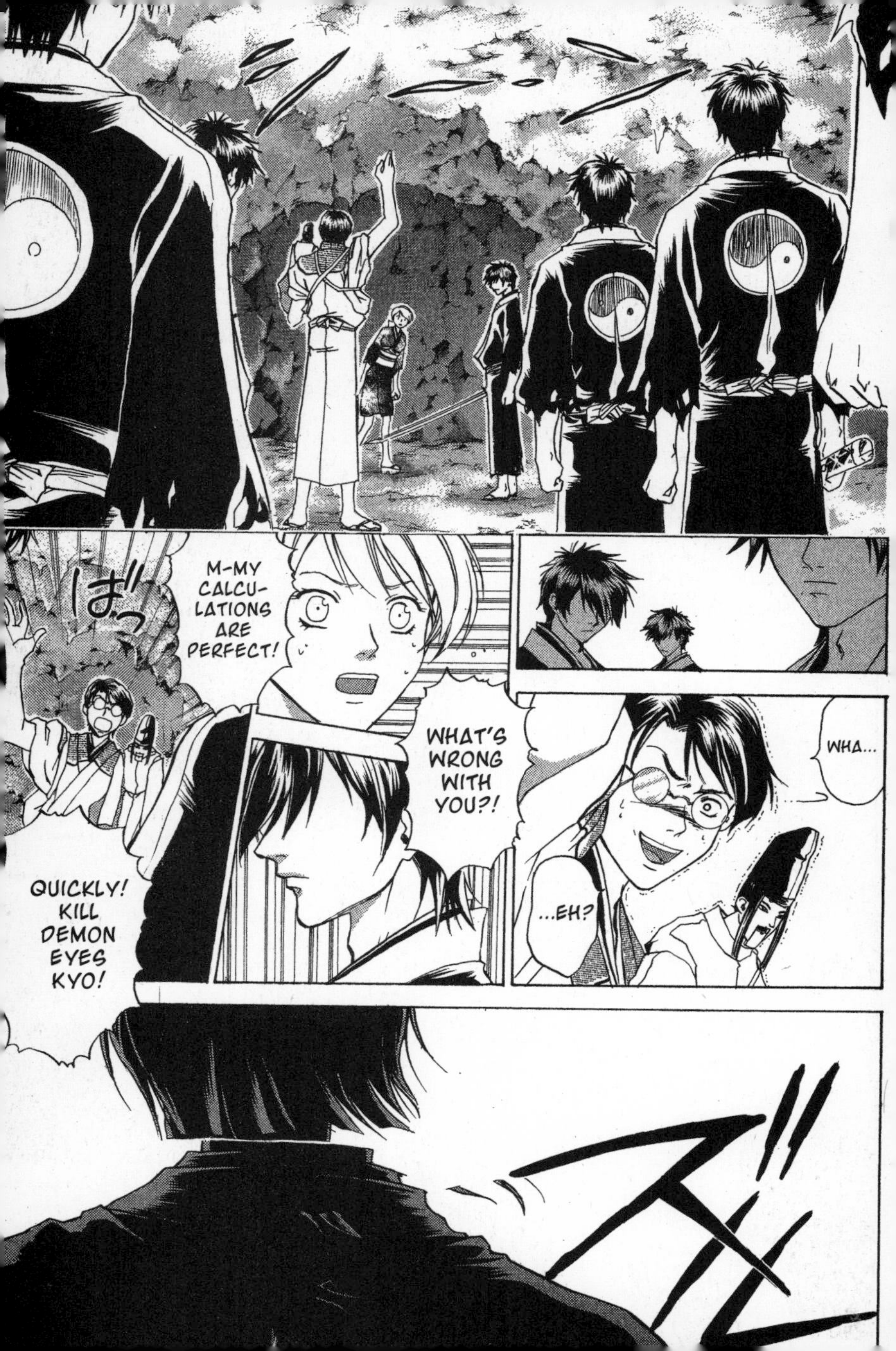
WHA...
...EH?
M-MY CALCU-LATIONS ARE PERFECT!
WHAT'S WRONG WITH YOU?!
ばっ
QUICKLY! KILL DEMON EYES KYO!
ズ

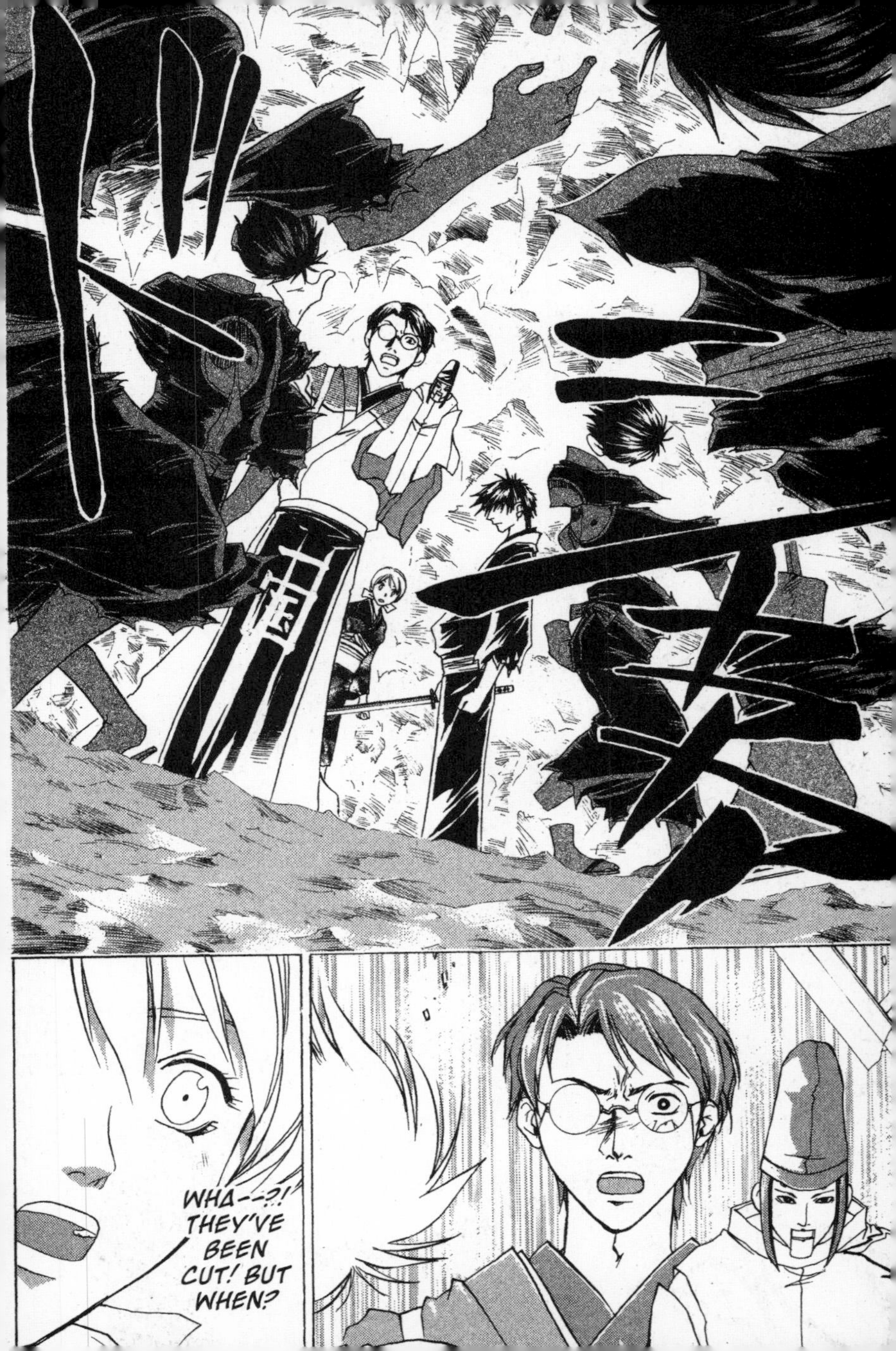
WHA--?! THEY'VE BEEN CUT! BUT WHEN?

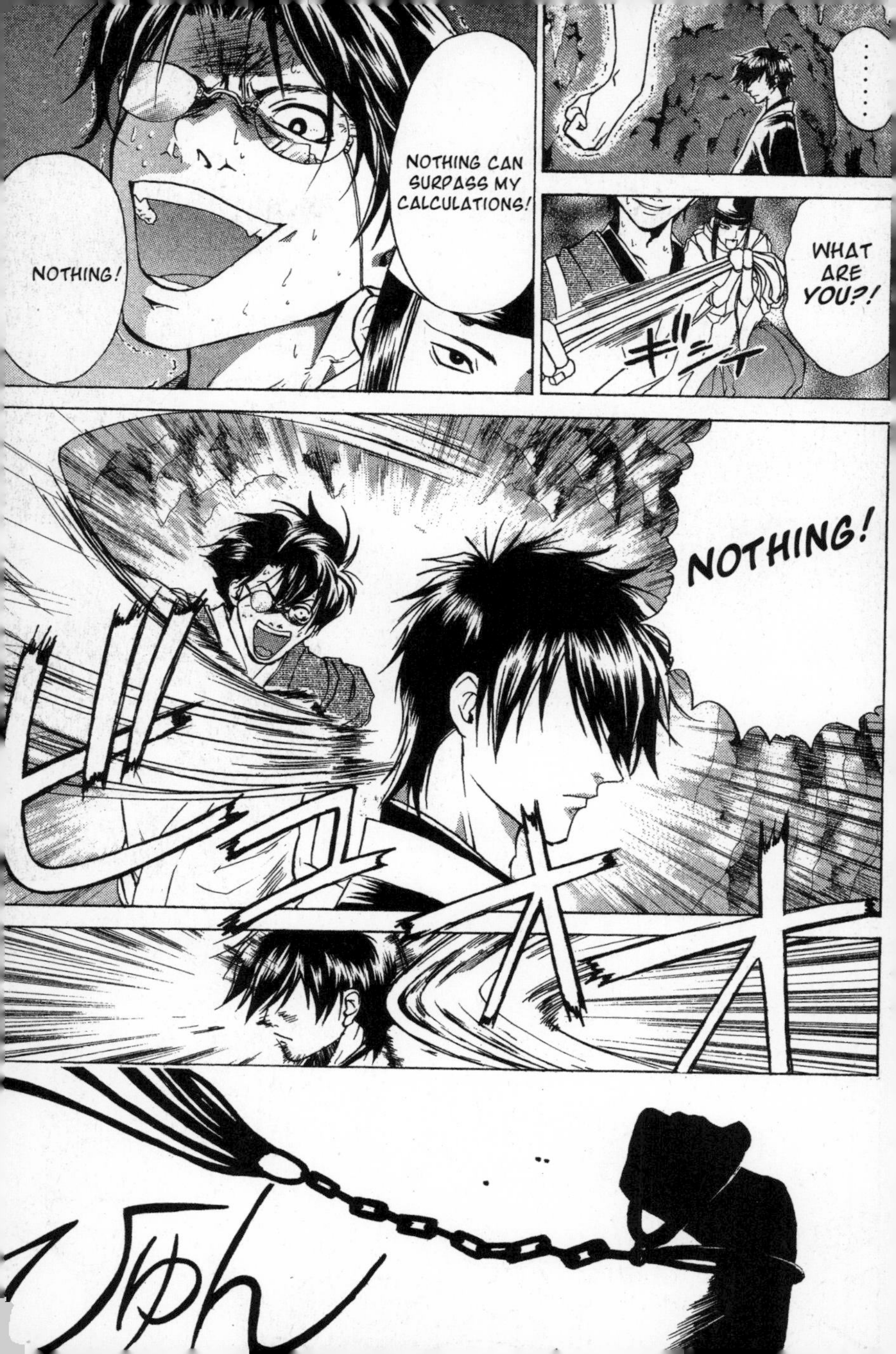

......
WHAT ARE YOU?!
ギシィ
NOTHING CAN SURPASS MY CALCULATIONS!
NOTHING!
NOTHING!
..

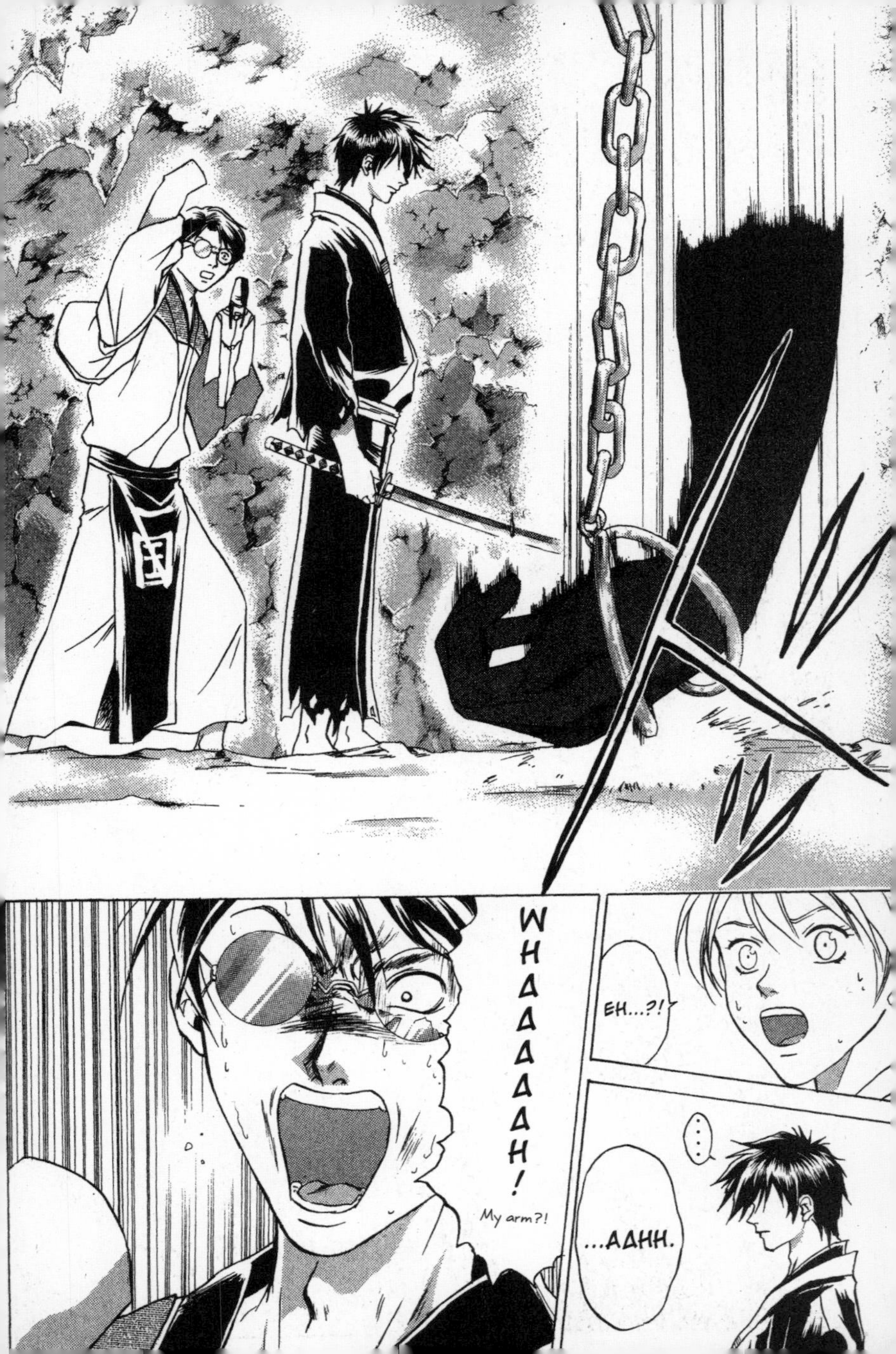
EH...?!
...
...AAHH.
WHAAAAAH!
My arm?!

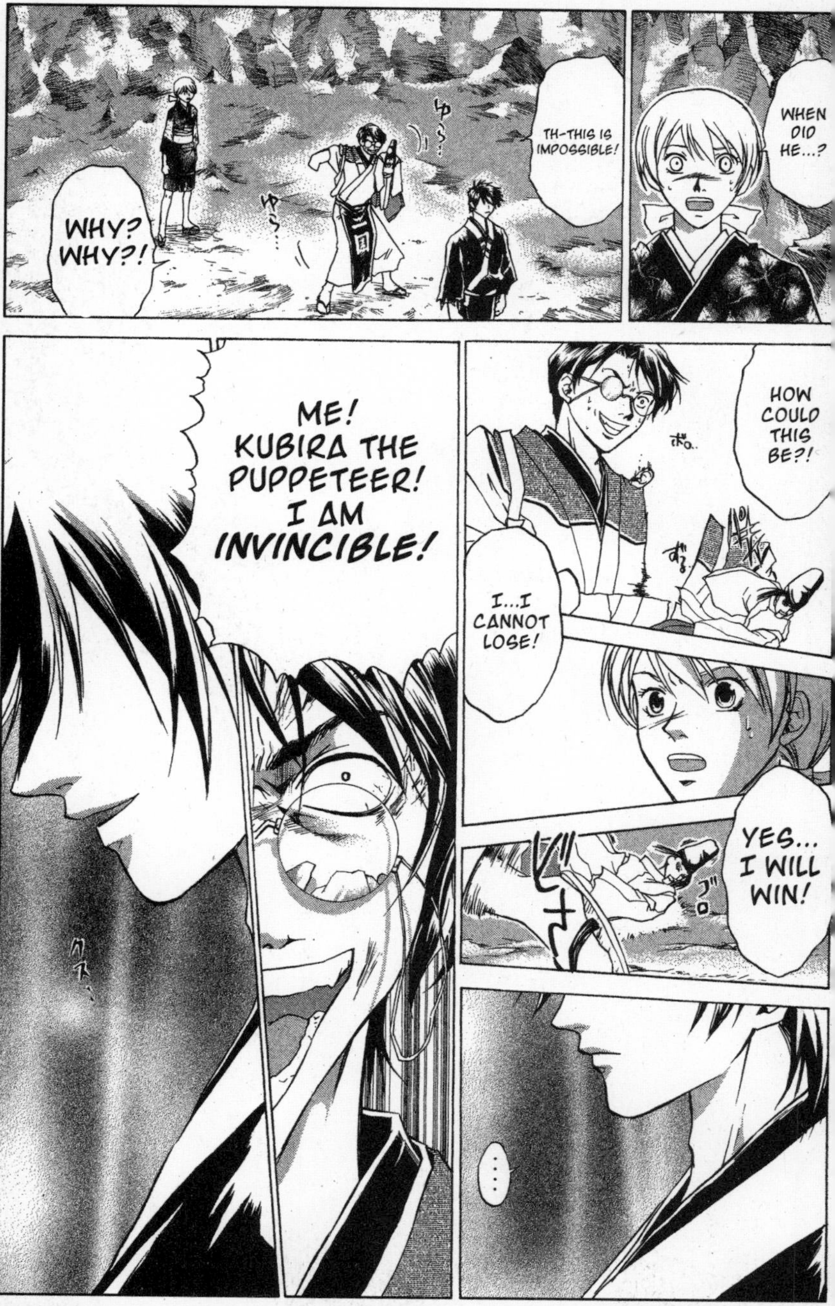

WHEN DID HE...?
TH-THIS IS IMPOSSIBLE!
WHY? WHY?!
HOW COULD THIS BE?!
I...I CANNOT LOSE!
YES... I WILL WIN!
....
ME! KUBIRA THE PUPPETEER! I AM *INVINCIBLE!*

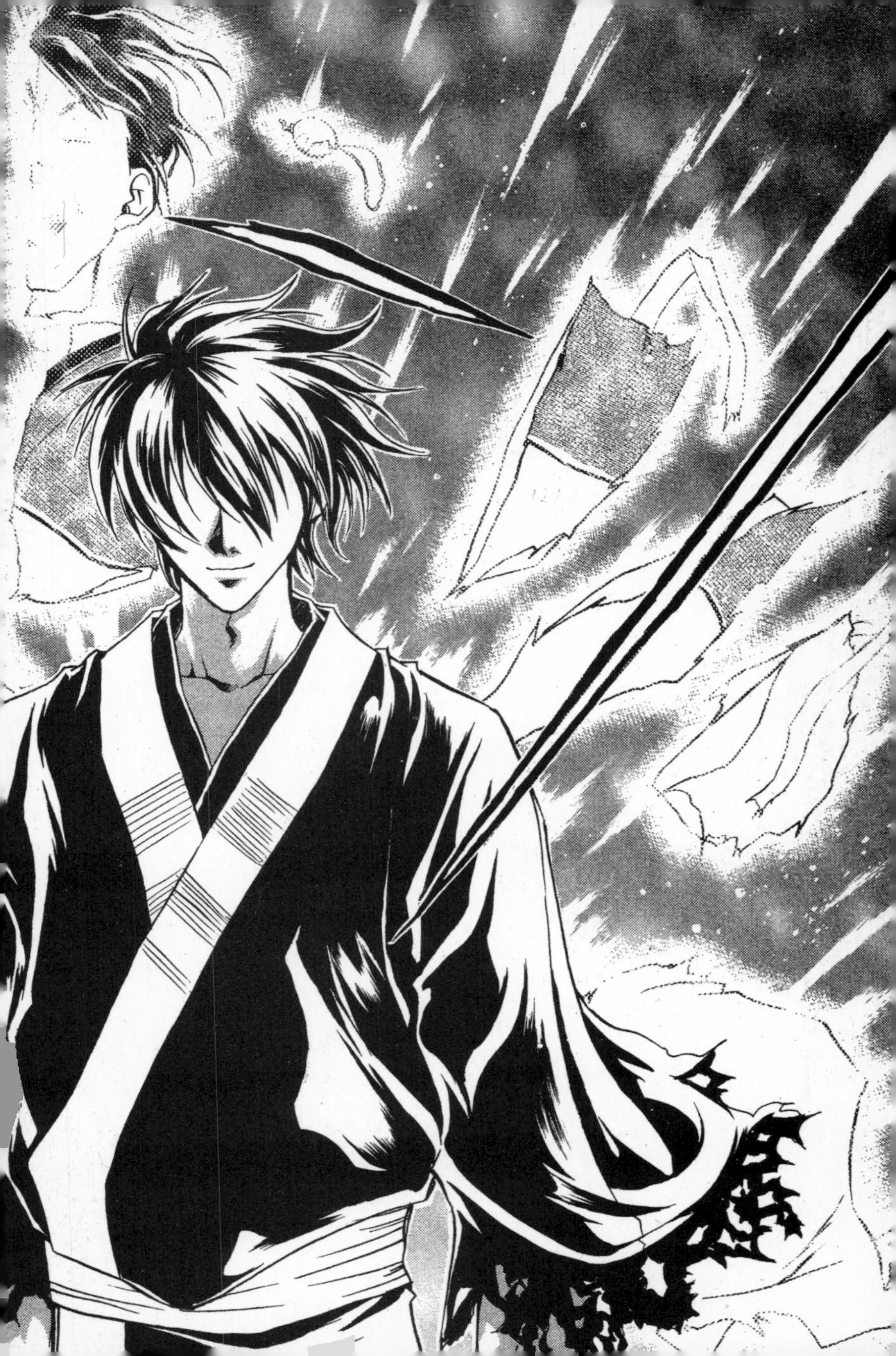

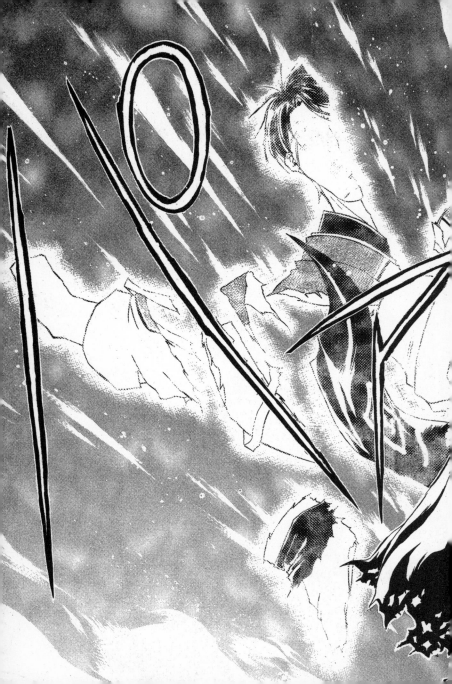

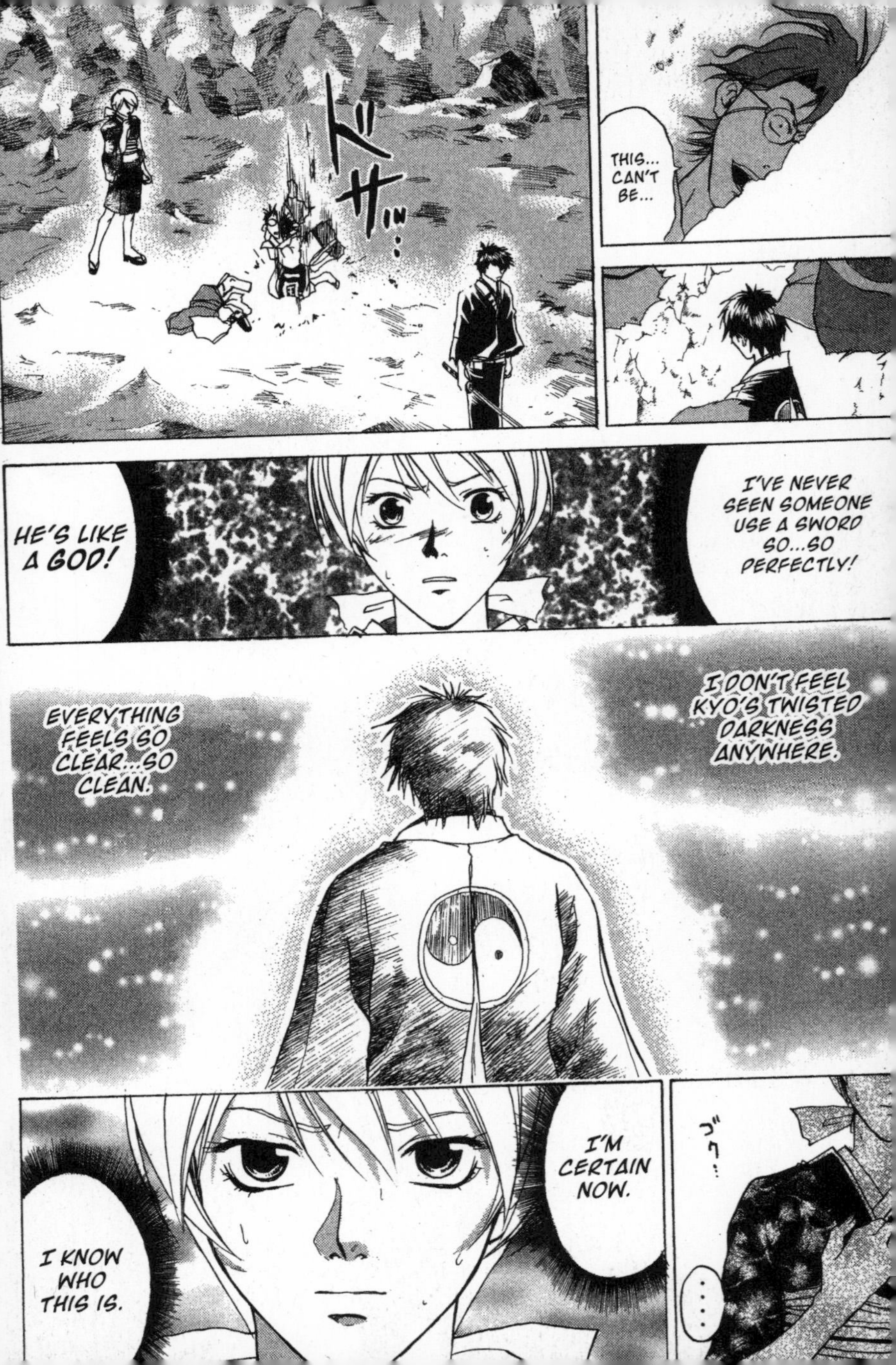
THIS... CAN'T BE...
I'VE NEVER SEEN SOMEONE USE A SWORD SO...SO PERFECTLY!
HE'S LIKE A GOD!
I DON'T FEEL KYO'S TWISTED DARKNESS ANYWHERE.
EVERYTHING FEELS SO CLEAR...SO CLEAN.
ゴク…
...
I'M CERTAIN NOW.
I KNOW WHO THIS IS.

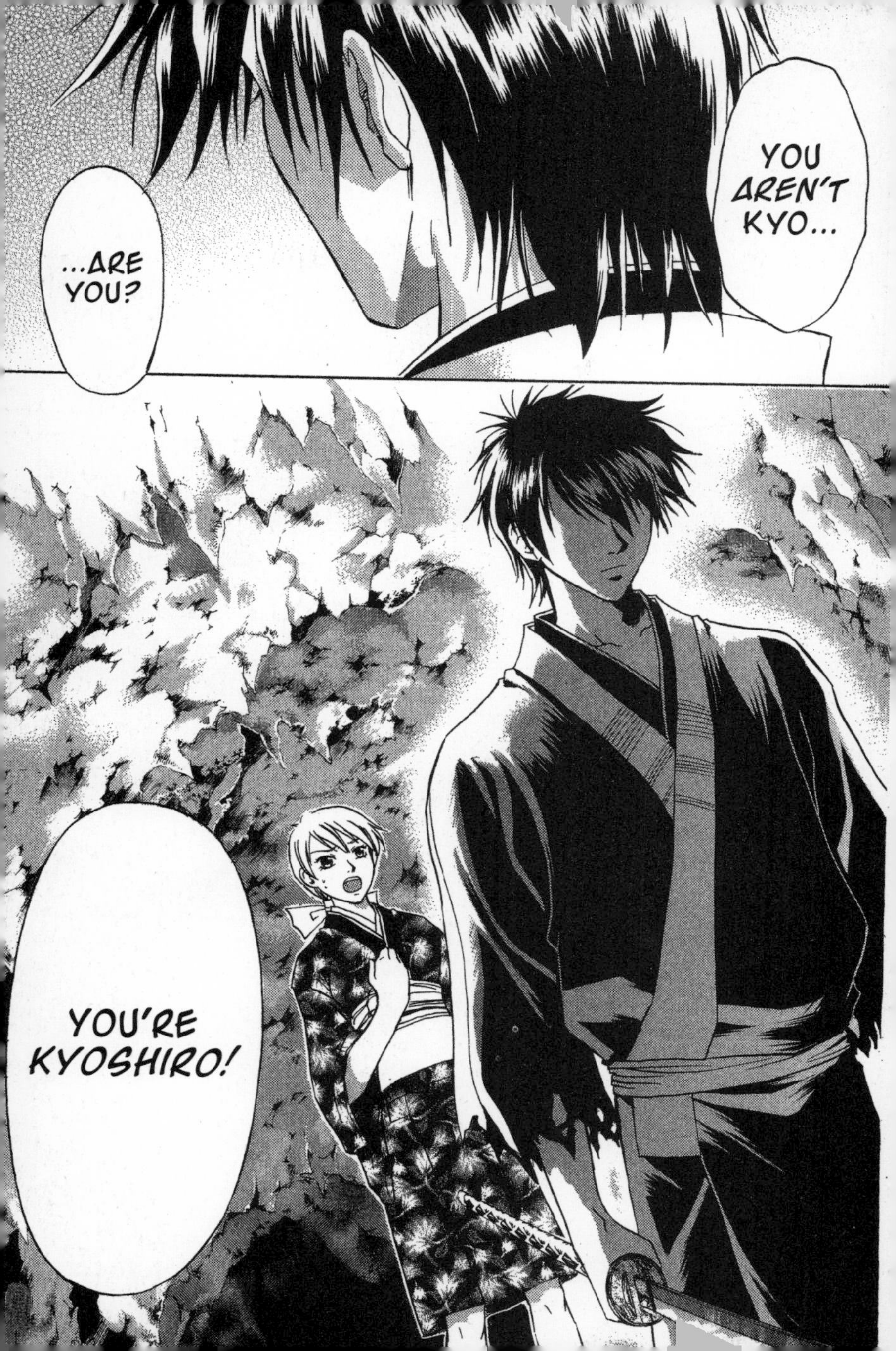
YOU AREN'T KYO...
...ARE YOU?
YOU'RE KYOSHIRO!

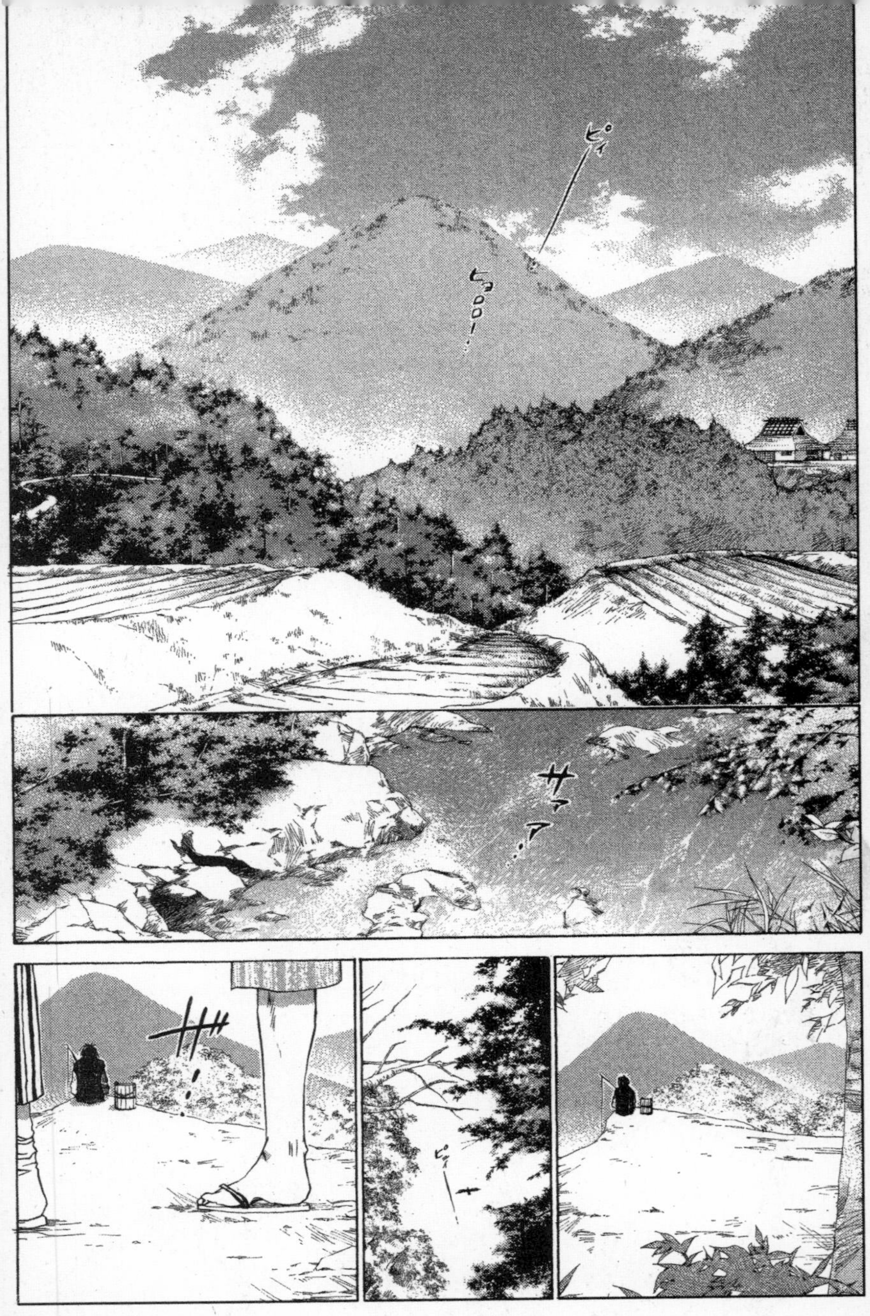
ピィ―
ヒョロロー…
ザァア…
ピィ―
ザ…!

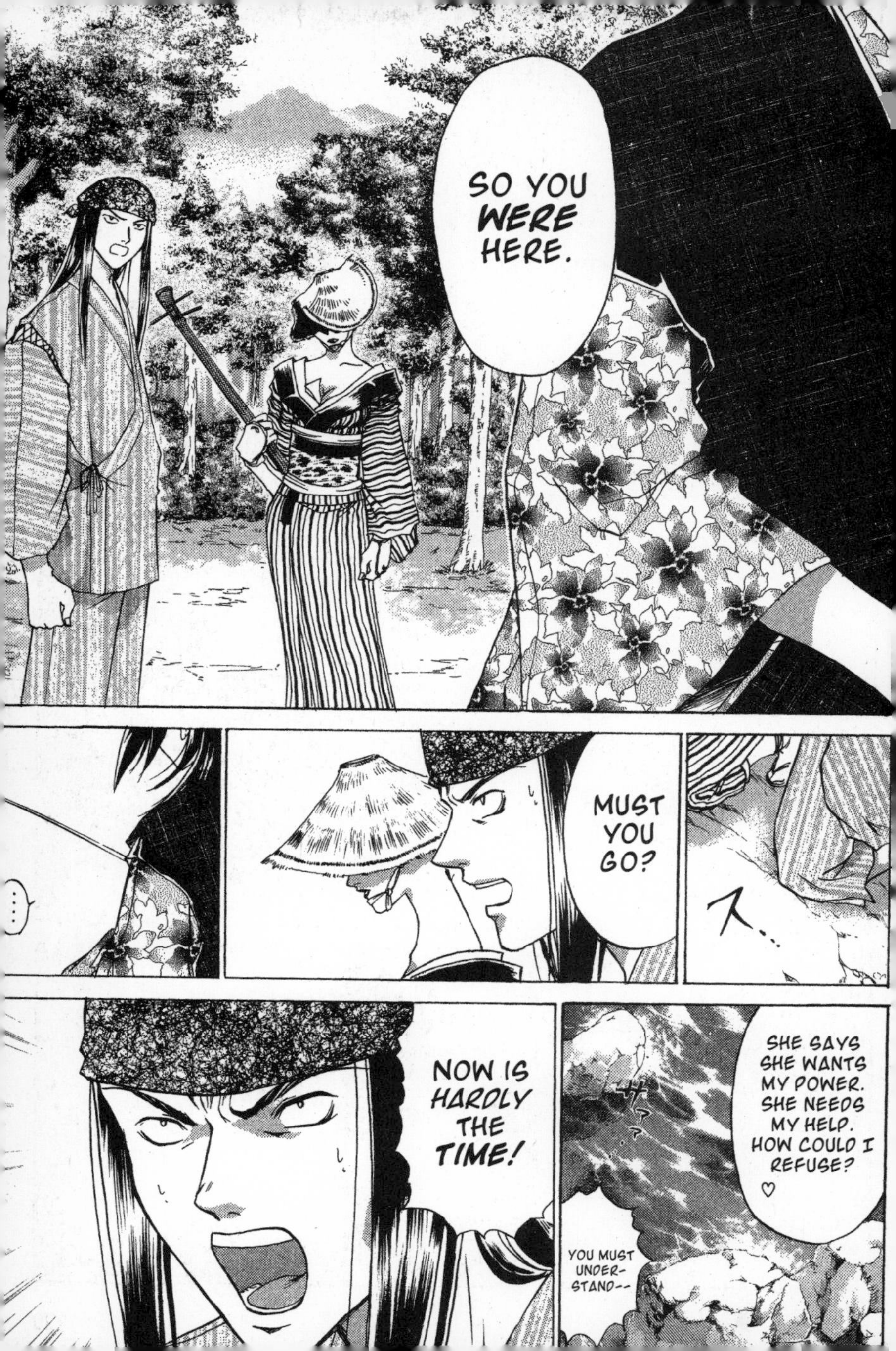
SO YOU WERE HERE.
MUST YOU GO?
......
SHE SAYS SHE WANTS MY POWER. SHE NEEDS MY HELP. HOW COULD I REFUSE? ♡
YOU MUST UNDER-STAND--
NOW IS HARDLY THE TIME!

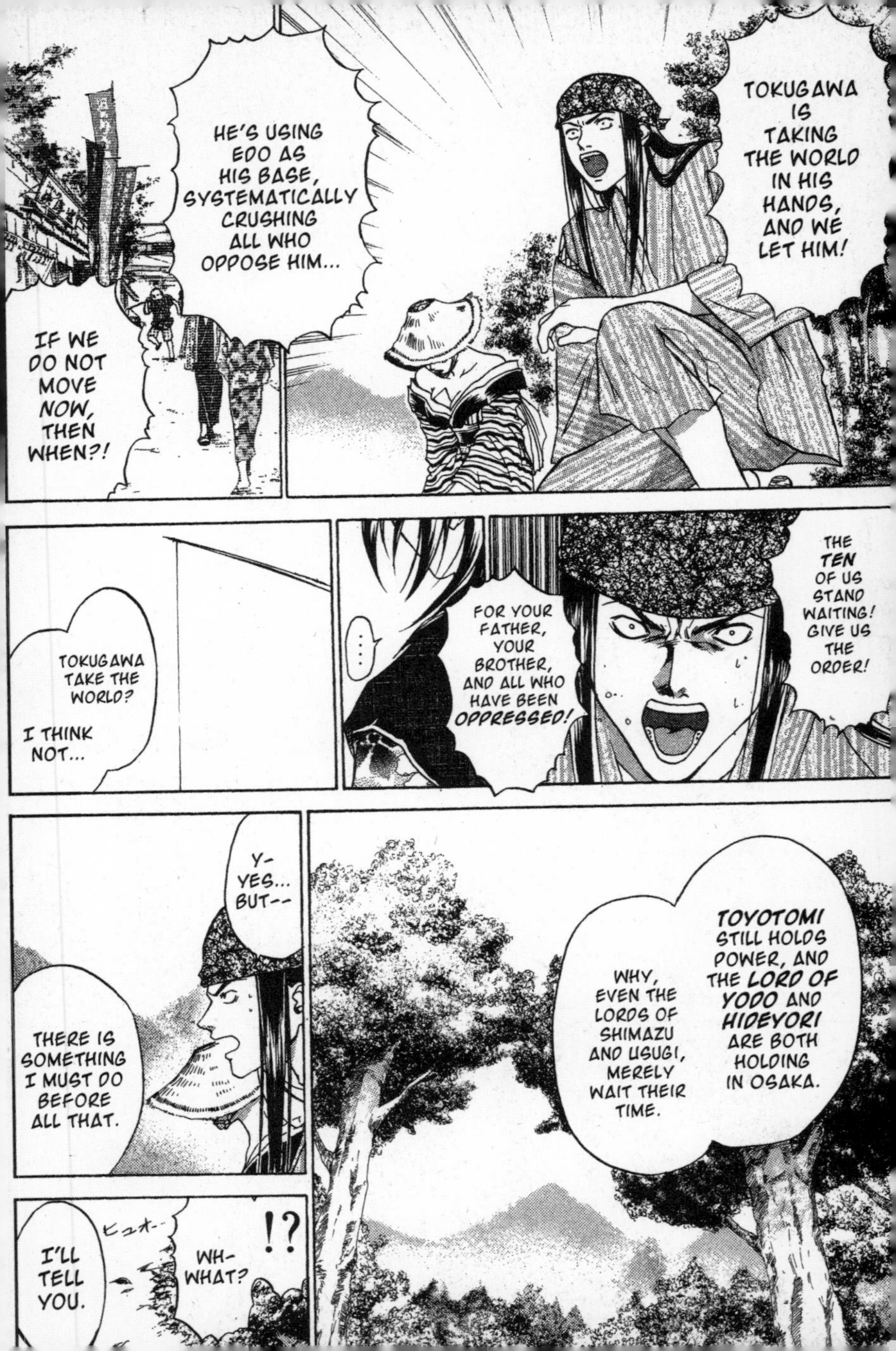
TOKUGAWA IS TAKING THE WORLD IN HIS HANDS, AND WE LET HIM!
HE'S USING EDO AS HIS BASE, SYSTEMATICALLY CRUSHING ALL WHO OPPOSE HIM...
IF WE DO NOT MOVE NOW, THEN WHEN?!
THE TEN OF US STAND WAITING! GIVE US THE ORDER!
FOR YOUR FATHER, YOUR BROTHER, AND ALL WHO HAVE BEEN OPPRESSED!
.....
TOKUGAWA TAKE THE WORLD?
I THINK NOT...
TOYOTOMI STILL HOLDS POWER, AND THE LORD OF YODO AND HIDEYORI ARE BOTH HOLDING IN OSAKA.
WHY, EVEN THE LORDS OF SHIMAZU AND USUGI, MERELY WAIT THEIR TIME.
Y- YES... BUT--
THERE IS SOMETHING I MUST DO BEFORE ALL THAT.
!?
WH- WHAT?
ヒュオー..
I'LL TELL YOU.

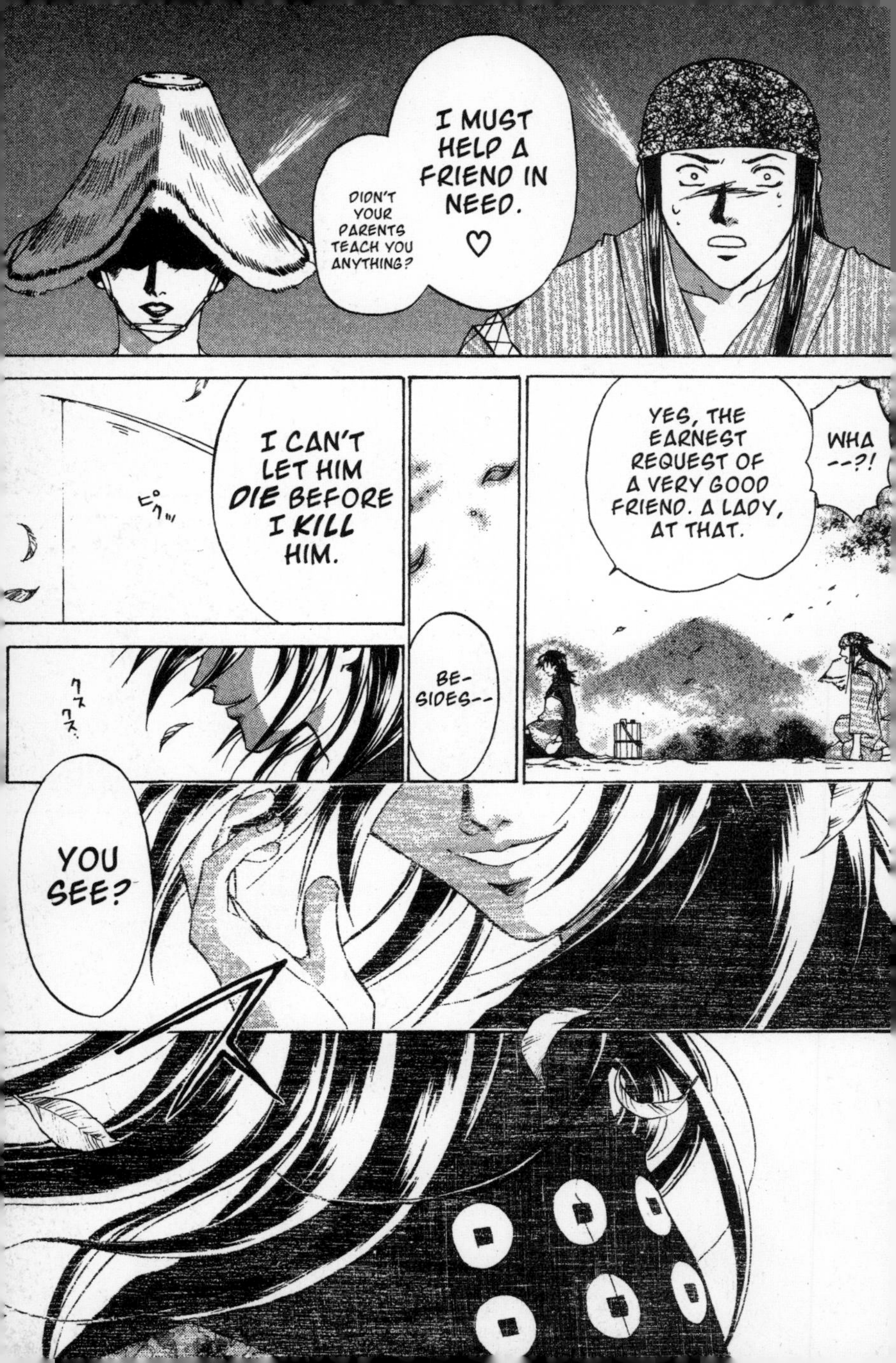
I MUST HELP A FRIEND IN NEED. ♡
DIDN'T YOUR PARENTS TEACH YOU ANYTHING?
WHA--?!
YES, THE EARNEST REQUEST OF A VERY GOOD FRIEND. A LADY, AT THAT.
I CAN'T LET HIM DIE BEFORE I KILL HIM.
ピクッ
BE-SIDES--
クス クス
YOU SEE?

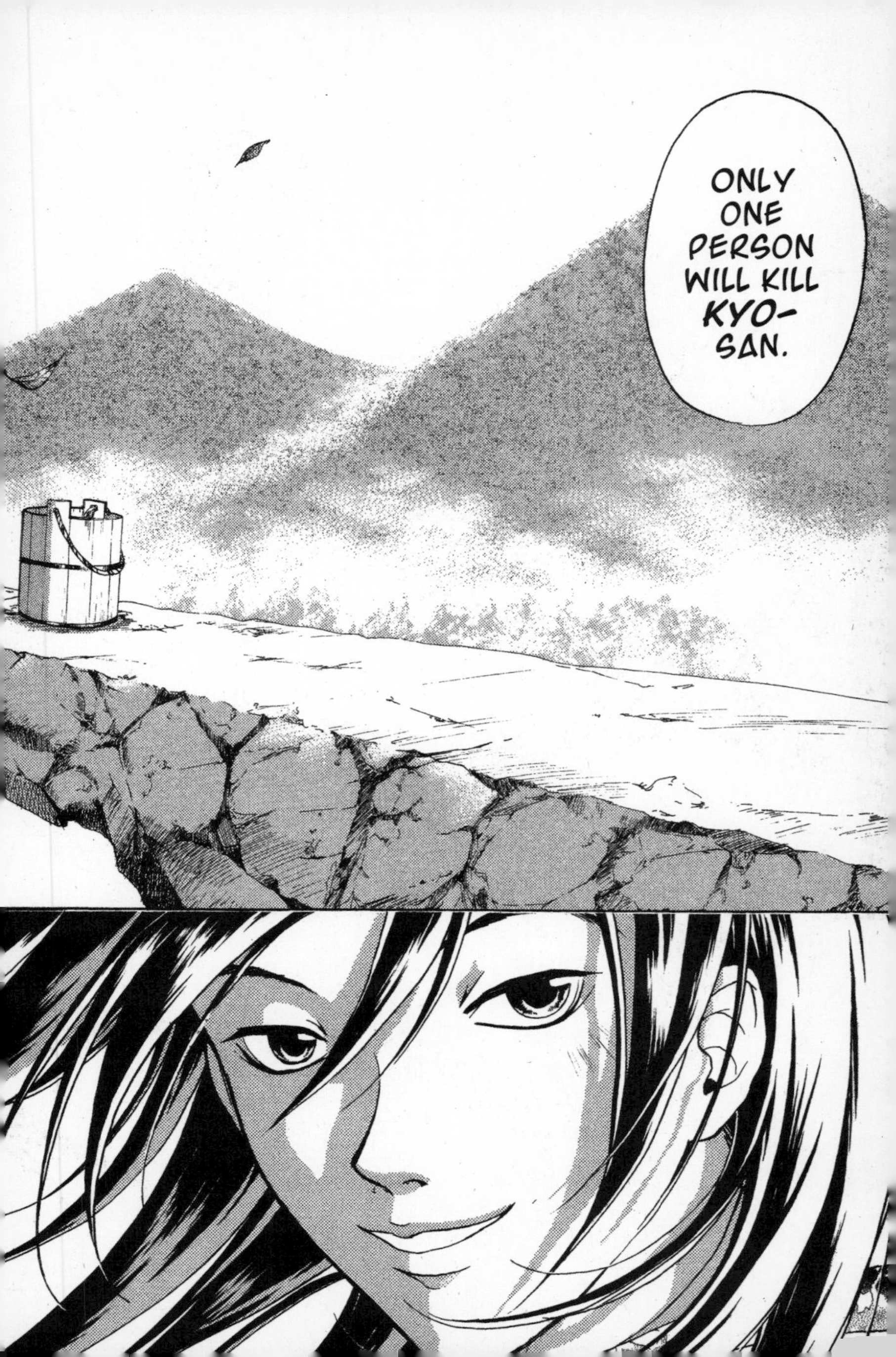
ONLY ONE PERSON WILL KILL KYO-SAN.

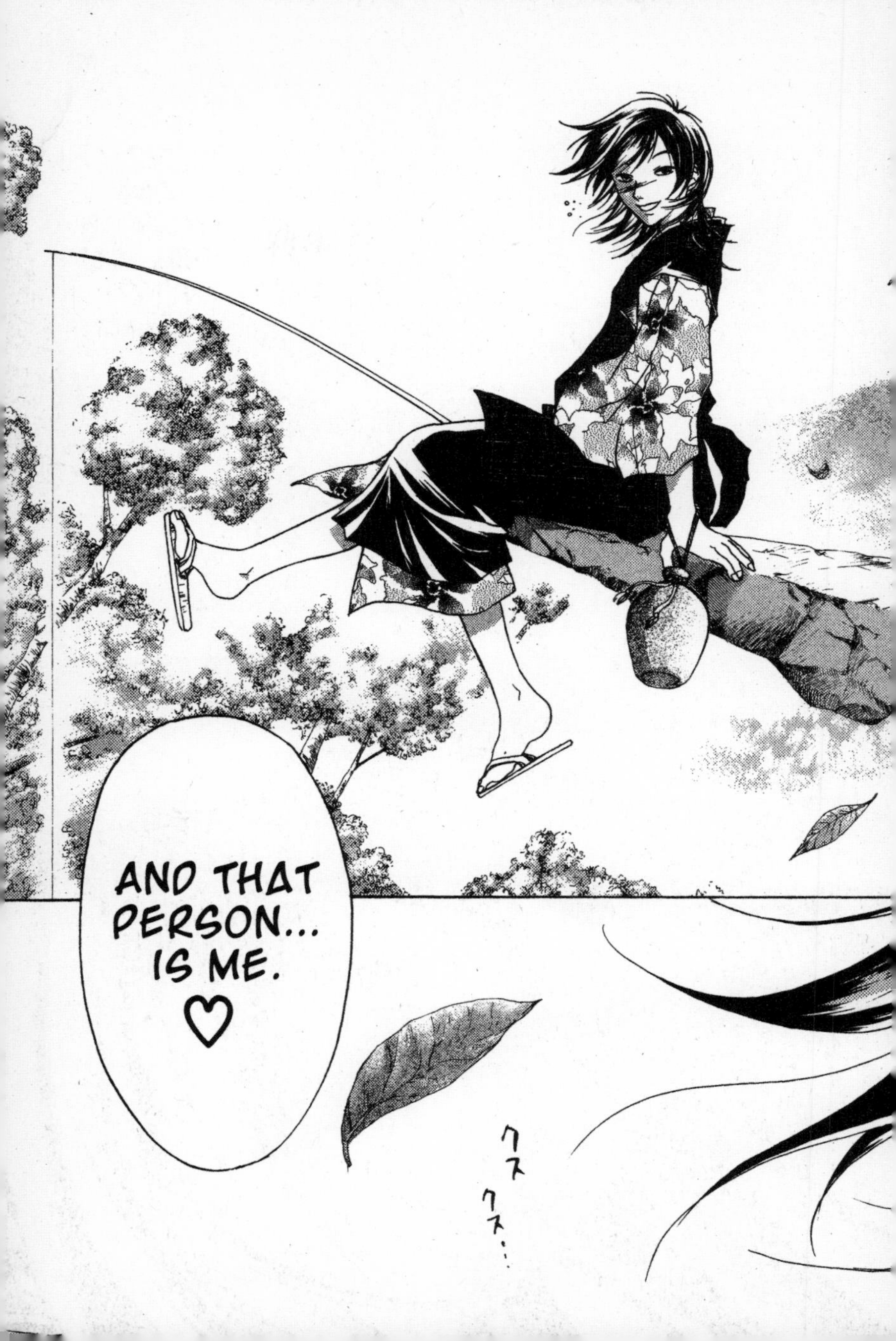
AND THAT PERSON... IS ME. ♡
クス クス...

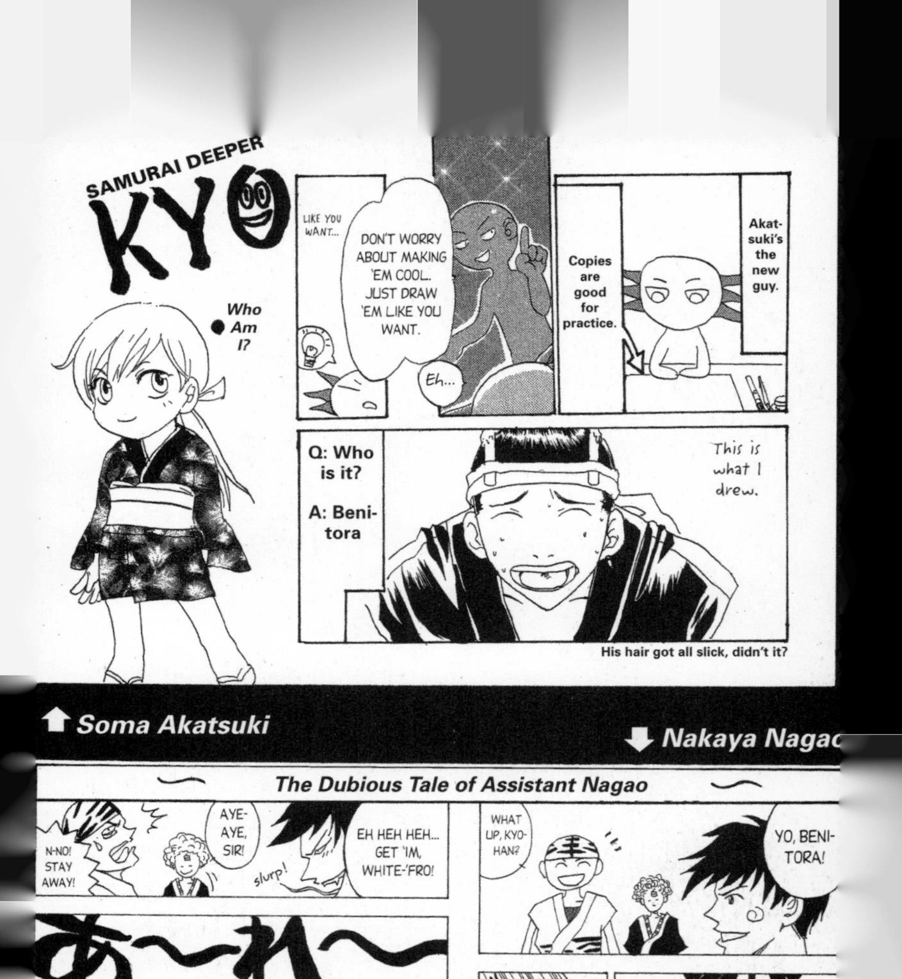

SAMURAI DEEPER KYO
Akat-suki's the new guy.
Copies are good for practice.
DON'T WORRY ABOUT MAKING 'EM COOL. JUST DRAW 'EM LIKE YOU WANT.
LIKE YOU WANT...
Eh...
This is what I drew.
Q: Who is it?
A: Beni-tora
His hair got all slick, didn't it?
Who Am I?

⬆ Soma Akatsuki

⬇ Nakaya Nagao

The Dubious Tale of Assistant Nagao

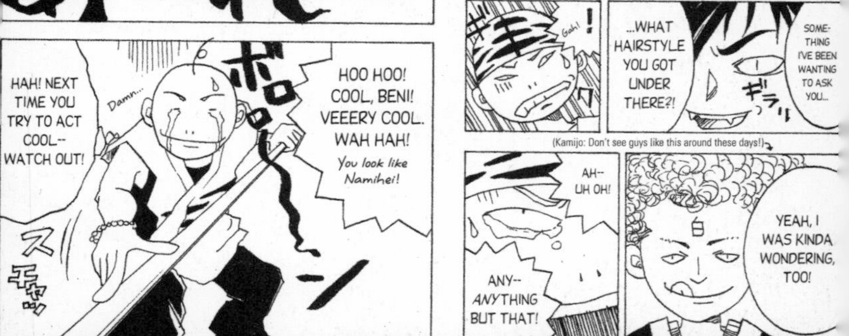

YO, BENI-TORA!
WHAT UP, KYO-HAN?
SOME-THING I'VE BEEN WANTING TO ASK YOU...
...WHAT HAIRSTYLE YOU GOT UNDER THERE?!
Gah!
(Kamijo: Don't see guys like this around these days!)
YEAH, I WAS KINDA WONDERING, TOO!
AH--UH OH!
ANY--ANYTHING BUT THAT!
EH HEH HEH... GET 'IM, WHITE-'FRO!
slurp!
AYE-AYE, SIR!
N-NO! STAY AWAY!
あ～れ～
HOO HOO! COOL, BENI! VEEERY COOL. WAH HAH!
You look like Namihei!
Damn...
HAH! NEXT TIME YOU TRY TO ACT COOL--WATCH OUT!

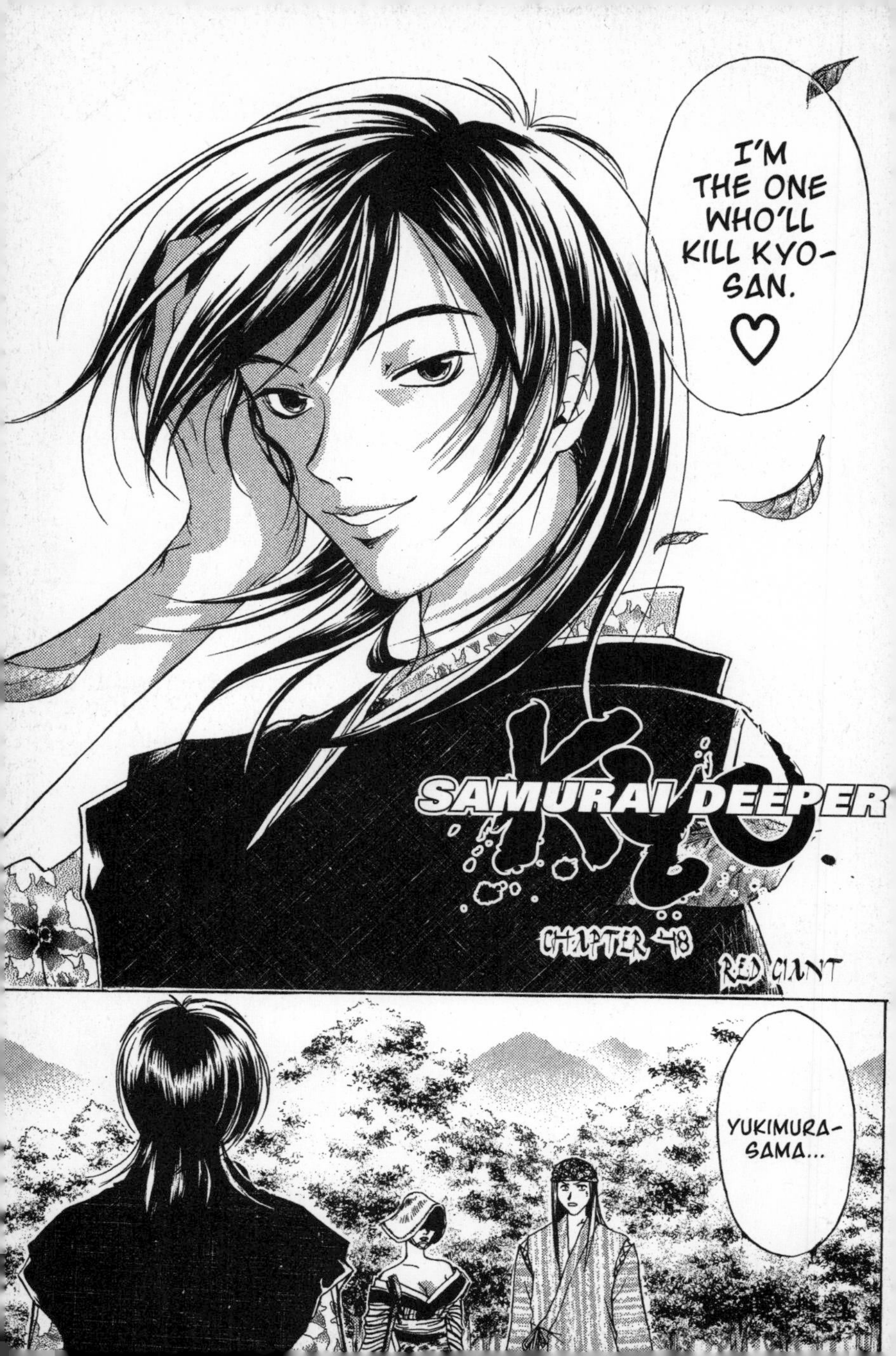
I'M THE ONE WHO'LL KILL KYO-SAN. ♡
SAMURAI DEEPER KYO
CHAPTER 48
RED GIANT
YUKIMURA-SAMA...

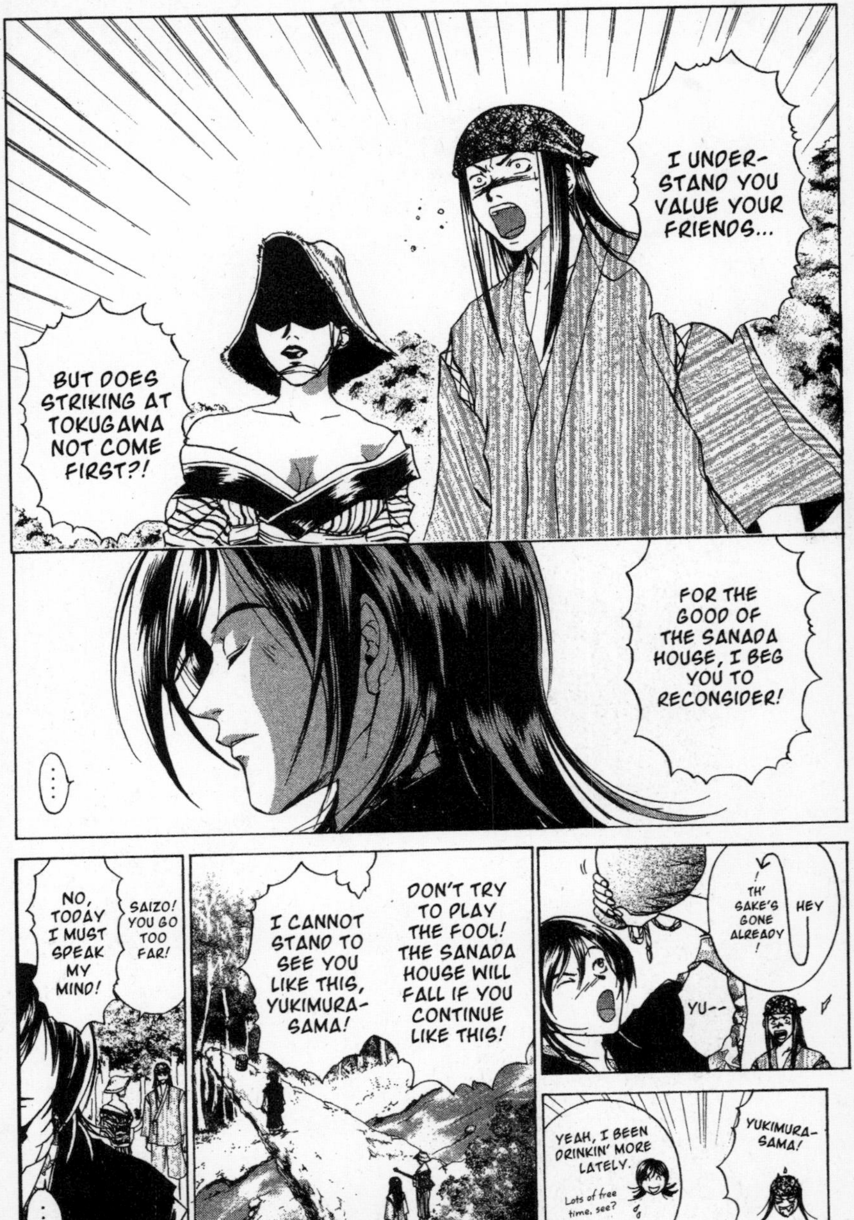
I UNDER-STAND YOU VALUE YOUR FRIENDS...
BUT DOES STRIKING AT TOKUGAWA NOT COME FIRST?!
FOR THE GOOD OF THE SANADA HOUSE, I BEG YOU TO RECONSIDER!
....
HEY
! TH' SAKE'S GONE ALREADY !
YU--
YUKIMURA-SAMA!
YEAH, I BEEN DRINKIN' MORE LATELY.
Lots of free time, see?
DON'T TRY TO PLAY THE FOOL! THE SANADA HOUSE WILL FALL IF YOU CONTINUE LIKE THIS!
I CANNOT STAND TO SEE YOU LIKE THIS, YUKIMURA-SAMA!
SAIZO! YOU GO TOO FAR!
NO, TODAY I MUST SPEAK MY MIND!
....

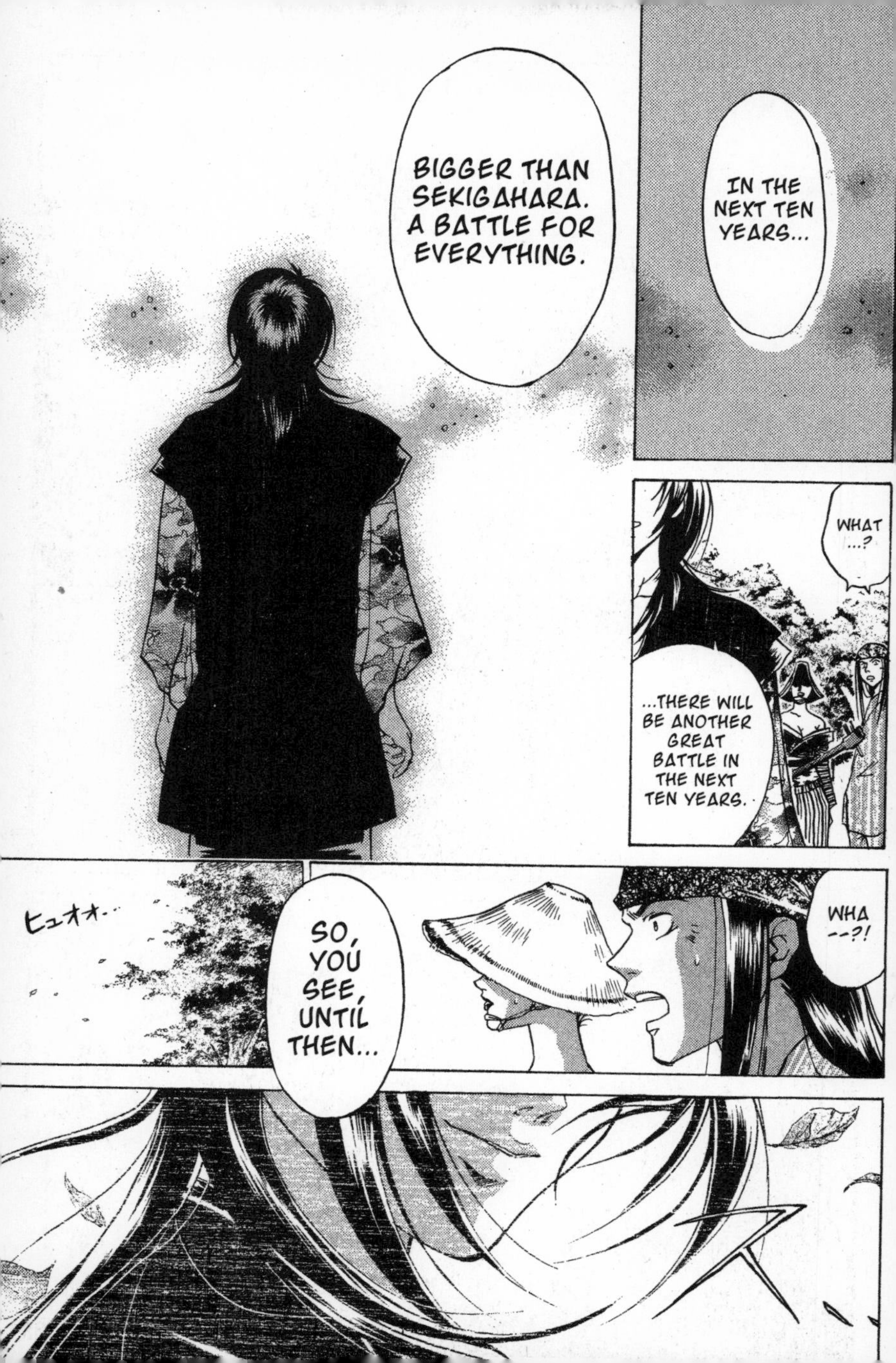
IN THE NEXT TEN YEARS...
WHAT ...?
...THERE WILL BE ANOTHER GREAT BATTLE IN THE NEXT TEN YEARS.
BIGGER THAN SEKIGAHARA. A BATTLE FOR EVERYTHING.
WHA --?!
SO, YOU SEE, UNTIL THEN...
ヒュオオ...

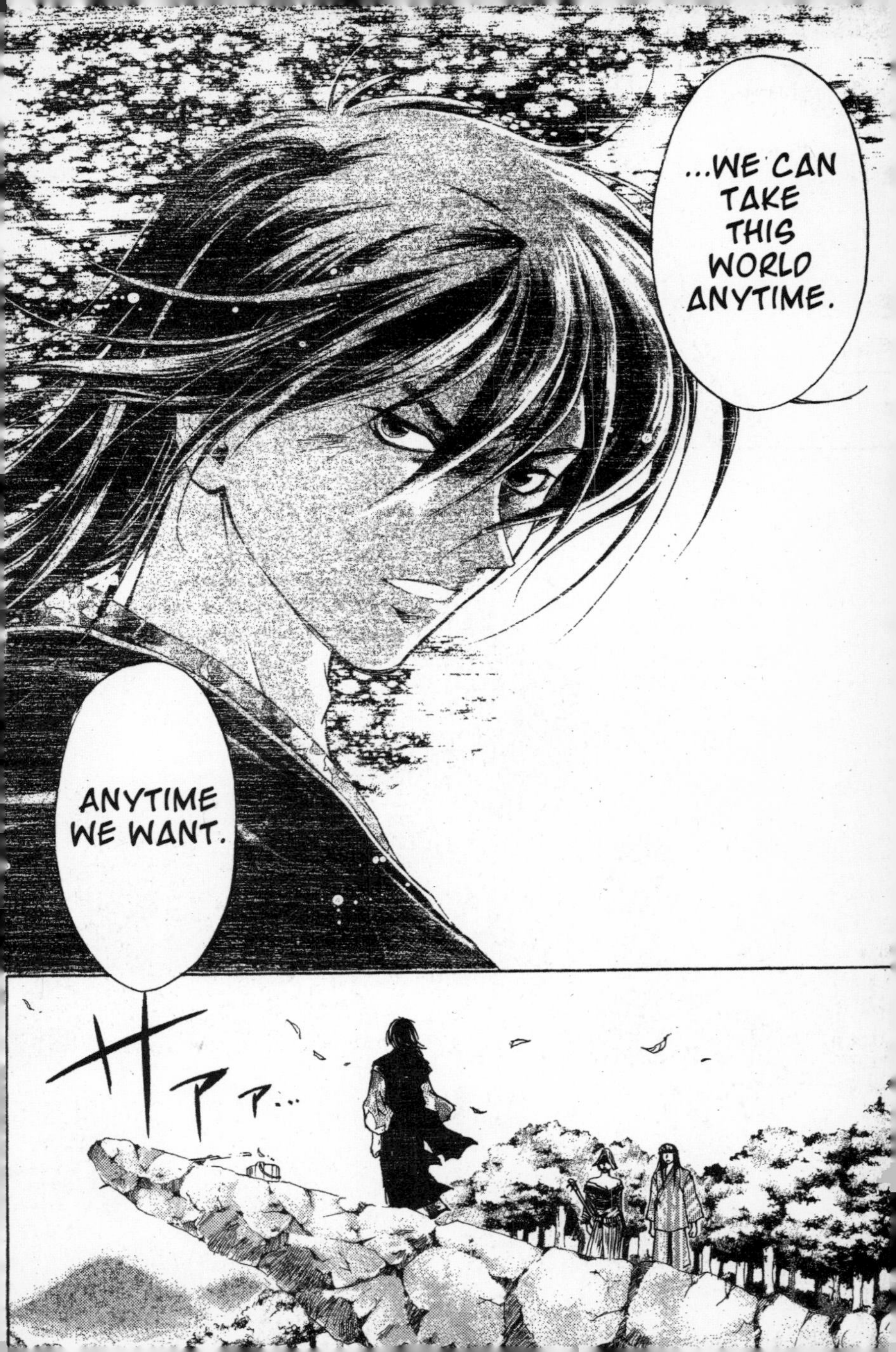
...WE CAN TAKE THIS WORLD ANYTIME.
ANYTIME WE WANT.
サァァ...

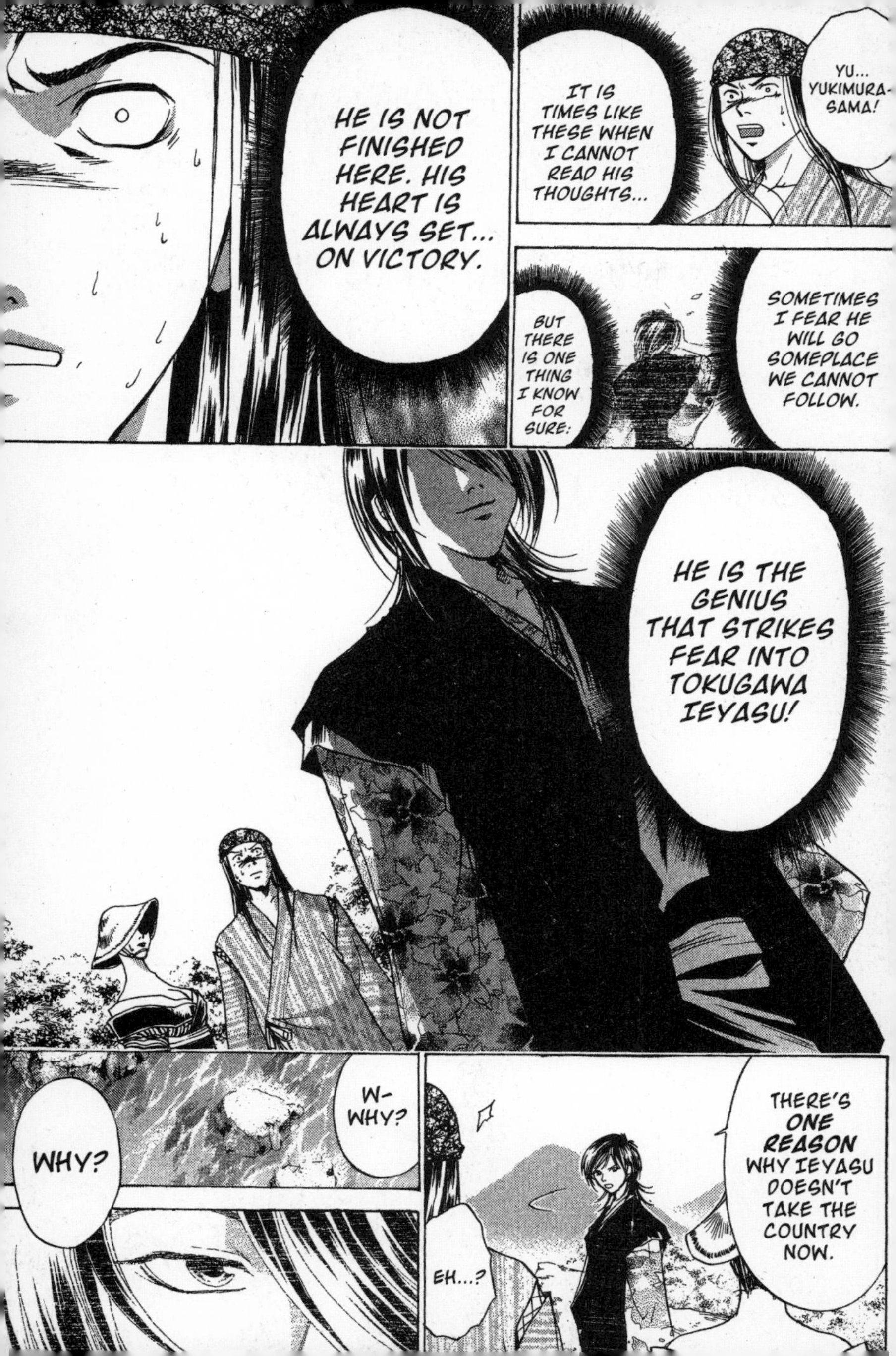
YU... YUKIMURA-SAMA!
IT IS TIMES LIKE THESE WHEN I CANNOT READ HIS THOUGHTS...
SOMETIMES I FEAR HE WILL GO SOMEPLACE WE CANNOT FOLLOW.
BUT THERE IS ONE THING I KNOW FOR SURE:
HE IS NOT FINISHED HERE. HIS HEART IS ALWAYS SET... ON VICTORY.
HE IS THE GENIUS THAT STRIKES FEAR INTO TOKUGAWA IEYASU!
THERE'S ONE REASON WHY IEYASU DOESN'T TAKE THE COUNTRY NOW.
EH...?
W- WHY?
WHY?

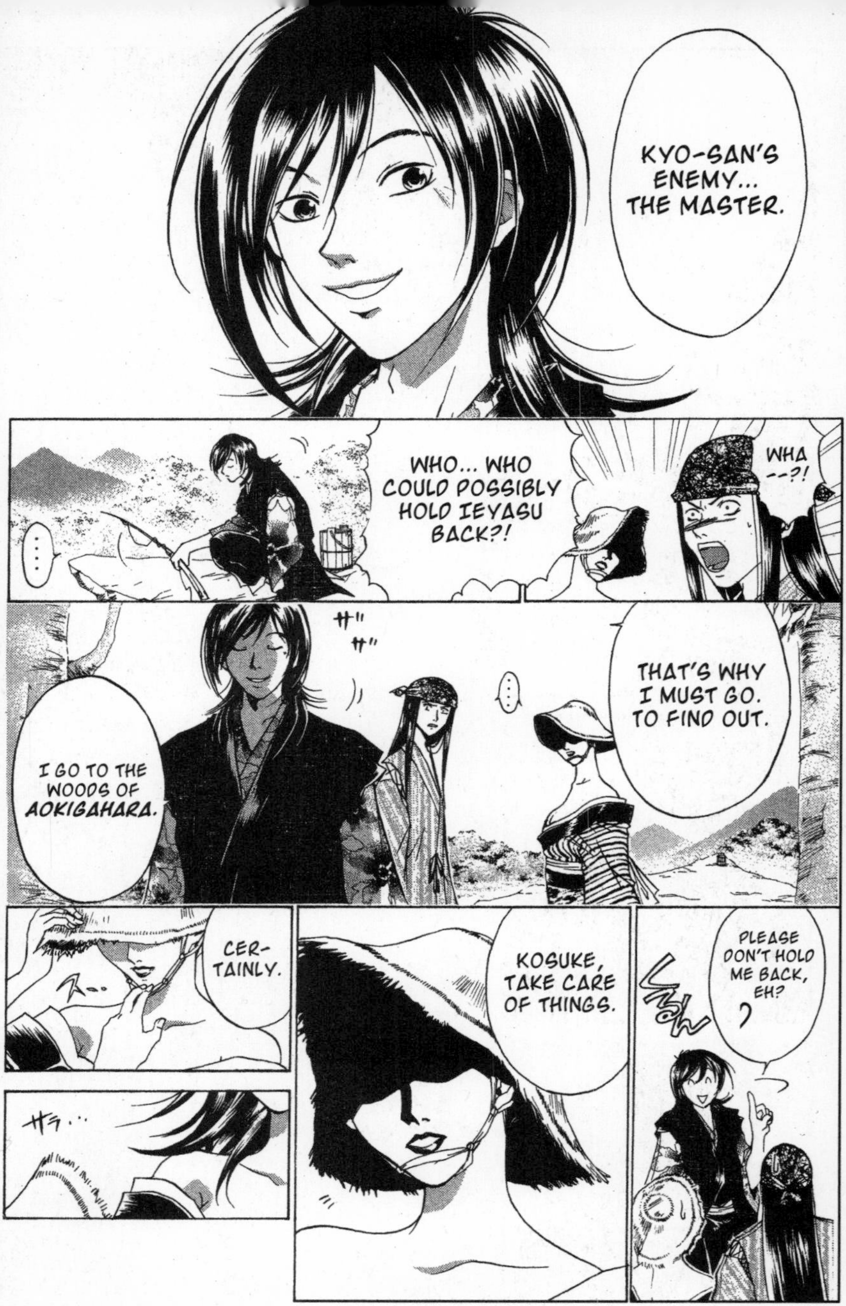
KYO-SAN'S ENEMY... THE MASTER.
WHA --?!
WHO... WHO COULD POSSIBLY HOLD IEYASU BACK?!
...
THAT'S WHY I MUST GO. TO FIND OUT.
ザ
ザ
...
I GO TO THE WOODS OF AOKIGAHARA.
PLEASE DON'T HOLD ME BACK, EH?
KOSUKE, TAKE CARE OF THINGS.
CER-TAINLY.
スー..
サラ..

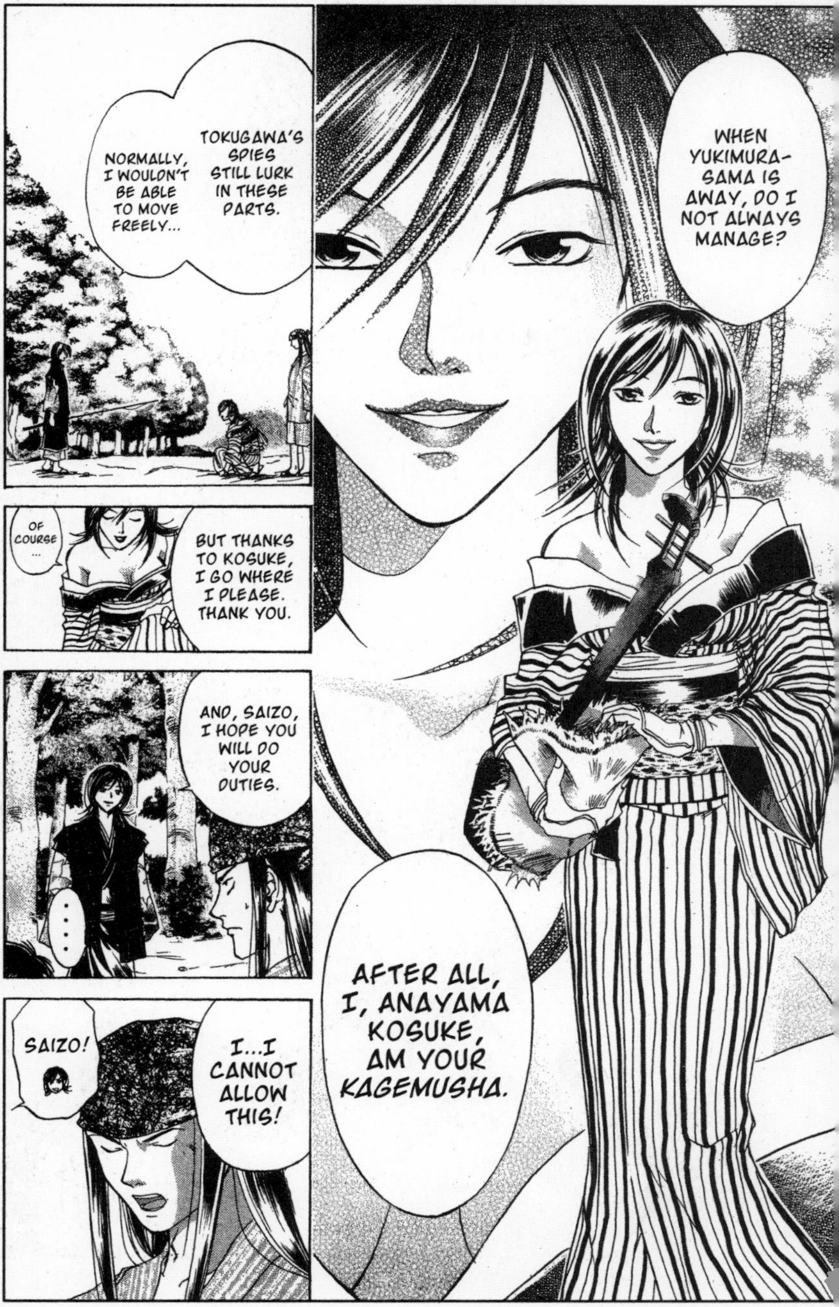
WHEN YUKIMURA-SAMA IS AWAY, DO I NOT ALWAYS MANAGE?
AFTER ALL, I, ANAYAMA KOSUKE, AM YOUR KAGEMUSHA.
TOKUGAWA'S SPIES STILL LURK IN THESE PARTS.
NORMALLY, I WOULDN'T BE ABLE TO MOVE FREELY...
BUT THANKS TO KOSUKE, I GO WHERE I PLEASE. THANK YOU.
OF COURSE...
AND, SAIZO, I HOPE YOU WILL DO YOUR DUTIES.
....
I...I CANNOT ALLOW THIS!
SAIZO!

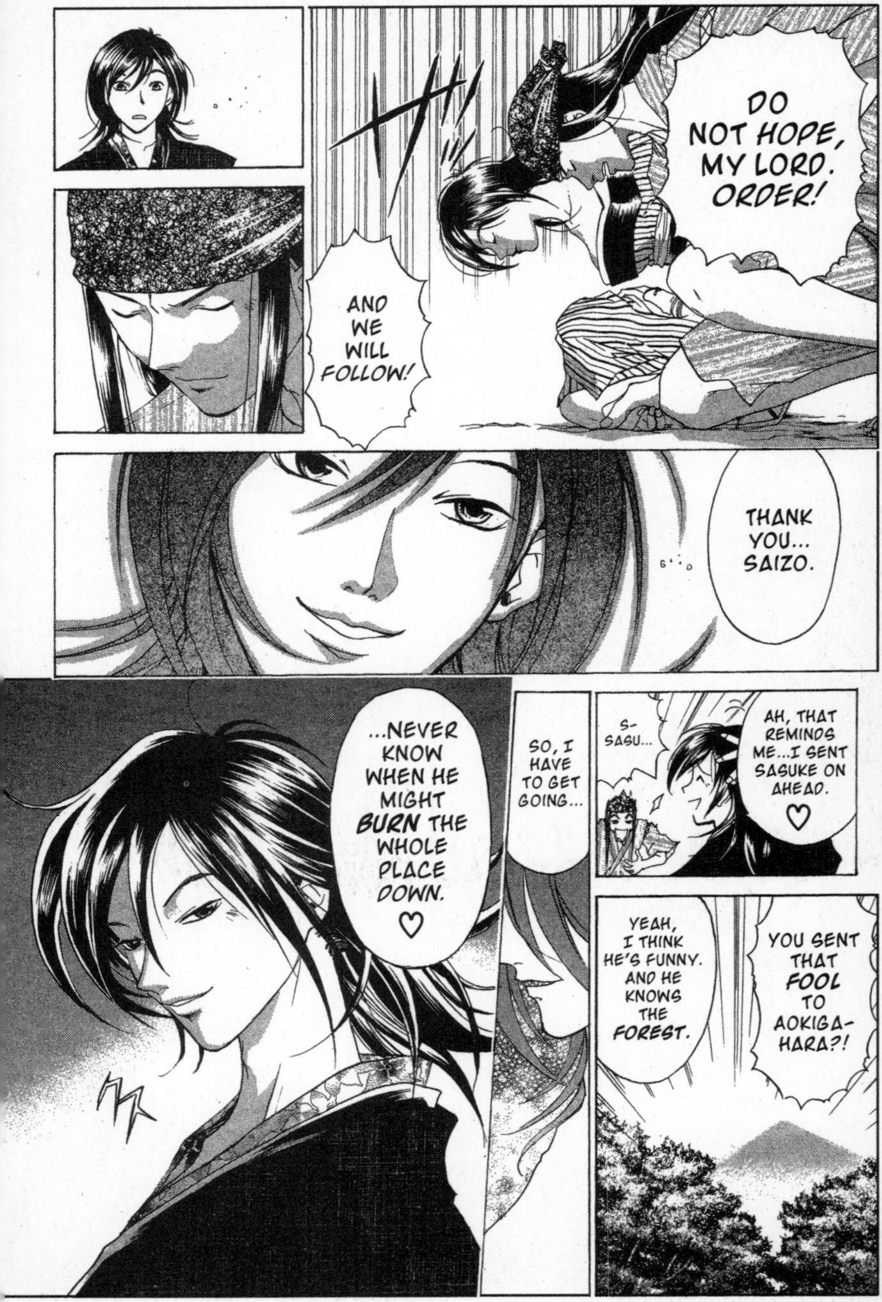

DO NOT HOPE, MY LORD. ORDER!
AND WE WILL FOLLOW!
THANK YOU... SAIZO.
AH, THAT REMINDS ME...I SENT SASUKE ON AHEAD. ♡
S-SASU...
YOU SENT THAT FOOL TO AOKIGA-HARA?!
YEAH, I THINK HE'S FUNNY. AND HE KNOWS THE FOREST.
SO, I HAVE TO GET GOING...
...NEVER KNOW WHEN HE MIGHT BURN THE WHOLE PLACE DOWN. ♡

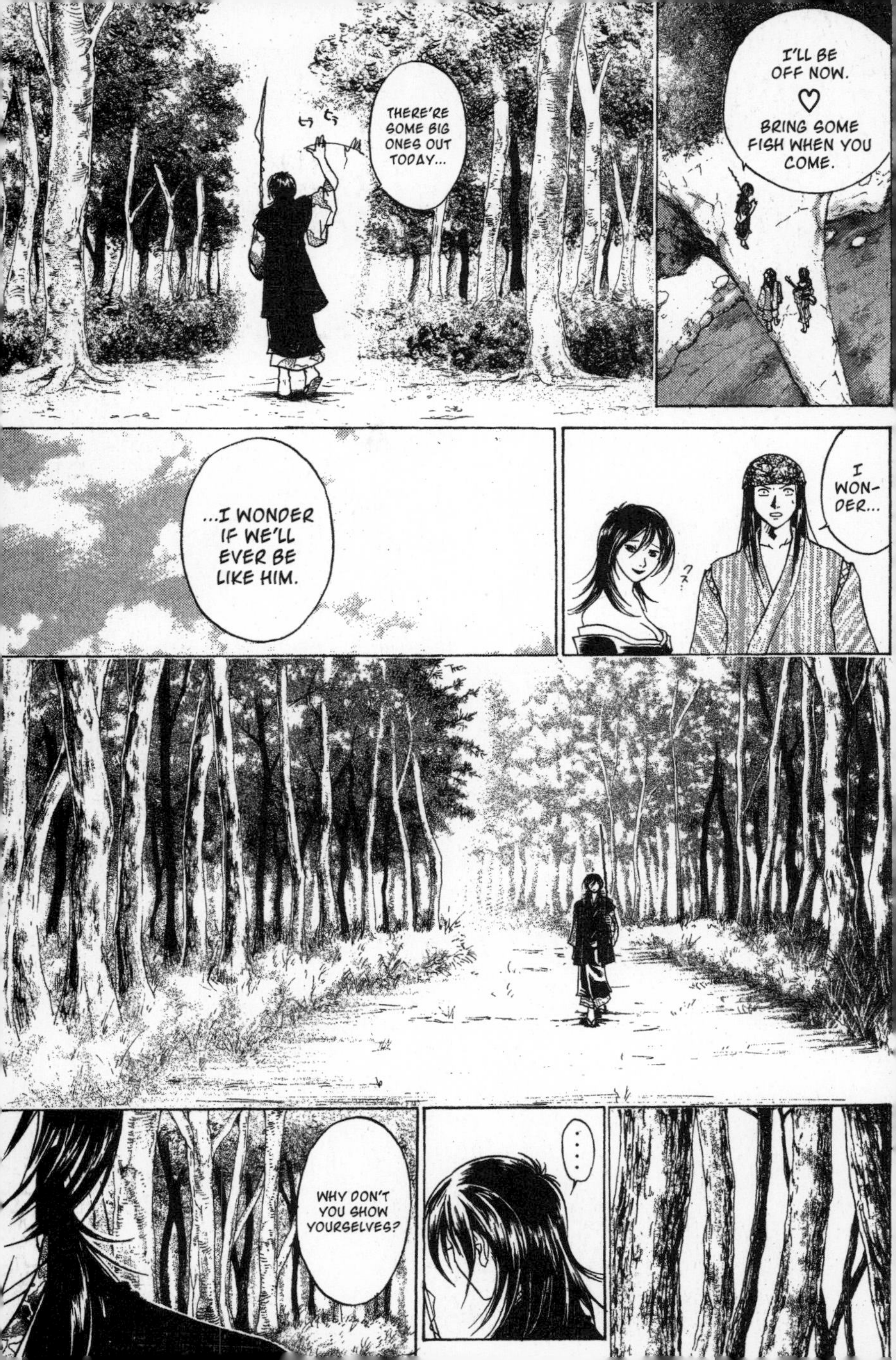
I'LL BE OFF NOW. ♡ BRING SOME FISH WHEN YOU COME.
THERE'RE SOME BIG ONES OUT TODAY...
I WON-DER...
...I WONDER IF WE'LL EVER BE LIKE HIM.
....
WHY DON'T YOU SHOW YOURSELVES?

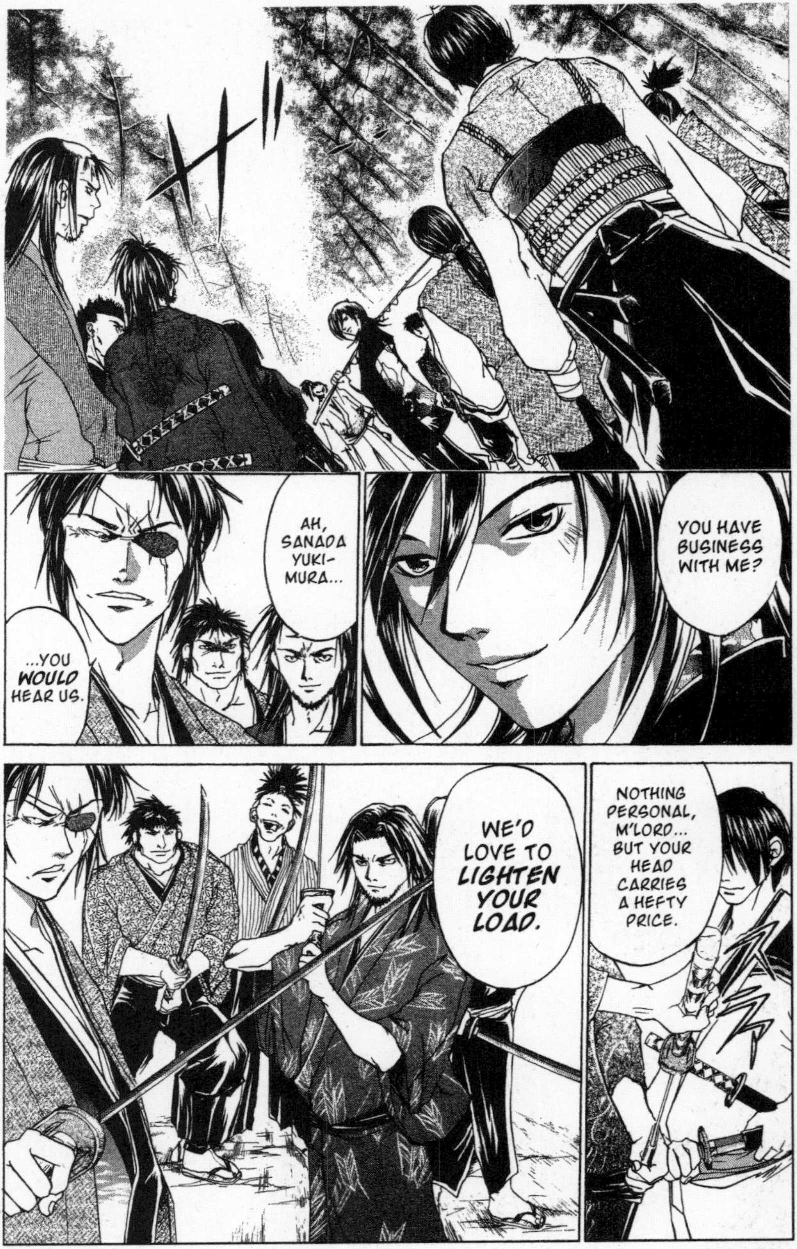
YOU HAVE BUSINESS WITH ME?
AH, SANADA YUKI-MURA...
...YOU WOULD HEAR US.
NOTHING PERSONAL, M'LORD... BUT YOUR HEAD CARRIES A HEFTY PRICE.
WE'D LOVE TO LIGHTEN YOUR LOAD.

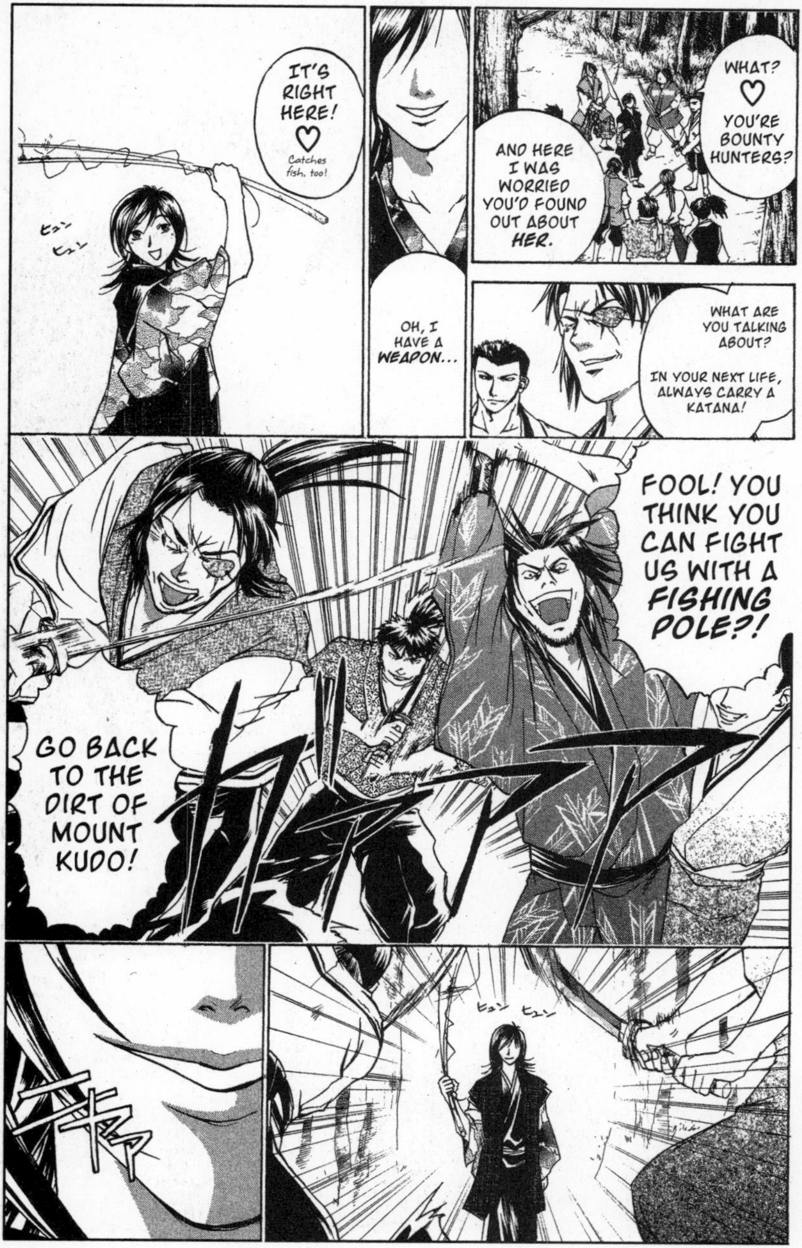
WHAT? ♡ YOU'RE BOUNTY HUNTERS?
AND HERE I WAS WORRIED YOU'D FOUND OUT ABOUT **HER.**
WHAT ARE YOU TALKING ABOUT?
IN YOUR NEXT LIFE, ALWAYS CARRY A KATANA!
OH, I HAVE A **WEAPON...**
IT'S RIGHT HERE! ♡
Catches fish, too!
ヒュン ヒュン
FOOL! YOU THINK YOU CAN FIGHT US WITH A ***FISHING POLE?!***
GO BACK TO THE DIRT OF MOUNT KUDO!
ヒュン ヒュン

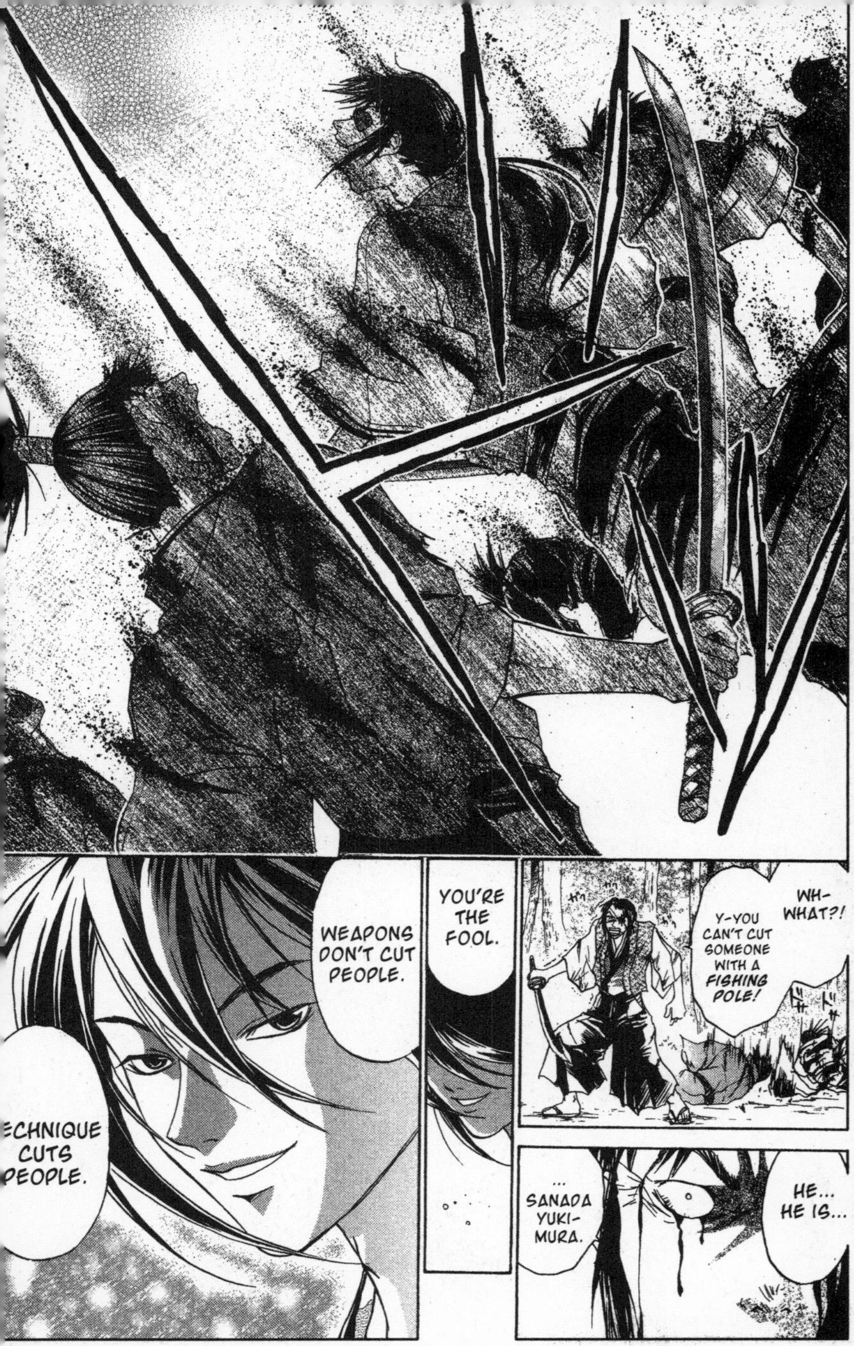
WH-WHAT?!
Y-YOU CAN'T CUT SOMEONE WITH A FISHING POLE!
HE... HE IS...
...SANADA YUKI-MURA.
YOU'RE THE FOOL.
WEAPONS DON'T CUT PEOPLE.
ECHNIQUE CUTS PEOPLE.

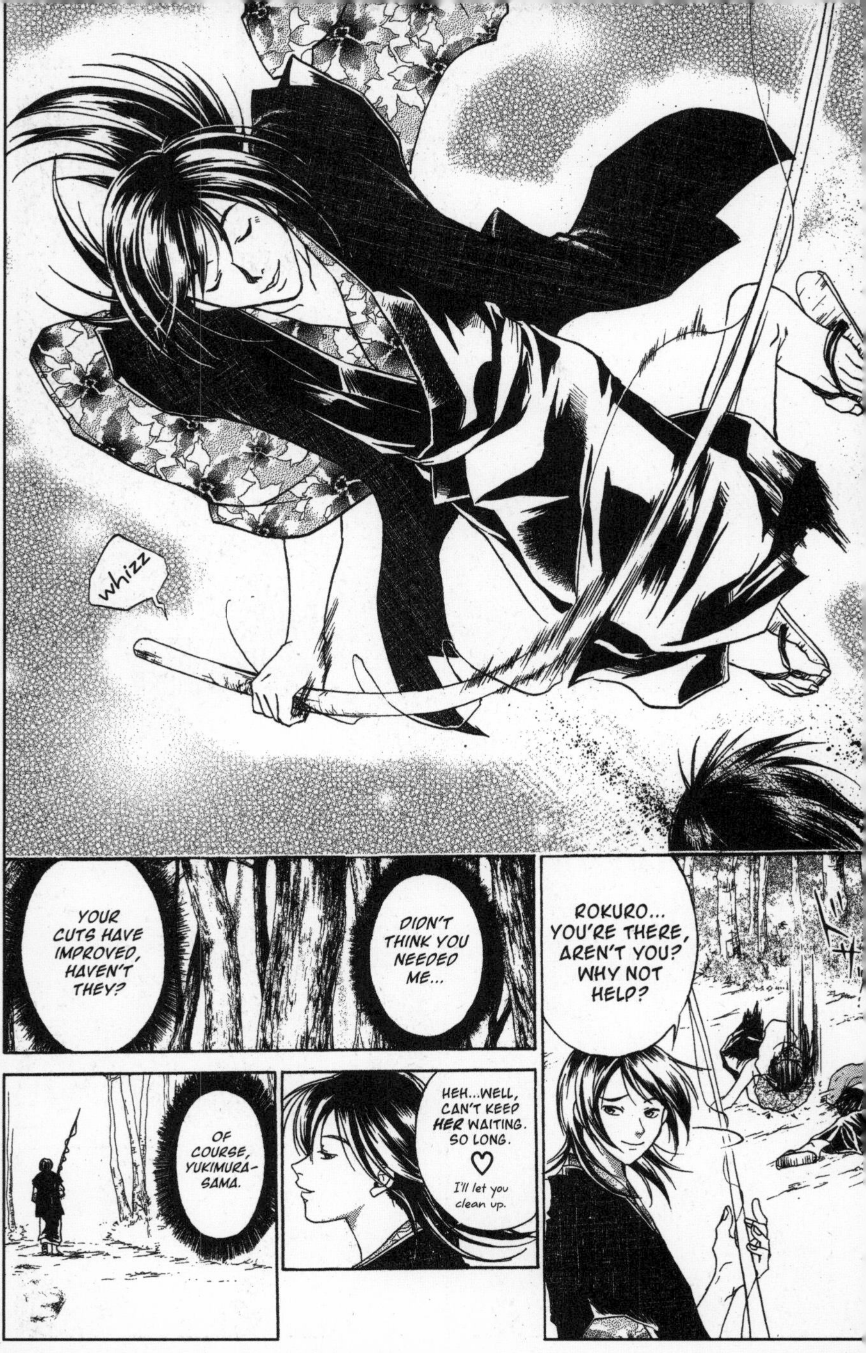
whizz
ROKURO... YOU'RE THERE, AREN'T YOU? WHY NOT HELP?
DIDN'T THINK YOU NEEDED ME...
YOUR CUTS HAVE IMPROVED, HAVEN'T THEY?
HEH...WELL, CAN'T KEEP HER WAITING. SO LONG. ♥
I'll let you clean up.
OF COURSE, YUKIMURA-SAMA.

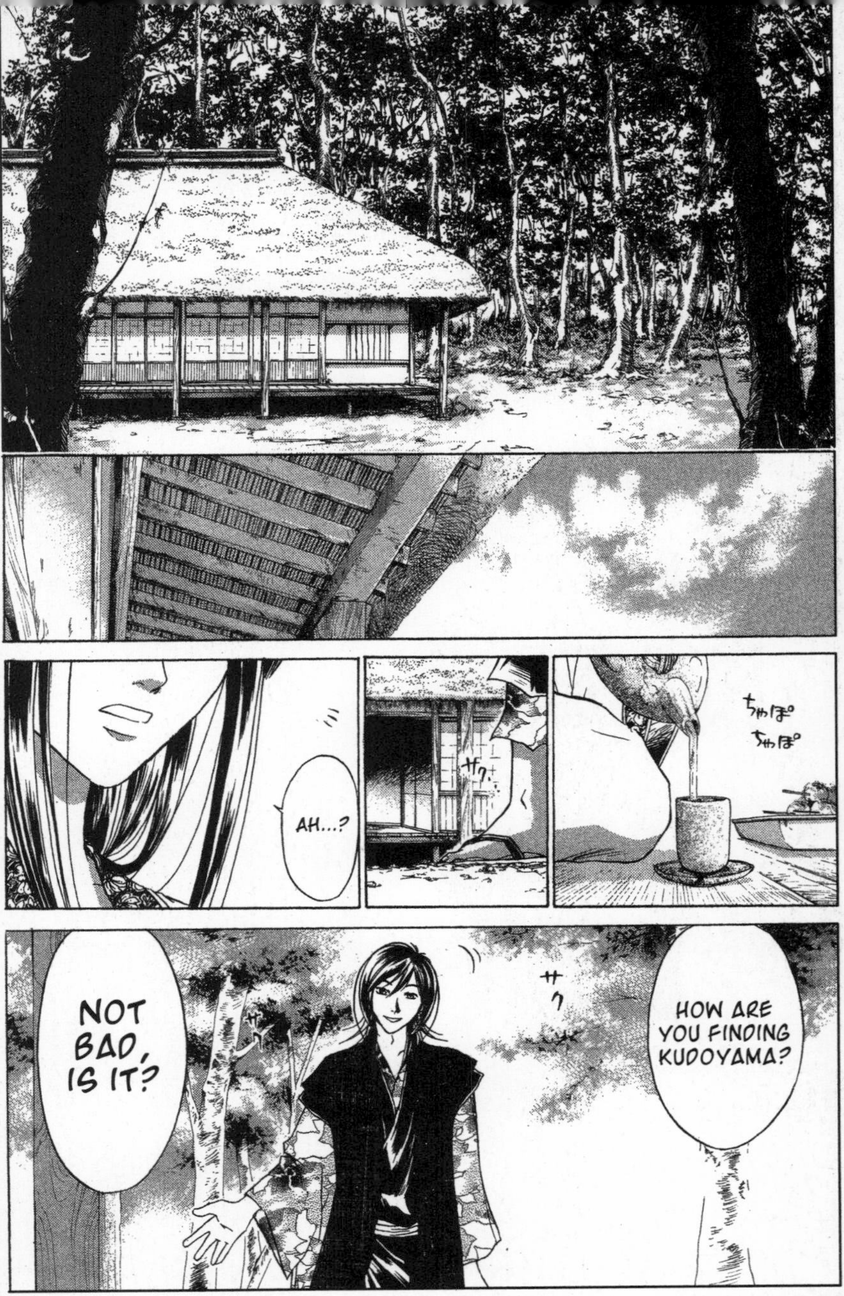
ちゃぽ
ちゃぽ
サク
AH...?
HOW ARE YOU FINDING KUDOYAMA?
サク
NOT BAD, IS IT?

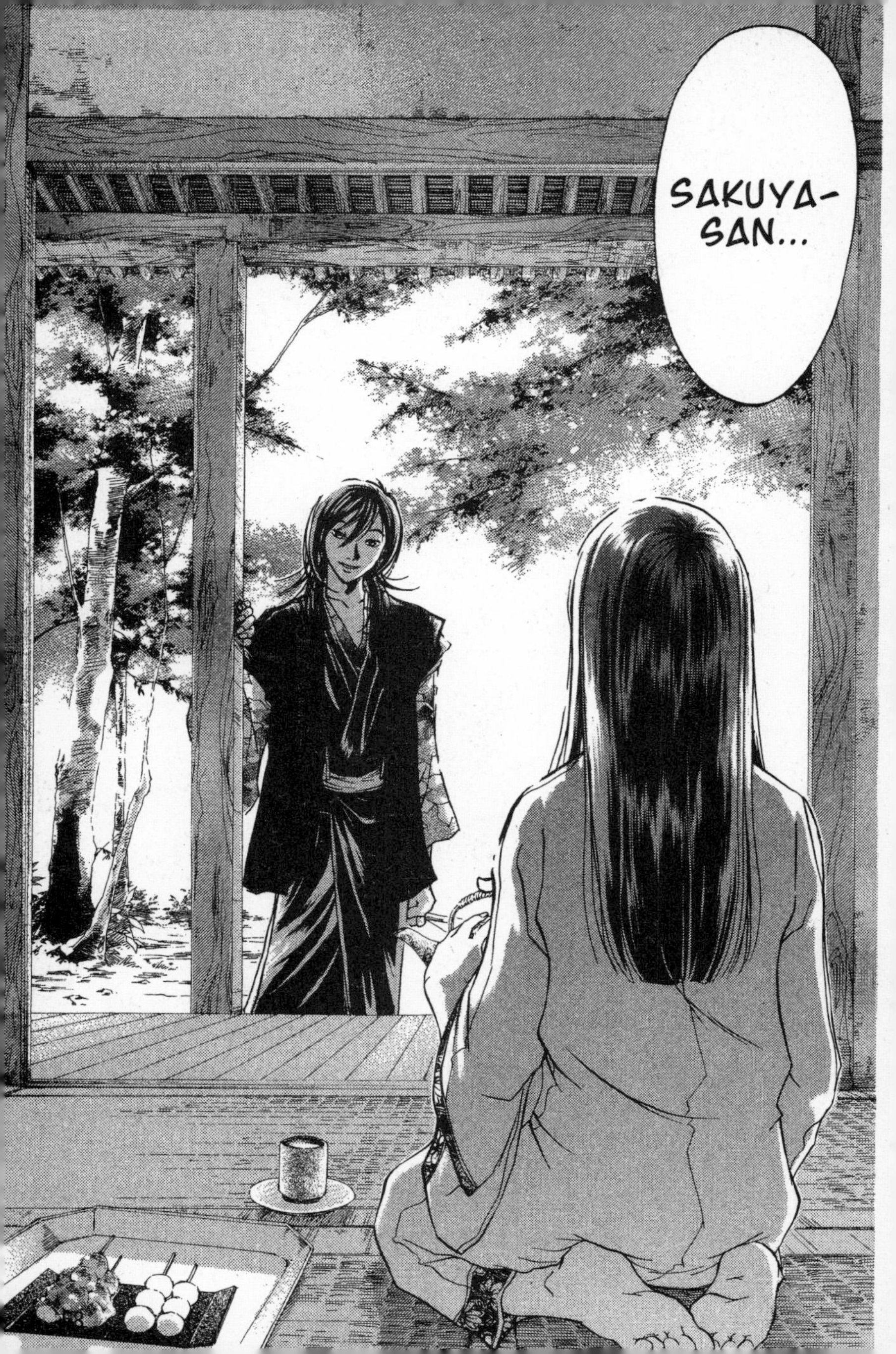
SAKUYA-SAN...

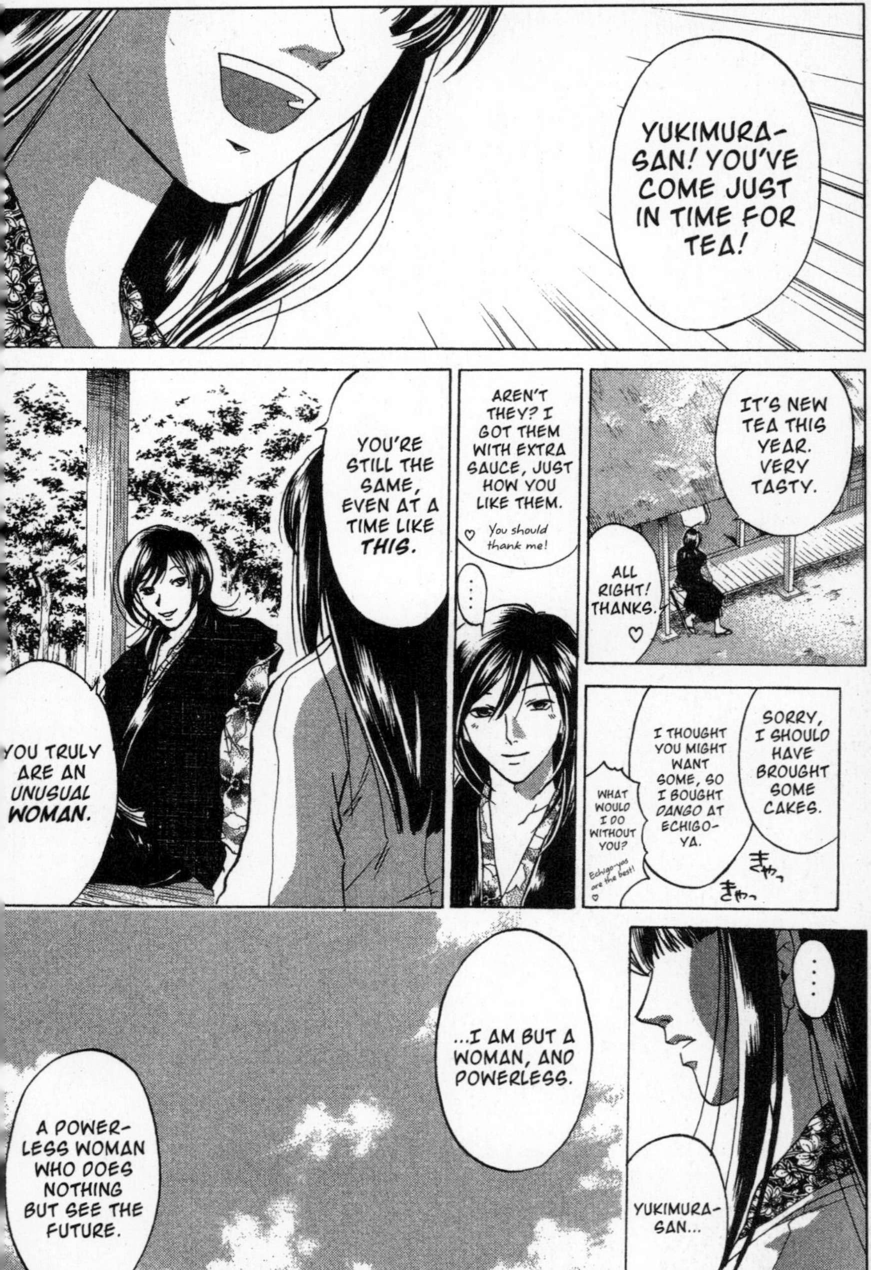
YUKIMURA-SAN! YOU'VE COME JUST IN TIME FOR TEA!
IT'S NEW TEA THIS YEAR. VERY TASTY.
ALL RIGHT! THANKS. ♡
SORRY, I SHOULD HAVE BROUGHT SOME CAKES.
I THOUGHT YOU MIGHT WANT SOME, SO I BOUGHT DANGO AT ECHIGO-YA.
WHAT WOULD I DO WITHOUT YOU?
Echigo-ya's are the best! ♡
きゃっ
きゃっ
AREN'T THEY? I GOT THEM WITH EXTRA SAUCE, JUST HOW YOU LIKE THEM.
♡ You should thank me!
....
YOU'RE STILL THE SAME, EVEN AT A TIME LIKE THIS.
YOU TRULY ARE AN UNUSUAL WOMAN.
....
YUKIMURA-SAN...
...I AM BUT A WOMAN, AND POWERLESS.
A POWER-LESS WOMAN WHO DOES NOTHING BUT SEE THE FUTURE.

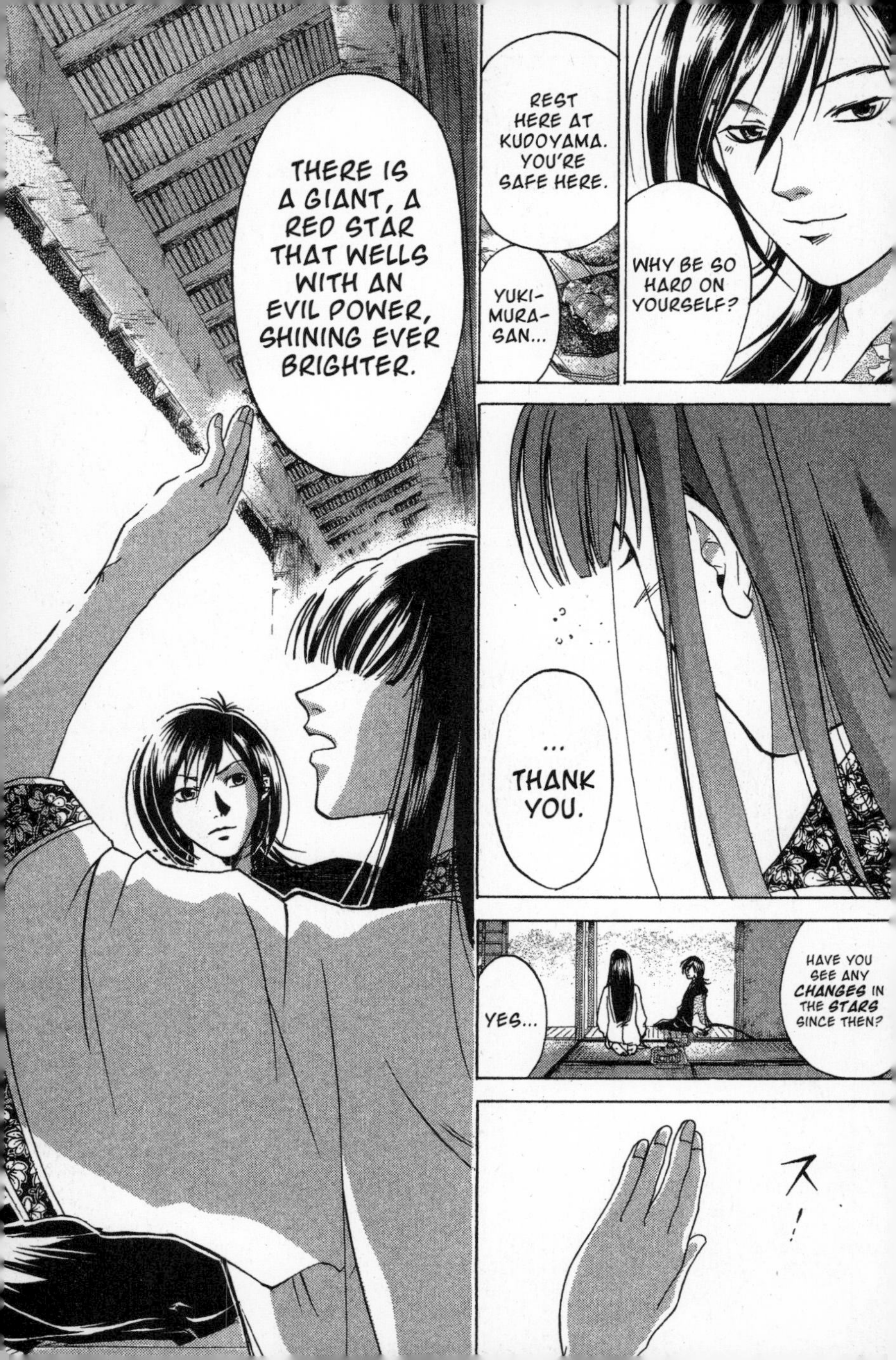
WHY BE SO HARD ON YOURSELF?
REST HERE AT KUDOYAMA. YOU'RE SAFE HERE.
YUKI-MURA-SAN...
... THANK YOU.
HAVE YOU SEE ANY **CHANGES** IN THE **STARS** SINCE THEN?
YES...
ス!
THERE IS A GIANT, A RED STAR THAT WELLS WITH AN EVIL POWER, SHINING EVER BRIGHTER.

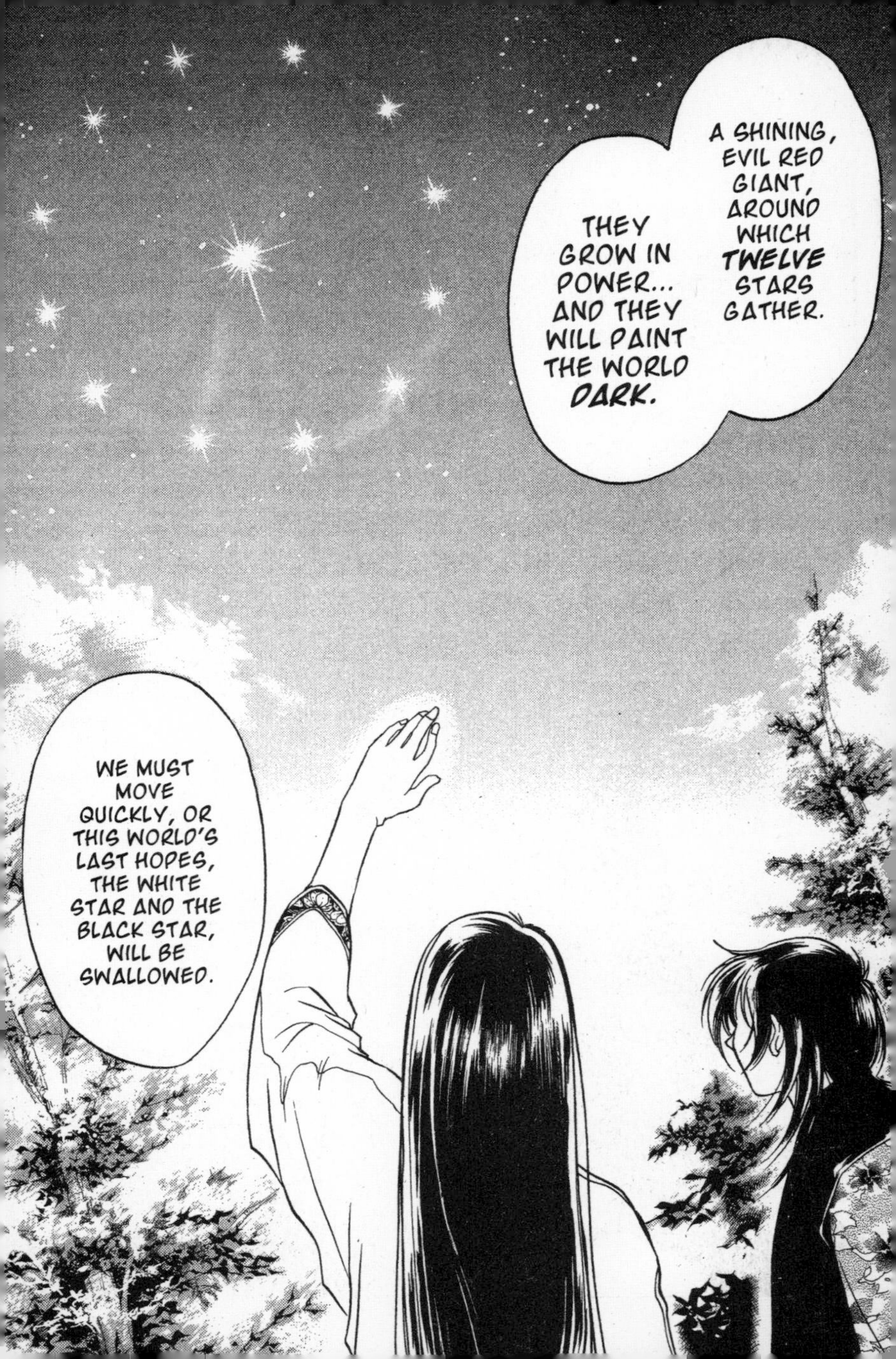
A SHINING, EVIL RED GIANT, AROUND WHICH TWELVE STARS GATHER.
THEY GROW IN POWER... AND THEY WILL PAINT THE WORLD DARK.
WE MUST MOVE QUICKLY, OR THIS WORLD'S LAST HOPES, THE WHITE STAR AND THE BLACK STAR, WILL BE SWALLOWED.

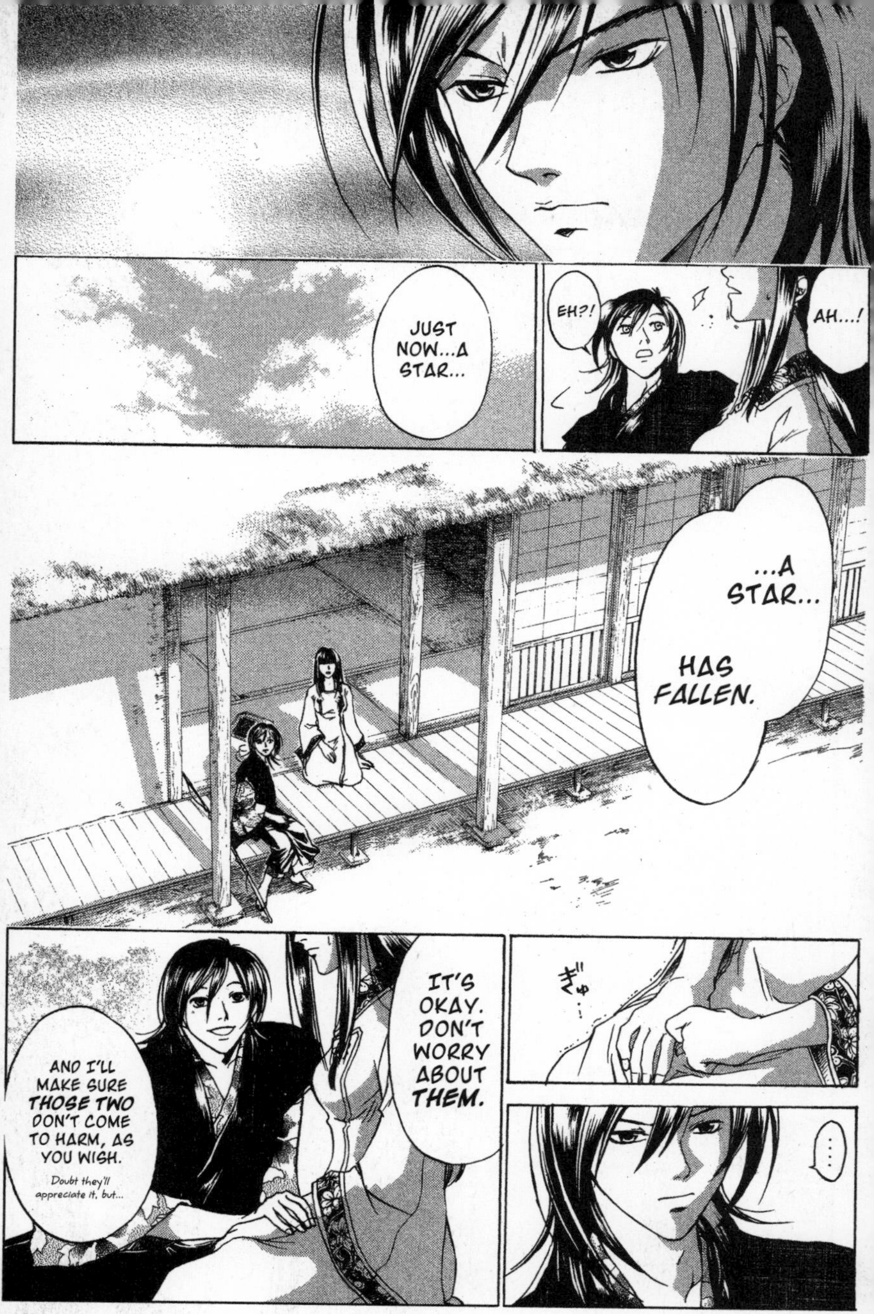
AH...!
EH?!
JUST NOW...A STAR...
...A STAR... HAS FALLEN.
ぎゅ...
....
IT'S OKAY. DON'T WORRY ABOUT THEM.
AND I'LL MAKE SURE THOSE TWO DON'T COME TO HARM, AS YOU WISH.
Doubt they'll appreciate it, but...

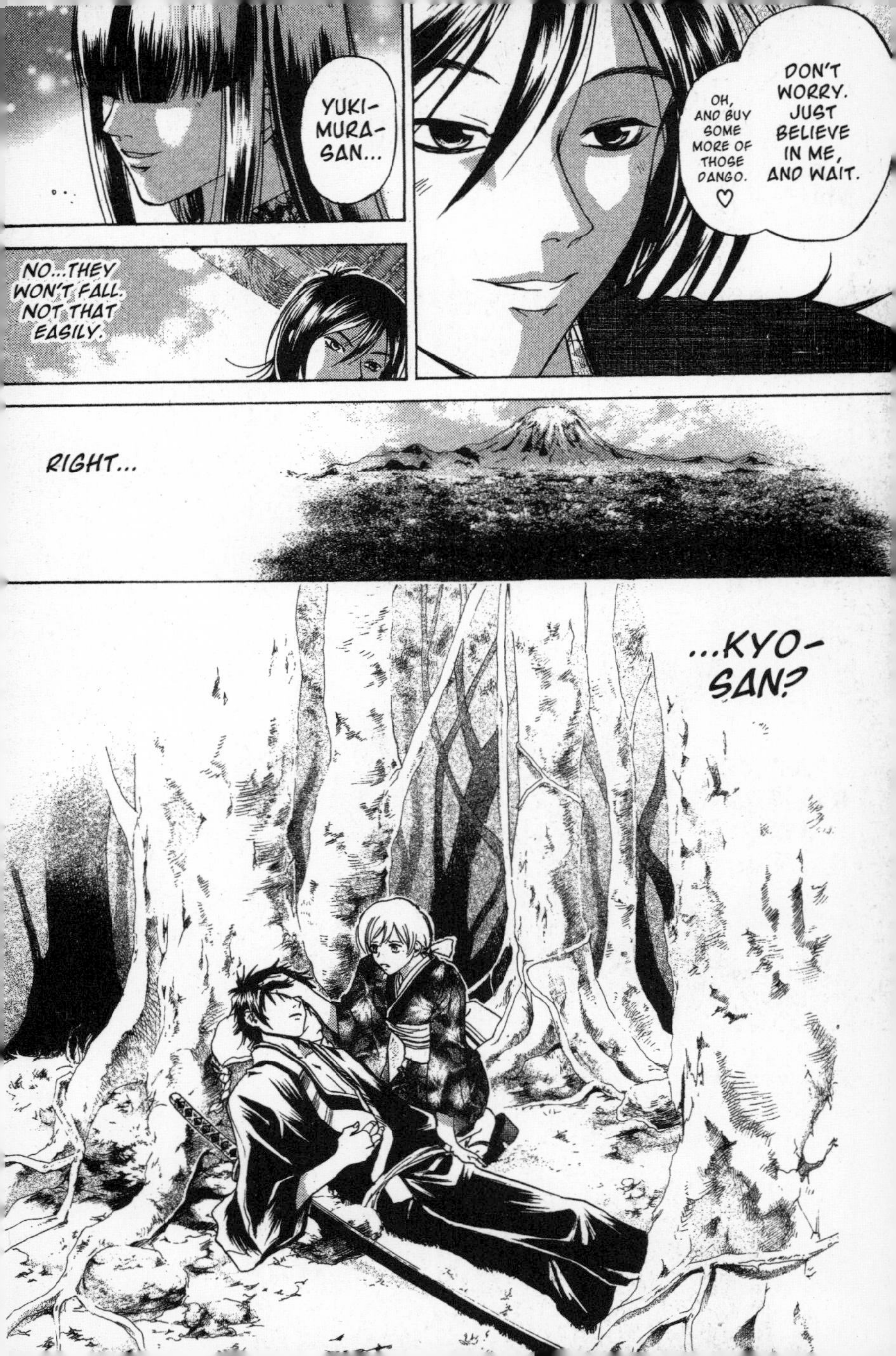
DON'T WORRY. JUST BELIEVE IN ME, AND WAIT.
OH, AND BUY SOME MORE OF THOSE DANGO. ♡
YUKI-MURA-SAN...
...
NO...THEY WON'T FALL. NOT THAT EASILY.
RIGHT...
...KYO-SAN?

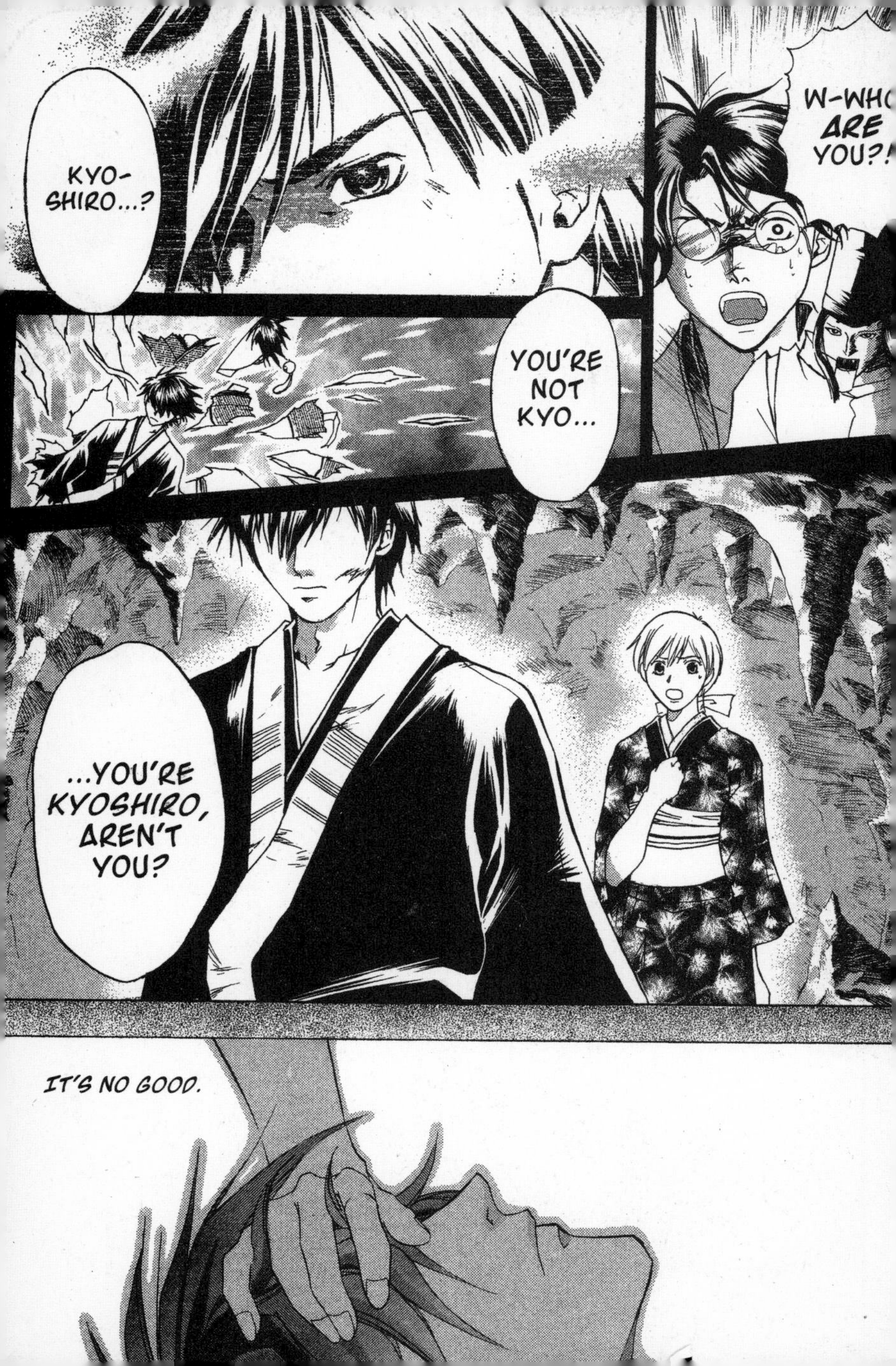
W-WHO ARE YOU?!
KYO-SHIRO...?
YOU'RE NOT KYO...
...YOU'RE KYOSHIRO, AREN'T YOU?
IT'S NO GOOD.

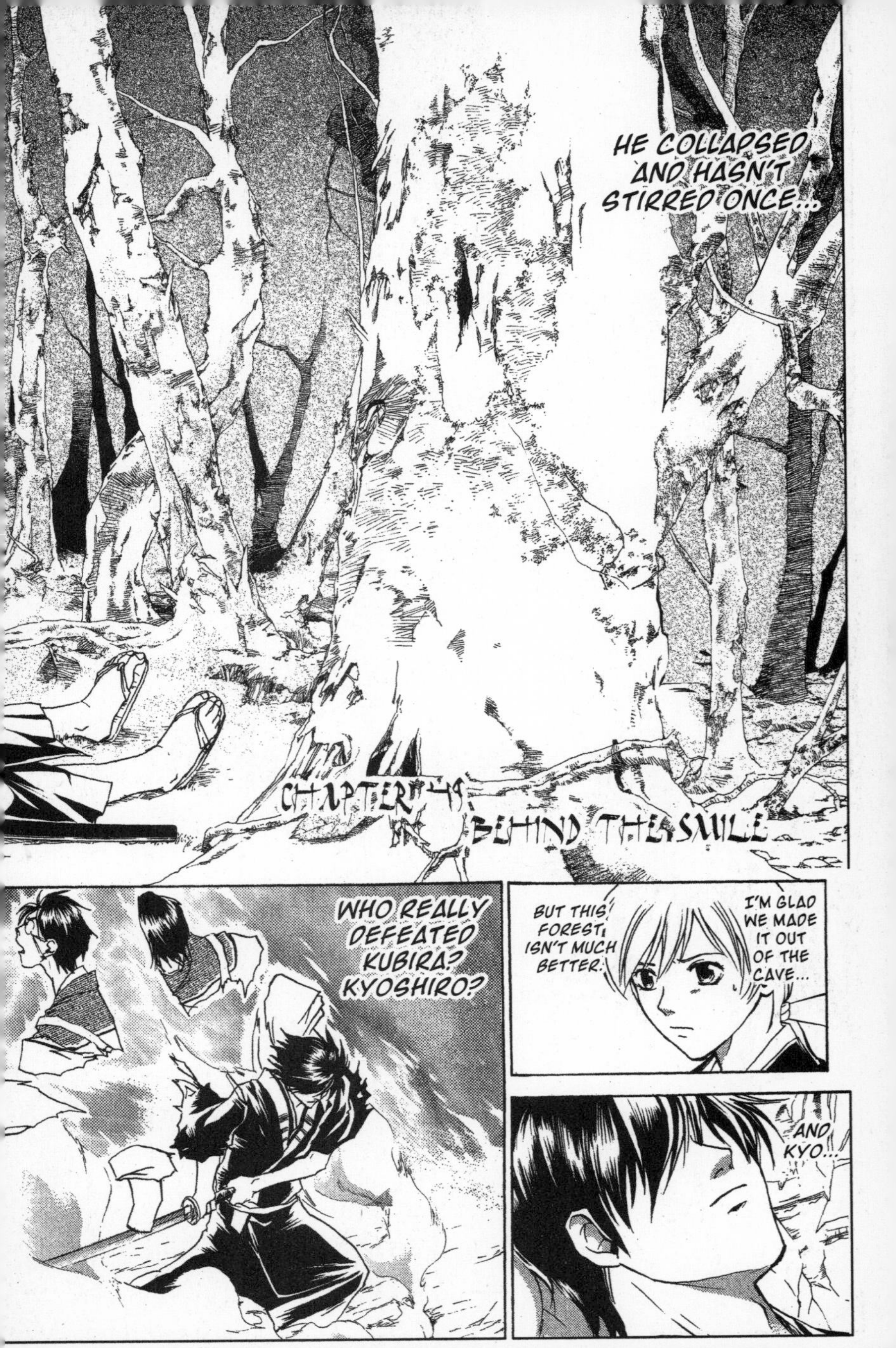
HE COLLAPSED AND HASN'T STIRRED ONCE...
CHAPTER 49
BEHIND THE SMILE
I'M GLAD WE MADE IT OUT OF THE CAVE...
BUT THIS FOREST ISN'T MUCH BETTER.
AND KYO...
WHO REALLY DEFEATED KUBIRA? KYOSHIRO?

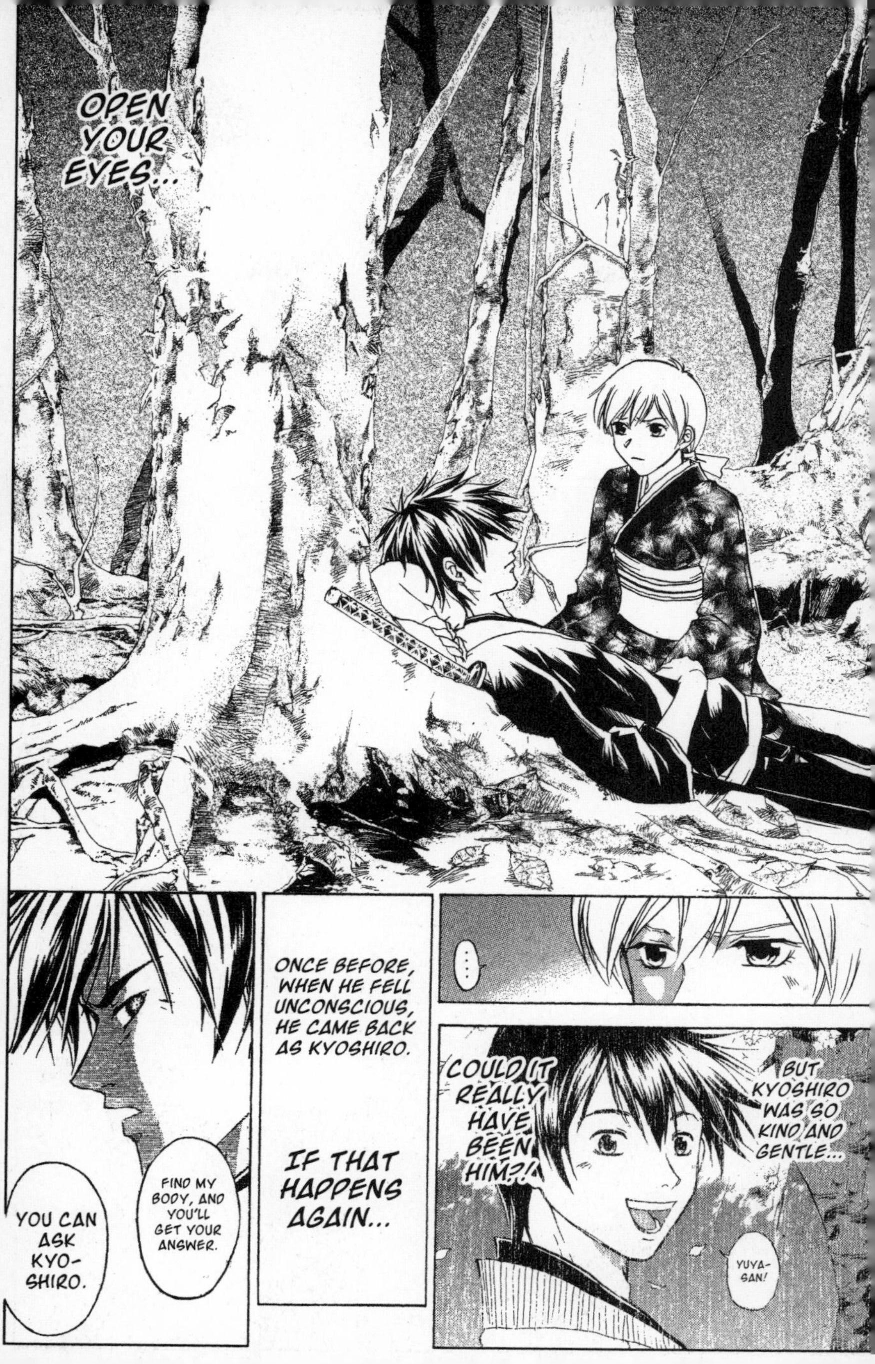
OPEN YOUR EYES...
...
BUT KYOSHIRO WAS SO KIND AND GENTLE...
COULD IT REALLY HAVE BEEN HIM?!
YUYA-SAN!
ONCE BEFORE, WHEN HE FELL UNCONSCIOUS, HE CAME BACK AS KYOSHIRO.
IF THAT HAPPENS AGAIN...
FIND MY BODY, AND YOU'LL GET YOUR ANSWER.
YOU CAN ASK KYO-SHIRO.

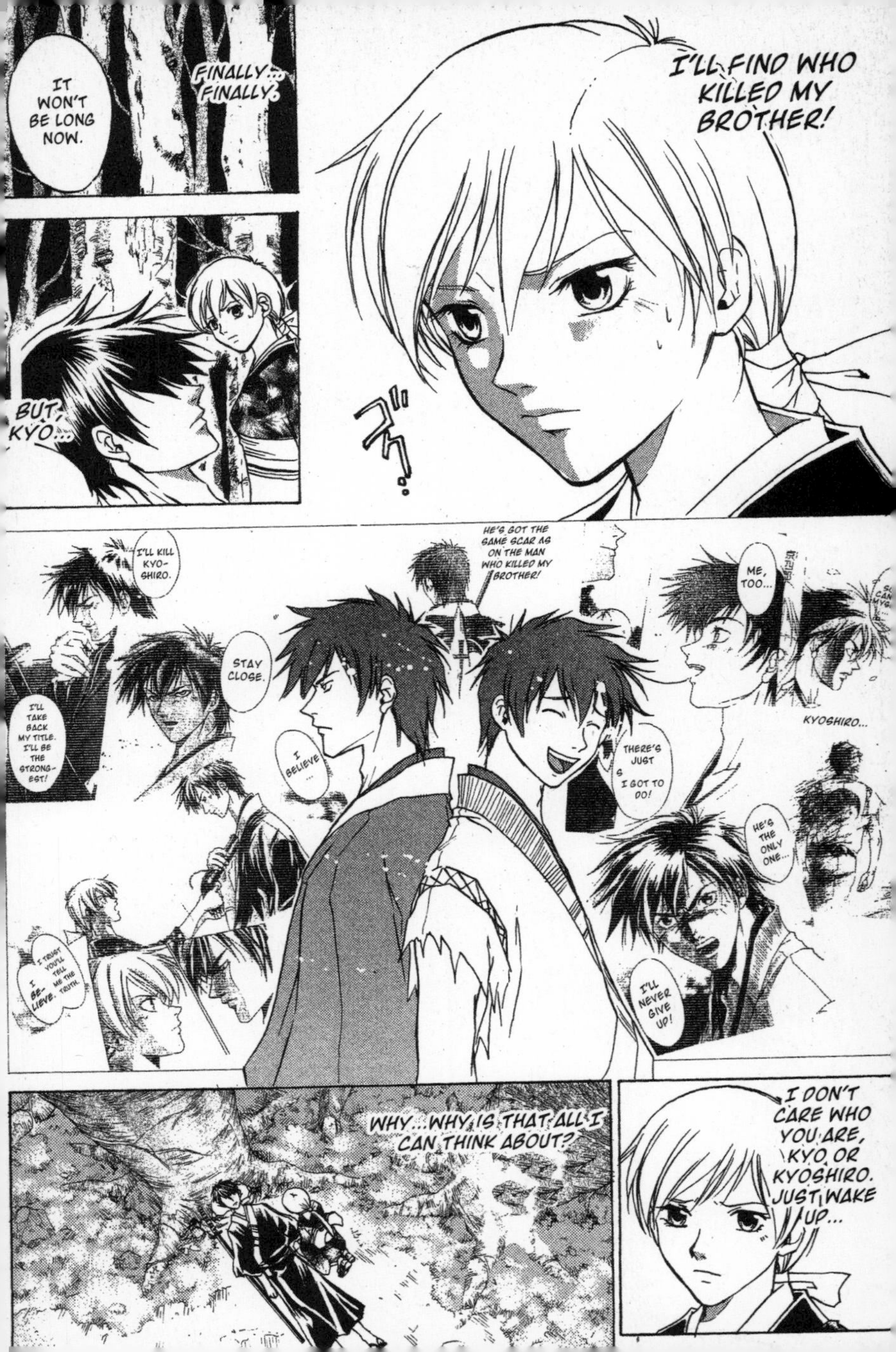

I'LL FIND WHO KILLED MY BROTHER!
FINALLY... FINALLY.
IT WON'T BE LONG NOW.
BUT, KYO...
ME, TOO...
KYOSHIRO...
HE'S GOT THE SAME SCAR AS ON THE MAN WHO KILLED MY BROTHER!
THERE'S JUST S I GOT TO DO!
HE'S THE ONLY ONE...
I'LL NEVER GIVE UP!
STAY CLOSE.
I BELIEVE...
I'LL KILL KYO-SHIRO.
I'LL TAKE BACK MY TITLE. I'LL BE THE STRONG-EST!
I TRUST YOU'LL TELL ME THE TRUTH.
I BE-LIEVE.
I DON'T CARE WHO YOU ARE, KYO OR KYOSHIRO. JUST WAKE UP...
WHY...WHY IS THAT ALL I CAN THINK ABOUT?

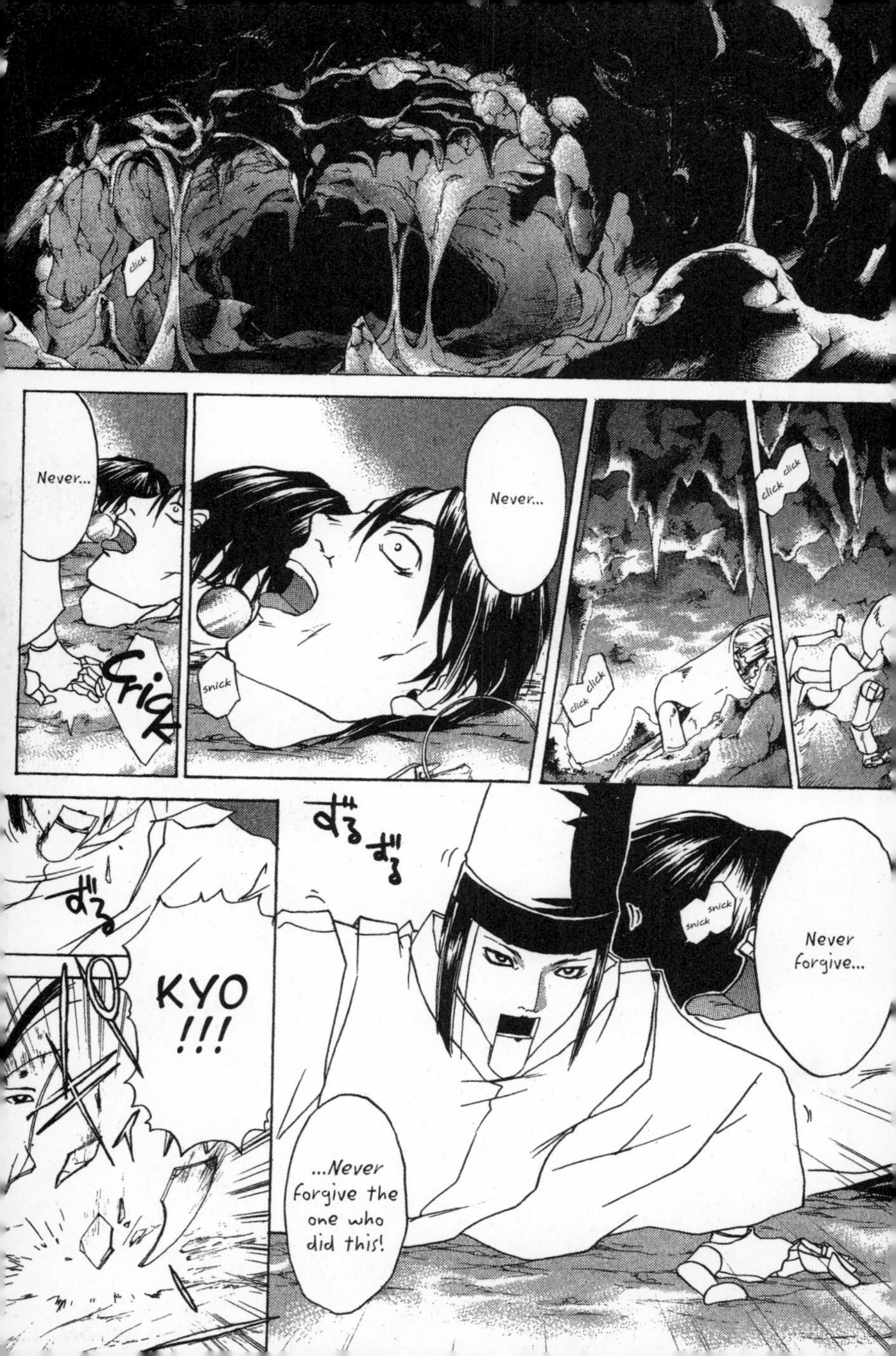
click
click click
click click
Never...
snick
Never...
CRICK
Never forgive...
snick snick
ずる ずる
...Never forgive the one who did this!
ずる
KYO !!!

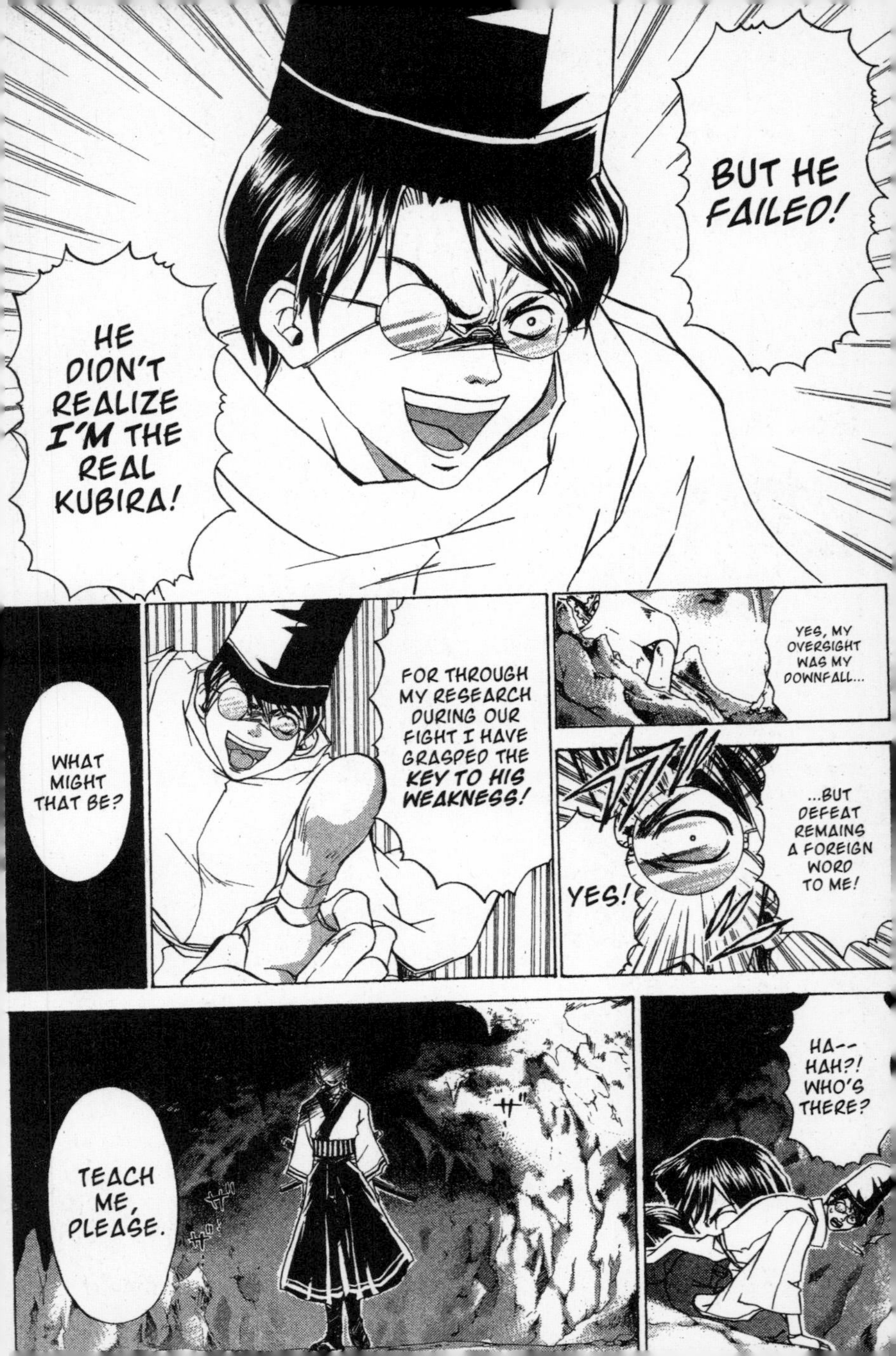
BUT HE FAILED!
HE DIDN'T REALIZE *I'M* THE REAL KUBIRA!
YES, MY OVERSIGHT WAS MY DOWNFALL...
...BUT DEFEAT REMAINS A FOREIGN WORD TO ME!
YES!
FOR THROUGH MY RESEARCH DURING OUR FIGHT I HAVE GRASPED THE **KEY TO HIS WEAKNESS!**
WHAT MIGHT THAT BE?
HA-- HAH?! WHO'S THERE?
TEACH ME, PLEASE.

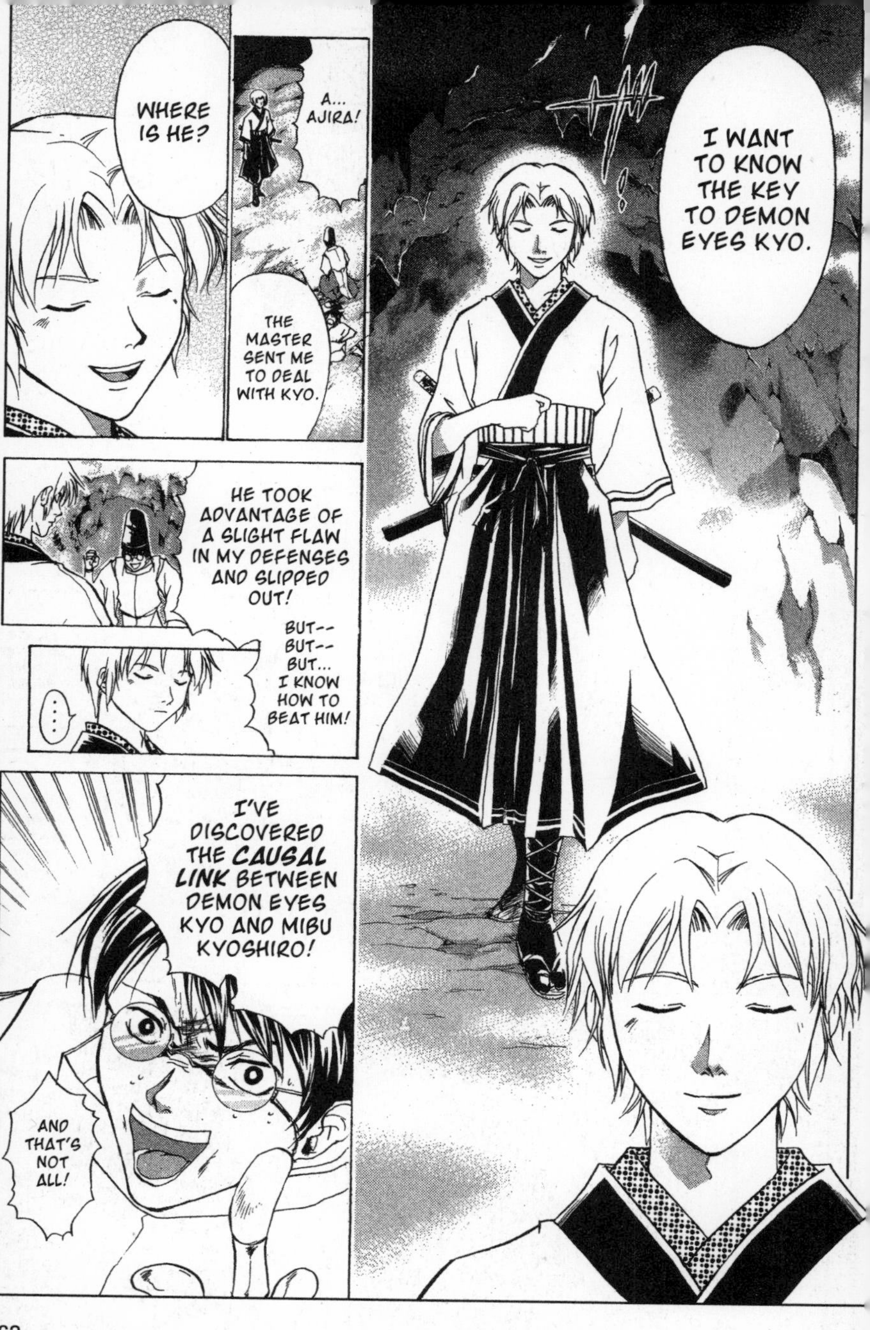
I WANT TO KNOW THE KEY TO DEMON EYES KYO.
A... AJIRA!
THE MASTER SENT ME TO DEAL WITH KYO.
WHERE IS HE?
HE TOOK ADVANTAGE OF A SLIGHT FLAW IN MY DEFENSES AND SLIPPED OUT!
BUT-- BUT-- BUT... I KNOW HOW TO BEAT HIM!
...
I'VE DISCOVERED THE ***CAUSAL LINK*** BETWEEN DEMON EYES KYO AND MIBU KYOSHIRO!
AND THAT'S NOT ALL!

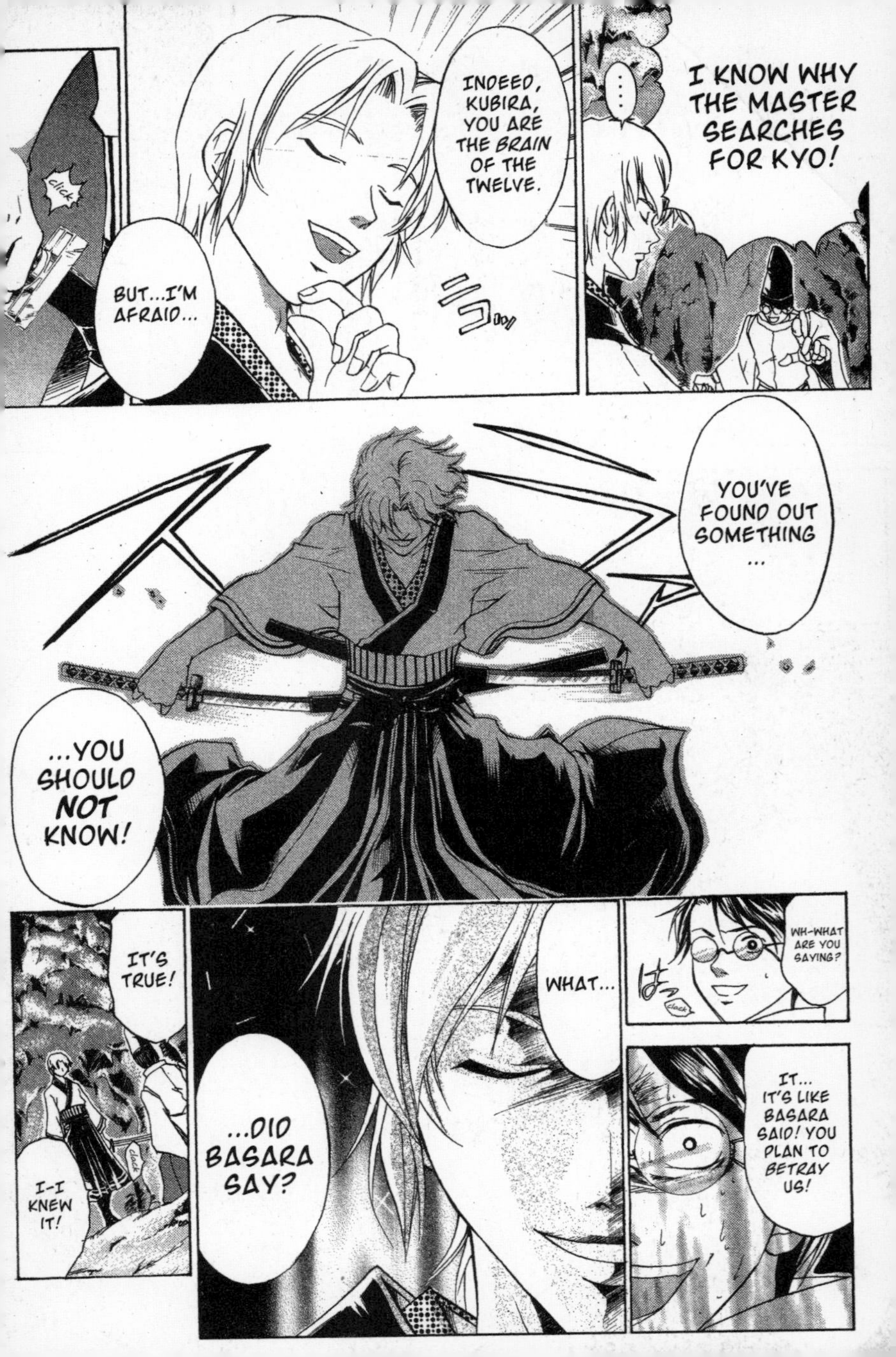

I KNOW WHY THE MASTER SEARCHES FOR KYO!
...
INDEED, KUBIRA, YOU ARE THE *BRAIN* OF THE TWELVE.
ニコッ
BUT...I'M AFRAID...
click
YOU'VE FOUND OUT SOMETHING ...
...YOU SHOULD **NOT** KNOW!
WH-WHAT ARE YOU SAYING?
はっ
clack
IT... IT'S LIKE BASARA SAID! YOU PLAN TO *BETRAY* US!
WHAT...
...DID BASARA SAY?
IT'S TRUE!
clack
I-I KNEW IT!

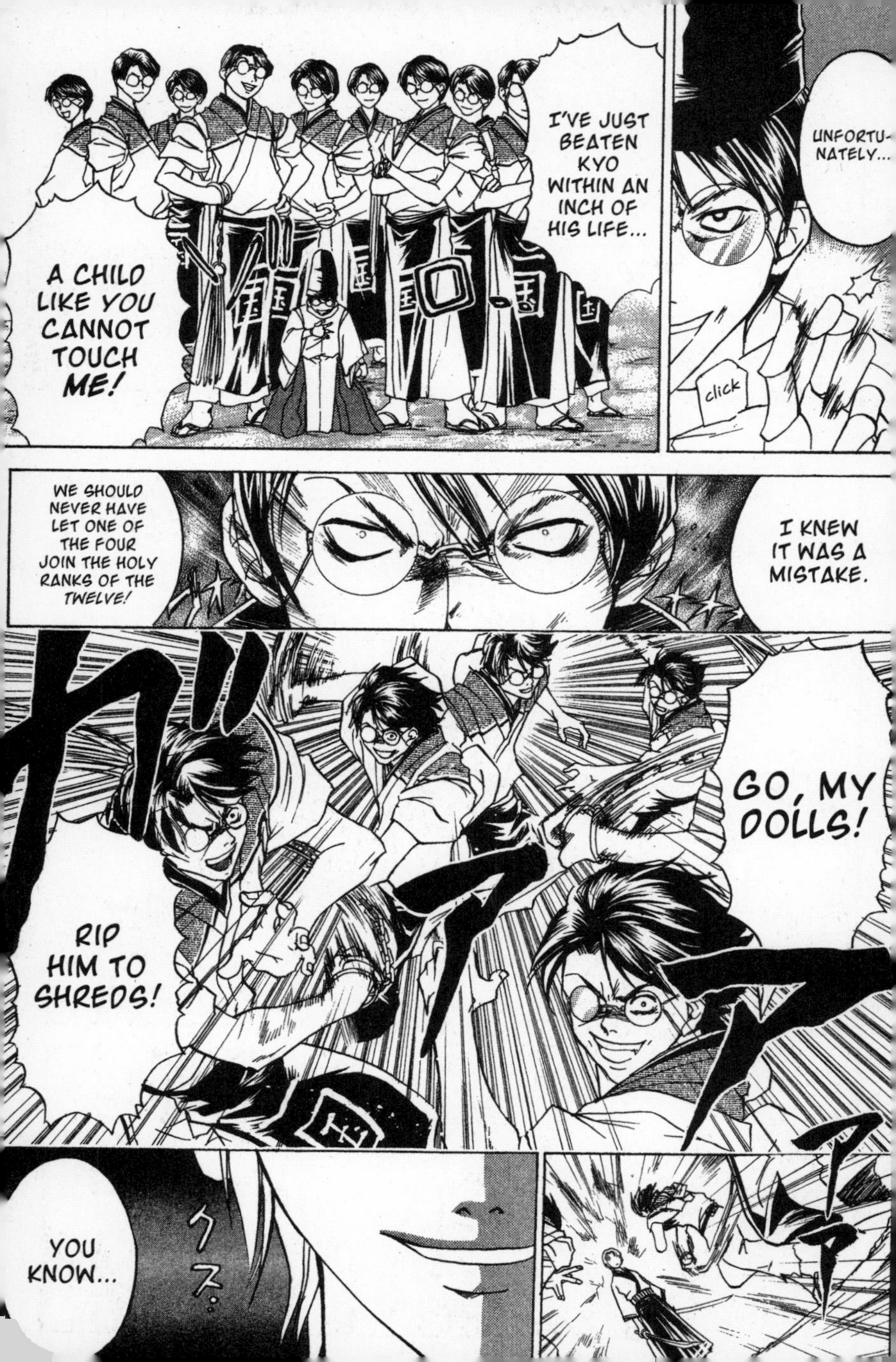

UNFORTUNATELY...
click
I'VE JUST BEATEN KYO WITHIN AN INCH OF HIS LIFE...
A CHILD LIKE YOU CANNOT TOUCH ME!
I KNEW IT WAS A MISTAKE.
WE SHOULD NEVER HAVE LET ONE OF THE FOUR JOIN THE HOLY RANKS OF THE TWELVE!
GO, MY DOLLS!
RIP HIM TO SHREDS!
YOU KNOW...

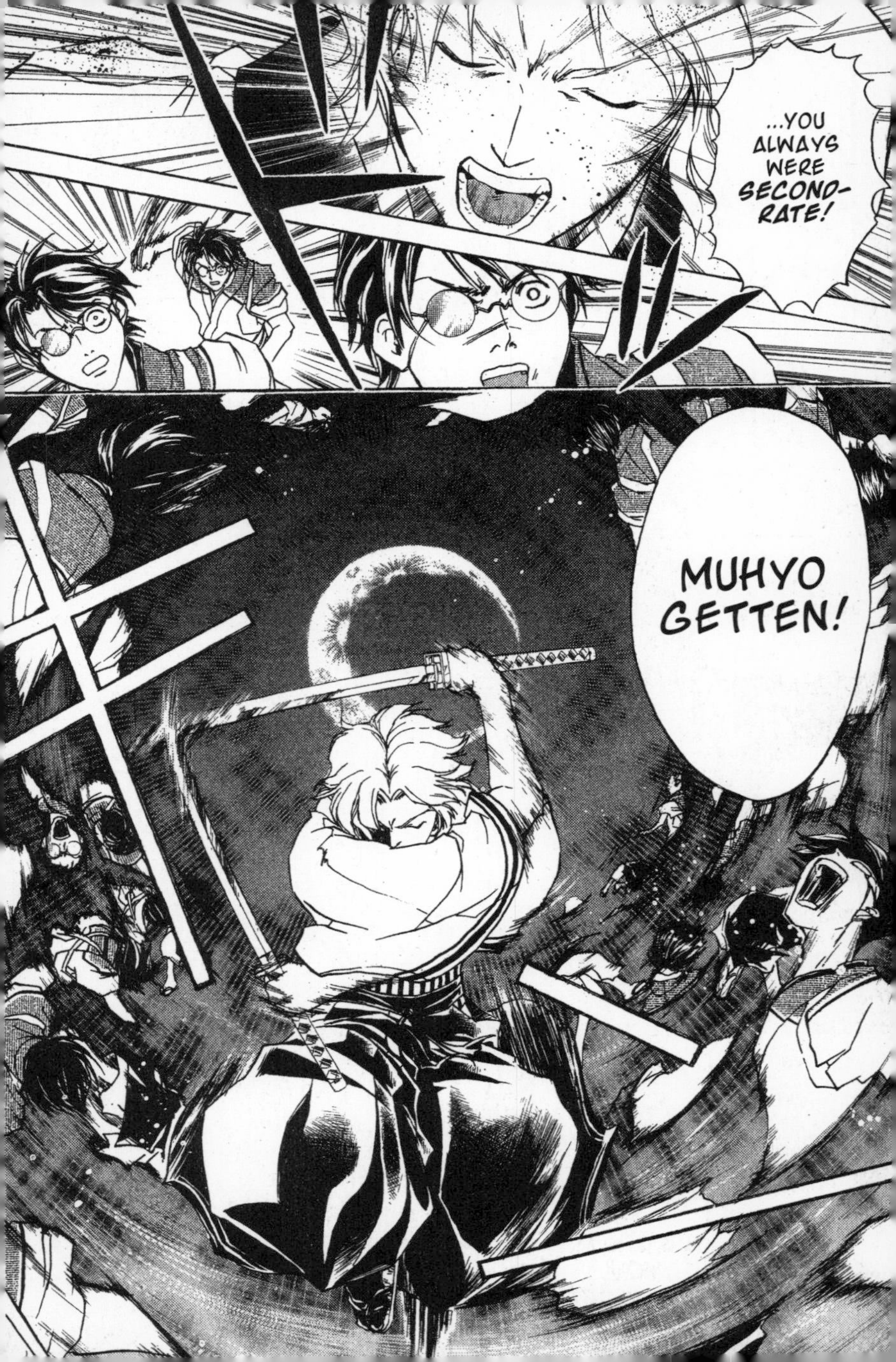
...YOU ALWAYS WERE SECOND-RATE!
MUHYO GETTEN!

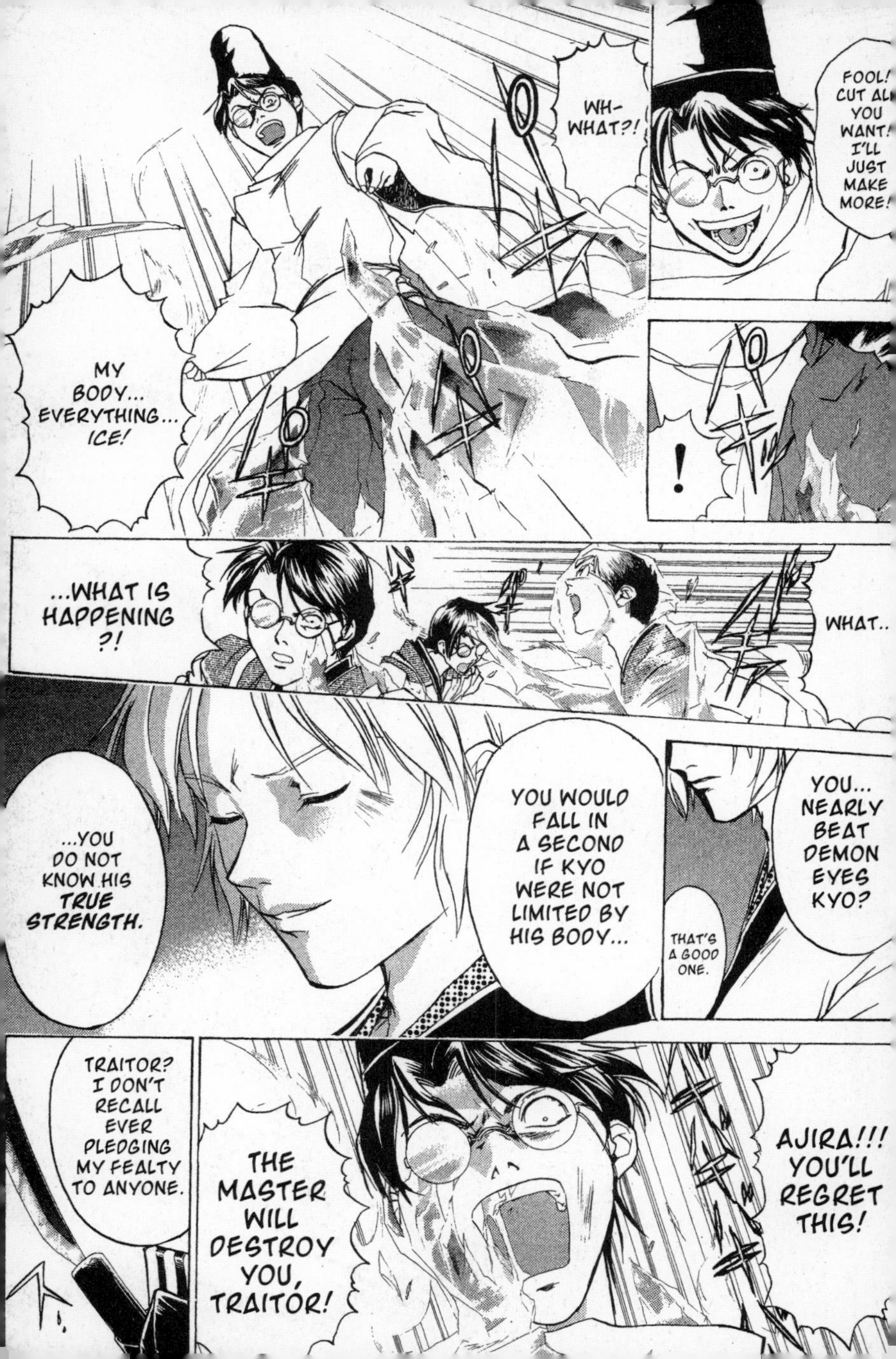
FOOL! CUT ALL YOU WANT! I'LL JUST MAKE MORE!
!
WH- WHAT?!
MY BODY... EVERYTHING... ICE!
WHAT..
...WHAT IS HAPPENING ?!
YOU... NEARLY BEAT DEMON EYES KYO?
THAT'S A GOOD ONE.
YOU WOULD FALL IN A SECOND IF KYO WERE NOT LIMITED BY HIS BODY...
...YOU DO NOT KNOW HIS **TRUE STRENGTH.**
AJIRA!!! YOU'LL REGRET THIS!
THE MASTER WILL DESTROY YOU, TRAITOR!
TRAITOR? I DON'T RECALL EVER PLEDGING MY FEALTY TO ANYONE.

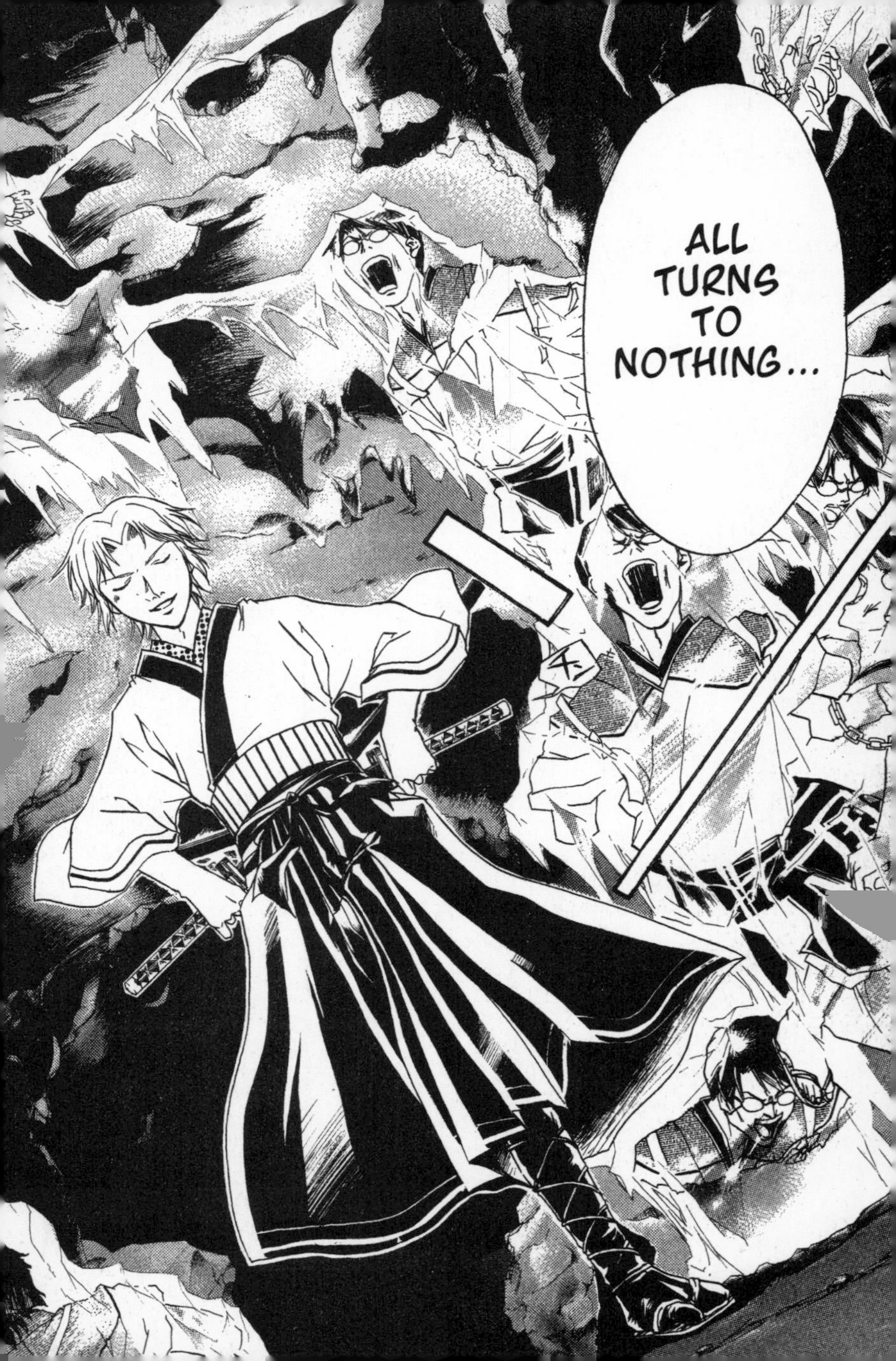
ALL TURNS TO NOTHING...

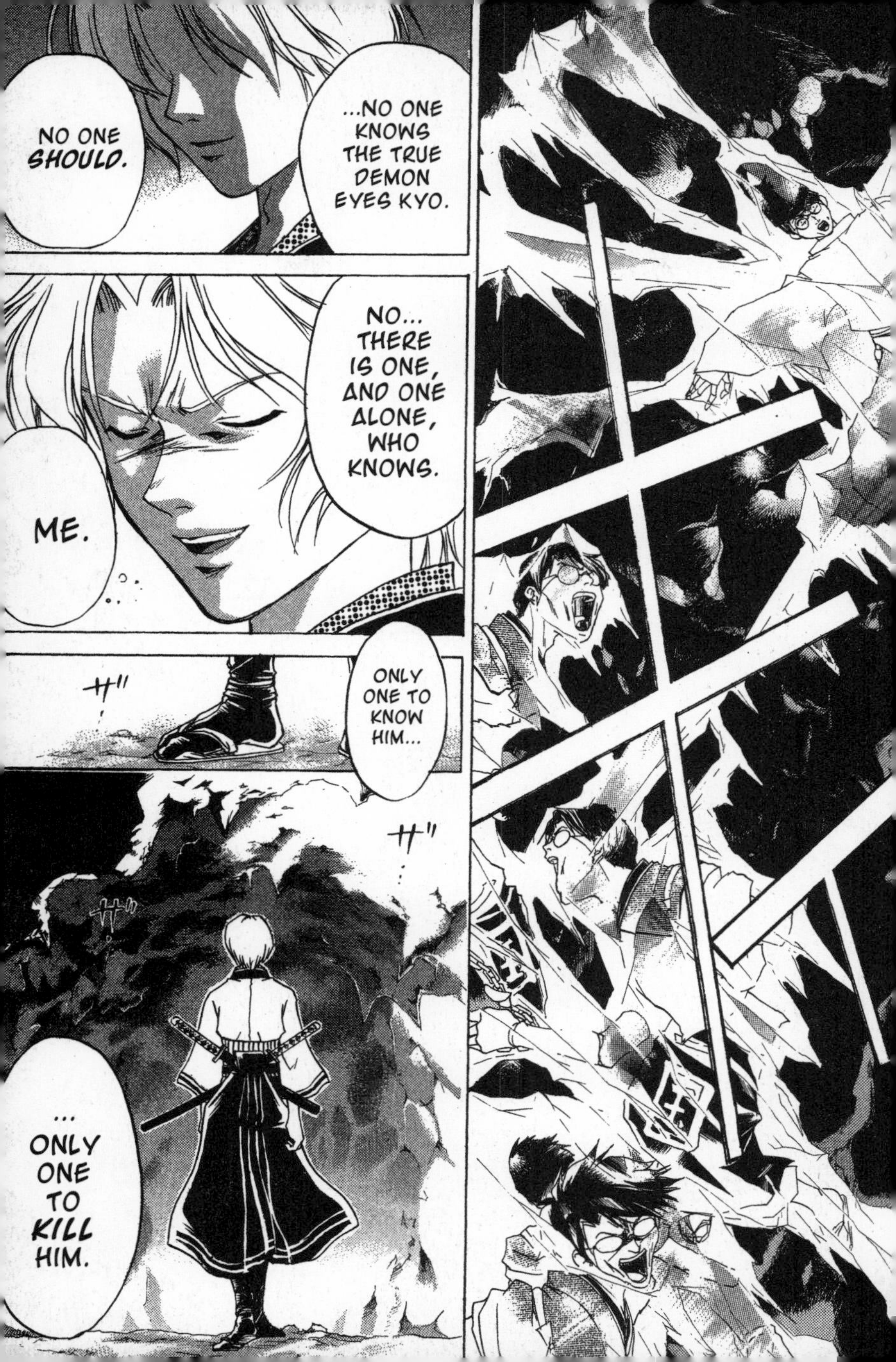
...NO ONE KNOWS THE TRUE DEMON EYES KYO.
NO ONE SHOULD.
NO... THERE IS ONE, AND ONE ALONE, WHO KNOWS.
ME.
ONLY ONE TO KNOW HIM...
... ONLY ONE TO KILL HIM.

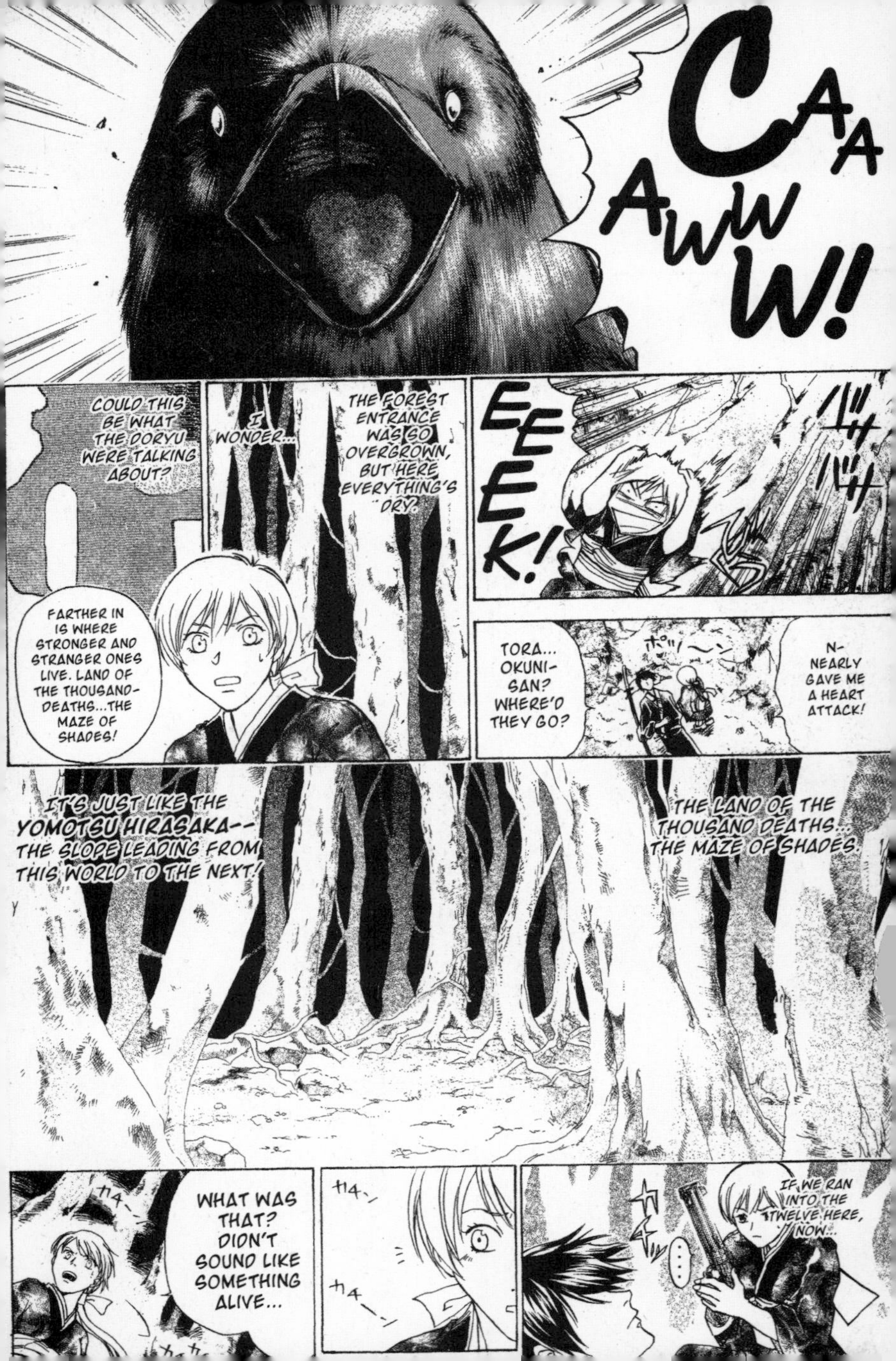
CAAAWWW!
EEEEK!
N-NEARLY GAVE ME A HEART ATTACK!
TORA... OKUNI-SAN? WHERE'D THEY GO?
THE FOREST ENTRANCE WAS SO OVERGROWN, BUT HERE EVERYTHING'S DRY.
I WONDER...
COULD THIS BE WHAT THE DORYU WERE TALKING ABOUT?
FARTHER IN IS WHERE STRONGER AND STRANGER ONES LIVE. LAND OF THE THOUSAND-DEATHS...THE MAZE OF SHADES!
THE LAND OF THE THOUSAND DEATHS... THE MAZE OF SHADES.
IT'S JUST LIKE THE YOMOTSU HIRASAKA-- THE SLOPE LEADING FROM THIS WORLD TO THE NEXT!
IF WE RAN INTO THE TWELVE HERE, NOW...
...
WHAT WAS THAT? DIDN'T SOUND LIKE SOMETHING ALIVE...

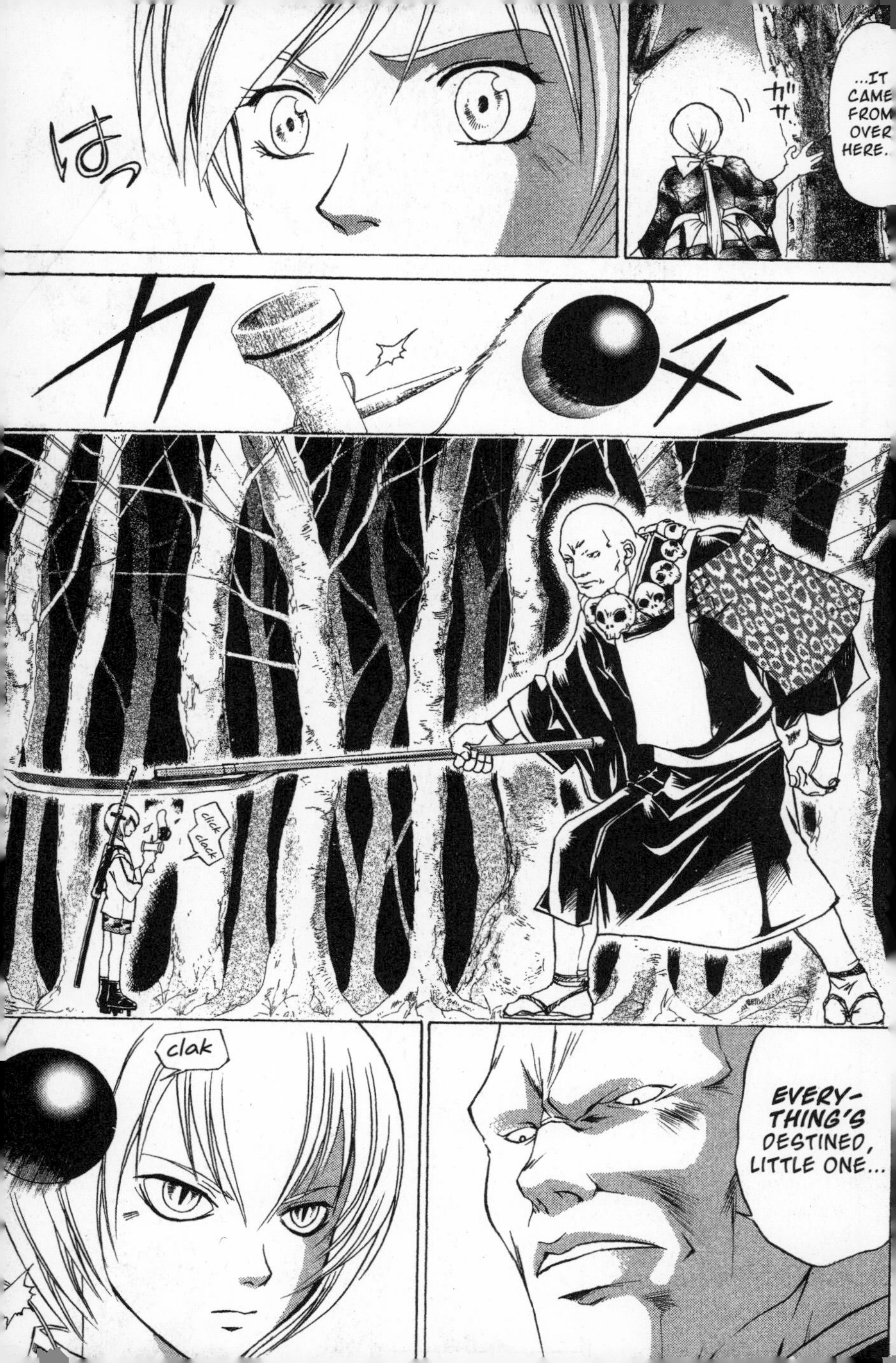
...IT CAME FROM OVER HERE.
ガサ…
はっ
カ
click
clack
EVERY-THING'S DESTINED, LITTLE ONE...
clak

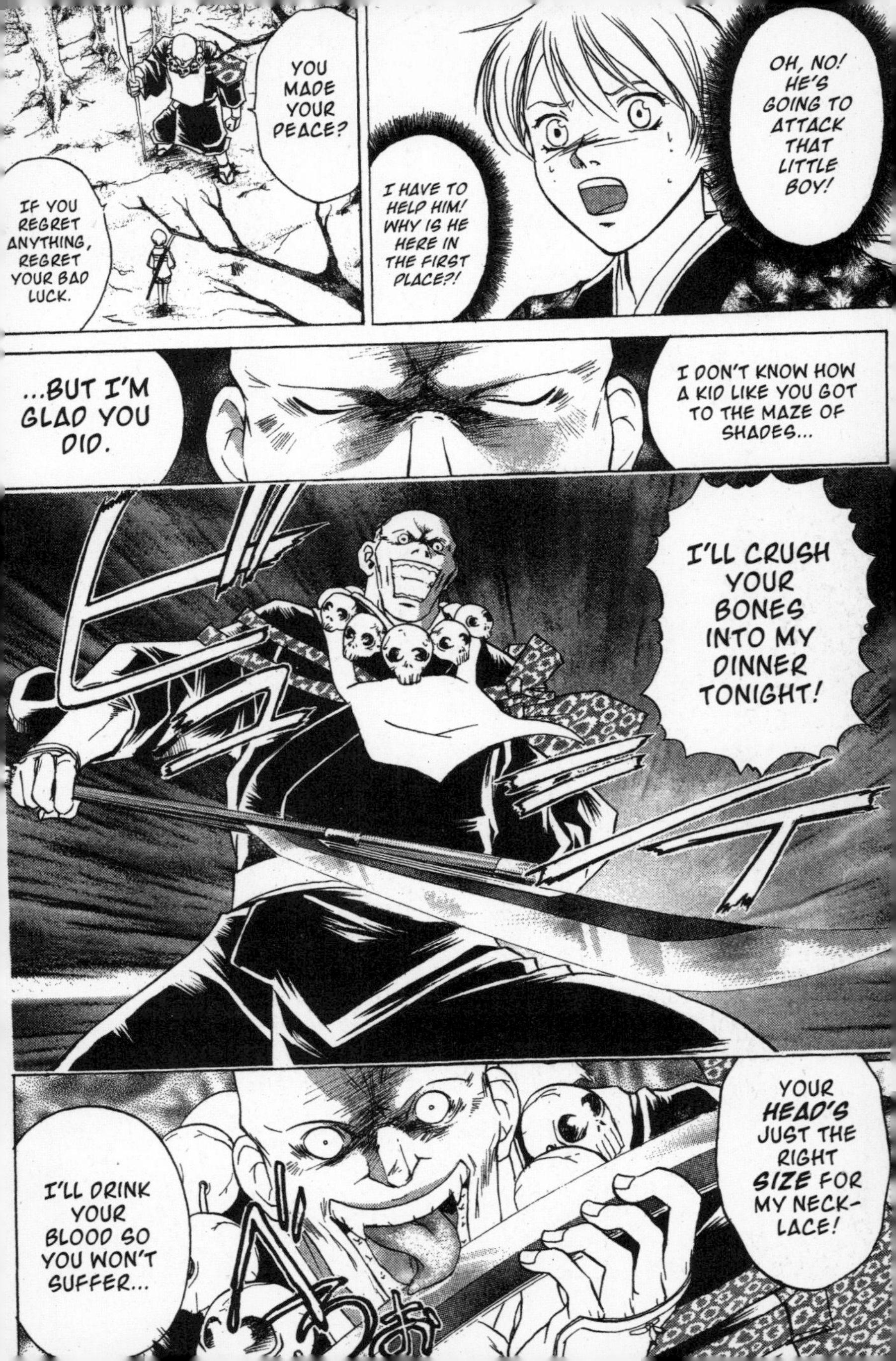
OH, NO! HE'S GOING TO ATTACK THAT LITTLE BOY!
I HAVE TO HELP HIM! WHY IS HE HERE IN THE FIRST PLACE?!
YOU MADE YOUR PEACE?
IF YOU REGRET ANYTHING, REGRET YOUR BAD LUCK.
I DON'T KNOW HOW A KID LIKE YOU GOT TO THE MAZE OF SHADES...
...BUT I'M GLAD YOU DID.
I'LL CRUSH YOUR BONES INTO MY DINNER TONIGHT!
YOUR HEAD'S JUST THE RIGHT SIZE FOR MY NECKLACE!
I'LL DRINK YOUR BLOOD SO YOU WON'T SUFFER...

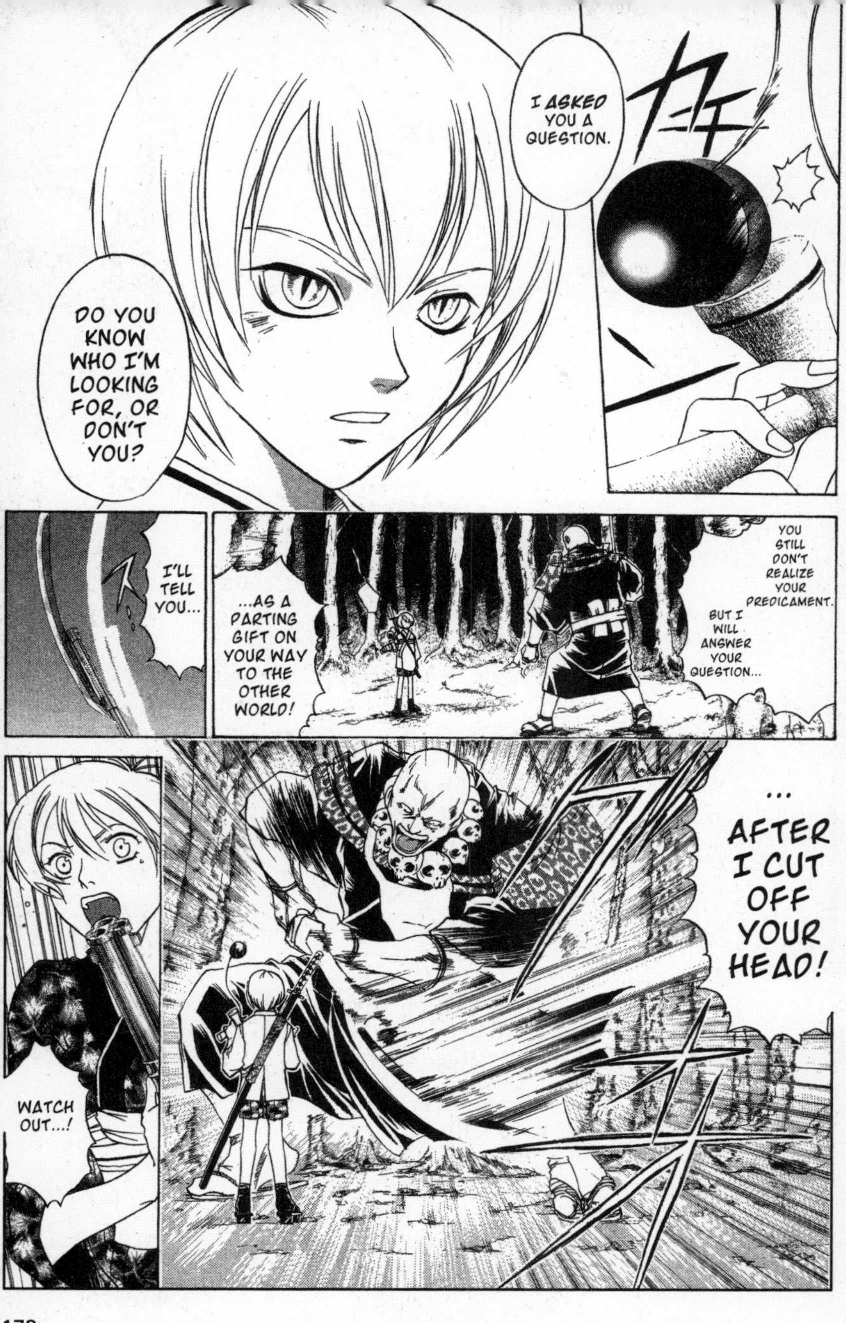
I ASKED YOU A QUESTION.
DO YOU KNOW WHO I'M LOOKING FOR, OR DON'T YOU?
YOU STILL DON'T REALIZE YOUR PREDICAMENT.
BUT I WILL ANSWER YOUR QUESTION...
...AS A PARTING GIFT ON YOUR WAY TO THE OTHER WORLD!
I'LL TELL YOU...
...AFTER I CUT OFF YOUR HEAD!
WATCH OUT...!

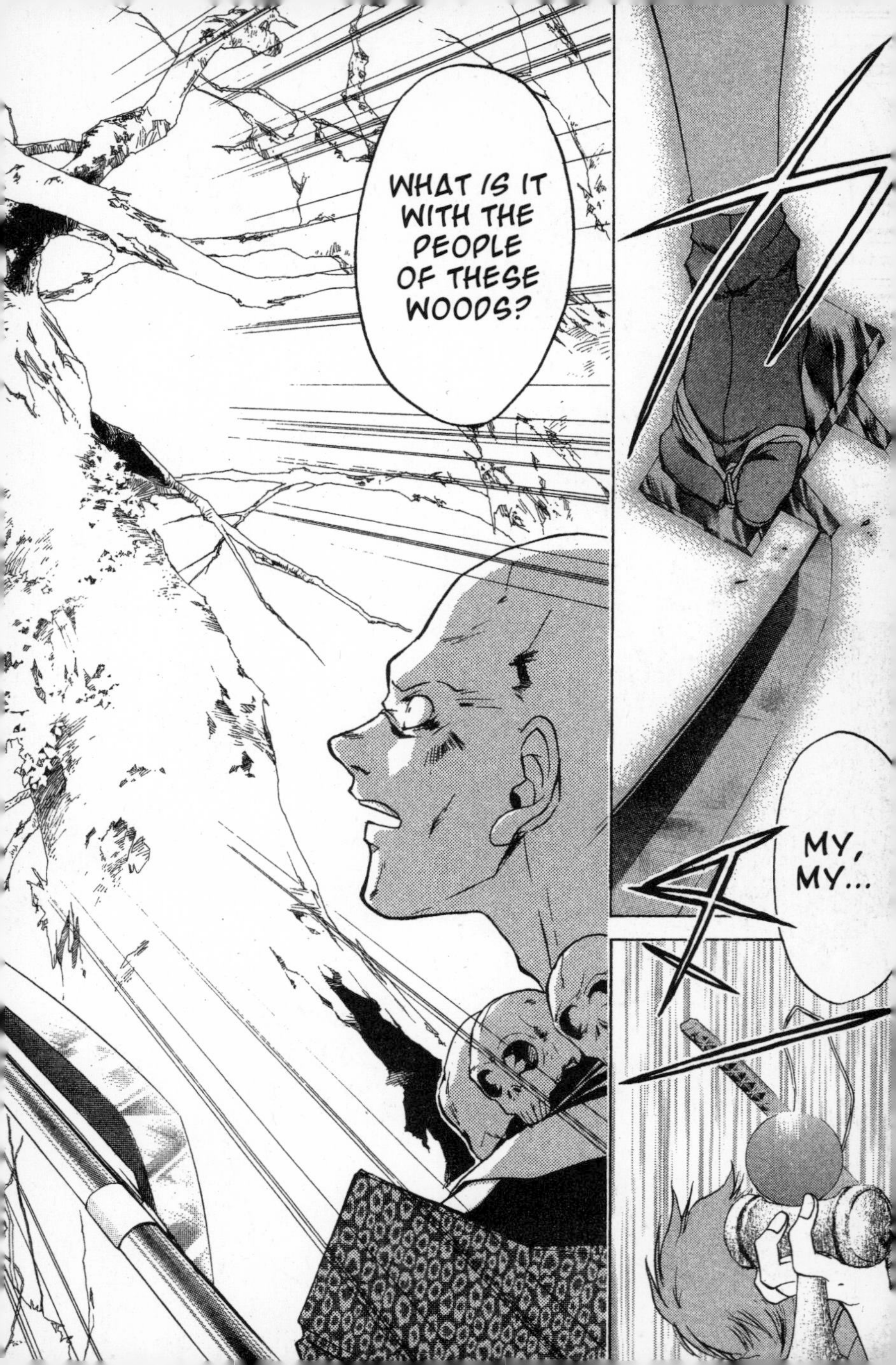
MY, MY...
WHAT IS IT WITH THE PEOPLE OF THESE WOODS?

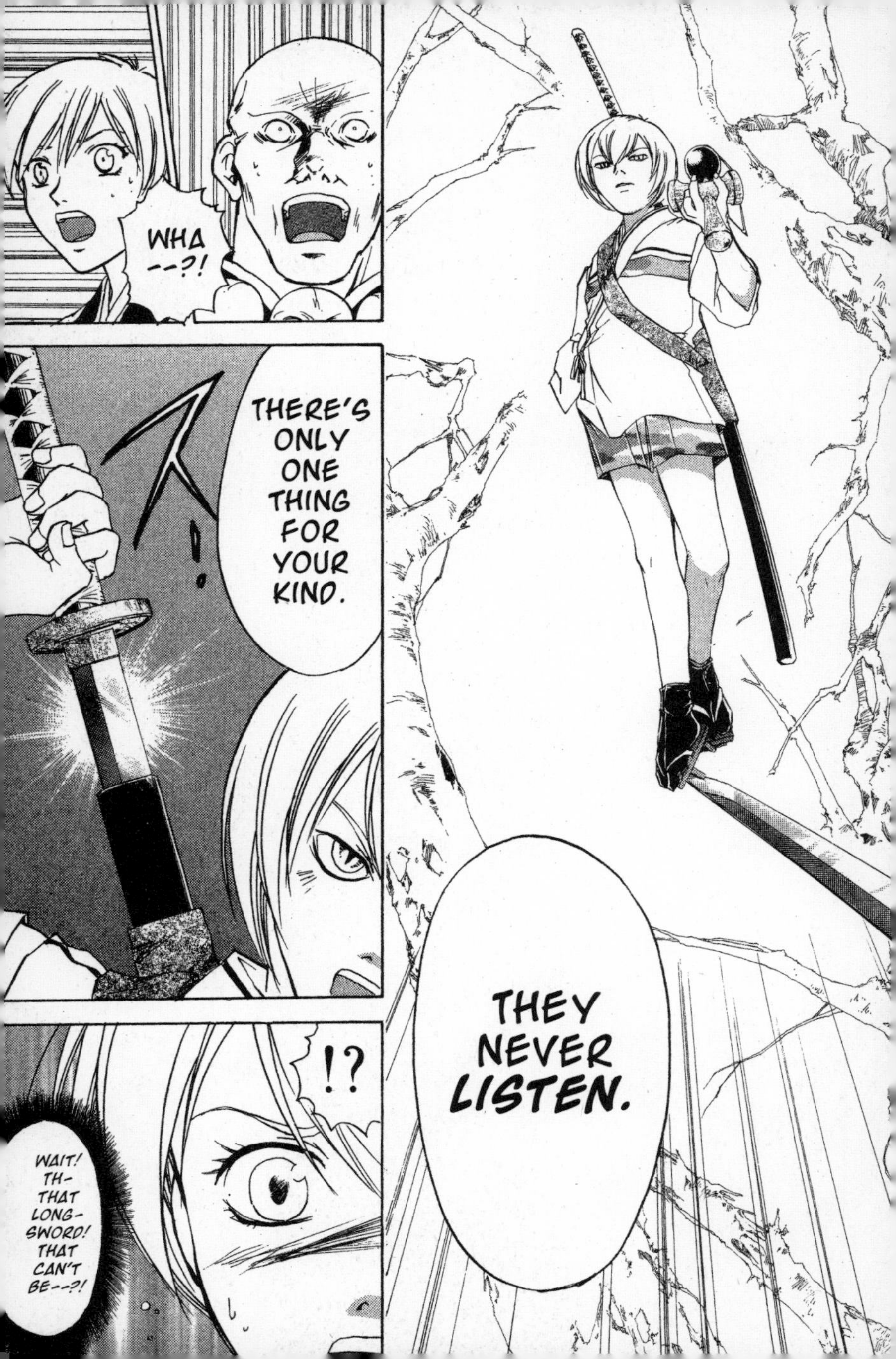
THEY NEVER LISTEN.
WHA--?!
THERE'S ONLY ONE THING FOR YOUR KIND.
!
!?
WAIT! TH-THAT LONG-SWORD! THAT CAN'T BE--?!

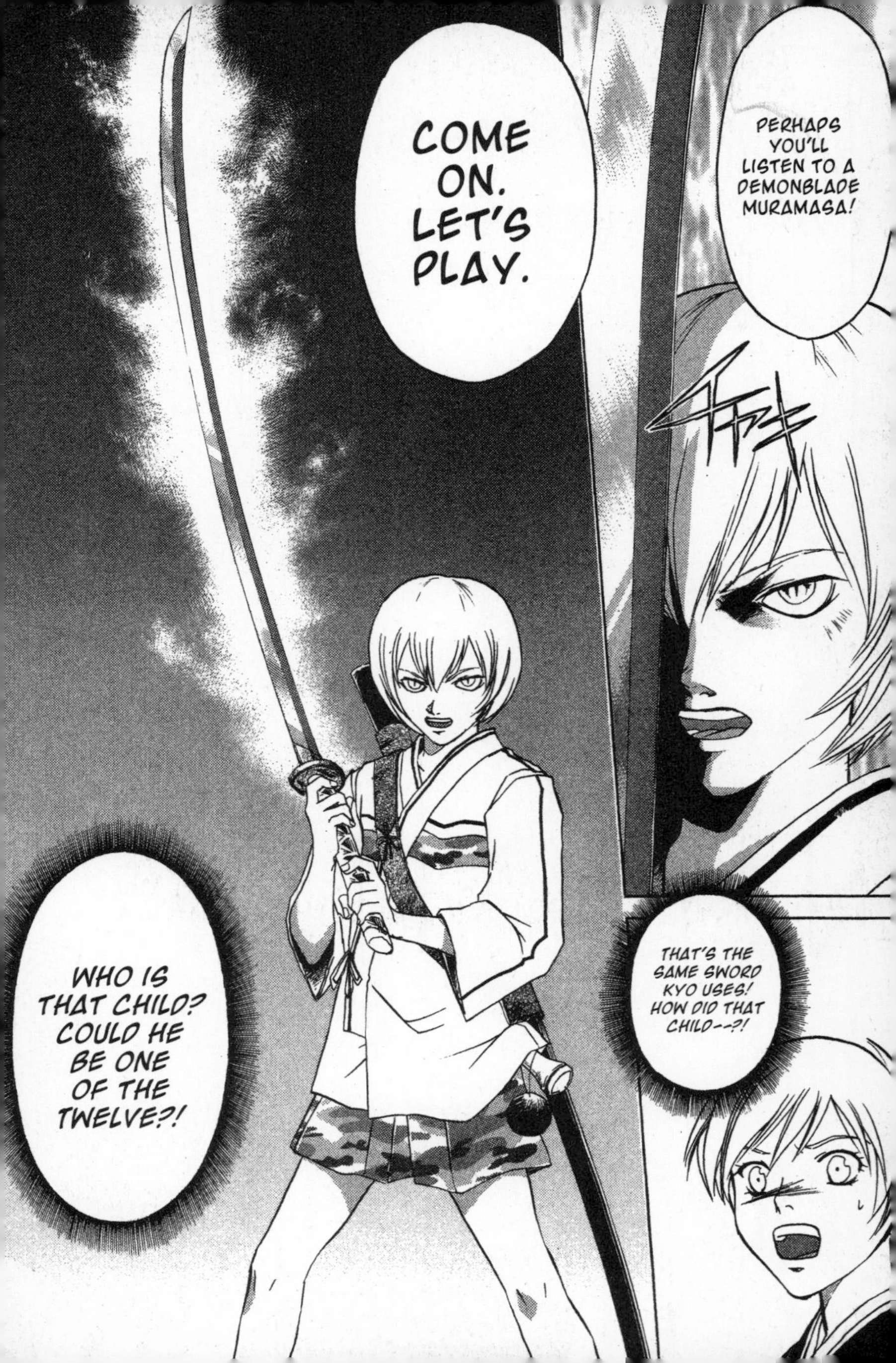
PERHAPS YOU'LL LISTEN TO A DEMONBLADE MURAMASA!
THAT'S THE SAME SWORD KYO USES! HOW DID THAT CHILD--?!
COME ON. LET'S PLAY.
WHO IS THAT CHILD? COULD HE BE ONE OF THE TWELVE?!

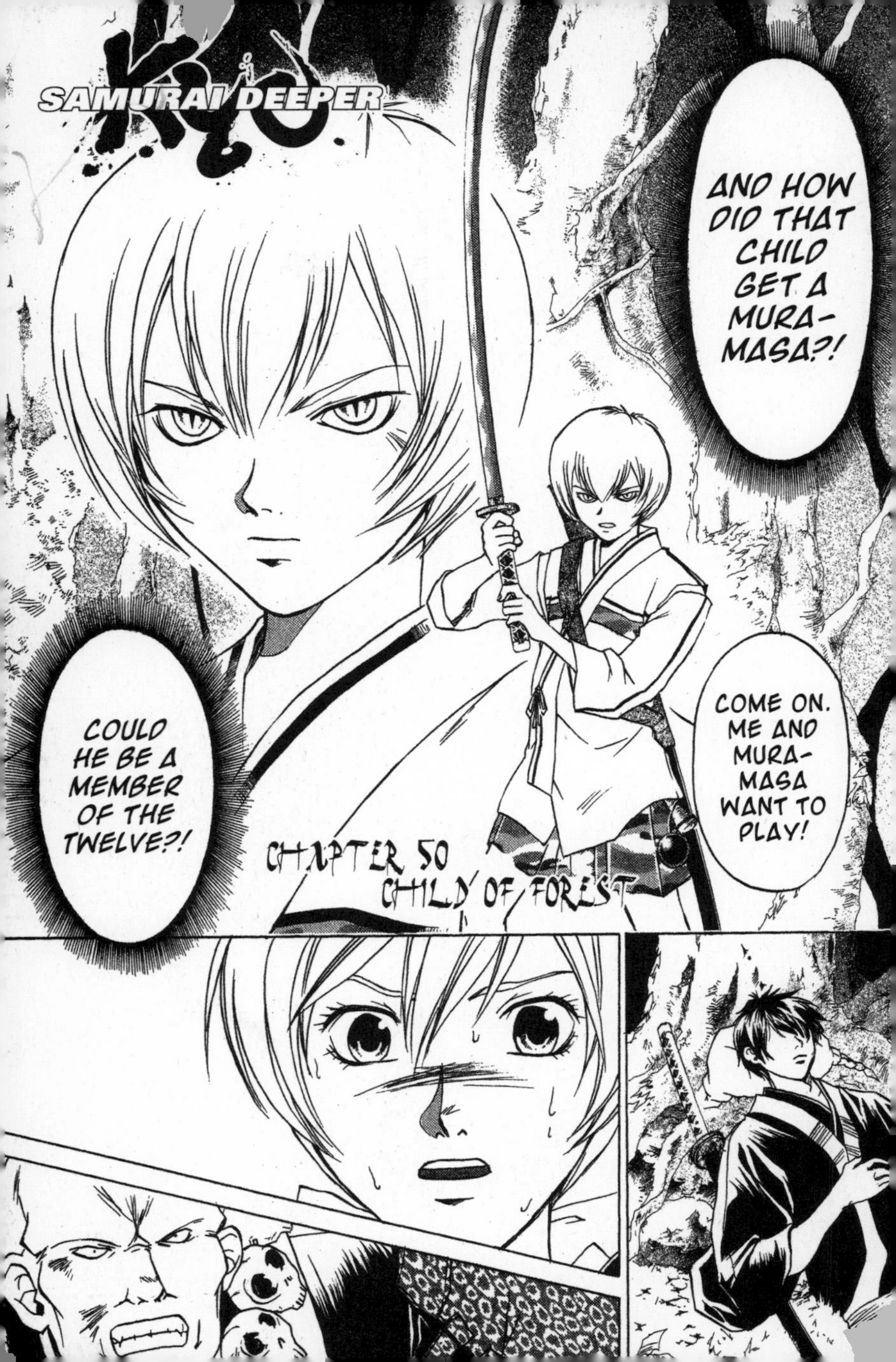
SAMURAI DEEPER KYO
AND HOW DID THAT CHILD GET A MURA-MASA?!
COME ON. ME AND MURA-MASA WANT TO PLAY!
CHAPTER 50 CHILD OF FOREST
COULD HE BE A MEMBER OF THE TWELVE?!

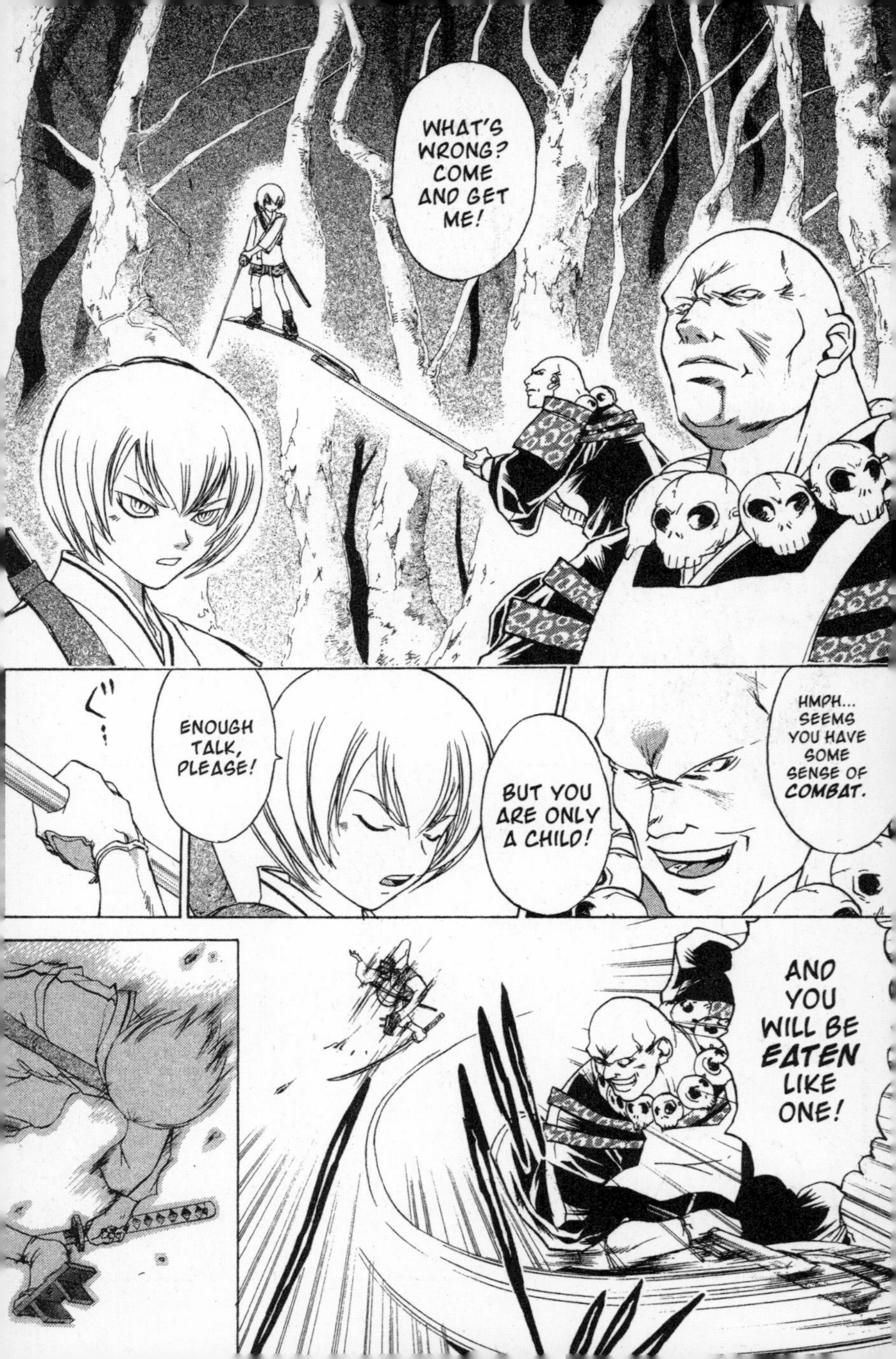
WHAT'S WRONG? COME AND GET ME!
HMPH... SEEMS YOU HAVE SOME SENSE OF COMBAT.
BUT YOU ARE ONLY A CHILD!
ENOUGH TALK, PLEASE!
AND YOU WILL BE EATEN LIKE ONE!

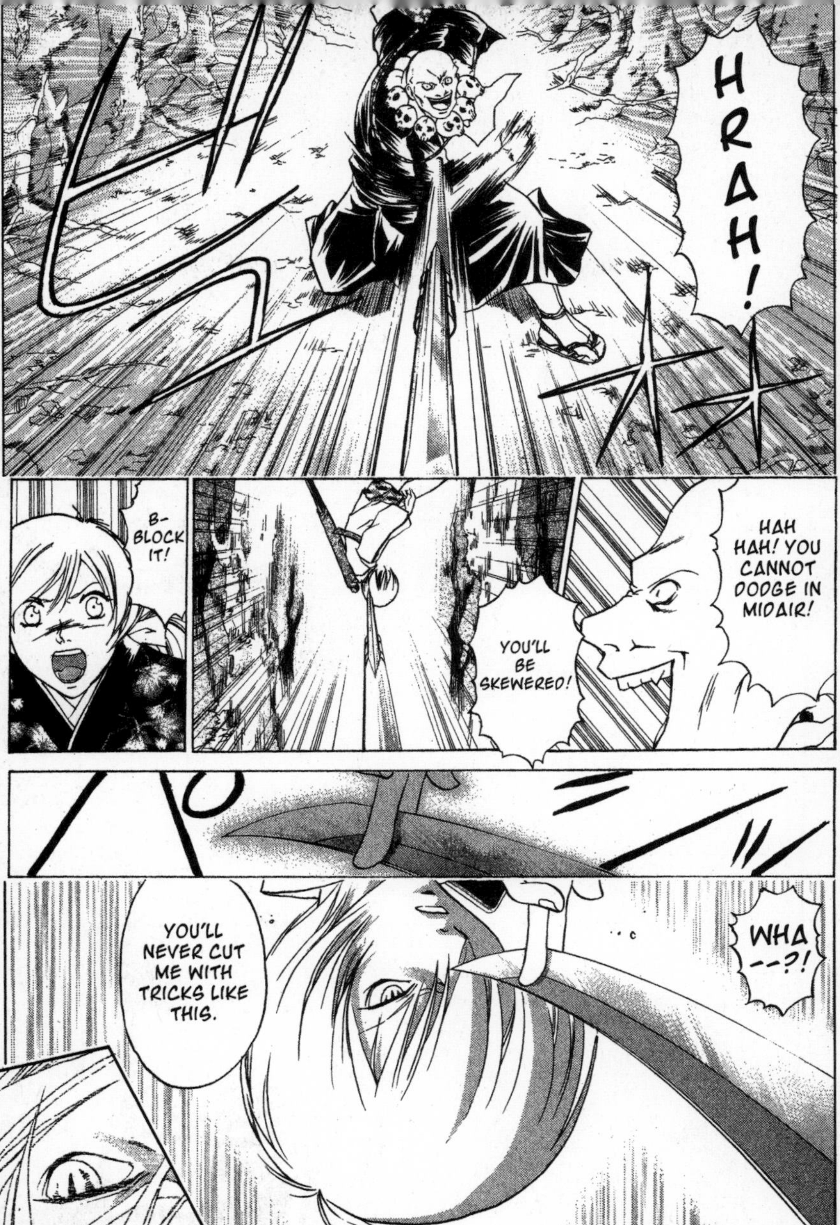
HRAH!
HAH HAH! YOU CANNOT DODGE IN MIDAIR!
YOU'LL BE SKEWERED!
B-BLOCK IT!
WHA--?!
YOU'LL NEVER CUT ME WITH TRICKS LIKE THIS.

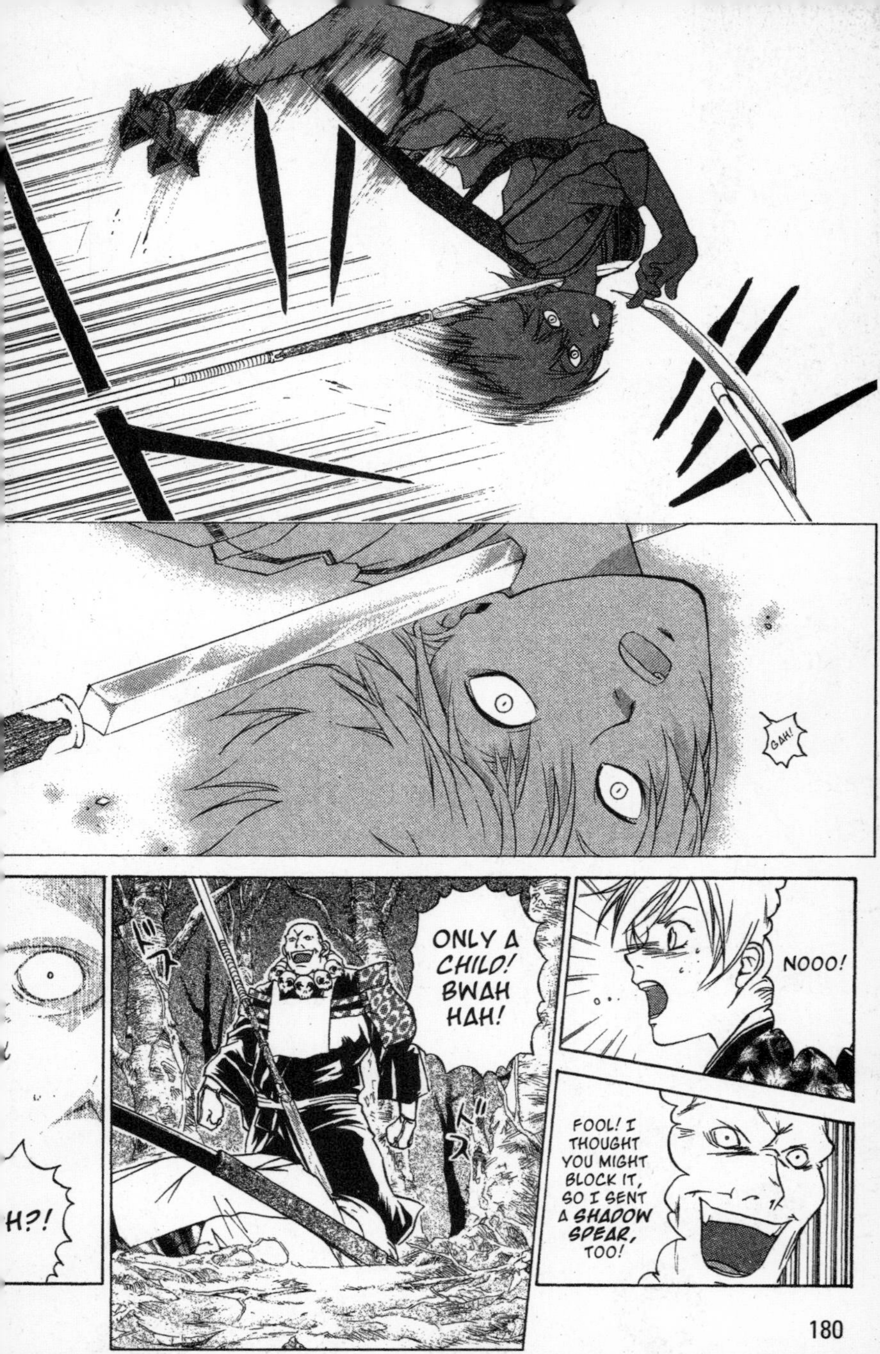
GAH!
NOOO!
FOOL! I THOUGHT YOU MIGHT BLOCK IT, SO I SENT A SHADOW SPEAR, TOO!
ONLY A CHILD! BWAH HAH!
H?!

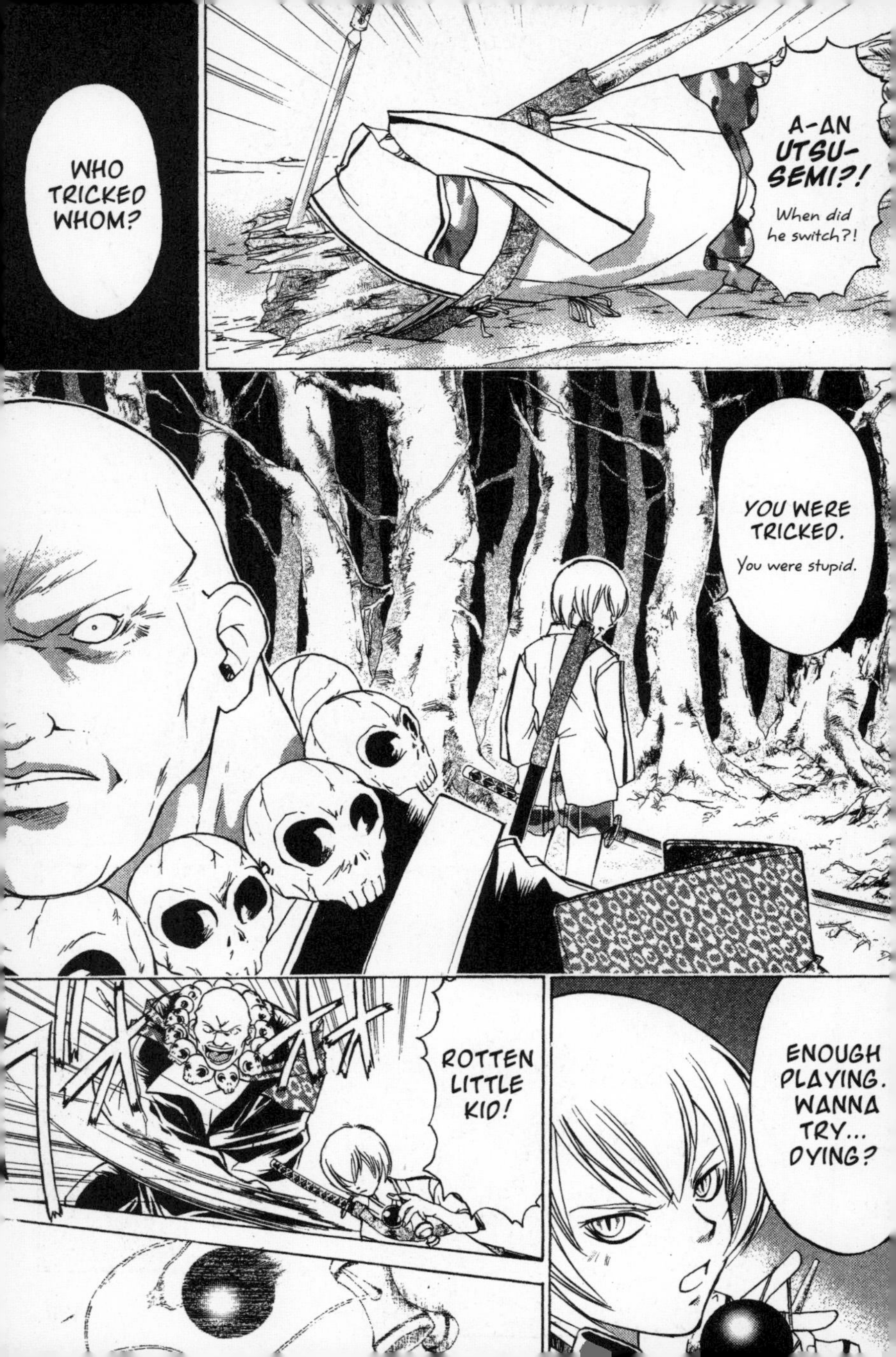
A-AN UTSU-SEMI?!
When did he switch?!
WHO TRICKED WHOM?
YOU WERE TRICKED.
You were stupid.
ENOUGH PLAYING. WANNA TRY... DYING?
ROTTEN LITTLE KID!

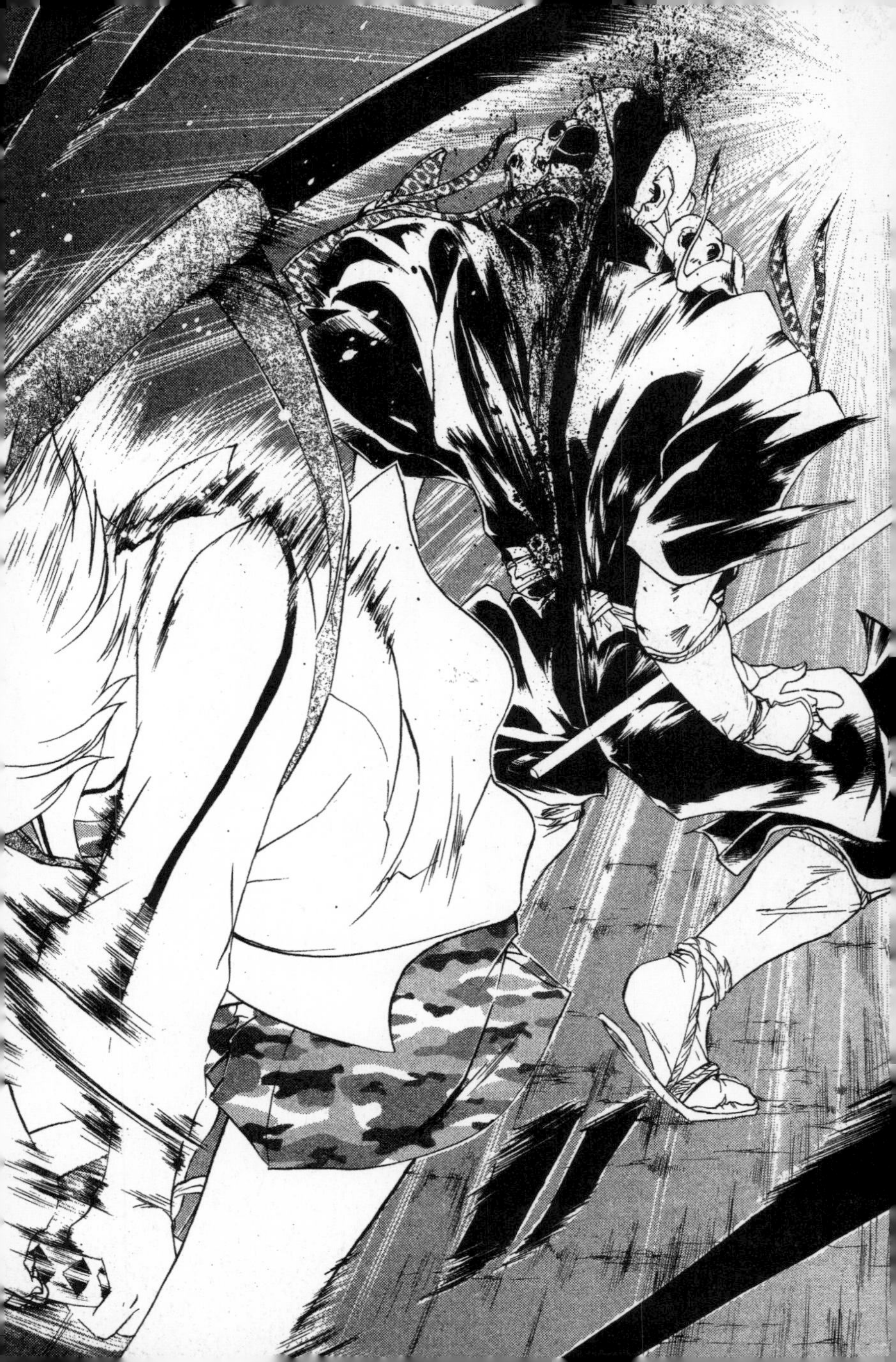

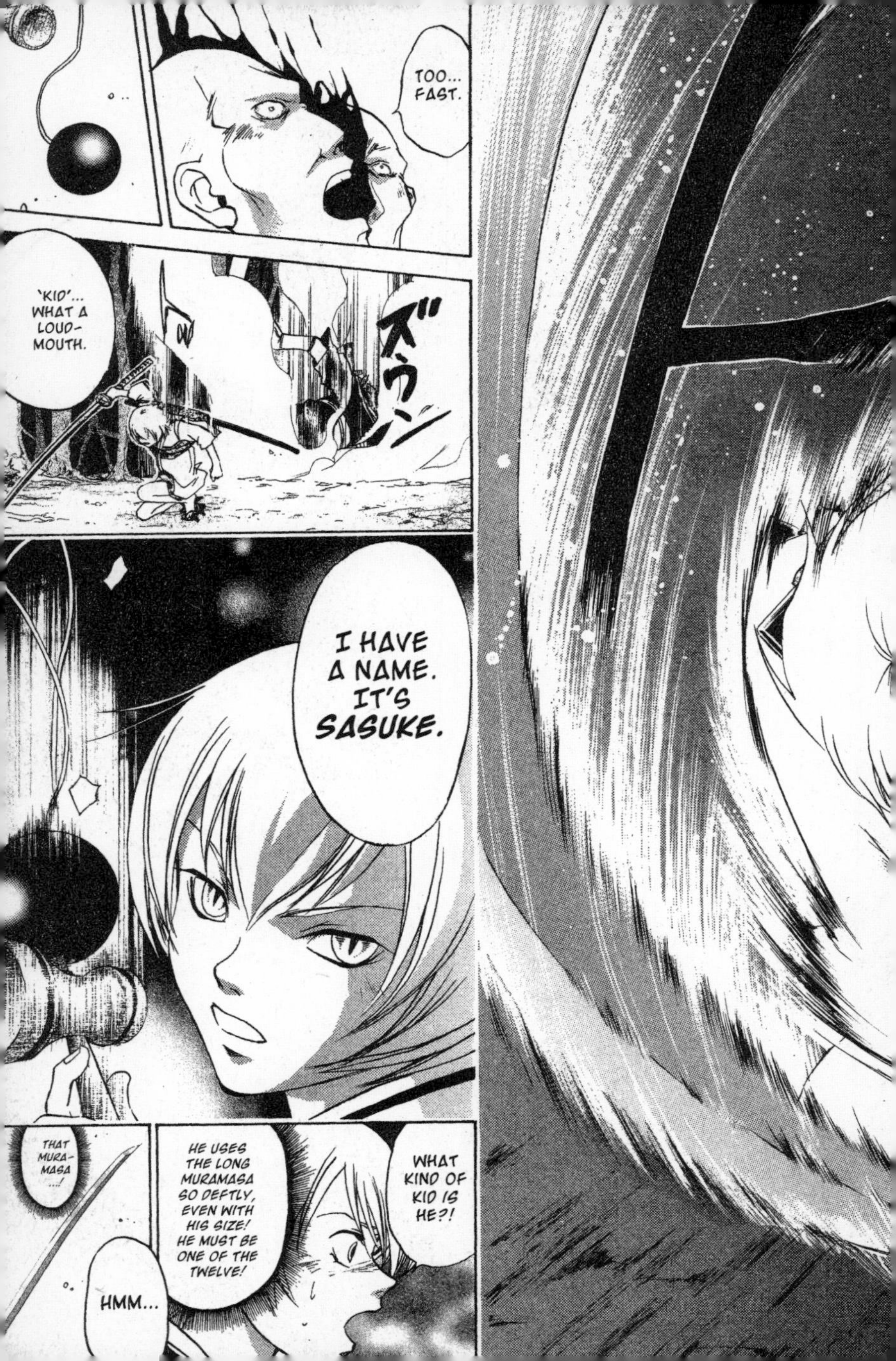
TOO... FAST.
'KID'... WHAT A LOUD-MOUTH.
ズウン
I HAVE A NAME. IT'S SASUKE.
WHAT KIND OF KID IS HE?!
HE USES THE LONG MURAMASA SO DEFTLY, EVEN WITH HIS SIZE! HE MUST BE ONE OF THE TWELVE!
HMM...
THAT MURAMASA...!

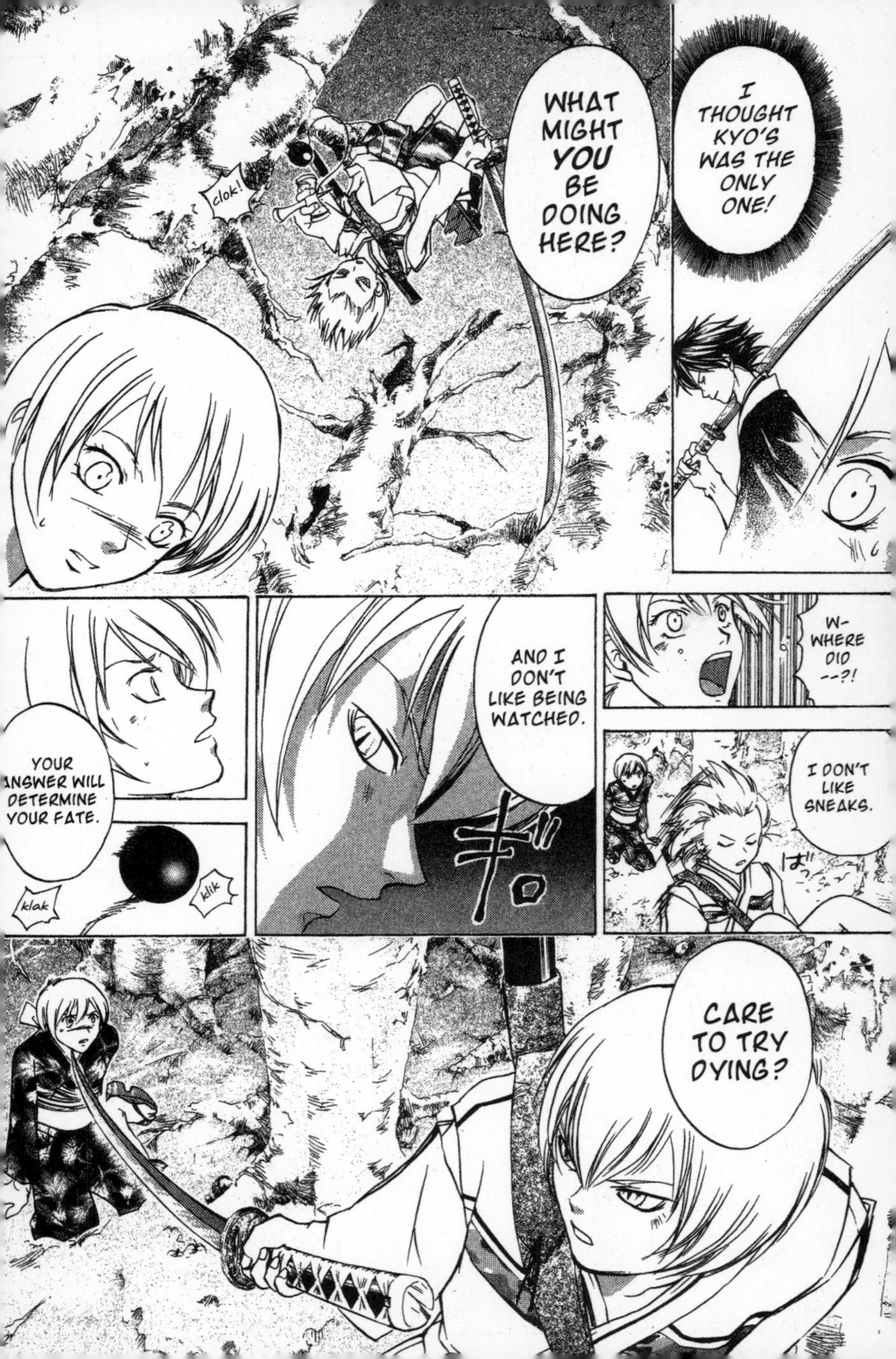
I THOUGHT KYO'S WAS THE ONLY ONE!
WHAT MIGHT YOU BE DOING HERE?
clok!
W-WHERE DID --?!
I DON'T LIKE SNEAKS.
AND I DON'T LIKE BEING WATCHED.
ギロ
YOUR ANSWER WILL DETERMINE YOUR FATE.
klik
klak
CARE TO TRY DYING?

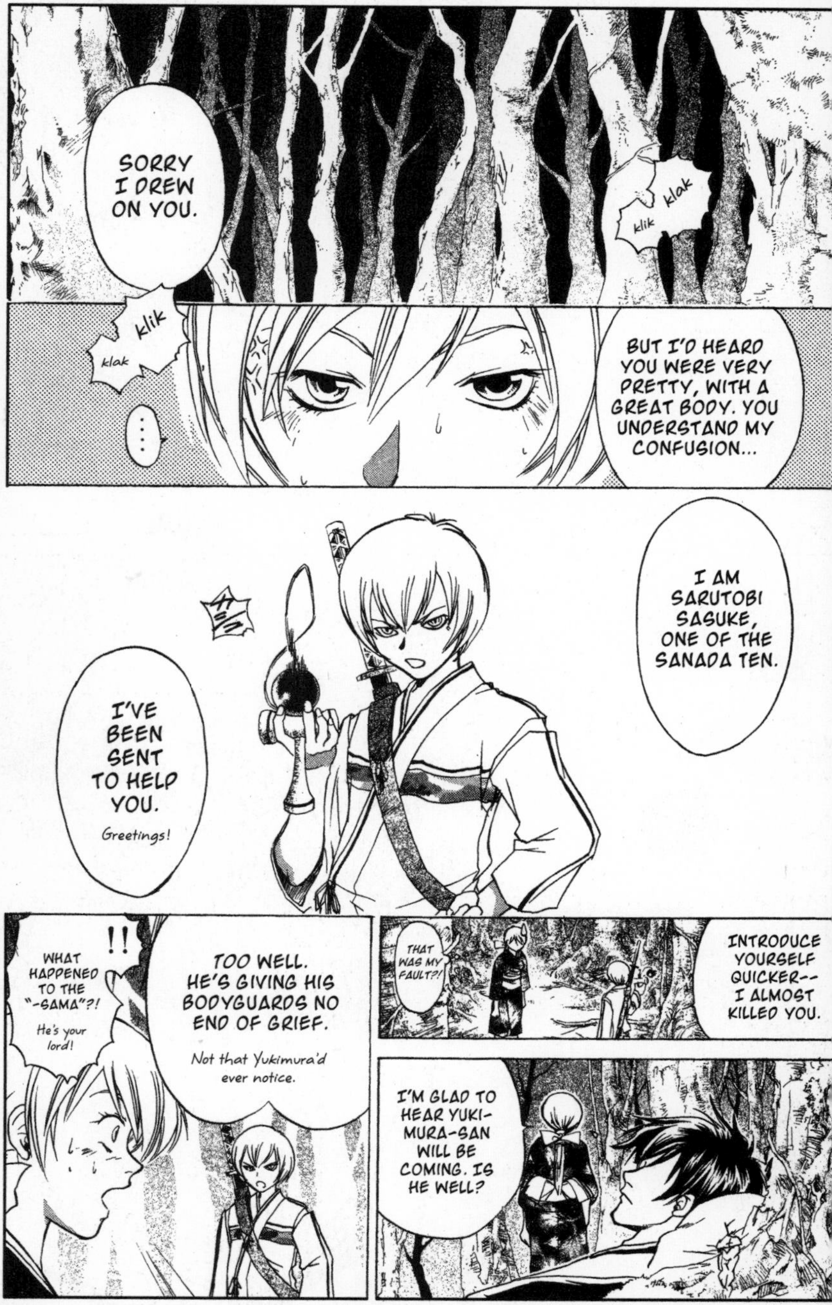
klik klak
SORRY I DREW ON YOU.
BUT I'D HEARD YOU WERE VERY PRETTY, WITH A GREAT BODY. YOU UNDERSTAND MY CONFUSION...
klik klak
....
I AM SARUTOBI SASUKE, ONE OF THE SANADA TEN.
I'VE BEEN SENT TO HELP YOU.
Greetings!
INTRODUCE YOURSELF QUICKER-- I ALMOST KILLED YOU.
THAT WAS MY FAULT?!
I'M GLAD TO HEAR YUKI-MURA-SAN WILL BE COMING. IS HE WELL?
TOO WELL. HE'S GIVING HIS BODYGUARDS NO END OF GRIEF.
Not that Yukimura'd ever notice.
!!
WHAT HAPPENED TO THE "-SAMA"?!
He's your lord!

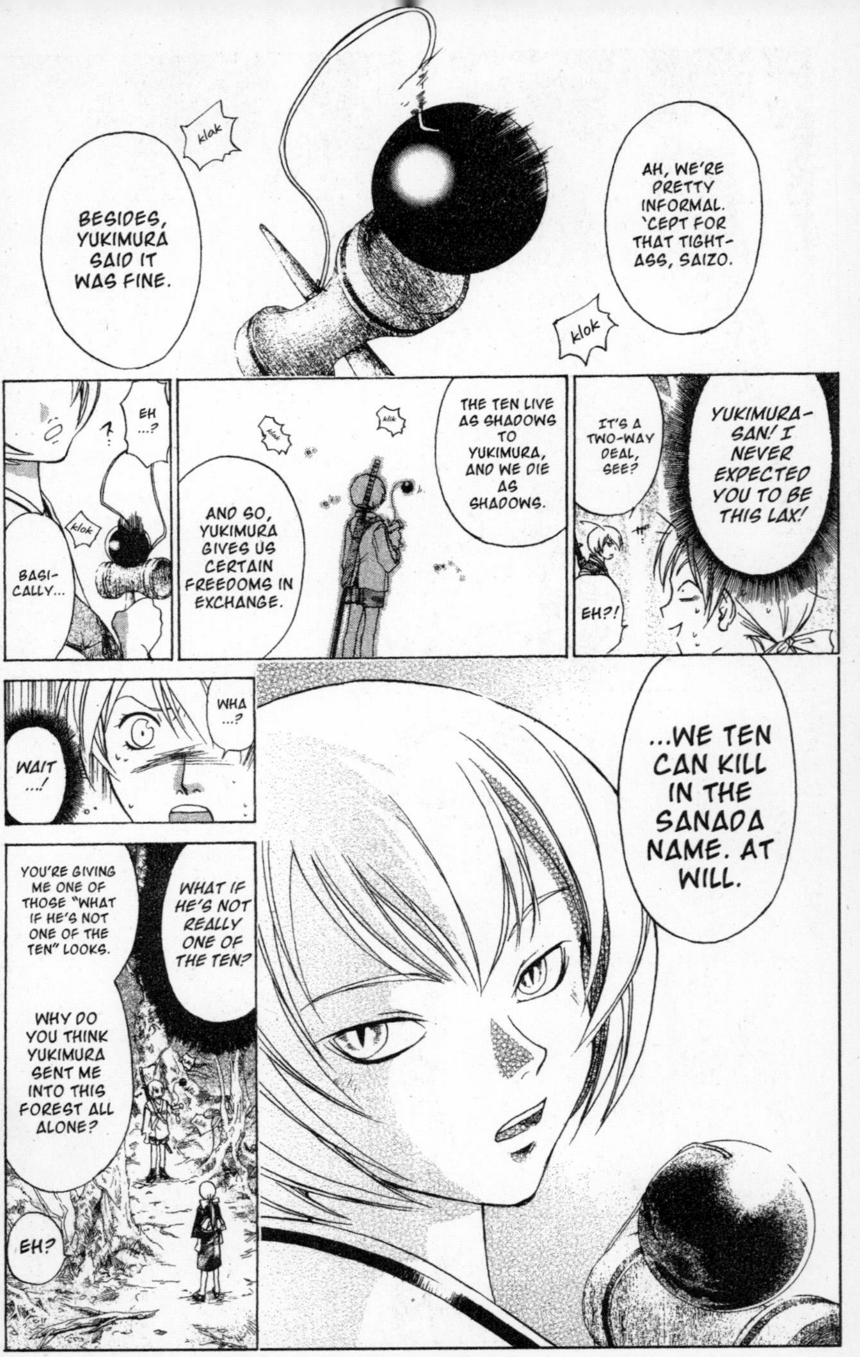
AH, WE'RE PRETTY INFORMAL. `CEPT FOR THAT TIGHT-ASS, SAIZO.
klok
klak
BESIDES, YUKIMURA SAID IT WAS FINE.
YUKIMURA-SAN! I NEVER EXPECTED YOU TO BE THIS LAX!
IT'S A TWO-WAY DEAL, SEE?
EH?!
THE TEN LIVE AS SHADOWS TO YUKIMURA, AND WE DIE AS SHADOWS.
klik
klak
AND SO, YUKIMURA GIVES US CERTAIN FREEDOMS IN EXCHANGE.
EH ...?
klok
BASI-CALLY...
...WE TEN CAN KILL IN THE SANADA NAME. AT WILL.
WHA ...?
WAIT ...!
WHAT IF HE'S NOT REALLY ONE OF THE TEN?
YOU'RE GIVING ME ONE OF THOSE "WHAT IF HE'S NOT ONE OF THE TEN" LOOKS.
WHY DO YOU THINK YUKIMURA SENT ME INTO THIS FOREST ALL ALONE?
EH?

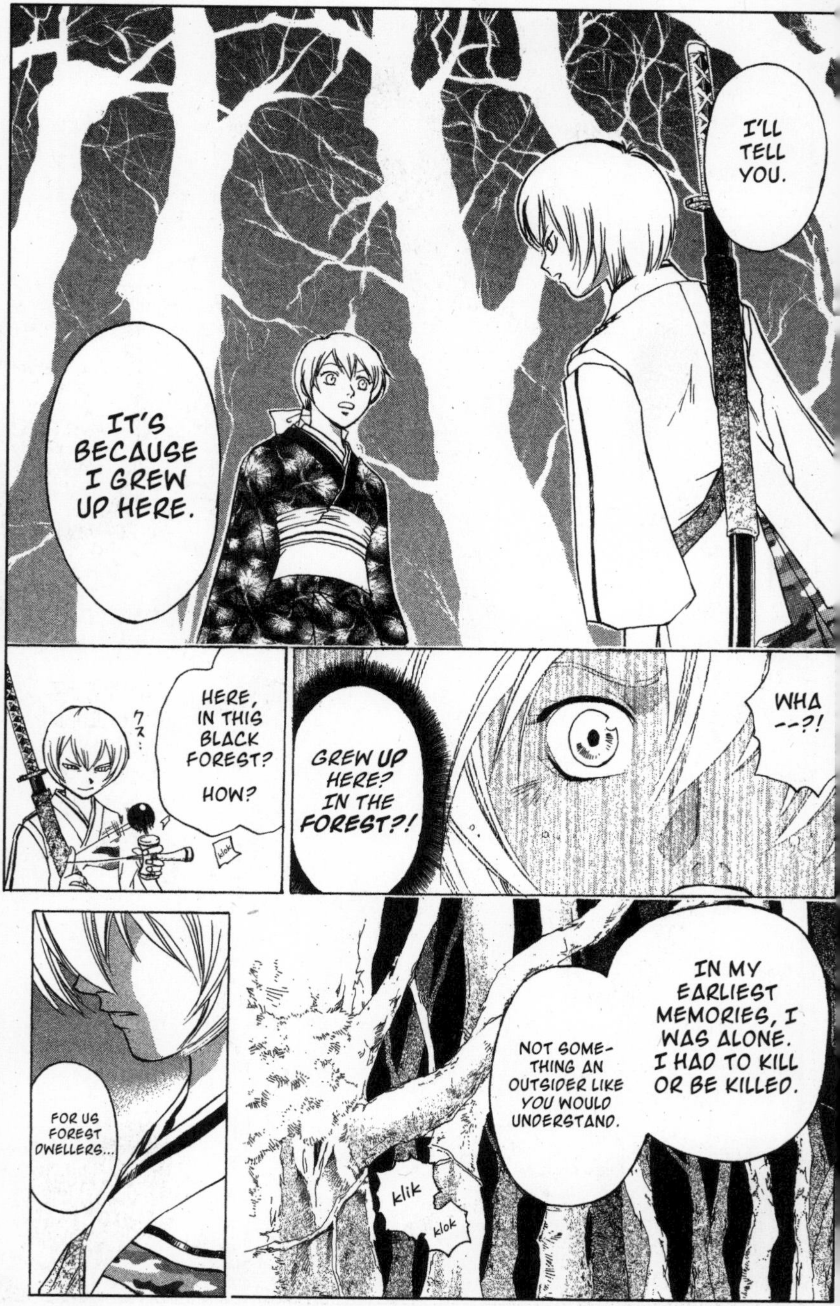
I'LL TELL YOU.
IT'S BECAUSE I GREW UP HERE.
WHA--?!
GREW UP HERE? IN THE FOREST?!
HERE, IN THIS BLACK FOREST? HOW?
クス…
klok
IN MY EARLIEST MEMORIES, I WAS ALONE. I HAD TO KILL OR BE KILLED.
NOT SOMETHING AN OUTSIDER LIKE YOU WOULD UNDERSTAND.
klik
klok
FOR US FOREST DWELLERS...

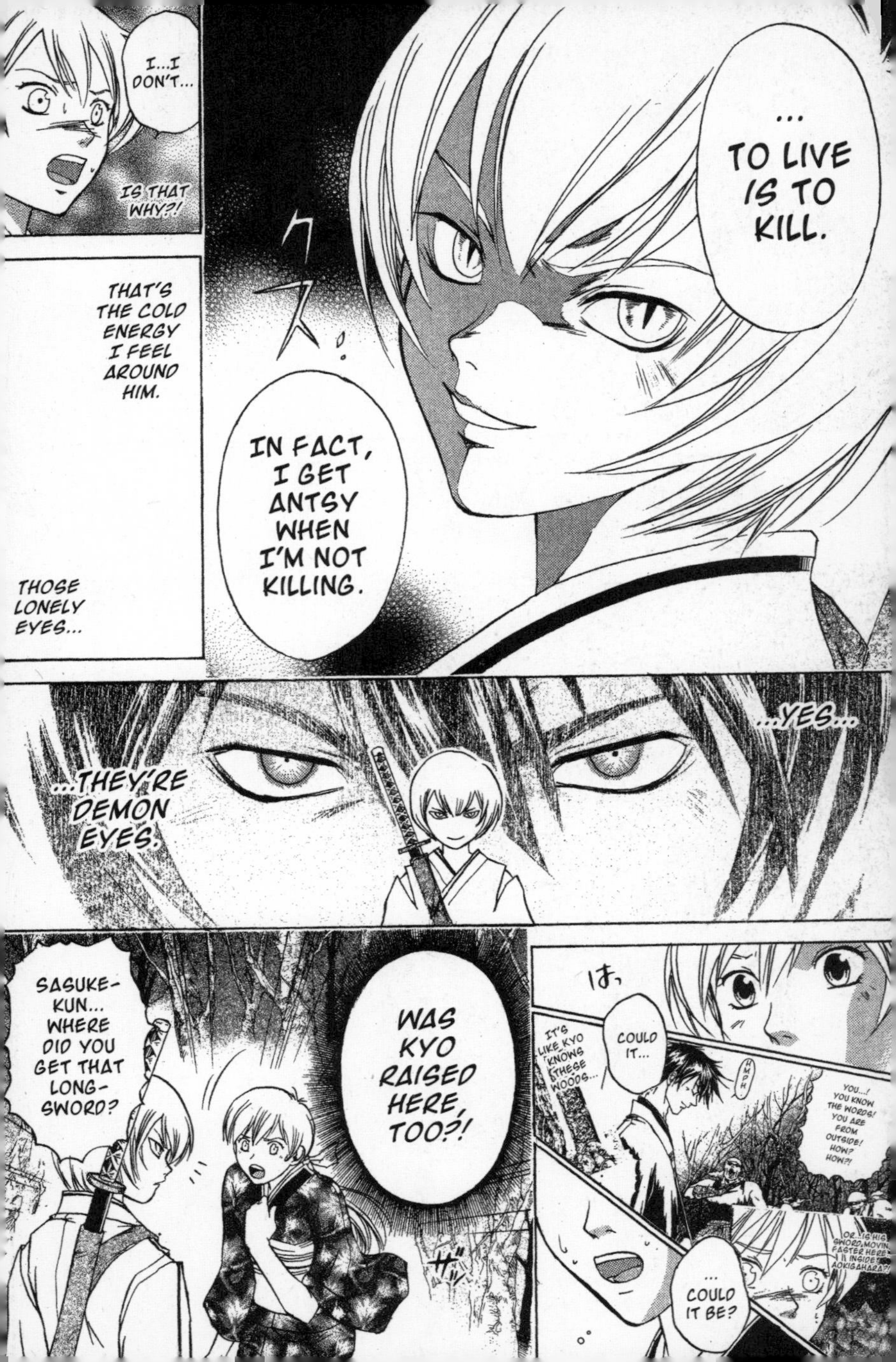
... TO LIVE IS TO KILL.
クス
IN FACT, I GET ANTSY WHEN I'M NOT KILLING.
I...I DON'T...
IS THAT WHY?!
THAT'S THE COLD ENERGY I FEEL AROUND HIM.
THOSE LONELY EYES...
...YES...
...THEY'RE DEMON EYES.
は、
COULD IT...
IT'S LIKE KYO KNOWS THESE WOODS...
HMPH.
YOU...! YOU KNOW THE WORDS! YOU ARE FROM OUTSIDE! HOW? HOW?!
OR...IS HIS SWORD MOVIN FASTER HERE INSIDE AOKIGAHARA?!
... COULD IT BE?
WAS KYO RAISED HERE, TOO?!
SASUKE-KUN... WHERE DID YOU GET THAT LONG-SWORD?
ザッ

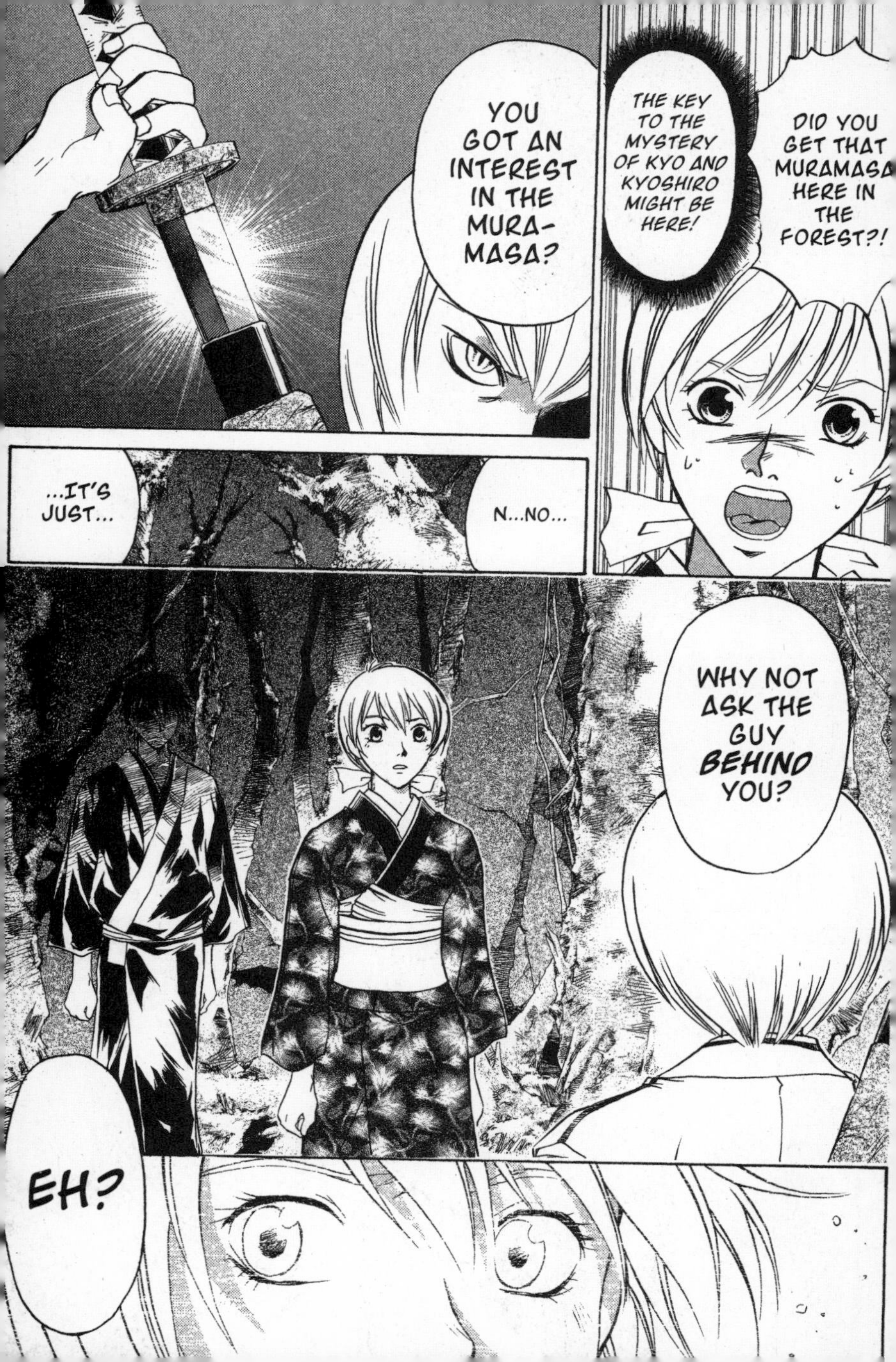
DID YOU GET THAT MURAMASA HERE IN THE FOREST?!
THE KEY TO THE MYSTERY OF KYO AND KYOSHIRO MIGHT BE HERE!
YOU GOT AN INTEREST IN THE MURA-MASA?
N...NO...
...IT'S JUST...
WHY NOT ASK THE GUY BEHIND YOU?
EH?

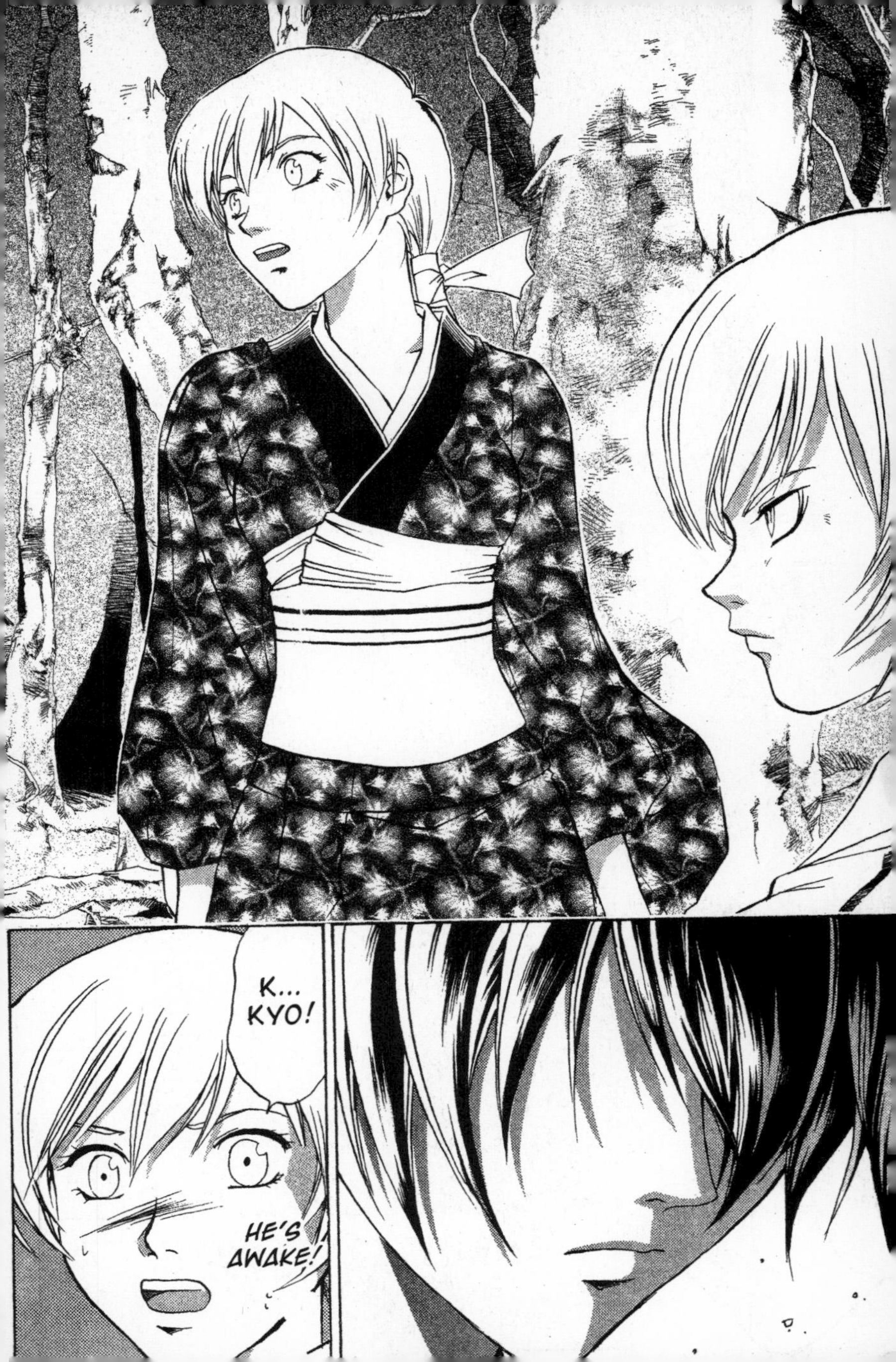
K...
KYO!
HE'S
AWAKE!

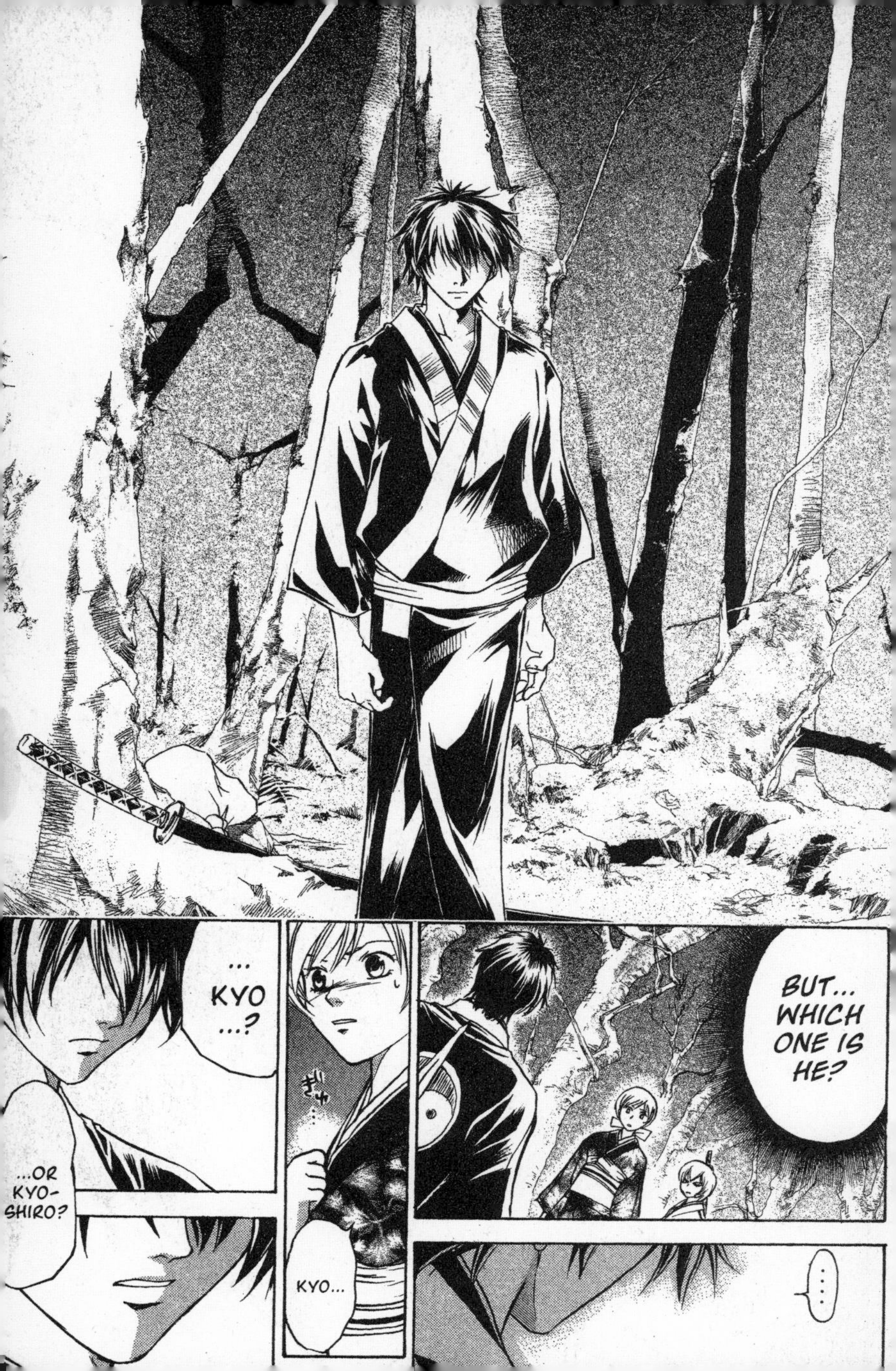
BUT... WHICH ONE IS HE?
....
KYO...
... KYO ...?
...OR KYO-SHIRO?

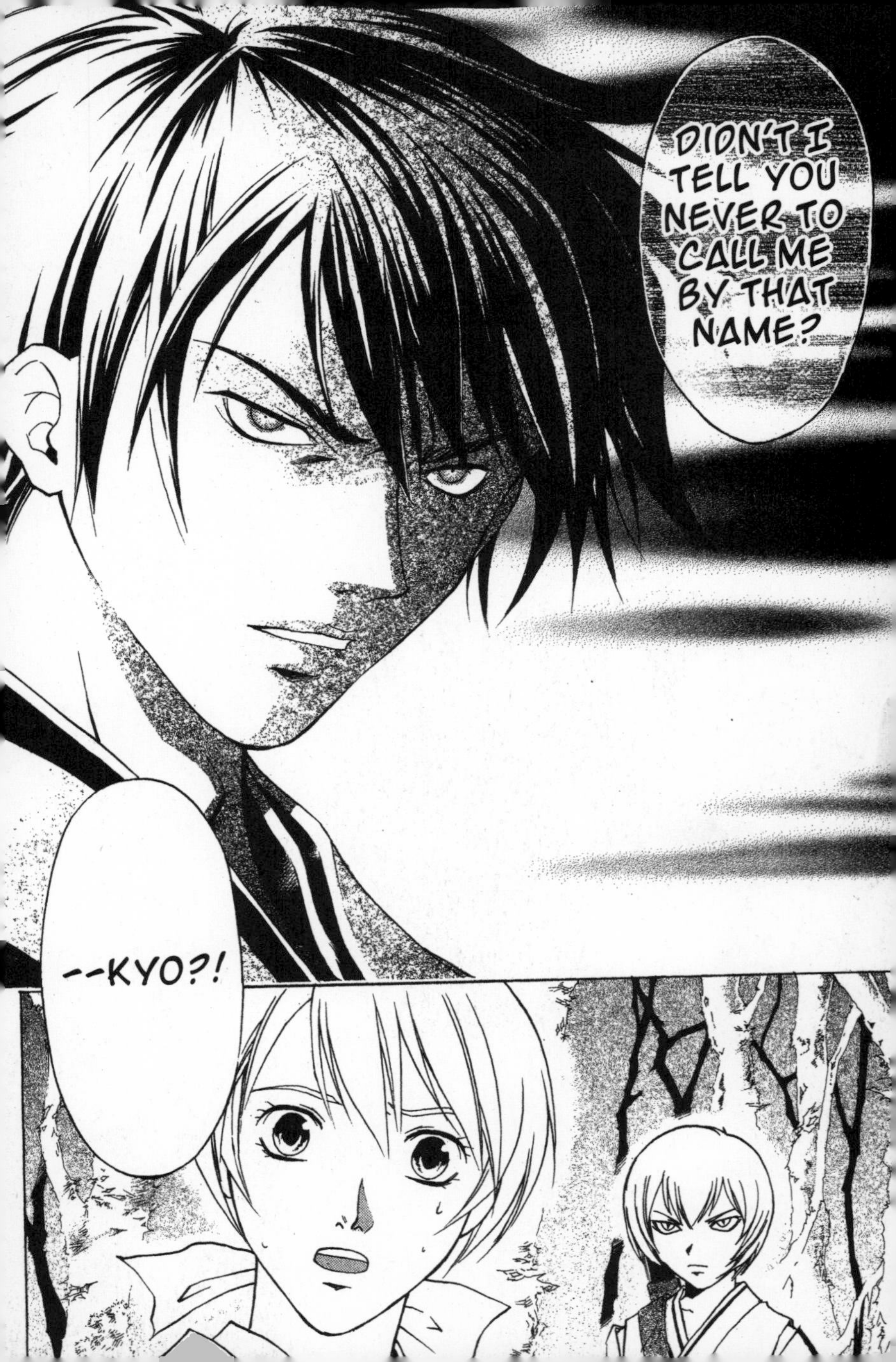
DIDN'T I TELL YOU NEVER TO CALL ME BY THAT NAME?
--KYO?!

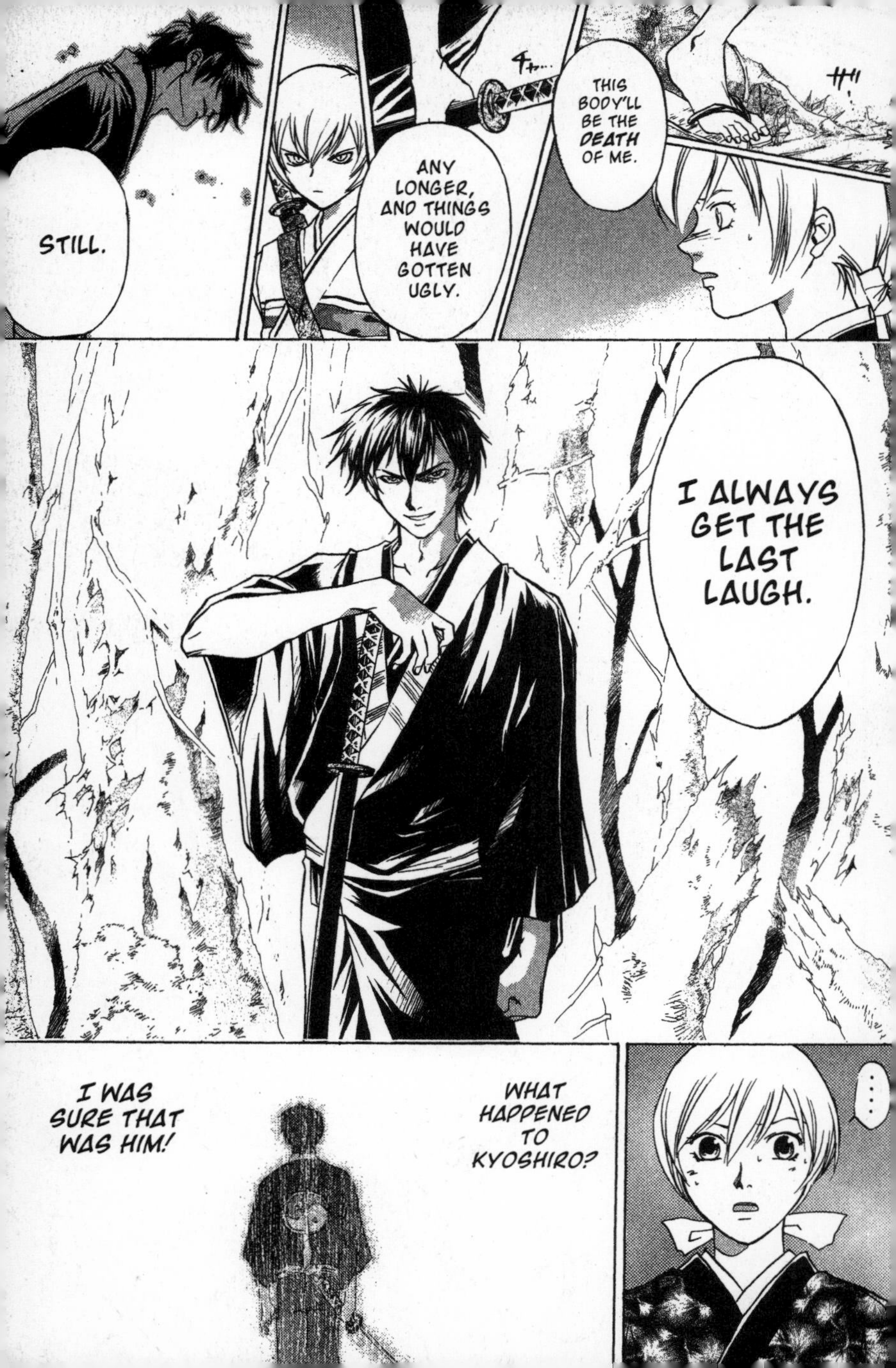
THIS BODY'LL BE THE DEATH OF ME.
ANY LONGER, AND THINGS WOULD HAVE GOTTEN UGLY.
STILL.
I ALWAYS GET THE LAST LAUGH.
....
WHAT HAPPENED TO KYOSHIRO?
I WAS SURE THAT WAS HIM!

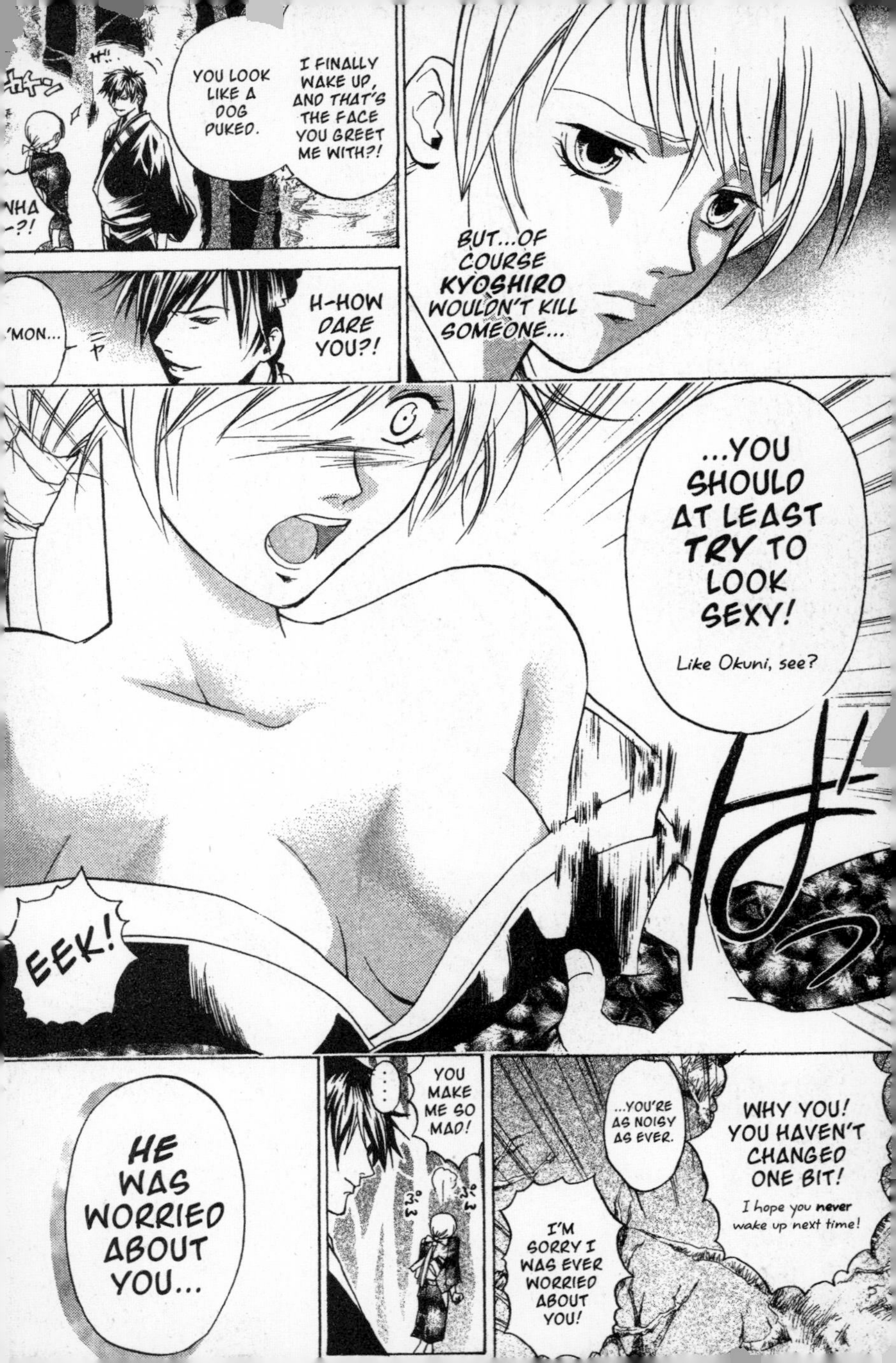
BUT...OF COURSE KYOSHIRO WOULDN'T KILL SOMEONE...
I FINALLY WAKE UP, AND THAT'S THE FACE YOU GREET ME WITH?!
YOU LOOK LIKE A DOG PUKED.
WHA-?!
H-HOW DARE YOU?!
'MON...
...YOU SHOULD AT LEAST TRY TO LOOK SEXY!
Like Okuni, see?
EEK!
WHY YOU! YOU HAVEN'T CHANGED ONE BIT!
I hope you never wake up next time!
...YOU'RE AS NOISY AS EVER.
I'M SORRY I WAS EVER WORRIED ABOUT YOU!
YOU MAKE ME SO MAD!
...
HE WAS WORRIED ABOUT YOU...

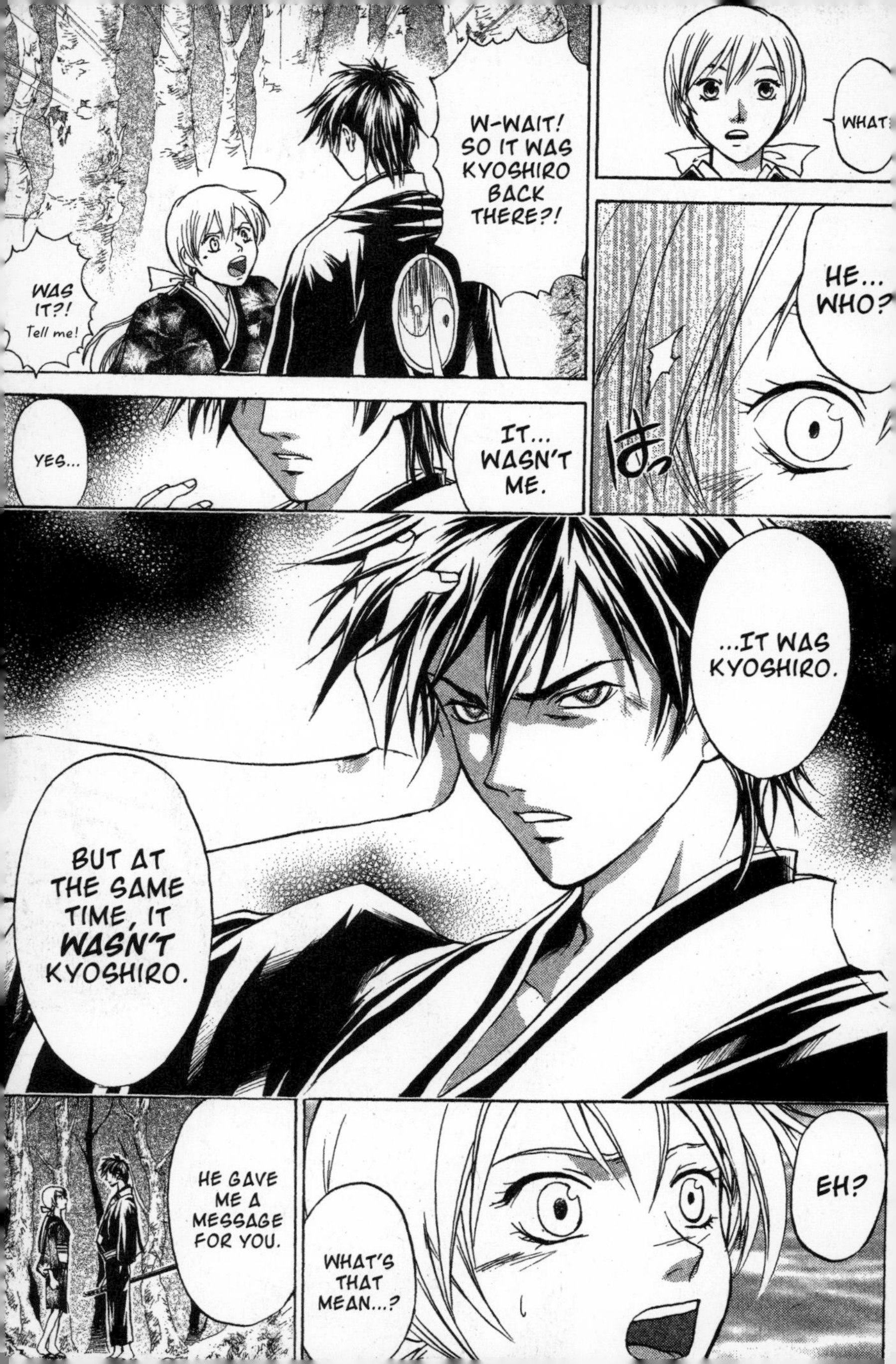

WHAT
HE... WHO?
W-WAIT! SO IT WAS KYOSHIRO BACK THERE?!
WAS IT?! Tell me!
IT... WASN'T ME.
YES...
...IT WAS KYOSHIRO.
BUT AT THE SAME TIME, IT WASN'T KYOSHIRO.
EH?
WHAT'S THAT MEAN...?
HE GAVE ME A MESSAGE FOR YOU.

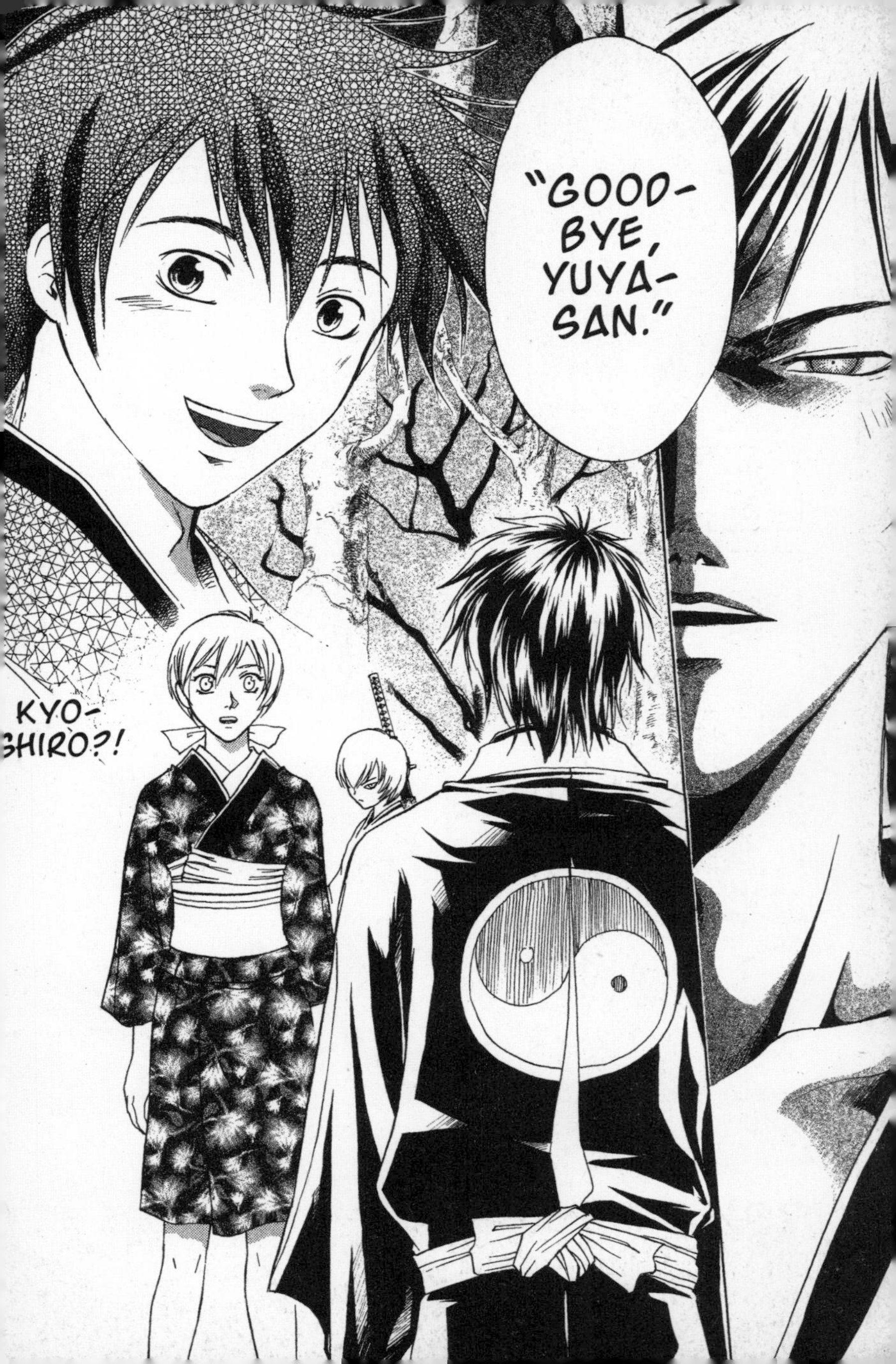
"GOOD-BYE, YUYA-SAN."
KYO-
SHIRO?!

上条事情。 Kamijyo Circumstances

IN THE LAST CHARACTER PROFILE, I FORGOT TO MENTION YUYA'S BLOOD TYPE AND AGE. SHE'S TYPE A, 16 YEARS OLD.
TYPE A GIRLS ARE GREAT, BY THE WAY. VERY ATTENTIVE, VERY SWEET... I'M BIASED, OF COURSE.

◉ *G'day. Kamijyo here. Thanks for reading! In volume 2, I asked for your questions, an I've received a lot, but I never get the time respond. I'll write up a page soon, promise*

◪ *The Birth of Yukimura...*

Yukimura's first scene...
CAN I REDRAW THE WHOLE PANEL WHERE YUKIMURA FIRST APPEARS? IT'S NOT GOING WELL...
SAY, WHAT DO YOU GUYS THINK?
The first time I ever asked my staff for their opinion...sorry!
It's a new look...
I faxed my sister, too...
WANNA KNOW WHY?
'CAUSE THIS IS THE REAL YUKIMURA!
Um, his hands are kinda small...
C'MON! IT'S A MANGA!
I'm sure that portrait's an exaggeration...
I spent forever on his hair...

According to one document, when he was at Kudoyama, Yukimura was so poor, he didn't even have fish to eat.

That's why I gave him a big fish in chapter 48.

CHARACTER PROFILE

Go for it.
I am a spy. Name: Izumo-no-Okuni. I'm a woman, height 168cm. Kamijo-san, you really shouldn't ask women their age and weight.. Maybe that's why you're so unpopular?

Eheh (rubs hands together). How about your sizes?
You've got hands. Use them.♡

Eh?! Y-you sure?!
No. I'm kidding. (glares)

..Sorry. How about your likes? Dislikes? Hobbies? Favorite Food? Fears?
I like strong men, I dislike weak men, my hobby is reading, and I fear nothing.

Umm. What kind of books?
Well...hee hee ♡

(What could she possibly like?...)
Um...I've got a letter here from a female reader who says you're kind of scary.
I can't stand that. She obviously has an inferiority complex.

Well, I'm not sure about that... Anything to say in parting?
Hee hee hee hee...♡

(Mysterious...very mysterious...)

出雲阿国
IZUMO OKUNI

夢

William L.
Cascade, VA
In William's original drawing, the eyes are painted red. Trust me, it's creepy.

KYO-
HAN

"Maki"
Grand Junction, CO
Cool looking Kyo. Looks like he could be in a band!

SAMURAI DEEPER KYO
FAN ART!

真田幸村

A.V.V.
Mawson, Australia
I've always heard that Aussies draw the sexiest Yukimuras, but I never believe it...until now. Damn! Very nice, A.V.V. Thanks for representing the AU.

SAMURAI DEEPER KYO
FAN ART!

"Pwca"
*Sweet looking Yukimura! Pwca also asks when we'll find out who Okuni works for. I think we can tell who her last employer was, but just who **is** the Master?*

SAMURAI DEEPER KYO

Christina K.
Racine WI
What a splitting headache Kyo must have! Sorry...

Celebrity Fan Art!

It's a postcard from Masashi-Asaki-sensei, Manga-ka of Psychometer Eiji!

W-what will I tell Shima-san this time?! (sweats x2)
Special Thanks

Leah P.
Kwajalein Atoll, Marshall Islands
It's rare, but sometimes you get fan mail that actually helps you improve your geography and history knowledge. For that, I thank you, Leah. Oh, and thanks for the bishi Benitora.

Kimberly H.
Honolulu, HI
Yeah, baby. Show some skin, Kyo!

Alicia G.
Princeville, HI
The sweet side of Yuya.
Will she ever get a break from Kyo

yuya-san

鬼眼の狂

DEMON-EYES KYOU

Shut up and get ready to die!

HE'LL SHOW YOU THE MEANING OF "CUTE."

THANK YOU FOR ALL THE AMAZING ART! PLEASE KEEP SENDING IT!

Message from the Editor:
♡

"Neko"
Tohatch, NM
So cute! I want to put Kyo in my pocket!

New Guidelines! Please read carefully

How to submit:
1) Send your work via regular mail (NOT e-mail) to:

SAMURAI DEEPER KYO FAN MAIL
C/O TOKYOPOP
5900 WILSHIRE BLVD., SUITE 2000
LOS ANGELES, CA 90036

2) All work should be in black and white and no larger than 8.5" x 11". (And try not to fold it too many times!) 3) Anything you send will not be returned. If you want to keep your original, it's fine to send us a copy. 4) Please include your full name, age, city and state for us to print with your work. If you'd rather us use a pen name, please include that too. 5) IMPORTANT: If you're under the age of 18, you must have your parent's permission in order for us to print your work. Any submissions without a signed note of parental consent will not be used. 6) For full details, please check out http://www.tokyopop.com/aboutus/fanart.php

Disclaimer: Anything you send to us becomes the property of TOKYOPOP Inc. and will not be returned to you. We will have the right to print, repro- duce, distribute, or modify the artwork for use in future volumes of Samurai Deeper Kyo or on the web without payment to you.

GLOSSARY

daifuku–A sweet rice cake, usually with a sweet bean paste filling, eaten as a snack or desert in Japan.

-dono–An honorific denoting you are speaking to someone of a higher rank than yourself. Generally, a higher show of respect than "-sama".

Edo–The new capital of Japan after Sekigahara. Present-day Tokyo.

Edo Era–(1603-1868) Japan's "golden era" of political and economic stability after the civil wars of the Sengoku Era. During the Edo Era, all Japan would be ruled by one Shogun. Samurai Deeper Kyo takes place at the start of the Edo Era.

dango–Japanese rice dumpling, often served with green tea. It makes an easy-to-make but satisfying snack for any season.

-han–the "-san" suffix as said with Benitora's kansai-ben inflexion.

Ieyasu Tokugawa–The historical first shogun of Japan. Certain...liberties... have been taken with his role in Samurai Deeper Kyo.

kagemusha–Literally "shadow warrior." A kagemusha is a body double for a political or military leader, intended to protect him or her from potential assassins.

Kansai-ben–Regional dialect of the Kansai era (Osaka, Kyoto, Kobe). Benitora speaks with this dialect, known for its fast-paced diction and unique slang.

-kun–An honorific label used when addressing close friends or children. Usually used towards boys.

Muramasa–Muramasa was the name of the student to the great sword maker, Masamune in Japanese history, turned myth. Muramasa was known as the insane and violent match of his gentle and peaceful master. It is said the swords he forged would bring out the bloodlust from its wielder.

-sama–Honorific denoting the person vis of a much higher status than the speaker. Similar to "lord" or "master" in English.

-san–An honorific that denotes that one is higher/older than the speaker. Similar to "Mr/Mrs."

Sekigahara–The greatest battle in Japanese history, the Battle of Sekigahara took place in the fall of 1600 and ended years of civil war.

Shinkage School—A school of swordsmanship that really existed in Japan, and had many branching schools, focusing on developing different techniques.

utsusemi—The ninja-technique of substitution. It involves replacing one's own body with a fake (usually a chunk of wood), which distracts your attacker long enough to get a good hit in.

SAMURAI DEEPER KYO NEXT!!

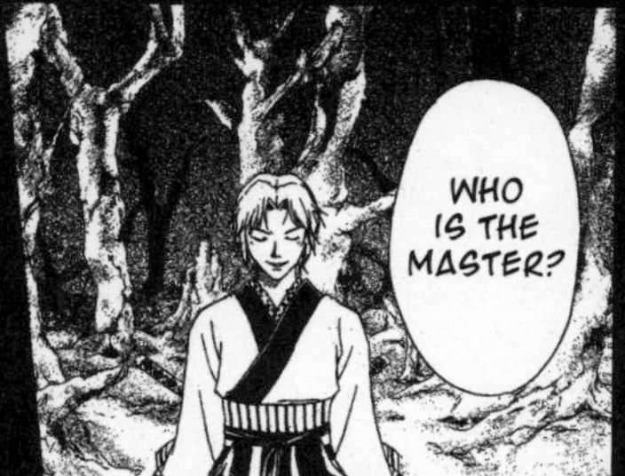
WHO IS THE MASTER?

Akira tells who the Master really is!!!

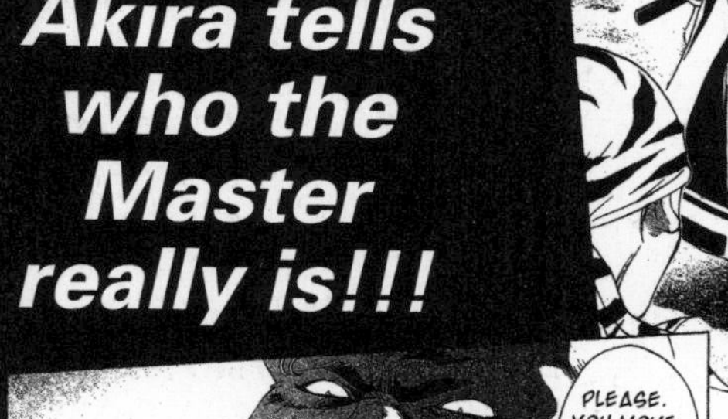
PLEASE. YOU MOVE SO SLOW A FLY COULD LAY EGGS ON YOU.
BUT THIS IS THE END.
BYE-BYE, KYO-SAN.
IT IS OVER...

Demon Eyes Kyo is in the biggest pinch yet!

The wild and wooly...SDK Vol 7. Don't miss it!!!

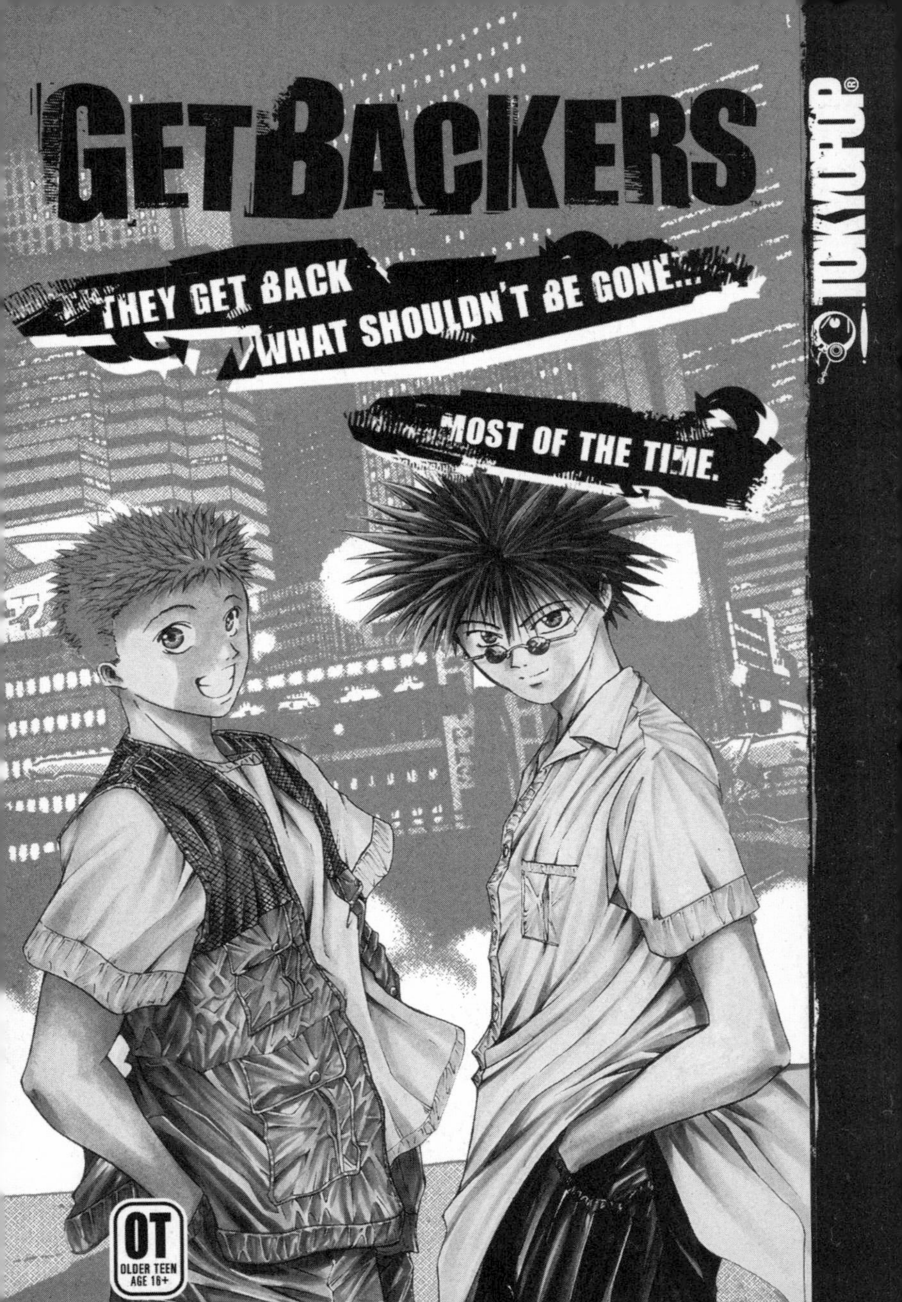
GETBACKERS™
THEY GET BACK
WHAT SHOULDN'T BE GONE...
MOST OF THE TIME.
TOKYOPOP®
OT
OLDER TEEN
AGE 16+
www.TOKYOPOP.com

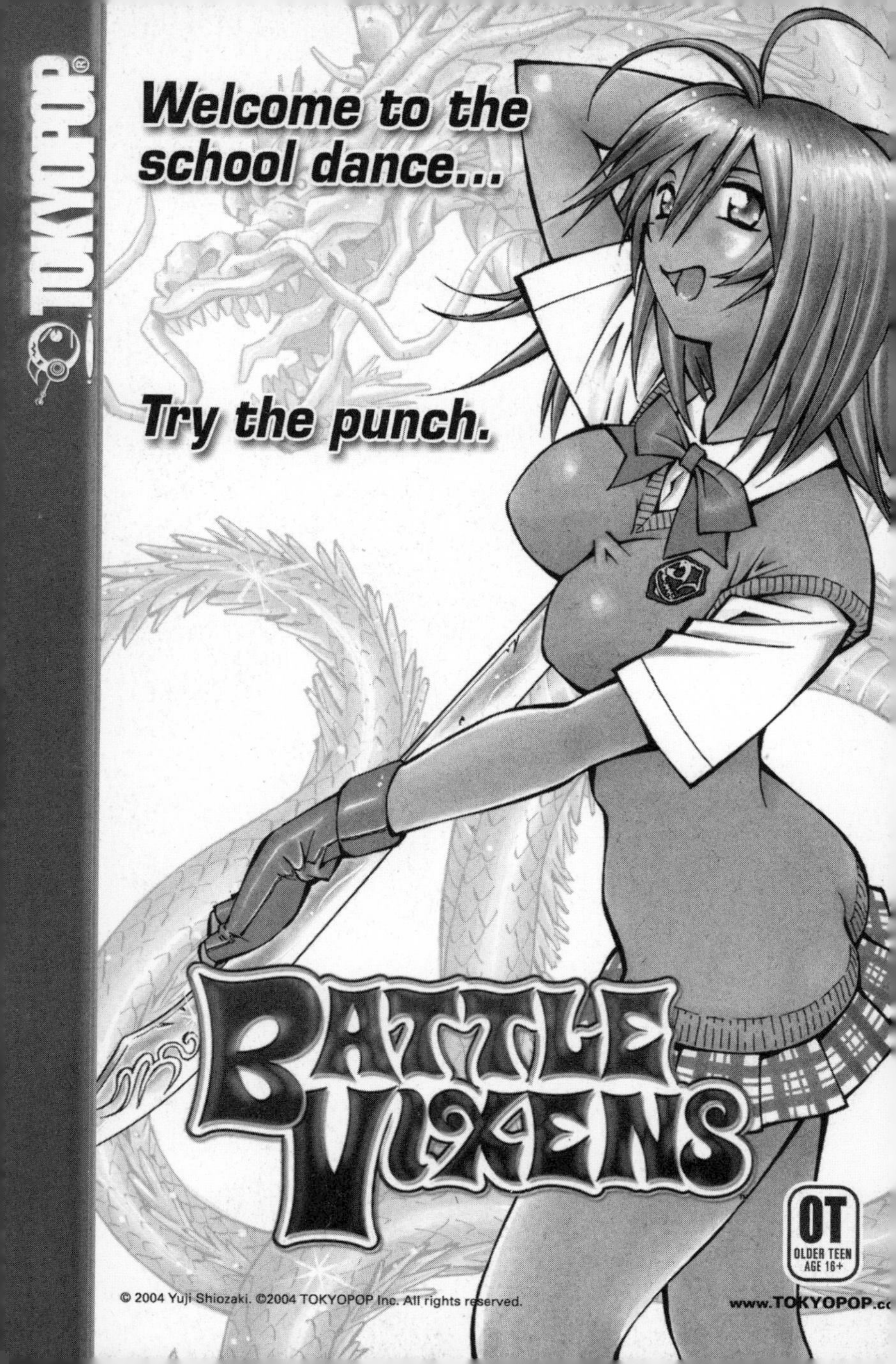
TOKYOPOP
Welcome to the school dance...
Try the punch.
BATTLE VIXENS
OT
OLDER TEEN AGE 16+
© 2004 Yuji Shiozaki. ©2004 TOKYOPOP Inc. All rights reserved.
www.TOKYOPOP.co

ALSO AVAILABLE FROM TOKYOPOP®

PRINCESS AI
PSYCHIC ACADEMY
RAGNAROK
RAVE MASTER
REALITY CHECK
REBIRTH
REBOUND
REMOTE
RISING STARS OF MANGA
SABER MARIONETTE J
SAILOR MOON
SAINT TAIL
SAIYUKI
SAMURAI DEEPER KYO
SAMURAI GIRL REAL BOUT HIGH SCHOOL
SCRYED
SEIKAI TRILOGY, THE
SGT. FROG
SHAOLIN SISTERS
SHIRAHIME-SYO: SNOW GODDESS TALES
SHUTTERBOX
SKULL MAN, THE
SMUGGLER
SNOW DROP
SORCERER HUNTERS
STONE
SUIKODEN III
SUKI
THREADS OF TIME
TOKYO BABYLON
TOKYO MEW MEW
TRAMPS LIKE US
TREASURE CHESS
UNDER THE GLASS MOON
VAMPIRE GAME
VISION OF ESCAFLOWNE, THE
WARRIORS OF TAO
WILD ACT
WISH
WORLD OF HARTZ
X-DAY
ZODIAC P.I.

NOVELS

CLAMP SCHOOL PARANORMAL INVESTIGATORS
KARMA CLUB
SAILOR MOON
SLAYERS

ART BOOKS

ART OF CARDCAPTOR SAKURA
ART OF MAGIC KNIGHT RAYEARTH, THE
PEACH: MIWA UEDA ILLUSTRATIONS

ANIME GUIDES

COWBOY BEBOP
GUNDAM TECHNICAL MANUALS
SAILOR MOON SCOUT GUIDES

TOKYOPOP KIDS

STRAY SHEEP

CINE-MANGA™

ALADDIN
ASTRO BOY
CARDCAPTORS
CONFESSIONS OF A TEENAGE DRAMA QUEEN
DUEL MASTERS
FAIRLY ODDPARENTS, THE
FAMILY GUY
FINDING NEMO
G.I. JOE SPY TROOPS
JACKIE CHAN ADVENTURES
JIMMY NEUTRON: BOY GENIUS, THE ADVENTURES OF
KIM POSSIBLE
LILO & STITCH
LIZZIE MCGUIRE
LIZZIE MCGUIRE MOVIE, THE
MALCOLM IN THE MIDDLE
POWER RANGERS: NINJA STORM
SHREK 2
SPONGEBOB SQUAREPANTS
SPY KIDS 2
SPY KIDS 3-D: GAME OVER
TEENAGE MUTANT NINJA TURTLES
THAT'S SO RAVEN
TRANSFORMERS: ARMADA
TRANSFORMERS: ENERGON

For more
information visit
www.TOKYOPOP.com

02.03.04T

ALSO AVAILABLE FROM 🌐TOKYOPOP®

MANGA

.HACK//LEGEND OF THE TWILIGHT
@LARGE
ABENOBASHI: MAGICAL SHOPPING ARCADE
A.I. LOVE YOU
AI YORI AOSHI
ANGELIC LAYER
ARM OF KANNON
BABY BIRTH
BATTLE ROYALE
BATTLE VIXENS
BRAIN POWERED
BRIGADOON
B'TX
CANDIDATE FOR GODDESS, THE
CARDCAPTOR SAKURA
CARDCAPTOR SAKURA - MASTER OF THE CLOW
CHOBITS
CHRONICLES OF THE CURSED SWORD
CLAMP SCHOOL DETECTIVES
CLOVER
COMIC PARTY
CONFIDENTIAL CONFESSIONS
CORRECTOR YUI
COWBOY BEBOP
COWBOY BEBOP: SHOOTING STAR
CRAZY LOVE STORY
CRESCENT MOON
CULDCEPT
CYBORG 009
D•N•ANGEL
DEMON DIARY
DEMON ORORON, THE
DEUS VITAE
DIGIMON
DIGIMON TAMERS
DIGIMON ZERO TWO
DOLL
DRAGON HUNTER
DRAGON KNIGHTS
DRAGON VOICE
DREAM SAGA
DUKLYON: CLAMP SCHOOL DEFENDERS
EERIE QUEERIE!
ERICA SAKURAZAWA: COLLECTED WORKS
ET CETERA
ETERNITY
EVIL'S RETURN
FAERIES' LANDING
FAKE
FLCL
FORBIDDEN DANCE
FRUITS BASKET
G GUNDAM
GATEKEEPERS
GETBACKERS

GIRL GOT GAME
GRAVITATION
GTO
GUNDAM BLUE DESTINY
GUNDAM SEED ASTRAY
GUNDAM WING
GUNDAM WING: BATTLEFIELD OF PACIFISTS
GUNDAM WING: ENDLESS WALTZ
GUNDAM WING: THE LAST OUTPOST (G-UNIT)
HANDS OFF!
HAPPY MANIA
HARLEM BEAT
I.N.V.U.
IMMORTAL RAIN
INITIAL D
INSTANT TEEN: JUST ADD NUTS
ISLAND
JING: KING OF BANDITS
JING: KING OF BANDITS - TWILIGHT TALES
JULINE
KARE KANO
KILL ME, KISS ME
KINDAICHI CASE FILES, THE
KING OF HELL
KODOCHA: SANA'S STAGE
LAMENT OF THE LAMB
LEGAL DRUG
LEGEND OF CHUN HYANG, THE
LES BIJOUX
LOVE HINA
LUPIN III
LUPIN III: WORLD'S MOST WANTED
MAGIC KNIGHT RAYEARTH I
MAGIC KNIGHT RAYEARTH II
MAHOROMATIC: AUTOMATIC MAIDEN
MAN OF MANY FACES
MARMALADE BOY
MARS
MARS: HORSE WITH NO NAME
METROID
MINK
MIRACLE GIRLS
MIYUKI-CHAN IN WONDERLAND
MODEL
ONE
ONE I LOVE, THE
PARADISE KISS
PARASYTE
PASSION FRUIT
PEACH GIRL
PEACH GIRL: CHANGE OF HEART
PET SHOP OF HORRORS
PITA-TEN
PLANET LADDER
PLANETES
PRIEST

02.03.04T

STOP!

This is the back of the book.
You wouldn't want to spoil a great ending!

This book is printed "manga-style," in the authentic Japanese right-to-left format. Since none of the artwork has been flipped or altered, readers get to experience the story just as the creator intended. You've been asking for it, so TOKYOPOP® delivered: authentic, hot-off-the-press, and far more fun!

DIRECTIONS

If this is your first time reading manga-style, here's a quick guide to help you understand how it works.

It's easy... just start in the top right panel and follow the numbers. Have fun, and look for more 100% authentic manga from TOKYOPOP®!